# Building/Object

# Building/Object

Shared and Contested Territories of Design and Architecture

EDITED BY CHARLOTTE ASHBY
AND MARK CRINSON

BLOOMSBURY VISUAL ARTS
LONDON • NEW YORK • OXFORD • NEW DELHI • SYDNEY

BLOOMSBURY VISUAL ARTS
Bloomsbury Publishing Plc
50 Bedford Square, London, WC1B 3DP, UK
1385 Broadway, New York, NY 10018, USA
29 Earlsfort Terrace, Dublin 2, Ireland

BLOOMSBURY, BLOOMSBURY VISUAL ARTS and the Diana logo are trademarks of
Bloomsbury Publishing Plc

First published in Great Britain 2022
Paperback edition published by Bloomsbury Visual Arts 2024

Selection and editorial matter copyright © Charlotte Ashby and Mark Crinson, 2022
Individual chapters © their authors, 2022

Charlotte Ashby and Mark Crinson have asserted their right under the Copyright,
Designs and Patents Act, 1988, to be identified as Author of this work.

For legal purposes the Acknowledgements on p. xi constitute an extension of this copyright page.

Cover design by Eleanor Rose
Cover image: Advertisement for Daikin split unit system in Our Home (1986)

All rights reserved. No part of this publication may be reproduced or transmitted
in any form or by any means, electronic or mechanical, including photocopying,
recording, or any information storage or retrieval system, without prior
permission in writing from the publishers.

Bloomsbury Publishing Plc does not have any control over, or responsibility for, any
third-party websites referred to or in this book. All internet addresses given in this
book were correct at the time of going to press. The author and publisher regret
any inconvenience caused if addresses have changed or sites have ceased to
exist, but can accept no responsibility for any such changes.

Every effort has been made to trace copyright holders and to obtain their permission for
the use of copyright material. The publisher apologizes for any errors or omissions.

A catalogue record for this book is available from the British Library.

Library of Congress Cataloging-in-Publication Data

Names: Ashby, Charlotte, 1979- editor. | Crinson, Mark, editor.
Title: Building/object: shared and contested territories of design and
architecture / edited by Charlotte Ashby and Mark Crinson.
Other titles: Building object
Description: London; New York: Bloomsbury Visual Arts, 2022. |
Includes bibliographical references and index. | Summary: "Building-Object
addresses the space in between the conventional objects of design and the conventional objects
of architecture, probing and reassessing the differences between the disciplines of
design history and architectural history Each of the 13 chapters in this book examine things which are
neither object-like or building-like, but somewhere in between - air conditioning; bookshelves;
partition walls; table-monuments; TVs; convenience stores; cars - exposing particular
political configurations and resonances that otherwise might be occluded. In doing so, they
reveal that the definitions we make of objects in opposition to buildings, architecture in
opposition to design, are not as fundamental as they seem. This book brings new aspects of the creative and
experiential into our understanding of the human environment"– Provided by publisher.
Identifiers: LCCN 2021053294 (print) | LCCN 2021053295 (ebook) |
ISBN 9781350234000 (hardback) | ISBN 9781350234048 (paperback) |
ISBN 9781350234017 (pdf) | ISBN 9781350234024 (epub) | ISBN 9781350234031
Subjects: LCSH: Design–Social aspects.
Classification: LCC NK1505.B85 2022 (print) |
LCC NK1505 (ebook) | DDC 745.2–dc23/eng/20220331
LC record available at https://lccn.loc.gov/2021053294
LC ebook record available at https://lccn.loc.gov/2021053295

ISBN: HB: 978-1-3502-3400-0
PB: 978-1-3502-3404-8
ePDF: 978-1-3502-3401-7
eBook: 978-1-3502-3402-4

Typeset by RefineCatch Limited, Bungay, Suffolk

COVER IMAGE
Detail of a 1986 advertisement for Daikin split unit system. *Our Home* (1986).
Courtesy of Daikin.

To find out more about our authors and books visit www.bloomsbury.com
and sign up for our newsletters.

# CONTENTS

*List of Illustrations* vii
*Acknowledgements* xi
*List of Contributors* xii

**Foreword** *Adrian Forty* xvi

**Introduction** *Mark Crinson and Charlotte Ashby* 1

**PART ONE** Grey Zones 19

1 A Good Shelf: The Material Culture of Reading in Colonial India *Swati Chattopadhyay* 21

2 The Power of Television in Modern Turkish Homes *Meltem Ö. Gürel* 43

3 Bin, Bag, Box: The Architecture of Convenience *Louisa Iarocci* 61

4 Atmospheric Exchanges: Air-conditioning, Thermal Material Culture and Public Housing in Singapore *Jiat-Hwee Chang* 77

5 Beyond Buildings and Objects: Reyner Banham's Freeway Ecology *Richard J. Williams* 97

**PART TWO** Dissolved Distinctions 115

6 Designing for a Nocturnal Banquet, Versailles 1674 *Panagiotis Doudesis* 119

7 Printed Objects and Ready-mades in the *Architectural Magazine* (1834–8) *Anne Hultzsch* 141

8 Entangled Histories of Buildings and Furniture: Knoll

International and the Production and Mediation of Modern Architecture in Post-war Belgium *Fredie Floré* 161

9 Disaster Relief and 'Universal Shelters': Humanitarian Imaginaries and Design Interventions at Oxfam, 1971–6 *Tania Messell and Lilián Sánchez-Moreno* 181

**PART THREE** Uneasy Difference 199

10 Regulation by Design: Reification and Building Regulations *Alistair Cartwright* 201
11 The Relational Object: Haus-Rucker-Co.'s Designs for Reshaping the Environment *Ross K. Elfline* 219
12 The Stylistic End-games of Modernism: High Tech Design in Criticism and History *Jane Pavitt* 237
13 Shared and Not Contested: Modern Erasures in Design and Architecture – History, Practice and Education in Brazil *Livia Rezende and Tatiana Pinto* 253

**Afterword – On Borrowed Time** *Ben Highmore* 273

*Index* 281

# ILLUSTRATIONS

| | | |
|---|---|---|
| 0.1 | Interior of the Mosque-Madrassa of Sultan Hassan, Cairo (1356–63). Photograph taken in 2019. Courtesy of Mohammed Moussa via Wikimedia Commons. | 3 |
| 0.2 | The *Festsaal* in the Bauhaus building, Dessau (1925–6). Photograph taken in 2011. Courtesy of Adrian Forty. | 5 |
| 0.3 | Behrens House, north–south section, Darmstadt (1901). *Deutsche Kunst und Dekoration* IX (1901–2): 162 | 14 |
| 1.1 | One of the bookshelves that once belonged to Ishwar Chandra Vidyasagar. Copyright Swati Chattopadhyay. | 22 |
| 1.2 | 'English Gentleman and his Munshi' (*c.* 1813). | 26 |
| 1.3 | Plan and elevations of the East India Company's Oriental Repository (*c.* 1797–8). Courtesy Victoria and Albert Museum. Accession no. D.1672–1898. | 30 |
| 1.4 | 'The East Offering its Riches to Britannia', East India House (1777). Courtesy British Library Board. Shelf mark: Foster 245: 1778 | 31 |
| 1.5 | Ishwar Chandra Vidyasagar's residence, Kolkata. Copyright Swati Chattopadhyay. | 36 |
| 2.1 | A salon with a door as the centre stage of a home, reserved only for the use of guests. | 45 |
| 2.2 | Plan of a flat with a fireplace, by architect Melih Pekel (1956). Courtesy of Konak Municipality Archives. | 46 |
| 2.3 | A TV set dictated the furniture layout and seating arrangements in the room. | 49 |
| 2.4 | A recent photograph showing satellite dishes attached to buildings. Courtesy of Meltem Gürel. | 54 |
| 2.5 | Television provided a cheaper means of entertainment for the middle class. | 55 |
| 3.1 | The world's first convenience store (*c.* 1928). Courtesy of 7-Eleven, Inc. | 64 |
| 3.2 | Tote'm Store of the late 1930s and early 1940s. Courtesy of 7-Eleven, Inc. | 65 |
| 3.3 | A typical 7-Eleven Store of the early 1950s. Courtesy of 7-Eleven, Inc. | 67 |
| 3.4 | A Fort Worth 7-Eleven Store (1951). Courtesy of 7-Eleven, Inc. | 69 |
| 3.5 | 'Leave the youngsters in the car? Why not? You can see them from anywhere in the store.' Courtesy of 7-Eleven, Inc. | 71 |

| | | |
|---|---|---|
| 4.1 | View of an access corridor in an HDB slab block. Courtesy of Tan Wei Ming. | 80 |
| 4.2 | A 1986 advertisement for Daikin split unit system. Courtesy of Daikin Air-conditioning Singapore. | 82 |
| 4.3 | Exterior view of the vertical stack of utility corners on a block of recently built HDB flats. Courtesy of Jiat-Hwee Chang. | 85 |
| 4.4 | HDB interior (1973). Courtesy of the Housing & Development Board. | 86 |
| 4.5 | Interior of a HUDC flat from 1992. Image courtesy of *HOMESTYLE* magazine 1992 Jan/Feb issue | 89 |
| 5.1 | Frame grab from One Pair of Eyes, 'Reyner Banham Loves Los Angeles', directed by Julian Cooper © BBC 1972. | 103 |
| 5.2 | Aerial view of 405/10 junction, Los Angeles. | 108 |
| 5.3 | View of freeway signage, Los Angeles. | 109 |
| 6.1 | Engraving depicting the nocturnal banquet at the Cour de Marbre, Versailles (1676). Courtesy of National Library of France/BnF. | 120 |
| 6.2 | Drawing for the *medianoche* machine (1674). Courtesy of National Museum of Fine Arts, Stockholm. | 121 |
| 6.3 | A pair of gilded limewood *guéridons* produced in The Hague (*c.* 1700). Courtesy of Rijksmuseum (CC0 1.0). | 128 |
| 6.4 | Funerary monument of Francesco d'Este (1658). Courtesy of National Library of France/BnF. | 130 |
| 6.5 | Lantern of Florence Cathedral (mid-fifteenth century). Courtesy of Birasuegi via Wikimedia Commons. | 131 |
| 7.1 | John Loudon's *Architectural Magazine*, vol. 1 (1834). Private collection. | 142 |
| 7.2 | Title page of *Mechanics' Magazine*, 2 October (1830). Private collection. | 146 |
| 7.3 | 'A Temporary Table, Or Ironing-Board, for Small Country Cottages' (1838). | 149 |
| 7.4 | Lamb's design of a piano (1838). | 150 |
| 7.5 | 'Marble Table, with a Cast-Iron Pillar, Constructed on an Economical Principle' (1834). Private collection. | 151 |
| 7.6 | Ornaments by Austin & Seeley (1834). Private collection. | 153 |
| 8.1 | ECSC house with Tubax furniture, International Annual Fair, Charleroi (1954). Courtesy of WVDM Archives/coll. A&D 50, Mechelen. | 164 |
| 8.2 | De Coene model home furnished with Knoll designs, Expo 58, Brussels (1958). Courtesy of Archive Stichting De Coene, Collection Verzameling De Coene nv., Rijksarchief Kortrijk, no. 179. | 166 |
| 8.3 | Knoll International Brussels showroom, Brussels (1954). Photograph by Serge Vandercam. *Bouwen en Wonen*, no. 12 (1958), 133. | 168 |

| | | |
|---|---|---|
| 8.4 | Knoll International Brussels advertisement (1954). Courtesy of Knoll, Inc. | 171 |
| 8.5 | Knoll International Brussels advertisement (1964). Courtesy of Knoll, Inc. | 173 |
| 9.1 | Blueprints for the Oxfam design study (1971). Source: Oxfam Archive, Bodleian Library, University of Oxford. Courtesy of Oxfam. | 188 |
| 9.2 | Visual representations for the Oxfam design study (1971). Source: Oxfam Archive, Bodleian Library, University of Oxford. Courtesy of Oxfam | 189 |
| 9.3 | Prototype of Oxfam's first 'igloo' Emergency House. Source: Oxfam Archive, Bodleian Library, University of Oxford. Courtesy of Oxfam. | 190 |
| 9.4 | New 'honeycomb' shaped Emergency Houses (1975). Source: Oxfam Archive, Bodleian Library, University of Oxford. Courtesy of Oxfam. | 192 |
| 10.1 | Celotex fibreboard panels (1950). | 210 |
| 10.2 | Demonstration of planning grid to be fed into computer programmed with Parker Morris standards (1966). | 213 |
| 11.1 | Haus-Rucker-Co., *Mind Expander II* (1968). Courtesy of Archive Zamp Kelp. | 220 |
| 11.2 | Haus-Rucker-Co., *Battleship* (1970). Courtesy of the Museum of Contemporary Crafts Archive, American Craft Council. | 224 |
| 11.3 | Haus-Rucker-Co., *Flyhead*, *View Atomizer* and *Drizzler* (1968). Courtesy of Archive Zamp Kelp. | 225 |
| 12.1 | Exterior of the Centre Pompidou, Paris, France (1977). Architects: Piano + Rogers. Structural and services engineers: Ove Arup & Partners. Photograph taken in 2017. Courtesy of Suicasmo via Wikimedia Commons. | 238 |
| 12.2 | Exterior of Hopkins House, London (1976). Photographer Matthew Weinrab. Courtesy of Hopkins Architects/Anthony Hunt Associates and Matthew Weinrab. | 239 |
| 12.3 | Loft bed by Morsa design team. Courtesy of Donato Savoie/Morsa. | 243 |
| 12.4 | 'The Look of the 1980s: Your House Will Never Be the Same' (1978). Courtesy of Carl Fischer and Esquire, Herst Communications, Inc. | 245 |
| 13.1 | Brasília's National Congress Tower under construction (1959). Photograph by Marcel Gautherot/Instituto Moreira Salles Collection. Courtesy of IMS – Instituto Moreira Salles. | 255 |
| 13.2 | Worker on the 28-storey National Congress Tower (1959). Photograph by Marcel Gautherot/Instituto Moreira Salles Collection. Courtesy of IMS – Instituto Moreira Salles. | 257 |
| 13.3 | Workers hand-finishing one of the domes of Brasília's National Congress complex (1959). Photograph by Marcel | |

|  | Gautherot/Instituto Moreira Salles Collection. Courtesy of IMS – Instituto Moreira Salles. | 259 |
|---|---|---|
| 13.4 | Migrants arriving to work on the construction of Brasília (1959). Courtesy of Arquivo Público do Distrito Federal. | 261 |
| 13.5 | Sacolândia, an informal settlement built by migrants and workers during Brasília's construction (1958). Photo by Marcel Gautherot/Instituto Moreira Salles Collection. Courtesy of IMS – Instituto Moreira Salles. | 264 |

# ACKNOWLEDGEMENTS

This book owes its gestation to a conference held at Birkbeck, University of London, in June 2019. We would especially like to thank the co-organizer of that conference, Jeremy Aynsley, and Milos Kosec who helped make everything run smoothly. The conference included talks by many speakers whose papers we could not include here, and was helped considerably by the work of session chairs and the guidance of a scientific committee and an organizing committee. We are grateful to them all for their ideas and enthusiasm: Lisa Godson, Jonathan Mekinda, Eleanor Rees, Tag Gronberg, Karolina Jakaite, Claire O'Mahony, Penelope Dean, Daniel Huppatz, Claire Jamieson, Jessica Kelly, Doris Behrens-Abouseif, Harriet Atkinson, Aurora Laurenti, Gabriele Oropallo, Katie Lloyd Thomas, Didem Ekici, Eeva-Liisa Pelkonen, Penny Sparke, Caroline Maniaque-Benton, Maarten Delbeke, Hilde Heynen and Josie Kane. The conference was supported by the Design History Society, the European Architectural History Network, and the Architecture Space and Society Centre (Birkbeck). It has been a real pleasure to work with our editors at Bloomsbury: Alex Highfield and James Thompson.

# CONTRIBUTORS

**Charlotte Ashby** is an art and design historian based at Birkbeck, University of London. She is the author of *Modernism in Scandinavia: Art, Architecture and Design* (2017) and co-editor of *Imagined Cosmopolis: Internationalism and Cultural Exchange, 1870s–1920s* (2019) and of *Nordic Design in Translation: The Circulation of Objects, Ideas and Practices* (2022).

**Alistair Cartwright** is a writer living in London. His PhD examined the experience of post-war London's rented rooms, with a focus on domestic space, subdivision, speculation and resistance. Recent articles have appeared in the *London Journal* (2020), *Architectural Histories* (2020) and *Jacobin* (2017). He writes regularly for Counterfire.org.

**Jiat-Hwee Chang**, Associate Professor of Architecture at the National University of Singapore, is the author of *A Genealogy of Tropical Architecture* (2016, awarded IPHS Book Prize 2018) and co-author (with Justin Zhuang and photographer Darren Soh) of *Everyday Modernism* (2022). He has also co-edited several books and special issues of journals. He is currently researching the socio-cultural histories and techno-politics of air-conditioning and climate change in urban Asia.

**Swati Chattopadhyay** is Professor of History of Art and Architecture at the University of California, Santa Barbara. She is a founding editor of PLATFORM, author of *Representing Calcutta: Modernity, Nationalism, and the Colonial Uncanny* (2005), *Unlearning the City: Infrastructure in a New Optical Field* (2012), and co-editor with Jeremy White of *City Halls and Civic Materialism: Towards a Global History of Urban Public* Space (2014) and *Routledge Companion to Critical Approaches to Contemporary Architecture* (2019).

**Mark Crinson** is Professor of Architectural History at Birkbeck, University of London. His books include *Modern Architecture and the End of Empire* (2003), *Stirling and Gowan: Architecture from Austerity to Affluence* (2012), *Rebuilding Babel: Internationalism and Modern Architecture* (2017), *Alison and Peter Smithson* (2018), and (with Richard J. Williams) *The Architecture of Art History – A Historiography* (2019). *Shock City: Architecture and Image in Industrial Manchester* will be published in 2022.

**Panagiotis Doudesis** is an architect and currently a PhD candidate at the Department of Art History, University of Cambridge, investigating the connections of early modern architecture and dining cultures. He has taught architectural design at the National Technical University of Athens and supervised courses at his faculty. His publications include essays such as 'Wedding Feasts' in *Feast & Fast: The Art of Food in Europe, 1500–1800* (2019).

**Ross K. Elfline** is Associate Professor of Contemporary Art History at Carleton College, USA. He has published widely on European and American Radical Architecture practices from the 1960s and 1970s. He is currently working on a book, tentatively titled *Common Ground, Common Time: Architectural Performance in the 1960s and 70s*, on the intersection of architecture and time-based media.

**Fredie Floré** is Professor of History and Theory of Interior Architecture at KU Leuven, Faculty of Architecture. Her books include *Lessen in goed wonen: woonvoorlichting in België 1945–1958* (2010). She co-edited (with Cammie McAtee) *The Politics of Furniture: Identity, Diplomacy and Persuasion in Post-war Interiors* (2017) and has published in *The Journal of Architecture, Architectural Theory Review, Journal of Design History, Design and Culture, Interiors* and *Architectural History*.

**Adrian Forty** is Professor Emeritus of Architectural History at the Bartlett School of Architecture, UCL and Honorary Curator of Architecture at the Royal Academy, London. He is the author of *Objects of Desire: Design and Society Since 1750* (1986), *Words and Buildings: A Vocabulary of Modern Architecture* (2000) and *Concrete and Culture: A Material History* (2012), and was President of the European Architectural History Network from 2010 to 2014.

**Meltem Ö. Gürel** is a professor and the Dean at Yaşar University's Faculty of Architecture, Izmir. She received her PhD in architecture from the University of Illinois, Urbana-Champaign. Her research is published in volumes and journals, including *The Journal of Architecture, Journal of Architectural Education, JSAH* and *Journal of Design History*. She is the editor of *Mid-Century Modernism in Turkey: Architecture Across Cultures in the 1950s and 1960s* (2016).

**Ben Highmore** is Professor of Cultural Studies in the School of Media, Arts and Humanities at the University of Sussex. His most recent books are *The Art of Brutalism: Rescuing Hope from Catastrophe in 1950s Britain* and *Cultural Feelings: Mood, Mediation, and Cultural Politics*, both published in 2017. His book *In Good Taste: How Britain's Middle Classes Found Their Style* will be published in 2022.

**Anne Hultzsch** leads the ERC-funded group 'Women Writing Architecture: Female Experiences of the Built, 1700–1900' at ETH Zurich. Among other publications, she has edited *The Printed and the Built: Architecture, Print Culture, and Public Debate in the Nineteenth Century* (with Mari Hvattum, 2018) and a special issue of *The Journal of Architecture* on the nineteenth-century architectural magazine (2020). She is the author of *Architecture, Travellers and Writers: Constructing Histories of Perception 1640–1950* (2014).

**Louisa Iarocci** is Associate Professor in the Department of Architecture at the University of Washington in Seattle. She is a licensed architect who has worked in architectural firms in the United States and Canada. She edited and contributed to the anthology *Visual Merchandising: The Image of Selling* (2013) and wrote the monograph *The Urban Department Store in America* (2014). Her current research focuses on the forms and operations of the material artefacts of commerce and storage.

**Tania Messell** is a design historian at the University of Applied Sciences and Arts Northwestern Switzerland, whose research focuses on design professionalization, design and globalization, and design for development in the long twentieth century. She currently investigates design and humanitarian governance as they intersected in disaster relief between 1960 and 1980. Author of several peer-reviewed publications, she is also the co-editor of *International Design Organisations: Histories, Legacies* (2022).

**Jane Pavitt** is a curator and Professor of Design and Architectural History at Kingston University. Her exhibitions and accompanying publications include *Cold War Modern: Design 1945–70* (V&A, with David Crowley, 2008), *Postmodernism: Style and Subversion 1970–90* (V&A, with Glenn Adamson, 2011) and *Superstructures: The New Architecture 1960–1990* (Sainsbury Centre for Visual Arts, with Abraham Thomas, 2018). Other books include *Fear and Fashion in the Cold War* (2008) and *High Tech Reassessed* (2022).

**Tatiana Pinto** is an architect, artist and independent researcher. Her main research interests revolve around social inequalities, the political aspect of space, and the responsibilities of architects in current societal struggles. Her transdisciplinary work combines architecture, art, activism, writing and public interaction. Previous work: *Dear You* (2017), *Trialogue* (2018), *Trialogue Act2* and *Act3* (2020). She teaches and works alongside DAAS (Decolonizing Architecture Advanced Studies) at the Royal Institute of Art, Stockholm, Sweden.

**Livia Rezende** is a design historian living on Gadigal land and working at the University of New South Wales, Sydney. She is the co-founder of OPEN, an art and design decolonial praxis collective. Her publications feature in *Iberoamericana* (2021), *Designing Worlds* (2016), *Cultures of International Exhibitions* (2015), *Design Frontiers* (2014) and the *Journal of Design History* (2015, 2017), of which the special issue *Locating Design Exchanges in Latin America and the Caribbean* (2019) she co-edited.

**Lilián Sanchez-Moreno** is a design researcher at the Centre for Sustainable Design, University for the Creative Arts, Farnham. She was awarded a PhD from the School of Architecture and Design at the University of Brighton in 2021, where she explored the professionalization of social responsibility within design discourse and practice from the mid-1960s to the late 1970s. Lilián has co-authored peer-reviewed journal articles and exhibition reviews.

**Richard J. Williams** is Professor of Contemporary Visual Cultures at the University of Edinburgh. His books include *The Anxious City* (2004), *Brazil: Modern Architectures in History* (2009), *Sex and Buildings* (2013), *The Architecture of Art History – A Historiography* (with Mark Crinson, 2019), *Why Cities Look the Way They Do* (2019), *Reyner Banham Revisited* (2021) and *The Culture Factory: Architecture and the Contemporary Art Museum* (2021).

# FOREWORD

## Adrian Forty

In a book about buildings and objects, it would be as well to start by reflecting on the two sets of apparatus that we have evolved for studying them: their convergences and their divergences. Having contributed to both disciplines, I offer some recollection of how their relationship has appeared to me, from the time when I started out in the early 1970s.

Fifty years ago, design history did not exist. As a practice, design of non-architectural objects then was for the most part so addicted to progress as to be in denial about even having a past. Apart from a few specialized areas – such as typography and, more covertly, fashion – designers were only concerned with the future. In this respect, design differed from architecture, forever obsessed with its own history, even when it has claimed not to be. To bring 'history' into design went against the grain – and there were few models for how to do it.

The available existing disciplines all had their limitations. Art history, in some ways the most obvious, was – at that time, at least – too preoccupied with questions of authorship to deal with a class of objects whose authors were mostly unknown. Moreover, art history's emphasis on the origins and creation of works, rather than their afterlife, was unhelpful to a field whose primary concern was the circulation of its products in the world once they had been finished. Nor was the discipline of history all that much use, for while it had much to say about the social relations and economics of production, when it came to the varied characteristics of individual products and their specificities it remained mute, regarding these as too trivial a matter to be concerned with.

In my own case, it was Le Corbusier's *L'art décoratif d'aujourdhui* (1925), with its profusion of images of anonymous artefacts, that set me off in pursuit of a history of design. Le Corbusier used these artefacts as the authority for a new aesthetic – an aesthetic from which 'decoration' was banished. He claimed that these artefacts had become the 'typical' objects of the age, that they defined what it was to be modern. But he never once asked how this had come about. Where had these objects come from? Why had they been given these forms? It certainly was not, as Le Corbusier claimed, through some internal law of mechanical selection that mimicked Darwinian evolution. And how had they come to be part of the landscape of modern life? By what process had they 'taken'? And what were the results of introducing them into everyday life? If they were indeed iconic objects, then one wanted to know how they might have affected the people who used them or encountered them in the course of their daily lives.

To try to find answers to these questions was, in 1970, a challenge. First of all, looking back on a pre-internet age, without online databases or searchable archives, one should not underestimate the difficulties of doing research into 'anonymous history'. A lot of time was spent turning the pages and adverts of trade magazines, and following up the remotest of leads. But far more of an obstacle than the difficulty of finding data was the absence of any theory through which to interpret whatever one might find. Yes, there was Marx's theory of commodity fetishism, but no guidance as to how to apply this to any actual artefact. Walter Benjamin and Georg Simmel were as yet unknown to us – they hadn't yet started to be translated into English. Baudrillard's *System of Objects* had come out in France in 1968, but I only found out about that later. Making sense of mass culture without the benefit of these thinkers now seems inconceivable, yet that is what we had to try to do. The steps by which I set about trying to construct an enquiry are almost too painful for me now to recall.

Inspiration, and rescue of a kind, came from two sources in particular. One was the weekly magazine *New Society*, published in Britain from 1962 to 1988, its best years under the editorship of Paul Barker between 1965 and 1975. Ostensibly it was a magazine for social work, and much of its content concerned social issues and education. It reflected the apogee of the welfare state, when education and social work attracted people with ideas, and ideals, and there was much experiment in these areas. But if we take a typical issue, like that of 14 January 1971, we find just how wide-ranging it was: this particular issue contained articles on the planning of Jerusalem following the Yom Kippur war; gentrification in London; the East Thames Tunnel; Museum charges; and, surprisingly, the Santa Monica pier. There was also typically quite a lot about things that hadn't happened, speculation about 'what if?', and a strong sense that the world was open to being reshaped for the better. Above all, *New Society* presented a concept of the environment, a totality made up of people, places, territories, ideas, apparatuses. It covered many different things, and suggested that they were all connected. To me, at the time, this was revelatory, that there could be a total object of study, made up of many individual discrete objects that were all related, each one of which could only be understood fully by taking them all into account. Characteristic of this was the article on the Santa Monica pier – in fact Reyner Banham's inaugural lecture at UCL. From this very unremarkable structure, Banham strung a whole discussion as to how one might think about the environment, suggesting that the significance of buildings lay in the relation to the land upon which they stood, quoting the architect Richard Llewelyn Davies' 'rock-bottom' definition of architecture as 'that which changes land use'. It is astonishing that a magazine for a general readership should have carried ideas more radical, more speculative, than could be found in any *academic* journal at the time.

*New Society* also ran pieces on mass culture. These included John Berger's pioneering article on female nudity 'Sight and Sex', anticipating his own *Ways of Seeing* in 1972, and a variety of articles by Reyner Banham on items as various as potato crisps, clipboards, sunglasses and kitchen mixers. *New Society* gave me the confidence that one could study ubiquitous, anonymous artefacts other than through art history.

The other source of hope was Roland Barthes's *Mythologies*, which I came across in 1970. Although first published in 1957, it was not translated into English until 1972. Barthes's book was a revelation; it showed that it was possible to treat seemingly ephemeral things that didn't fit into any then known disciplinary framework – washing powders, plastic, steak – in a way that was both rigorous and systematic, but also entertaining. For ever after, Barthes remained an inspiration, for his tone – the reluctant theorist, who doesn't want to take up a 'position' – as much as for his content.

These two exemplars, *New Society* and *Mythologies*, gave me confidence that one could research designed artefacts, and find a way to situate them historically. As it started to emerge as a discipline in the 1970s, design history was divided into two camps: those who came out of cultural studies, and those who came out of art history. The cultural studies people were primarily interested in media, and for them, mass-produced goods had significance because they were objects of media attention – they appeared on TV, in advertising, etc. Initially, the cultural studies approach to media was directed towards understanding the formation of ideologies of social class, though later it started to include gender issues, and these choices impacted on design history. On the other hand, there were the art history people, who were more interested in provenance, in where things came from, who had designed them, what references they had used in designing them, etc. The relationship between these two groups was not always particularly comfortable, and I can remember some notable stand-offs.

Although I had come from the art history side, I didn't really align myself with either group, and tried as far as possible to avoid affiliation with one or the other. I was interested in effects – in what artefacts did once they were in the world, in how they did or didn't change things. The cultural studies people for their part were interested in how the media set up or reinforced social relations, which was a slightly different question. For me, *physical objects* were always the centre of attention, whereas for cultural studies, it was the *media*. And, as I have already made clear, I had my differences with the art historians' approach too. My book *Objects of Desire*, written in the late 1970s, came out of the friction between these two groups, as I experienced it then.

As I moved away from design history towards architectural history, I did not abandon what I had learnt from design history, although I was looking at a different kind of object. I carried on being interested in the same question that I had started with in design history, only now it became not 'what do artefacts do?', but 'what does architecture do?'. I simply shifted to asking how buildings performed. And still today, the first question I would ask about any building, as of any new design, is 'what does it change?'.

Llewelyn Davies' rock-bottom definition of architecture as 'that which changes land use' suggested one sort of answer to that question, but that is not the only thing that architecture, or design, changes – both change how people see themselves, how they see each other, how they see their place in the world, the balance of wealth, of resources. All these, and more, seem to be equally worth addressing and, for me, architectural history or design history scholarship is to be judged by how well, or badly, it answers these questions. One does not have to be an architectural behaviourist to acknowledge that architecture *performs*; it does things to our perceptions of and relationship with the world, for better or for worse. Wanting to be able to give some account of the consequences that buildings and objects have is what has kept me interested in architecture and its history, and design and its history, for the best part of fifty years.

Although I brought with me to architecture the same questions as had been prompted by design history, let us be clear that the two disciplines are not the same. There are some fundamental differences between works of architecture and mass-produced goods. For all that people have pushed analogies between the two, or tried to blur the distinction between them, one cannot get away from the fact that they remain fundamentally different. First of all, as the building economist Duccio Turin, quoted by Banham in his Santa Monica pier article, said, buildings are fixed to the ground, whereas artefacts aren't. They're mobile. And secondly, buildings are unique objects. Only perhaps in the most extreme forms of mass-prefabrication do buildings become multiples, but even then, there are often slight differences between individual buildings of the same type. On the other hand, consumer goods are by their very nature mass-produced. The unique object is the exception, and belongs to another category: 'craft'. Design history specializes in studying very large sets of identical objects that are widely diffused. This fact, which presents a very particular kind of opportunity – the opportunity to follow how the same article is appropriated and used in different circumstances – is quite specific to design history.

One of the motives for this collection of essays was whether there was any convergence between architectural history and design history, and to ask where the overlaps might be. Whatever the answers, I think it is important not to lose sight of these two fundamental differences – the fixity and uniqueness of buildings, the mobility and multiplication of artefacts – in how we go about shaping the future of the two disciplines.

# Introduction

## Mark Crinson and Charlotte Ashby

We can indicate something of what is at stake when we relate objects and buildings by starting with two passages from novels:

> It was a large, well-proportioned room, handsomely fitted up. Elizabeth, after slightly surveying it, went to a window to enjoy its prospect. The hill, crowned with wood, from which they had descended, receiving increased abruptness from the distance, was a beautiful object. Every disposition of the ground was good; and she looked on the whole scene, the river, the trees scattered on its banks, and the winding of the valley, as far as she could trace it, with delight. As they passed into other rooms these objects were taking different positions; but from every window there were beauties to be seen. The rooms were lofty and handsome, and their furniture suitable to the fortune of their proprietor; but Elizabeth saw, with admiration of his taste, that it was neither gaudy nor uselessly fine; with less of splendour, and more real elegance, than the furniture of Rosings.
> JANE AUSTEN, *Pride and Prejudice*, 1813

> ...the postal official from Klein-Reifling, accustomed to shabby surroundings, can't just flick a switch and really believe that this room is for her, this extravagantly scaled, exquisitely bright, colourfully wallpapered room, with open French doors like crystalline floodgates, the light cascading through. The unchecked golden torrent covers every corner of the room, every object in it is bathed in a deluge of fire. The polished surfaces of the furniture sparkle like crystal, friendly reflections glint on brass and glass, even the carpet with its embroidered flowers breathes with the lushness and naturalness of living moss.
> STEFAN ZWEIG, *The Post Office Girl*, 1930s, first published 1982

These are worlds hyperbolically at peace with themselves. As Zweig writes, 'The room glows like a morning in paradise'. Elizabeth Bennet and Christine the post office worker see their unfamiliar surroundings as having so much harmony that the object world, bathed in golden light, encompasses neighbouring hills as much as furniture, and includes even perhaps the women's own bodies. But these worlds are entered and perceived as harmonious by those socially askew from them, strangers to them, those who don't belong, or not yet. And so their continuums of objects, buildings and landscapes conceal other worlds, where people are 'in the wrong place', where objects are out of sorts, too ill-fitting for their rooms, and where buildings are in a state of shabbiness, declining to their separate parts.[1] There, in those other worlds, it's almost a category mistake to think that objects and buildings have some smooth relationship.

Despite such imagined worlds, buildings are not generally referred to as objects, and when we name something as an object – whether *naturalia* (found) or *artificialia* (made) – we don't usually think of it as having the scale of a building. There are, at once, exceptions: the building as an 'object in the landscape', for instance, which draws attention both to a sense of apartness and to the building's relation to something that is, in turn, larger than it. Building and object are clearly not antonymous. Often, one is so integral to the other that they are only conceivable as separate objects when one or the other enters a different object world – think of the mosque lamp as inseparable from the mosque whose interior spaces and ensemble of other objects it lights, but also often sold in the street (a tourist souvenir, a domestic decoration (Figure 0.1)). And think also of those items literally prised loose from the mosque and also commodified: tiles, wooden fittings, stucco-work. The object has some object-ivity, some wholeness, some separateness or there-ness, some perceivable limits, but these are mutable. And we can usually say the same of the building. Once the building's interior and its inhabitable capacities are reckoned in, then all thought of buildings as objects apparently disappears; they come to have an interiority which, it is imagined, is like intruding into another's mind. To be surrounded by objects in these interiors is to seem to know the difference between them and what contains them.

Calling something an 'object of design' implies that the object has resulted from a different order of human intent and making – indeed, that there was someone who played the role of designing that object. Something similar happens in the difference between building and architecture. To call something a building, at least according to one way of thinking, is to place emphasis on the making rather than the designing – for that we tend to use the word 'architecture'. And 'design', for both architecture and objects, carries an emphasis on the process of giving form (aesthetic) to an idea. The designer of objects and the architect of buildings have a kind of equivalence, or we might say that they have acquired this equivalence over the last few hundred years. This, and indeed how we think of buildings and objects, has nothing natural or inevitable about it.

FIGURE 0.1 *Interior of the Mosque-Madrassa of Sultan Hassan, Cairo (1356–63). Photograph taken in 2019. Courtesy of Mohammed Moussa via Wikimedia Commons.*

In this book, *Building/Object*, we attempt to scrutinize this relationship, to put it under some pressure and to awaken different potentials in it. It's a relationship both between objects and buildings and between the disciplines by which we try to understand them. These are *shared and contested territories*, as our subtitle puts it, because of the ways in which academic interest in buildings and objects has tended to divide them at the level of scale or portability or some other category, or because of professional divisions which at times make a great deal of sense but at others are unnecessarily constraining. The disciplines we primarily speak to here are design history and architectural history, although others are invoked too. But it is the disciplinary impulse itself (or the related impulse to autonomy or media specificity) that is constantly at stake or at question in the spectrum of topics discussed here.

In what follows we will introduce the book, first by showing how building/object relationships have been transferred into the terms of disciplinary relations. Then we will relate how categorization or classification can marginalize disciplinary distinctions, as well as how the issue of scale relativizes them.

## Disciplines

Objects and buildings are, supposedly, different orders of things. The difference is sometimes claimed as ontological: between the mobile and the fixed, the serial and the unique, commodified things and things determined by land use. Architecture, it is often said, shelters or frames human activities, while objects punctuate those activities and articulate them in closer relation to specific needs. Objects are designed to function within environments (built or at least marked by human usage), while buildings are built to provide enclosing environments for the activity or objects they house. In both cases objects and buildings can be understood as responses to the projected human activities they are designed to serve. Acting in the other direction, human activity can be shaped and directed by the spaces in which it occurs and by objects that prompt certain kinds of interaction. So those effects are always knocking on from one to the other and back and forth between building, object and human interaction.

Building/object differences clearly often have historical causes and political motivations, visible at different times. In William Morris's formulation – less an ontological difference than a recognition of a historical divide with class connotations – architecture had become closer to the 'intellectual' arts, while 'decorative art' was 'intended primarily for the service of the body'.[2] This was written within the framework of a socialist politics that understood industrial society as separating the worker from objective life through the commodification both of objects and of labour power; alienation was itself the loss of the object and of the capacity for sensuous engagement.[3] And so 'design' became a term that signified the non-material, the pure work of mind, as separate from labour.[4]

The tensions of a modernity that seemed to separate the economic world from the sensuous or formal one also provided the rich soil in which the discipline of art history, as a project encompassing art, architecture and design, emerged in Germany.[5] This coincided with efforts through the nineteenth century to formalize the professional identity, first of the architect and, later, of the designer. The former was marked by emphasis on architecture as an art and by strenuous efforts to create and police distinctions between architects and those who merely build. This project carried echoes of earlier endeavours to position the artist as a practitioner of the liberal arts, rather than a craftsperson, with a consequent rise in esteem and economic rewards. The development of professional structures, educational institutions, qualifications, scientific societies and specialist publications all sought to safeguard the distinctive value of the services provided by the architect, but yet to keep the spectre of architecture as a commodity at arm's length. Even with the formation of the new design schools – many of which expressed as a core purpose the advancement of the quality of manufactured goods – the terms on which this was to be done (superiority of artistry or idea) perpetuated the distinction between 'good' design and the tawdry, profit-driven making of things.

Modernists attempted to reconcile some of these tensions through the new intermedialities of 'total design', itself dialectically related to the nineteenth-century interior 'supporting [the bourgeois] in his illusions'.[6]

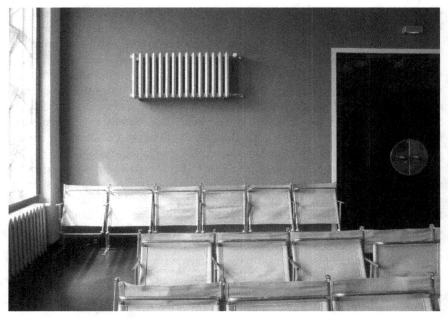

**FIGURE 0.2** *The* Festsaal *in the Bauhaus building, Dessau, Walter Gropius (1925–6). Photograph taken in 2011. Courtesy of Adrian Forty.*

Closely bound to disciplinary knowledge responding to industrial culture – and with profound implications for architecture and design – total design also involved the abandonment of ornament and the elevation of the status of everyday objects.[7] (The Bauhaus's famous radiators, 'skied' at the rear of its lecture theatre, can stand for this development. (See Figure 0.2.))[8]

These changes, although they welcomed new objects into the purview of professional consideration (the home, the vehicle and the city), did not disturb earlier hierarchies so much as they positioned the designer, and most particularly the architect, at the apex of all forms of design and making. (Much the same thing might be said about the recent return of ornament as the 'overall property of the [building] envelope'.)[9] The extension, or 'implosive design', of his (not accidentally gendered) attention to the small and domestic was counterbalanced by the 'explosive design' or synoptic quality of his vision and ambition, with the architectural profession positioned as uniquely capable of resolving the problems of modernity.[10] At almost the same moment (and shifted across the Atlantic) emerged a criticism that acclaimed the autonomous conditions of different art forms, but which allowed architecture the potential to transcend all the rest, to encompass within it the bounds of art and science. The celebrated breadth of the modern architect's competence remained, in reality, highly selective. 'Total design' remained within narrow bounds of professionalized and monetized practice, subsuming many different specialisms and trades within a hierarchical system. This structure and its boundaries were tacitly affirmed in surrounding professional discourse and criticism, which celebrated the integration of design elements, just as the people behind those elements were erased from the record. A superficially similar phenomenon can be found recently in what Hal Foster has called the 'inflation of design', but now in the conditions of post-Fordist neoliberalism and the 'perpetual profiling of the commodity'.[11] So we might say neither disciplinary and medial autonomy nor intermedial and interdisciplinary attitudes are inherently positive or negative; much depends on their relation with historical and cultural context.

The development of architecture and design as professional career paths was marked by the construction and naturalization of boundaries, even where they were laid over practices of making and building that were (and frequently remained) much more fluid. Academic discourse came to follow those boundaries, intentionally or simply through habit, and ignore their artificiality and persistent permeability. But this was not how it had always been. The founding figures of both disciplines were based in art history, and would either not have recognized their separation or would have seen it as insignificant in their search for the deeper historical connections between human societies and their cultural productions. In the tradition of *Kunstwissenschaft*, or the critical history of art, the objects of design and architecture (as well as fine art objects) were considered of equal significance and requiring equal attention. It was this tradition – even with its different camps and oppositions – that provided some of the key figures for both present-day design history and present-day architectural history, among them Gottfried Semper, Alois Riegl, Erwin Panofsky and Nikolaus Pevsner. (Even later figures like Reyner Banham might be understood as displaced products of this tradition.) But the logic and even the will behind this intermediality had been lost by the mid-twentieth century – so much so that, in the 1970s, design history was expressly founded in resistance to art history's aversion to the mass-produced and mundane object (and, more implicitly, to architectural history's 'custodial relationship' to design).[12] But though art history, architectural history and design history have all moved on from this in various ways, the echoes of these conceptual divisions persist in the primacy given to the artist/architect/designer over those who make or build, as well as to artefacts shaped by a vision over those whose realization is more accidental or solutions-focused. The maintenance of these boundaries in the histories we write reifies them and obscures their historical reality as recent and partial constructions. These boundaries are not merely arbitrary; they also have the potential to be pernicious. The aura of authority gathered around the term 'discipline' masks the historical specificity of the assumptions and biases around which disciplinary knowledge is produced and organized.[13]

The nineteenth-century roots of this academic disciplinary structure and so many of the other institutions that shaped the formation of architecture and design as professional categories should not be forgotten. The relationship between the act of design and the society it was produced for was envisioned first and foremost to naturalize the nation as a conceptual category and project a teleological vision of progress in which the autonomous, white, male creator would justly employ the labour of the working classes and the resources of colonized territories and people. This discipline-shaping ideology is not so easily displaced, leading to persistent blind spots when it comes to things like raw materials, supply chains, labour, transnational cultural exchange, appropriation, translation and environmental impact. The maintenance of disciplinary boundaries has, baked in, a tendency to obscure the contributions and transformations enacted by all those groups who lie outside of narrowly defined realms of professional practice (that is, on the basis of class, race, or gender).

Disciplines often – and for perfectly good reasons – have an interest in staying distinct. Design historians and architectural historians have some stake in the separation of domains; publishers have their separate series; journals define their remit so as to distinguish themselves in the academic market; professional societies promote the interests of the profession they represent. Museums have often structured their collections, especially as they reach the more modern periods, into departments divided by medium and discipline. The concept of disciplinary integrity or coherence masks the underlying economic compulsion of competition for funding and the attention of fee-paying student-customers. And all these, of course, institutionally enforce differences between objects and buildings. But, despite the actions of what Aby Warburg termed 'border guards', disciplines have never wholly limited or contained what can be done within them.[14] Overlaps frequently occur where historical agents – architects, designers, makers, clients – can be seen either as working together or working on each others' patch, and indeed where the assumption was that the buildings and the objects within them should be designed by the same person. And then there are the historians and theorists in either camp who work interchangeably on objects and on buildings without any felt need to justify or credentialize their competence in handling changing topics. Can one have a clear ontological distinction between disciplines and a more free-and-easy a-disciplinarity in the breach? Clearly, the answer must be yes, indeed that the distinction and the diffuseness are both necessary.

Large fields of practice already exist where distinctions between building and object are routinely bridged, if not ignored. Material culture studies will be discussed below, but to this could be added craft studies, archaeology and anthropology, as well as pre-modern period specialisms within art and design history. Many researchers don't think twice about whether the subject of their research is 'real' architecture or the 'proper' focus for a design historian or whether it encompasses legal history, political history, economic history, medical history, history of the workers' movement, history of science, or elements of all of these. But at the same time there may be penalties for thinking this way: students whose research interests are considered problematic for the awarding of a degree in one subject or another, colleagues who are considered as not fitted for a teaching job in a particular discipline or whose research work is difficult to publish because it is too much/not enough design history, women's history, medical history, etc.

At a conceptual level, boundaries create margins and therefore risk marginalizing the work that takes place at or over these boundaries. Professionalization and discipline formation were, at least in part, intended to secure economic advantage through the establishment of defensible credentials. Economic survival within academia remains tied to teaching posts and curricula that are slow to stray from traditional heartlands. This jeopardizes the future of scholars whose work is considered marginal or difficult to house. But an ability to work in this way is the pre-condition for many of academia's most pressing contemporary challenges: to decolonize, to pursue social justice and to address the climate crisis.[15]

A great deal of the human environment, of our experiences of it, and our ways of making sense of it, is neither uniquely architectural nor uniquely object-like – not-buildings, not-objects, or not exclusively so but sitting across or between designed objects and buildings. Hence many of the objects and topics addressed in this book: air-conditioning, bookshelves, the absence of a female toilet from a government building, an ephemeral table-monument, televisions and how they affect room use, convenience stores, emergency shelters. And hence too those moments in cultural history when such interdisciplinary experiences or zones have been the subject of sometimes colonizing, sometimes questioning work: whether in the technological aesthetic of High Tech, the environmental branding of Knoll, a Victorian journal devoted as much to objects as to buildings, the development of building and building component regulations, the disruptive potentials of the domestic object for radical architects, or the experience of freeway driving. As many of our contributors show, these objects and moments expose particular political configurations and resonances that otherwise might be occluded. Every definition we make of objects in opposition to buildings, architecture in opposition to design, turns out not to be as fundamental as once it might have seemed.

This book comes out of a sense that both this interzone and this questioning work needs to be more carefully explored.[16] Although it is largely a parochial concern, it is worth briefly returning to the relation between architectural history and design history in their institutional forms a few decades ago. Design history's separation from art history was declared necessary less to find an alternative niche as to assert a more varied set of methods and interdisciplinary approaches than had seemed permissible in what then appeared to be a limited and inward-looking discipline. The new *Journal of Design History* (launched in 1988) was notably downbeat about his its ambitions; design historians were used to marginality as well as 'the contingency of many disciplines', but social history now offered it better foundations or 'coherence' as a historical study. Architectural history's situation was different. Effectively separated – at least in English-speaking countries – from the intellectual course of art history since the mid-twentieth century, architectural history had already created its disciplinary armature and largely empirical practices while continuing in its difficult relation with architectural education. Other disciplines, theories and approaches impacted on design history, but generally their reception by architectural history was more belated and more uneven.

One disciplinary area that has opened up since the 1980s and that has come closest to dealing with the zone overlapping, and yet somehow also between, architecture and design is material culture studies. If this has a parent discipline it is really anthropology, which coined the term in the nineteenth century to identify ways that objects might help in the analysis of human society. As the *Journal of Material Culture* (launched in 1996) described its remit, it is 'concerned with the relationship between artefacts and social relations irrespective of time and place and aims to systematically explore the linkage between the construction of social identities and the production and use of culture'. Its editors gloried in having 'no obvious genealogy of ancestors to whom we should pay homage, and [we] are not concerned to invent any'.[17] It would be fair to say that there has probably been more interplay between material culture studies and design history than there has been between the former and architectural history, which when it looks towards anthropology has tended to engage with different traditions within it.

Materiality, or material practice, is understood in largely different ways by material culture studies than by design and architectural history. In the latter two, the traditions and founding concepts of art history can still be found in the emphasis on the particular phenomenal aspects of objects, on their description as a mode of interrogation and understanding, and in a concern with the specifics of historical context and location. Buildings and objects are understood through their processes of design and production (making, but also institutional constraints). Clients, patrons and public (often represented by critics) all play central roles, their intentions seen as umbilically linked to the forms taken by objects and buildings. There is also a largely different set of evidence adduced to understand all this, with priority given to the products of the personal hand (the drawing or letter), those documents close to the points of origin and making, and to a set of documents produced by the professions and trades concerned or those in their close contextual ambit (planners, manufacturers, and so on). Of course, much of this has been challenged in recent decades, but it is remarkable how much remains central.

Just as important for this book, there are many areas of history and many kinds of sensual and spatial material which have slipped our attention because the disciplinary separations and other dichotomies have obscured or prevented a serious and continuous engagement with the nature of the objects and situations and their actual historical implications.[18] Often these material elements correspond closely with the dimensions of a building that directly affect users and condition their experience and understanding of architecture, or they correspond to the dimensions of objecthood that give it the more pervasive effects and experiences we think of as environmental. The marginalization of such material, as a consequence, can exclude key aspects of the creative and experiential from our understanding of the human environment. Without intending to, these disciplinary boundaries often contribute to the perpetuation of regimes of value that have their foundations in the hegemony of capitalism and white supremacy – that 'real' architecture is made of brick, stone or concrete, not wood, bamboo, corrugated iron or other found and combined materials, and that 'important' design is produced by professionally trained designers and admirable in terms of form and not simply function.[19]

Building on what has been learnt from feminist interventions in scholarship and the necessity to go beyond an 'add women and stir' approach, we recognize that it is necessary to interrogate the parameters and assumptions we work within rather than just try to squeeze new things into them. This is imperative if we are to move towards architectural and design histories that adequately address the Global South, the climate crisis, and the vast inequalities that the buildings and objects that surround us continue to manifest and perpetuate.

## Categories

Specialist disciplinary knowledge, like most taxonomies, was designed to lay order over the inchoate, and is thus necessarily freighted with ideological assumptions as to what order looks like. It divides understanding and experiences into groups and units, replete with hierarchical interrelationships and cascades that can create arbitrary links between entities. But classification can be a way of rethinking as much as separating, bringing about new proximities and putting distance between things previously viewed as intrinsically aligned. In the mathematical field of topology, occasionally of interest to designers and architects in recent decades,[20] what is called the 'genus' is a highly essentialized characteristic of an object: how many holes it has, and therefore handles, closed surfaces and boundaries. Famously, in topology a coffee cup and a doughnut could share the same genus, and it's conceivable that a temple and a sieve might also. But classification need not be so formalist or at least not so instrumentally reductive; it might be something closer to the lingering theory of typology in architecture, even if that serves ultimately as a rigid separation of architecture from the mutability of time and the everyday. The type-object is a similar mythology, while a typology of objects has held out an unfulfilled promise of classification.[21] Where typology functions as cross-sectional analysis it allows for the consideration of what is there to be found, outside of preconceived notions of significance or worth or even discipline. The artist Ed Ruscha's typological series offer one possible version: parking lots, gas stations, swimming pools, sugar cubes, fabric swatches, even perhaps 'various small fires and milk'. Indifferent to object or building status, each series is limited only by the numbered quantity in its title.[22]

There is no single methodological solution to addressing the ingrained biases of disciplines. Rather it is increased flexibility of methodologies, experimentation and the employment of different lenses that will enable us to see differently. Classification systems create divisions between things that might, at first glance, look very similar (that sharks are fish and dolphins are not). An alternative perspective can bypass such divisions, such as an environmental category like marine biology. What is indicated here is not the dissolving of all distinctions, but more thought and flexibility in what distinctions are applied. In biology, 'genus' indicates taxonomic rank; above this, in the Linnaean system at least, would be kingdoms, classes and orders, and below genus would be species. So, within this, types of objects might be termed species. But how are we to go about defining species of objects? We might instead try an artistic-literary term like 'genre', which shares the same etymology. Are there genres of objects and can they include buildings? What about an environmental category?

Around a suburban house are a number of objects that abut onto the house in a variety of ways, which are not part of its architecture but are certainly within its close ambit – objects that extend or modify its performance. There might be water butts, benches, a lean-to for firewood and another for bikes, large pots and trellises for plants that scale the walls, a (possibly forlorn) nesting box, bins for different types of rubbish, a satellite dish, and so on. We might call these 'building-limb objects', but they could just as well be understood as extensions from the house's surrounds onto it and its dwelling practices, means of engaging it with a garden, a neighbourhood, with bird life, the weather, transmitted media, local waste collection, sources of energy, and so on. And they relate to another set of objects that belong more closely to the skin of the house: the guttering and other means of drainage, the fitted wiring and boxes for power supplies, extensions of the house in the form of an added conservatory, bay window, or just a screened-in porch. In each of these might be found quasi-anthropological structures of belief and practice, some of quite local cultural significance, others of wider, not to say universal import; each has an industry of suppliers or of ad hoc personalized solutions, and each a history of its emergence, development and possible decline.[23] And for the suburban house and its practices of dwelling, we might substitute, say, the nineteenth-century factory, the airport, the shopping mall, the power station, and so on. Each of these represents an environment, an ecosystem or 'décor' of designed elements to which the analytical skills of the architectural and design historian can readily be applied, in concert with other approaches.[24] And when considered in this way, margins are redrawn, creating different spaces for things to be noticed, for different questions to be raised. But there is in them all not only a tension between generic and particularized elements, but also between investment in the self-sufficient thing and the necessity of totality. That the latter remains even in conditions of extreme alienation between objects and buildings is well illustrated in the film *Nomadland* (2020), when, towards the end, the character Fern (played by Frances McDormand) visits Empire, the company town she had left in the Great Recession. Her old house, emptied of all objects (which are now in a storage unit), is nothing except echoing walls of board. But the desert that runs from the backyard of the house to the mountains is the same as she now sits in outside her van. The film constantly fixes on objects, habitations and landscapes; the elegiac mode barely contains the flux and disjointedness that are the effects of financial crisis and deindustrialization.

If neither a set of species nor of genres, perhaps objects might be understood as the 'simple forms' of human material life. This way of thinking about our material environment offers a perspective on buildings and objects, not as discrete units or sets of units, but as cultural manifestations of human experience. Borrowed from the German cultural historian André Jolles, 'simple forms' are modes of engagement with the world that, emerging from primordial gestures, have taken on structuring roles in literary narratives: jokes, saga, sayings, cases, riddles, and so on.[25] Jolles almost seems to encourage the analogy we are making not just by his emphasis on the links between the labour of language and the labour that produces objects, but by linking his simple forms with appropriate objects: relics (legends), runes (riddles), the cabin or forest clearing (fairy tales), newspaper clippings (anecdote), caricatures (jokes), and so on.[26] Similarly, though without the iconographic tendency in Jolles's suggestions, different categories of object help to structure human engagement with the material world, and they point to a set of associated social entities and collective experiences (home, travel, gathering, sleep). And simple forms, unlike biologically derived categories, allow for change: for emergence and adaptation, exhaustion and disappearance, and above all to be understood as manifestations of history.

## Scale

Perhaps the most readily drawn distinction between the building and the object is the most apparently simple: scale. Buildings are, on the whole, larger than objects – capable of the 'majestic', to use Kant's genre-specific term.[27] But though scale might be measurable, it is also relative and thus unstable. As the Zweig and Austen quotes at the start of this Introduction illustrate, scale is about relationships, about making one thing comparable to another, relative to it.[28] This sense of scale – mediate, intermediate, supermediate – has many repercussions. One of the distinctive features of modern architectural training was that architectural students very often started their education with exercises in designing objects like a chair, then worked up over the years towards the larger scales of building and even city. In that scaling up they were learning about the architect's sovereign realm, the aspiration for architecture to be *the* discipline to reconcile the forces of modernity. This is very much a control of scale or scaling up within the terms of a profession that often wanted more power, either for self-protective reasons in the face of incursions by other disciplines, professions or trades, or because of the aptitudinal logic of their sovereign control, leading as much to the colonial and neocolonial planning consultants of the mid-twentieth century as to the bathetic 'bigness' of the work of contemporary starchitects.[29]

In direct opposition to this is the notion of cooperation across the crafts and professions, as epitomized in the Arts and Crafts movement and Art Nouveau, for instance, where the emphasis lay in the encounter between the human and the material. In both making and use, scale was marginal to the immersive experience of tonality and patina.[30] Both these models, though, tend towards maintenance of a centre of gravity located in the intention or vision of the designer, the self-contained world of the mega-structure or *Gesamtkunstwerk*. A feature article on the Behrens House, by Peter Behrens, in *Deutsche Kunst und Dekoration* exemplifies this celebration of sole authorship (Figure 0.3).

Even when placed in the context of key actors such as Ernst Ludwig, the Grand Duke of Hesse, who initiated the enterprise of the Darmstadt Colony, or Alexander Koch, the publisher, the *Gesamtkunstwerk* ideal of the Behrens House still obscures the necessary contribution of myriad craftsmen and craftswomen, tradespeople, typesetters, draftsmen, the photographer, and Behren's wife and daughter, whose presence in photographs lent verisimilitude to imagery of an exhibition home that was, in fact, never occupied.[31]

Resisting the pull of the illusory clarity of solo-authorship allows us to focus instead on the intersections that permeate and pierce the integrity of such imagined worlds, drawing attention to what have too often been categorized as service spaces, as appendages or ancillary crafts, and therefore too often sublimated or marginalized. Such a 'geography of small spaces', as Swati Chattopadhyay has called it, works against the colonizing effects of the large, particularly in architectural history and particularly in relation to the assumption that significance, disciplinary importance, can only be found by going big.[32] Talking instead about the extremes of large scale or the miniature – macro-design, micro-architectures – also offers ways of bypassing disciplinary perspectives. To think of the encompassing landscape or of the punctuating detail, to think of environmental conditions or the workings of technology,[33] to think of infrastructure at the transcontinental level or at the level of its interface with homes or workplaces, to think of materiality as a relational not an inherent category,[34] all these do not so much render meaningless the distinctions of designed object and architecture

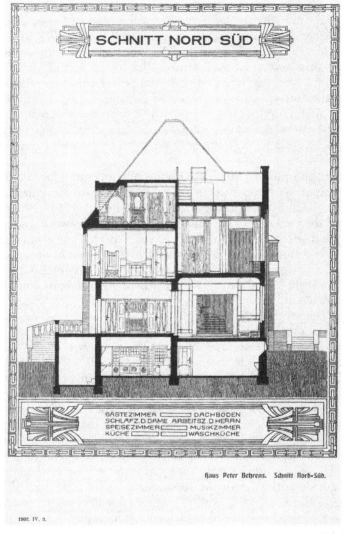

FIGURE 0.3 *Behrens House, north–south section, Darmstadt, Peter Behrens (1901). Deutsche Kunst und Dekoration IX (1901–2): 162.*

but place them in parentheses. It is not possible to encompass the history of everything. Parameters entail exclusions. But shifts of scalar setting – the church as gimmick, the smartphone's environment – can dissolve assumptions and dynamize interpretation.[35]

The idea of scale also affects how the surroundings, the explanatory contexts, are considered; how background becomes foreground. In one of the classics of modern design history, *Objects of Desire* (1986), Adrian Forty satirized simplistic approaches to the relation of design and architecture to society by using the analogy of an aquarium.[36] The fish in it are, as it were, the objects of design, but a rich and complex understanding of them as interrelated with many other things and conditions has been replaced by reduced stand-ins – the gravel at the bottom of the tank, a few weeds, the equivalent, say, of a sprinkling of political affairs, or a sketch of social change, neither of which is made to relate meaningfully to the chosen object of analysis. If the satire was well aimed, at the same time it was unfair in its choice of analogical object. How big an aquarium would be required, and how rich and varied would its contents need to be – how filled with animate life, with 'assemblages' – to satisfy contextual understanding? It would seem either to imply an equivalent world or a very different model, one perhaps where the framework, the glass walls, would somehow be dissolved. However – and tellingly, as John Bellamy Foster has shown – the beginnings of an ecological understanding of nature started in the nineteenth century precisely with aquariums. They were 'a way of understanding species within whole environments', especially when scaled up to huge size – made into architecture – like the popular aquarium opened at Brighton in 1872 (and much admired by Karl Marx) and the state-funded Marine Biological Laboratory opened at Plymouth in 1888 specifically for ecological research (and famous for its work on the ecology of plankton).[37] What would a controlled study be, where would an argument about determining conditions end, if the aquarium had to become an ocean in miniature? Contemporary biology and environmental sciences (not to mention big data) have developed new methods to grapple with the complexities of scale, across both space and time. But, as that which 'surrounds' the object, the problem of context and its ever refined or expanded parameters remains.

Ecology, like other thematic, issue-based approaches, requires movement outside disciplinary constraints. It needs to, as many other themes need to, if it is to be made to bear upon the theme's full consequences. Disciplines can seem starved and self-interested by comparison, their journals, academic departments and professional organizations too easily appearing inward-looking and irrelevant. This is ironic in relation to the discipline-building impulse to secure and defend a specialist preserve and the distinct authority to answer certain types of question. The danger is that these may not be the questions anyone wants the answers to. Instead, new and pressing questions arise that demand answers and that push at the boundaries of disciplinary knowledge: migration, slavery, waste, global trade, social media, empire, pandemics and health systems – all of these involve architecture and design or have implications for them, but they need often to be grounded in experiences and literatures produced with no necessary relation to architecture and design. Relatedly, there are even bigger themes such as the unconscious, class, identity, gender, which overarch disciplines, while at the same time often being aimed at their objects. And all these have, of course, their speculative thinkers and creators of systems and methods, the most influential of which are always discipline breaking (though they may also be – sometimes without intent – discipline making).

## Notes

1. Stefan Zweig, *The Post Office Girl*, trans. Joel Rotenberg (London: Sort Of Books, 2009), 39. The Austen quote is in Jane Austen, *Pride and Prejudice* (1813; London: Penguin, 1994), 188.
2. William Morris, 'Art Under Plutocracy', in William Morris, *Art and Society – Lectures and Essays by William Morris*, ed. Gary Zabel (1883; Medford, Mass.: George's Hill, 1993), 20–1.
3. Franck Fischbach, *La production des hommes: Marx avec Spinoza* (Paris: Vrin, 2014), 20–1.
4. Adrian Forty, 'Design' in *Words and Buildings: A Vocabulary of Modern Architecture* (London: Thames & Hudson, 2000), 136–41.
5. Mark Crinson and Richard J. Williams, *The Architecture of Art History – A Historiography* (London: Bloomsbury, 2019).
6. Walter Benjamin, *Charles Baudelaire – A Lyric Poet in the Era of High Capitalism*, trans. Henry Zohn (London and New York: Verso, 1983), 167.
7. Alina Payne, *From Ornament to Object: Genealogies of Architectural Modernism* (New Haven and London: Yale University Press, 2012).
8. Interestingly, the radiators were never connected up – they were purely ornamental. Thanks to Adrian Forty for this information.
9. Antoine Picon, *Ornament – The Politics of Architecture and Subjectivity* (Chichester: Wiley, 2013), 17–58.
10. Mark Wigley, 'Whatever Happened to Total Design?', *Harvard Design Magazine* 5 (1998): 1–8.
11. Hal Foster, *Design and Crime and Other Diatribes* (London: Verso, 2002), 17–26.
12. Penelope Dean, 'No Strings Attached', *Harvard Design Magazine*, 35 (2012): 22; Crinson and Williams, *Architecture of Art History*, 13–33; Clive Dilnot, 'The State of Design History. Part I: Mapping the Field' and 'The State of Design History. Part II: Problems and Possibilities', *Design Issues*, 1, no.1 (Spring, 1984): 4–23 and 1, no.2 (Autumn, 1984): 3–20.
13. David Shumway and Ellen Messer-Davidow, 'Disciplinarity: An Introduction', *Poetics Today* 12, no.2 (1991): 201–25.
14. E. H. Gombrich, 'Aby Warburg: His Aims and Methods', *Journal of the Warburg and Courtauld Institutes*, 62 (1999): 270.
15. For a related call for closer work between design history and environmental history see Kjetil Fallan and Finn Arne Jørgensen, 'Environmental Histories of Design: Towards a New Research Agenda', *Journal of Design History*, special issue on 'Environmental Histories of Design' 30, no.2 (2017): 103–21.

16  For another examination of the disciplinary intersections see Jessica Kelly and Claire Jamieson, 'Practice, Discourse, and Experience: The Relationship between Design History and Architectural History', *Journal of Design History* special issue on 'The Relationship of Design History and Architectural History', 33, no.1 (February 2020): 1–15.

17  Editorial, *Journal of Material Culture* 1 no.1 (March 1996): 5–6.

18  It was not a disciplinary demarcation that led Asa Briggs to separate out the subjects of his great – and in its own way revisionist – trilogy *Victorian People* (1953), *Victorian Cities* (1963), and *Victorian Things* (1988), but rather a certain understanding of context as the panorama of *the same*. Likewise, this book largely takes its distance from new materialist approaches in which things are ventriloquised and have their own (weightless) volition, while the human context of their meaning or making is deemed mythological: eg Maria Voyatzaki (ed.), *Architectural Materialisms – Nonhuman Creativity* (Edinburgh: Edinburgh University Press, 2018), 17, 308–9; Francesca Hughes, *The Architecture of Error: Matter, Measure, and the Misadventures of Precision* (Cambridge, MA and London: MIT Press, 2014), 105, 126–7; Lorraine Daston, 'Introduction' in Lorraine Daston (ed.), *Things That Talk: Object Lessons from Art and Science* (Brooklyn, NY: Zone Books, 2004), 7–24.

19  Mainak Ghosh, 'Built Environment in Response to the Ecology, Design, and Perception of the Global South' in *Perception, Design and Ecology of the Built Environment: A Focus on the Global South,* ed. Mainak Ghosh (Cham: Springer Nature, 2020), 1–22.

20  For very different takes on the 'topological turn' see John Roberts, *Revolutionary Time and the Avant-Garde* (London: Verso, 2015), 194–248; and Lars Spuybroek, *The Architecture of Continuity* (Rotterdam: NAI Publishers, 2008).

21  See Jean Baudrillard, *Le Système des Objets* (Paris: Gallimard, 1968).

22  On Ruscha and typology see Sianne Ngai, *Our Aesthetic Categories: Zany, Cute, Interesting* (Cambridge, MA and London: Harvard University Press, 2012), 147–9.

23  For comparative material see the essays in Robin Schuldenfrei (ed.), *Atomic Dwelling: Anxiety, Domesticity, and Postwar Architecture* (London: Abingdon, 2012). Schuldenfrei is our source for the term 'practices of dwelling': Ibid, xi. One could equally well compare these object–house relations to those (described in Charles Moore's preface as 'allies in inhabitation') in Junichiro Tanizaki, *In Praise of Shadows*, trans. Thomas J. Harper and Edward G. Seidensticker (London: Vintage, 2001), 1, 5ff.

24  Décor is Antoine Picon's term for an expanded sense of the coordination of ornaments and objects: Picon, *Ornament*, 122–6.

25  André Jolles, *Simple Forms*, trans. Peter J. Schwartz (1929; London: Verso, 2017). For discussion of Jolles's work see Fredric Jameson's Foreword in this translation, and for its use in elaborating a category of objects see Steve Edwards, 'Making a Case: Daguerreotypes', *British Art Studies* 18 (November 2020), https://doi.org/10.17658/issn.2058-5462/issue-18/sedwards

26 Jolles, *Simple Forms*, 8–18.

27 Immanuel Kant, *Critique of the Power of Judgment*, trans. Paul Guyer and Eric Matthew (Cambridge: Cambridge University Press, 2000), 228.

28 Darcy Grimaldo Grigsby, *Colossal: Engineering the Suez Canal, Statue of Liberty, Eiffel Tower and Panama Canal* (Pittsburgh and New York City: Periscope, 2012), 17.

29 On the historical development of the sovereign architect see Brian Hanson, *Architects and the 'Building World' from Chambers to Ruskin* (Cambridge: Cambridge University Press, 2003). For 'bigness' see Rem Koolhaas, 'Bigness or the Problem of Large', in Rem Koolhaas and Bruce Mau, *S, M, L, XL: OMA* (London: Taschen, 1997).

30 Claire O'Mahony (ed.), *Symbolist Objects: Materiality and Subjectivity at the Find de Siècle* (High Wycombe: The Rivendale Press, 2009).

31 Susanne Deicher, 'Imaginary Practice: Ideology and Form in the Unlived-in House of Peter Behrens on the Mathildenhöhe in Darmstadt', trans. Iain Boyd Whyte, *Art in Translation* 3, no.2 (June, 2011): 224.

32 Swati Chattopadhyay, 'Architectural History or a Geography of Small Spaces?', 2021 Eduard F. Sekler talk, Society of Architectural Historians, https://www.sah.org/2021-virtual-conference/eduard-f-sekler-talk

33 The pioneering text here remains Reyner Banham's *The Architecture of the Well-tempered Environment* (London: Architectural Press, 1969).

34 Antoine Picon, *The Materiality of Architecture* (Minneapolis: University of Minnesota Press, 2020), 10–20.

35 Here work within media theory is particularly relevant: Friedrich Kittler, *Gramophone, Film, Typewriter*, trans. Geoffrey Winthrop-Young and Michael Wutz (1986; Stanford: Stanford University Press, 1999); Reinhold Martin, *The Urban Apparatus: Mediapolitics and the City* (Minneapolis: University of Minnesota Press, 2016).

36 Adrian Forty, *Objects of Desire: Design and Society from Wedgwood to IBM* (London: Thames & Hudson, 1986), 8.

37 John Bellamy Foster, *The Return of Nature – Socialism and Ecology* (New York: Monthly Review Press, 2020), 38, 58.

# PART ONE

# Grey Zones

In Part One, Grey Zones, we find those things which are themselves in some conceptual inbetween zone – neither the conventional objects of design nor those of architecture. These entities are often neglected or not given much attention, either because of the disciplinary differences that have developed between design history and architectural history, or because they have simply not been regarded as worthy of attention as a result of their lowly status or ubiquity. They exist in the spaces of the ignored and taken-for-granted, the contact points between differently categorized zones of culture, neither one thing nor the other.

The first chapter by Swati Chattopadhyay explores interrelations in form and scale as they play between language and inscription, or printed word; from volume or manuscript to chest or bookshelf; from Royal Treasury to Oriental Repository and on to the emblematic function of the private library in the English-style house of an Indian intellectual. The chapter places the bookshelf in the context of its relationship to the colonial public sphere. Object acquisition and display is repeatedly reframed as an articulation of authority, and architecture plays a key role in making this visible and legible. At the same time, small objects retain their power. The preference for a wooden sandal over a leather shoe may function to bar the threshold to an institution. In this way, the chapter serves to remind us of the significance of the small-scale.

In Chapter Two by Meltem Ö. Gürel, we encounter an example of the way a now-ubiquitous object transformed domestic space and spatial practice in Turkey in the 1970s. The new technology of television engendered a new form of sociability within the home. Rather than being peripheral to the architecture, the popularity of television viewing made the object a centre of gravity that drew the occupants of the house together and reconfigured the surrounding furniture and architecture. Radiating out from this, privately owned televisions transformed the wider city, both through the infrastructure of individual aerials and satellite dishes and through a preference for entertainment within the home.

In Chapter Three by Louisa Iarocci, we are invited to consider the convenience store as a building type shaped, at a fundamental level, by developments in food and transport technologies. The advent of product branding was immediately absorbed into the architectural form, blurring the boundary between building and commodity. Both buildings and objects were shaped by the same forces: the development of food preservation technologies, refrigeration, electrification, and the rise in private automobile ownership. As such, the convenience store can only be understood as part of this wider consumer ecology. Rarely designed by professional architects, it is an example of the sort of building that has no place in the canon. Unlike the department store or the petrol pump, its evolution from nineteenth-century grocer's shop denies it a moment of emergence as a new form.

In Chapter Four, Jiat-Hwee Chang explores another overlooked form of domestic technology: the air-conditioning unit. Like the television, the air-conditioning unit had profound repercussions for the development of architectural form and spatial practices. Not just a new technology that needed to be accommodated within apartment design and the accompanying framework of legal regulation and utilities provision of the public housing authorities, air-conditioning altered the ambient environment of the home. This transformation had knock-on effects, as the design of homes in Singapore shifted from a dominant principle of airiness and porosity to one of enclosed cosiness, and from responsiveness to the external environment to reactions to the mechanically cooled interior.

In the last chapter in Part One, Richard J. Williams explores the ways in which automobile driving prompted a reconceptualization of public space in the 1960s. The focus here is not on vehicle design but on the transport infrastructure of the road network, particularly the freeway or motorway and its impact, transforming both the physical and the immersive landscape. The chapter explores how Reyner Banham and other thinkers were propelled by their experience of driving to understand the relationship between people, objects, urban infrastructure, space and time in a new way, as a design ecology or environmental category.

The grey zone is a blurring of boundaries. It reminds us of the knock-on effects that reverberate back and forth between people, things, buildings and their environment, and further to the wider infrastructure, transportation networks, utilities, legal frameworks, new forms of media and political systems within which all these effects take place.

# CHAPTER ONE

# A Good Shelf:
# The Material Culture of Reading in Colonial India

*Swati Chattopadhyay*

The Bangyia Sahitya Parishat Library in Kolkata is home to a collection of books that once belonged to Ishwar Chandra Vidyasagar (1820–91), a luminary of the nineteenth-century public sphere of Calcutta (Kolkata). The books are housed in twenty-four bookshelves that Vidyasagar had custom-made for his Sanskrit, Hindi, Bengali and English books as well as his collection of *puthi* (manuscript scrolls).[1]

A renowned Sanskrit scholar, social reformer, educator, author and publisher, Vidyasagar had intended his book collection to be donated or sold after his death. According to the instruction in his will, he wanted the person or institution acquiring his book collection to take the books *with* the bookcases in which he kept them. Those bookshelves ultimately arrived at the Bangiya Sahitya Parishat Library with much of the original collection still intact.[2]

Perhaps Vidyasagar anticipated that his heirs would not understand or heed the integrity of his book collection, and that is why he put in the clause about bookshelves in his will. He did not want his book collection to be dispersed, scattered and forgotten. Perhaps they were bequeathed to future generations of literary Calcutta as a mark of his scholarly range and taste. The books, he hoped, would acquire real value in transmission. Perhaps we would get to know him by the company of books he kept. We do not know why he made this decision, but it is evident from contemporary sources that he went to great lengths to accommodate those bookshelves. He had a new residence built to house this large collection.[3]

**FIGURE 1.1** *One of the bookshelves that once belonged to Ishwar Chandra Vidyasagar, presently in the Bangiya Sahitya Parishat Library, Kolkata. Copyright Swati Chattopadhyay.*

I stood in front of one of these bookshelves on a dimly lit stair-landing at the Bangiya Sahitya Parishat Library, hoping to find something extraordinary (Figure 1.1). The dark varnish of the solid wood spoke of age. The stout legs of the bookshelf made room for a few inches of space between the bottom shelf and the floor, making it convenient to clean underneath. The frame itself was unadorned. The clear glass door-leaves of the bookshelf were locked. I peered through the glass to see the titles of the volumes inside. Nothing appeared exceptional about the object, except a solemn presence.

Rather than consider the bookshelf as an isolated object of historical significance, I use Vidyasagar's bookshelf as an entrée into the nineteenth-century material culture of reading. It helps us unfold the relation between architecture (the building) and the object (bookshelf) as a set of practices – economic, social, political – that shaped the culture of empire. My focus is the relation between the bookshelf as a spatial container of books and the space in which the bookshelf was located. This relation accrued peculiar meanings in the nineteenth-century colonial milieu. Here I bring together a few historical strands that created such spatial specificities.

The changing practice of storing books – specifically, the gradual obsolescence of the practice of storing books in chests, hampers and wall niches, and the emergent practice of keeping books in rows of horizontal shelves either set inside a wall or as free-standing furniture – is key to this story. While the use of wall niches and cupboards for storing books continued, the widespread use of the shelf specifically meant for books was coeval with the rapid growth of the print industry in the late eighteenth and nineteenth centuries that transformed habits of reading, collecting and keeping books. It was also a consequence of global 'bibliomigrancy' – the movement of books from one language to another and across the world, made possible by modern colonialism.[4]

The social significance of bibliomigrancy exceeded its literary content. An entirely new set of social relations of race, class and caste – between colonizer and colonized, Indians and Europeans, intellectual elites and the barely literate – was created around the mode of storing books. The bookshelf, first as a tool of display and second as an emblem of knowledge acquisition and transmission, emerged as a central reference in calibrating power relations.

The location of the collection – in a secluded space as opposed to a public space, in the domestic realm or oriented towards a public sphere – was paramount to the attribution of meaning.[5] As a fragment linked to the public world of letters and of colonial collecting, the bookshelf in the colonial milieu framed the contentious relation between public and private spheres. Viewed in relation to an intended user/audience, it helped articulate both a new public display of colonial power and a new idea of literary space within domestic confines. The bookshelf in this sense emerged as a new *figure of space* that mediated relations of power.

By figure of space, I mean the constitution of space around a social role – when a space is attached to a social role and thus becomes connotative of an expected performance of power relations, and through this linkage becomes tropic. This is the case of the housewife and the drawing room in nineteenth-century literature on domesticity, the veranda as a site of European authority in the colonies, and the salon in the space of bourgeois domesticity that negotiated the line between public and private spheres. Though historically specific, a figure of space exceeds its particular spatial parameters to signal an expanded social imaginary where debates on social ideals and expectations may be launched.

The balance of the chapter is divided into four parts. The first section places the culture of bibliomigrancy in the colonial context of the long nineteenth century and the role of the bookshelf in mediating knowledge acquisition and language competency. The second section traces the shift in the practice of book collecting by focusing on the library of Tipu Sultan

(1750–99) as a site of cultural encounter between British colonizers and a vanquished ruler to demonstrate the spatial implication of the mode of storing and displaying books. The third section delves into the role of bookshelves in articulating the literary culture of nineteenth-century Calcutta and returns to Vidyasagar's library as the centrepiece of discussion. The concluding section focuses on the articulation of a new figure of space in the staging of an encounter between two public figures – Vidyasagar as a scholar and reformer, and the nineteenth-century mystic-saint Sri Ramakrishna (1836–86) – in a conversational vignette that addresses the object of seeking knowledge in a colonial milieu. In each of these sections, we see the relation between the bookshelf and the library as a repository of knowledge and a space of colonial accumulation being turned around to perform a different task. In each of these, the bookshelf as space and the architecture of the room in which the bookshelf was located were projected onto a larger landscape of colonial relations – of governance, sovereignty and public good.

## Bibliomigrancy

At the outset, let me establish how the bookshelf as a figure of space was particular to the colonial milieu and differed from the comfortable cosmopolitanism that pervaded the practice of book collecting in the nineteenth and early twentieth centuries. Let's take Walter Benjamin's essay, 'Unpacking My Library' (1931), for example.[6] Benjamin endowed the contingent act of collecting with a quasi-mystical aura, and noted that collections are dwelling spaces in the maelstrom of capitalism. As his bookscape extended from the personal to the larger world of Europe, Benjamin assumed the universality of the bookshelf as space: his cosmopolitanism would not allow anything short of that.

We see Benjamin sitting amid the crates in which the books had arrived: 'The books are not in shelves yet, not yet touched by the mild boredom of order', ready to be paraded in front of an audience. Until then Benjamin could rejoice in the disorder of the crates that had been 'wrenched open, the air saturated with the dust of wood, the floor covered with torn paper'.[7] The books would see light after two years of crate-life: the tactile pleasure of opening the crates and handling the books is what presumably prompted Benjamin to reflect how this collection was acquired and the legacy of that transmission; through remembrance he could travel to the cities and auction houses where he found his treasured editions. The most valued works had distinctive proprietary lineage or they were treasured family inheritance. No surprise there. A personal history of collecting as a form of self-fashioning is necessarily connected to the larger history of printing and collecting. In contrast, the bookshelf is the place of stasis, waiting to be disturbed by the owner-reader's volitions. In Benjamin's world, the bookshelf as container is rather too obvious, taken for granted. It disappears from view and enables us to contemplate the significance of the act of collecting.

Benjamin had inherited a culture of book collecting in which bibliomigrancy was both assumed and expected. The ability to fill the empty space of the bookshelf with works from all over the world and from all times gave the bookshelf a universal space–time feature not shared by any other space in the house until much later.[8] However, if for a moment we leave Benjamin's twentieth century for the nineteenth-century colonial world, the assumption of universality appears fraught. Not everyone could claim their literary heritage so assuredly without being reminded of the power relations of bibliomigrancy shaped by the 'command of languages and languages of command', to borrow Bernard Cohn's phrase.[9]

Advocating the introduction of English education in India in 1835, lawmaker and historian Thomas Babington Macaulay remarked that 'a single shelf of a good European library . . . is worth the whole of the native literature of India and Arabia'.[10] Macaulay acknowledged that he had no knowledge of these other languages, but he was satisfied with the opinion of orientalist scholars who advocated the study of Sanskrit, Persian and Arabic – none of whom would apparently contradict his assessment of the superiority of European languages. He was not discussing specific works; he did not have the language competency to do so. The comparison in which the whole of 'native' literature fell short of Macaulay's 'good' shelf was a connoisseurial space; it could be filled in by the reader's imagination and verified by their literary taste and judgement. Macaulay's single shelf of books was a synecdoche of empire – the basis for claiming the superiority of European language, law, justice.

That the authority of the written word would be used to justify European superiority ought not to be a surprise; much has been written about the interface between literate and non-literate cultures and between different language systems in shaping regimes of conquest.[11] The space in which Macaulay sought to intercede, however, was a scribal culture of governance with a complex system of rules and hierarchies, and a literate culture in which libraries already functioned as power symbols. Libraries of princes and elites as well as monastic institutions were well known and their valuable collections eagerly sought by European adventurists and Orientalists. By the time Macaulay penned his 'Minute', classics of Persian, Arabic and Sanskrit had already made their way into Europe to adorn personal libraries and fatten state and corporate archival holdings. The eighteenth- and early nineteenth-century orientalists prized their collection of oriental books and manuscripts.

What was at stake for Macaulay was not just the colonial state's support of schools that taught Oriental languages but the expectation that the British administrator in India would have to learn Indian languages.[12] In 1800, Governor General Richard Wellesley instituted the Fort William College in Calcutta to teach newly arrived British civilians Indian languages – Persian,

FIGURE 1.2 'English Gentleman and his Munshi' (c. 1813). Sir Charles D'Oyly, The Costumes and Customs of Modern India *(London: Edward Orme, 1825)*.

Arabic, Sanskrit, Urdu, Bengali and others. A first-hand knowledge of Indian languages, it was argued, would not only aid the work of governance, but was a necessary antidote to the untrustworthiness of Indian personnel who manned the expanding bureaucratic apparatus of the colonial state. Here European professors taught alongside Indian scholars who prepared texts, grammars and dictionaries. Language instruction at Fort William College formalized the informal process through which British administrators and merchants in the eighteenth century acquired familiarity with the principal languages of the subcontinent.[13]

The culture of knowledge accumulation and exchange that characterized these pre-1835 decades is depicted in an 1813 lithograph by Charles D'Oyly (Figure 1.2). Here we see a young European man learning the Arabic alphabet from an elderly *munshi* (language instructor). The *munshi* sits in a dignified manner as a person of authority with a book in hand, while the young man appears exhausted in his attempt to master the first steps of language preparation. In the background is John Gilchrist's *Grammar of the Hindoostanee Language* (1796). A bookcase against the wall provides a literal and metaphorical background of bibliomigrancy. The open bookcase as artefact designates the space as a study/office. Its rows of uniformly bound volumes, conforming to the practice of having books custom-bound for one's library, represent the authority of the world of European texts. That world of ideas, however, has to be mediated through the language practices of the colonized if it is to gain salience. The relation between the European *sahib* and the Indian *munshi* is presented in a subtle tension, as the hierarchy between the ruler and ruled appears skewed when the colonized teaches the language of command to the ruler. Macaulay's 'Minute' sought to change the terms of exchange portrayed in this image.

The new nexus of language and governance imagined by Macaulay was grounded in powerful currents of bibliomigrancy that had been set in motion in the late eighteenth century. Now I turn to one such event of pivotal significance: the looting of Tipu Sultan's library in Seringapatam (Srirangapatnam) and its subsequent re-establishment in London.

## Tipu's library and sovereignty

When the Battle of Seringapatam (1799) concluded the Fourth Anglo-Mysore War (1798–9) with a decisive British victory, Tipu Sultan was dead and his library of between 3,000 and 4,000 volumes was scattered, a substantial portion destroyed.[14] Of these, a collection of about 2,000 manuscripts in Persian (court language), Kannada (language of administration), Marathi, Telegu, Arabic, French and English was removed to Fort William College Library in Calcutta. Governor General Wellesley used Tipu's collection to buttress his decision to found Fort William College without the East India Company (EIC) Court of Directors' permission and to post-facto justify waging the Fourth Anglo-Mysore War. After Wellesley's term as governor general ended, the EIC asked for the collection at Fort William College to be sent to London, where it was placed in the company's Oriental Repository. Few originals and a large number of copies remained in Calcutta at the Fort William College and the Asiatic Society. The remains of Tipu's library in Calcutta and London would anchor the emergent vision of British imperial sovereignty.

Wellesley's acquisition and distribution of Tipu's library was an old and tried method of appropriating the signs of authority to justify the right of conquest. In this case, he wanted access to the documents in Tipu's library to establish the Mysore ruler's venality and determination to destroy British presence in India in order to justify the Fourth Anglo-Mysore War. The territorial and inquisitorial became linked in an assertion of the library as a representation of sovereignty: the right to rule. In a 2020 article, historian Joshua Ehrlich points out that in the eighteenth century libraries were emblems of power as repositories of *both knowledge and beauty*. In turning the plunder of Tipu's library into greater ideological use, beyond the monetary worth of the books, the EIC's administrators were appropriating the value that Tipu himself placed on his fine book collection as a mark of his sovereignty.[15]

Tipu had acquired this collection from the libraries of vanquished rulers and had manuscripts prepared at his court. He employed calligraphers, bookbinders and illustrators to reproduce works, which were then distributed. The works in the collection were marked with his imperial seal, individually wrapped, and kept in chests. This method of storage was common in collections attached to monasteries and religious institutions in the subcontinent and ensured 'excellent preservation'.[16] Following a much older and widespread practice of marking paintings and books with the owner's seal, in placing his royal stamp next to previous seals, Tipu was claiming dynastic legitimacy.[17] This legitimacy exceeded affairs of the state and contained a personal impress of rulership.

The relation between buildings and objects is key to understanding this articulation of sovereignty. Unlike the treasury (*toshakhana*), which was located behind the audience hall facing the public courtyard, the library was located in the inner courtyard of the palace.[18] Besides books and manuscripts, the library also contained state papers, legal digests and private correspondence.[19] In combining the functions of a *muhafizkhana* (record room) and a *kitabkhana* (library), the collection strode the line between public affairs of the state and the personal/dynastic collection of a king. This collection was carefully ordered and maintained by managers who were obliged to provide daily reports. From this repository of knowledge – literary, historic, scientific, legal – Tipu's sons were instructed in the affairs of the state.[20]

The narratives of British encounter with this collection suggest a reversal of meaning in how the space of the library was received and accorded value by the British. These narratives register both the value of the library as a *treasure house* and its difference from contemporary European libraries. To those who first encountered the library after the war it looked like a warehouse:

> The library and depôt of manuscripts, was a dark room, in the S.E. angle of the upper virandah of the interior quadrangle of the palace. Instead of being beautifully arranged, as in the Bodleian, the books were heaped together in hampers, covered with leather; to consult which, it was necessary to discharge the whole contents on the floor.[21]

The distinction between Tipu's library and the Bodleian resides in the use of bookshelves in the latter. Bookshelves here are synonymous with an enlightened institutional order, facilitating a methodical placement and display of books, providing easy access to that repository of knowledge. At the same time, bookshelves define the space of the modern library. They enable a collection to be turned into a library: here books may be placed in the light to engender the acquisition and dissemination of knowledge. In the absence of shelves, the vision of a library as a space of knowledge and enlightenment appeared errant. Tipu's library was seen as a dark space in which valuable content was secreted away, and seemingly betrayed Tipu's character: his coveting of beautiful objects, as well as his cunning and cruelty. Pairing the racialized metaphors of darkness and light with (heathen) ignorance and (Christian) knowledge, the distinction between the architecture of a depot and a library is used to signal the move from despotism to enlightened occupation.

The reference to the beauty of the Bodleian library is important in this context. Beauty itself was a matter of adjudication. While a 'Hindu goldsmith' was retained for providing a valuation of the treasury jewels, the inspection of the books in Tipu's library was presumably undertaken without the presence of an Indian scholar. British officers in charge selected from the larger collection over 300 manuscripts 'of the choicest description' for delivery to the EIC.[22] Penmanship and fineness of illustration were considered the chief criteria of value. The status of the books as artwork was prior to their importance as treatise. In this regard the valuation of the works in the library was akin to the valuation of jewels in the treasury.[23] Unlike the jewels, however, the books were not distributed among the officers and soldiers. Their status as art *and* information – something potentially more revealing – demanded a different kind of processing.

Tipu's state papers and the rest of the library were considered invaluable as reflective of his personal character. His peculiar 'barbarity', Alexander Beatson wrote, following William Kirkpatrick who translated some of the papers, could be deduced from state correspondence and a journal of dreams 'written in his own hand'.[24] The discovery of Tipu's library in a dark vault-like space was thus an encounter with the figure of Tipu as a ruler. The description corresponds with the much-publicized depiction of General Baird discovering the body of Tipu in a dimly lit dungeon-like space: English victory brings light to the dark spaces of Oriental despotism.[25]

That collections and characters were seen as mutually constitutive is not surprising. There is a much longer pre-eighteenth-century history going back to antiquity of thinking of a library as peculiarly reflective of the collector's intellectual and social dispositions.[26] What is striking in this instance is the intent behind disturbing the extant order of a collection. The actions of the British officers on the scene were a demonstration of the ability to appropriate, invert and disseminate a new order. Captain Price, one of the officers in charge of the operation, concluded his discussion of the princely library with an anecdote:

> As it was something in illustration of character, I cannot forbear mentioning that one day, while Maj. Ogg and myself were turning over the leaves of these multifarious M.SS. one of the young princes who had

been permitted to look in upon us, was overheard, in rather audible whisper, to observe to his attendants – 'Only see how these hogs are allowed to contaminate my father's books'.[27]

That the indiscriminate handling of the royal library was considered a desecration was evident to Captain Price. He placed this anecdote just before his description of the looting of the '*zennaunah*' or women's quarter located diagonally across from the library.[28]

When the library was transferred to the Oriental Repository at the East India House in London, it was displayed in shelves in a well-appointed room dressed in 'gold and azure' (Figure 1.3).[29] This room consisted of three compartments with two symmetrically arranged spaces flanking a domed square central space. Each room was furnished with bookshelves set within the walls. Generous windows in the side compartments admitted light. In the central space visitors were given a glimpse of Tipu's library.[30] They could

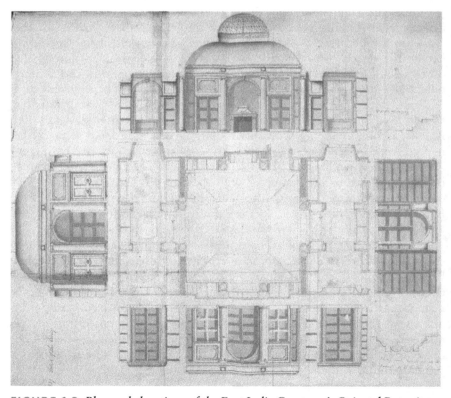

FIGURE 1.3 *Plan and elevations of the East India Company's Oriental Repository, Richard Jupp (c. 1797–8). Courtesy Victoria and Albert Museum. Accession no. D.1672–1898.*

FIGURE 1.4 'The East Offering its Riches to Britannia': Allegorical ceiling piece commissioned by the East India Company for the Revenue Committee Room in East India House (1777). Courtesy British Library Board. Shelf mark: Foster 245: 1778.

also see, alongside bound volumes, 'specimens of various ores and fossils which Major Ogg collected from the Mysore country'.[31]

At first glance, the distinction between the library as a state vault in Seringapatam and the library as the trophy of a mercantile corporation in London appears stark. While they both served the goals of claiming sovereignty, the Oriental Repository was meant as a visual display that extended the existing iconography of the decorative programme at the East India House, most clearly demonstrated by the ceiling painting that greeted visitors to the building: Spiridione Roma's 'The East Offering its Riches to Britannia' (1778) (Figure 1.4).[32]

Painted decades before the consolidation of empire, Roma's painting presented colonial trade and plunder as 'gifting': figures personifying India, Persia, China willingly offer their riches – tea, porcelain, bales of cotton, pearls – to Britannia as if they have recognized and accepted her innate superiority. Expropriation and gifting became unified in the figure of the library as a commodity on display.

This grand display of books alongside minerals and miscellaneous plundered treasures drew sharp criticism from one observer, Peter Gordon. A staunch critic of the EIC, Gordon disapproved of the repository on two counts. The collection as trophy transplanted to the 'metropolis of the conqueror' stood as an insult to the Indian who 'cannot visit the depot in which the spoil of his country is exhibited'. Note that Gordon describes the repository as a 'depot' exactly in the manner that Tipu's library was described by the English soldiers. Gordon also recorded the 'affecting sight' he had witnessed when Tipu's son, Jamal-ud-Din, visited the library and stood 'in the midst of the plunder of Seringapatam'; on one side of the prince 'lay Tipu's dream register, to another lay one of Tipu's illuminated Qurans'.[33] For the visitor, the original scene of plunder could be relived and reimagined.

The idea of the repository as alienated patrimony was reinforced by its ineffective insertion in Britain's public life. Gordon noted that the collection amounted to a national treasure: 'The most valuable collection of Oriental manuscripts in existence in Europe or in Asia'. Yet the directors possessed no recognition of such a valuable collection. The repository severely limited public access.[34] The short hours of the library, the paucity of qualified personnel, its lack of suitable reference books, even its location in the city far away from 'every other oriental establishment' made it ill-suited as a public library.

The functioning of the Oriental Repository, Gordon argued, mirrored the EIC's mercenary motives and its history of corruption.[35] The mere placement of books on shelves was not sufficient evidence of their availability for public enlightenment. The superficial emphasis on the library as a trophy detracted from the acquisition of knowledge that such a collection promised. Gordon was not troubled by the seizure of Tipu's library per se, but with the library's inadequate interface with the public (both in England and in India) and its utter neglect of public interest, that is, the failure of the library as an institution. The Court of Directors had reduced the collection to a hidden space once more; 'except the venerable librarian, no person knows what treasures it contains'.[36] Gordon saw in the library's lack of public access a mirror of that Oriental excess and despotism that so coloured the history of Tipu Sultan. If bibliomigrancy depended on circulation of books, travel between languages, and the exchange of ideas – the bases of an emergent nineteenth-century public sphere – the Oriental Repository thwarted these possibilities. The commodification of the library in the imperial metropolis that drew Gordon's critique was a constant refrain in descriptions of libraries in colonial India. Its spatial articulation, however, carried different meanings.

## Vidyasagar's library and the colonial public sphere

The diffusion of printed books in India in the late eighteenth century, beyond the confines of royal courts and European factories and missions, changed the spaces of reading, publishing, literary exchange and archiving.[37] For a while, as in the Western world, books, loose folios and manuscript scrolls jostled for space in trunks, chests and wall niches, before the bookshelf became a standard piece of household furniture.[38] The newness of the form of the bookshelf in the first decades of the nineteenth century was clearly articulated in Bhavanicharan Bandopadhyay's *Kalikata Kamalalaya* (Calcutta the Abode of Lakshmi, the Goddess of Prosperity), a didactic tract published in 1823.[39] Set as a conversation between a city dweller and a country dweller (newcomer to the city) about new modes of socialization that the upper-caste Hindus appeared to be undertaking in early nineteenth-century Calcutta, the text takes the form of two archetypal characters discussing the emergence of a new Bengali society in which religious rituals appear to have taken a back seat. The main point of contention is contamination: the pollution of the sacred Hindu household caught in the socio-economic nexus of the colonial city where men spend long hours performing salaried work in the office, neglecting the religious duties of the householder. Their speech, clothing, modes of socialization and the material culture of their residences betray foreign influence – hence the fear of ritual contamination. The outside world of the foreign colonizers is seen as invading the inner world of ritual observance, thereby posing a threat to the household's caste status.

One piece of furniture that serves as a point of discussion is the bookshelf. The visitor to the city asks in puzzlement about the fashion of buying books in Parsi, English and Arabic to fill one- and two-leaf glass-door 'almirahs'. The orderly display of the expensive collection appears in inverse relation to its use – seemingly the books are only handled by the manager and binder. Is this the educational equivalent of the practice of building temples – some do it for cultivating virtue and others to display wealth? – asks the country dweller.[40] At this, the city dweller irritably responds: there is no reason for a person of means to use a collection all the time; he does it when he needs to – his livelihood does not depend on daily use of books. And, of course, there are those whose livelihoods depend on daily perusal of books.

Three points are noticeable in this staged conversation. The English word bookshelf is not used, but the Portuguese/old English word almirah or almery (which by that time had become indigenized in Bengali as *almari*) is used to refer to the bookcase, suggestive of a process of cultural incorporation. Of course, all kinds of valuable goods could be stored in an *almari*. A book *almari* conveys the transformation of an older article of household furniture to meet the specific purpose of storing books.[41] Second, a distinction is made between the symbolic role of personal libraries comprising elegant bookshelves as markers of wealth and desire for knowledge acquisition, and the utilitarian use of collections for the sake of livelihood. Neither case, we are given to understand, presents a risk of contamination: books concern dealings with the outside world where economic and social norms of the rulers have to be followed. Not all wealthy people have libraries, we learn later. While the colonial marketplace has created opportunities for economic advancement for all castes and professions, not every man of means is invested in literary pursuits. The presence of a library in a house and its use differentiate upper-caste/classes from the merely wealthy. Third, there is no mention of Bengali books in this new library. Publication of Bengali books was a new enterprise, in which Bhavanicharan as writer, editor, publisher was one of the pioneers.

The library in nineteenth-century mansions of the Indian elite in Calcutta and provincial towns in Bengal would usually be located in the outer, public compartments of the house linked to the sphere of male sociality.[42] By the late nineteenth century bookshelves had also become common in middle-class households and residences of the burgeoning professional class of lawyers, educators and doctors.[43] While the library might still be located near the space of male sociality – the *baithakkhana* (salon) – it was just as likely to be a connecting piece between public (outer/male) and private (inner/female) compartments, as an increasing number of women were educated and fostered ambitions of partaking in the public sphere of letters.[44]

Vidyasagar's library did not fully accord with this spatial distinction between inner and outer compartments. Nor did Vidyasagar's understanding of public and private worlds comply with the distinction articulated by Bhavanicharan. Vidyasagar's book collection was not confined to a room designated as a library, but consisted of several rooms on the upper floor of his two-storey house. The scale, scope and organization of his library were noted by contemporaries. In addition to collecting books and manuscripts in Indian languages, he sourced English books directly from London, where booksellers were instructed to send him the books uniformly bound. The books were organized by subject – history, literature, philosophy – and represented this 'Sanskrit pundit's deep affection for Western history, science and philosophy'.[45]

The singular feature of Vidyasagar's life as an educator, author, publisher and social reformer was his nonconformism – his refusal to obey caste, religious and political norms simply because it would have been convenient to acquiesce for economic or social succour. Secular biographies and reminiscence of Vidyasagar read the spatial organization of his orderly library and its furniture arrangement as an index of his bibliomigrancy, rational outlook and upright disposition in matters both public and personal. Take this description, for example. In 1883, a young Muhammad Reazuddin Ahmad (1861–1933) came to meet Vidyasagar and was led into a large room in which ten to twelve glass-case almirahs were filled with books, all bound beautifully and with golden lettering. A servant was taking the books out one at a time and wiping each with a clean cloth. A massive table with twelve or thirteen chairs completed the room's furnishing. After a few minutes, the young man was 'led into another room also lined with almirahs filled with books' where Vidyasagar was sitting erect on a chair next to a large table.[46] In another reminiscence, these two rooms are described as his library and study. Though set up for both private reading and meeting with friends and guests, the rooms did not represent the *baithakkhana* of the

Bengali household, where men sat on a large carpet (*jajim*) on the floor. The *baithakkhana* had a connotation of gentlemanly indolence with which Vidyasagar, though known for his conversational aptitude, did not identify.[47]

The spatial articulation of the public self and the distinction between private and public spheres took on a peculiar configuration in nineteenth-century Bengal. Political theorist and historian Partha Chatterjee has argued that the distinction between an inner 'spiritual' domain and an outer 'material' domain was the leitmotif of nineteenth-century Bengali nationalism.[48] The spiritual domain that Bhavanicharan described as the domain of the household and caste community by the second half of the nineteenth century was redefined as a domain of the 'cultural'. This cultural domain had to be protected from colonial intrusion, whereas the material domain was the outer sphere of politics and statecraft in which European superiority had to be recognized, replicated and ultimately superseded. Long before the Bengali nationalist elite launched a political struggle in the outer domain, it began its self-definition in the domain of the cultural. Education and the purpose and value of education were some of the most debated aspects of this self-definition. Vidyasagar's library entered the history of Bengali thought as a site of such debate. The event was his legendary meeting with Sri Ramakrishna narrated by Mahendranath Gupta (1854–1932) in *Sri Sri Ramakrishna Kathamrita* (translated into English as *The Gospel of Shri Ramakrishna;* hereafter *RK*).

## A new figure of space

The meeting was initiated at Ramakrishna's request. Perpetually curious about spirituality and religious experience, he wanted to meet the man so famed for his erudition and kindness (Vidyasagar literally means 'ocean of learning' and his other sobriquet was *karunasagar*: 'ocean of kindness'). The narrative of this meeting was posed as an encounter between two divergent modes of being in the colonial world and two different paths to salvation. Although both were Brahmins, Ramakrishna, unlike Vidyasagar, had little education. He was a poor priest who had become, by the time this meeting took place, the most sought-after spiritual guide among the educated Bengali middle class. Increasingly disillusioned with the prospect of material advancement under colonial rule, they found refuge in Ramakrishna's teachings that emphasized freedom from salaried labour. Though usually dressed in a rustic manner, Ramakrishna had a fondness for fineries, particular Western leather shoes, an accessory that Vidyasagar famously never wore. The story of Vidyasagar's experience at the Asiatic Society Library where he was a member but was refused admission because he wore wooden sandals was already the stuff of lore.[49] Both men were living legends and 'worshipped' for two diametrically opposite reasons: one for his peculiar mix of kindheartedness and erudition, nonconformity and civic engagement,

FIGURE 1.5 *Ishwar Chandra Vidyasagar's residence, Kolkata. Copyright Swati Chattopadhyay.*

and the other for his godliness and sayings that combined the simplicity of rural speech with a dense body of theological scholarship.

*RK* is narrated in four registers. It contains the details of date, time and location and description of the physical settings. These documentary details written in formal urban Bengali attend to the historicity of the narrative and are interspersed with contextual and biographical information about the persons Ramakrishna met. When Mahendranath records Ramakrishna's speech he moves to rustic Bengali and 'surrenders himself completely in his journey with Ramakrishna through the fluid space of mythic time', making myriad connections across time and space.[50] It is also an explicitly bilingual text that repeatedly employs English terms to translate Ramakrishna's theological oeuvre for a Western-educated audience well versed in the traditions of European philosophy.[51] This narrative structure is deployed to a specific effect in the description of the meeting of Vidyasagar and Ramakrishna in August 1882.

When Ramakrishna arrived with Mahendranath and a few disciples at Vidyasagar's house, they encountered a two-storey building 'built in an English manner' (Figure 1.5). Unlike the Bengali urban courtyard house, Vidyasagar's residence was a free-standing three-bay structure with a central hall. Situated in the middle of the property enclosed by a boundary wall, the house was surrounded by a garden planted with flowering trees. The visitors' carriage stopped at the carriage entrance on the south. Ramakrishna was so 'impressed with this representation of bourgeois respectability'[52] that he asked Mahendranath if it would be okay to appear at this meeting with his shirt unbuttoned. Ramakrishna was assured that this would not pose a problem. Mahendranath then provides a description of the upstairs rooms – the hall, study and Vidyasagar's bedroom – all of which were filled with a 'valuable collection of books'. This scholarly setting would have been daunting for Ramakrishna:

> Vidyasagar is sitting on the north end of the hall facing south. A polished long rectangular table in front. On the east of the table is a bench with backrest. A few chairs on the south and west side of the table. Vidyasagar is conversing with a few friends. He stands up to greet Ramakrishna ...Thakur (Ramakrishna) stands on the east end (of the table), with his left hand on the table. He is intently looking at Vidyasagar as if he is an old acquaintance, smiling, in a trance-like state ... Soon the room is full of people.

Here the narrative pivots and we witness the emergence of a new figure of space centred around Ramakrishna. The people in the room serve as the frame, rather than the bookshelves. The next section of the narrative is titled 'Vidyasagar's worshipful offering (*puja*) and address to Sri Ramakrishna'. Ramakrishna emerges from his trance and speaks: 'Until now I have seen canals, ponds, puddles, rivers, today I see the ocean', referring to his host's title, 'ocean of learning'. Vidyasagar responds with a smile: 'then take away some salt water if you please'. In the long conversation that follows, Ramakrishna attempts to gauge Vidyasagar's position on spiritual matters, with Vidyasagar responding briefly, obliquely and with humour. The narrative is rigged in favour of Ramakrishna, but we sense the awkwardness of the meeting in which the two men with such divergent conceptions about the aim of life – public good and spiritual salvation – undertake a delicate 'public' performance of reason, knowledge, respect and reputation. What concerns us here is the technique of reframing the secular space of the library as a sacred space of spiritual encounter in *RK*.

Vidyasagar's library was his work space in which the bookshelves were a protective frame of sorts. The library was his refuge from the entanglements of family and society. The bookshelves also served as a key piece in his articulation of the self in relation to the colonial public sphere. The plan of his residence and his library, and the social life that he constructed around it, helped secrete a set of spatial layers between him and the literary public sphere that he helped construct and which remained in a heterogeneous relation to the colonial public sphere. In the narrative of his encounter with Ramakrishna, the bookshelves representing the expanding cosmopolitan network of knowledge are reframed to interrogate the ultimate object of knowledge acquisition. What begins as a detailed but factual description of the house is turned around as the two men meet face to face. Mahendranath's meticulous attention to the orientation of the house, the room and the positions of the protagonists serves to transform the library into a sacred topography in which orientation and cardinal directions are suffused with cosmic significance. The focus is turned away from the bookshelves to the library as a space of Ramakrishna's divine utterance.

## Conclusion

It is possible to configure two different spatial moves in the relation between books, bookshelves and buildings in the two sets of stories I have assembled above. The removal of Tipu's library from the 'dark' warehouse-like space to the 'gold and azure' display room of the Oriental Repository in London constitutes an architectural correspondence of the move from a secret collection of a barbaric monarch to a corporate library with an enlightenment promise that is ultimately thwarted by its logic of commodification. As the book collection moves from one space to another, the bookshelf mediates the construction of meaning between the object, building, institution and the universal claims of empire. The bookshelf here functions as the synecdoche of empire and helps create the colonial library as a figure of space around which questions of governance and the empire as public good could be launched.

In contrast, Vidyasagar's library, remembered for its orderly display, refutes that impress of empire and trajectory of knowledge acquisition. As a private library it took on a different agency and urgency in a colonial city where access to the nominally public libraries could not to be taken for granted. Vidyasagar imagined his bookshelves would define a new kind of residential space and help articulate a different set of relations between public, private and domestic space, determined neither by the racialized logic of colonial rule nor by the strictures of Bengali caste society. The bookshelves mediate these uneven relations to give the collection a unity and to affirm its collector's unique identity. But that articulation we have seen was not immune to contestation; the library as an object and space in the secular world was wrenched from its profane context and rendered susceptible to a different kind of universalism, away from public engagement and into the immaterial space of self-reflection and spiritual quest.

Seen through the lens of an emergent anti-colonial nationalism, these two invocations of the library were not entirely antithetical. Vidyasagar's bookshelves and book collection would find their way into Bangiya Sahitya Parishat Library, a public library instituted in 1893 as a nationalist response to colonial dominance. Those bookshelves, as objects of veneration, accommodate somewhat uneasily perhaps the secular meaning that Vidyasagar conferred upon them and the spiritual aura that Ramakrishna sought to induce within their architectural framing.

## Notes

1. The number of bookshelves is specified in his will, dated 1875. Santosh Kumar Adhikary, *Vidyasagarer Jibaner Shesh Dinguli* (Kolkata: Ananya Prakashan, 1986), 115.
2. Vidyasagar's son had carelessly sold off some of his books, ignoring the instructions in the will. Subsequently the Raja of Lalgola purchased the book collection and donated it to the Bangiya Sahitya Parishat Library in 1913. This collection of books from Vidyasagar's library at present contains, 324 Sanskrit and Bengali *puthi* (manuscript), 322 Sanskrit and Hindi books, 191 Bengali books, and 2910 books in English. Ramenkumar Sar, 'Bangiya Sahitya Parishade Vidyasagar Samgraha', Vidyasagar Special Issue, *Bangiya Sahitya Parishat Patrika* 126, no. 4 (2020): 206–8.
3. Sambhuchandra Vidyaratna, *Vidyasagar Jibancharit o Brhamanirash* (Kolkata: Chirayata Prakashan, 1992), 122.
4. B. Venkat Mani, *Recoding World Literature* (New York: Fordham University Press, 2017), 52.
5. For the spatial significance of the library in early modern England, see, Susie West, 'An architectural typology of the early modern country house library, 1660–1720', *Library* 14, no 4 (2013): 441–64.
6. Walter Benjamin, 'Unpacking my Library', *Illuminations*, trans. Harry Zohn (New York: Schocken Books, 1969).
7. Ibid., 59.
8. In this context see Amitav Ghosh, 'The march of the novel through history: the testimony of my grandfather's bookcase', *The Kenyon Review* 20, no. 2 (Spring 1998): 13–24.
9. Bernard S. Cohn, 'The Command of Languages and the Languages of Command', *Colonialism and its Forms of Knowledge: The British in India* (Princeton: Princeton University Press, 1995), 16–56.
10. Thomas Babington Macaulay, 'Minute on Education', 1835.
11. See for example, Angel Rama, *The Lettered City*, trans. John Charle Chasteen (Durham: Duke University Press, 1996); Elizabeth Hill Boone and Walter D. Mignolo, eds., *Writing without Words: Alternative Literacies in Mesoamerica and the Andes* (Durham: Duke University Press, 1994); José Rabasa, *Tell Me the Story of How I Conquered You: Elsewheres and Ethnosuicide in the Colonial Mesoamerican World* (Austin: University of Texas Press, 2011).
12. Modhumita Roy, 'The Englishing of India', *Social Scientist* 21 (May–June 1993): 36–62.
13. Instruction in Indian languages was also instituted at the East India College at Haileybury in 1807.
14. David Price, *Memoirs of the Early Life and Service of a Field Officer on the Retired List of the Indian Army* (London: W.H. Allen, 1839), 446. About the number of books in the library see the discussion in Joshua Ehrlich, 'Plunder and Prestige: Tipu Sultan's Library and the Making of British India', *South Asia: Journal of South Asia Studies* 43, no 3 (2020): 478–92.

15 Ehrlich, 'Plunder and Prestige'.
16 Ibid., 482–3.
17 Ibid., 483.
18 Incidentally the location of the library next to private compartments away from state rooms was a practice also followed in early modern English country houses. See Susie West, 'Studies and status: spaces for books in seventeenth-century Penshurst Place, Kent', *Transactions of the Cambridge Bibliographic Society* 12, no 3 (2002): 266–92.
19 Alexander Beatson, *A View of the Origin and Conduct of the War with Tippoo Sultaun* (London: W. Bulmer and Co, 1800), 179; Price, *Memoirs*, 446.
20 Ehrlich, 'Plunder and Prestige', 483.
21 Price, *Memoirs*, 445.
22 Ibid.
23 Ibid., 446. Capt. Price, one of the officers in charge of selecting manuscripts from Tipu's library, conveyed his desire to possess a book on magic which he considered to be 'an article of extraordinary rarity and value' because of its beautifully executed 'diagrams, and pictorial illustrations'.
24 Beatson, *A View of the Origin,* 179, 195–7.
25 David Wilkie, 'General Sir David Baird Discovering the Body of Sultan Tippoo Sahib after having Captured Seringapatam, on the 4th May, 1799' (1839), Scottish National Gallery.
26 Henry Petroski, *The Book on the Bookshelf* (New York: Alfred Knopf, 1999), 57–8.
27 Ibid.
28 Price, *Memoirs*, 447.
29 Ehrlich, 'Plunder and Prestige', 488.
30 Ibid., 488–9.
31 Peter Gordon, 'The Oriental Repository at the India House', typescript notes, British Library Mss Eur D 656, 3.
32 For a discussion of this image see Swati Chattopadhyay, *Representing Calcutta: Modernity, Nationalism, and the Colonial Uncanny* (Routledge: New York, 2005), 37–8.
33 Ehrlich, 'Plunder and Prestige', 491.
34 Peter Gordon, 'The Oriental Repository', 13.
35 Ibid., 15.
36 Ibid., 14.
37 Abulfazal M. Fazle Kabir, 'English libraries in eighteenth-century Bengal', *The Journal of Library History* 14, no 4 (Fall 1979): 436–56.
38 Purnima Thakur, *Thakurbarir Gaganthakur* (Kolkata: Punascha, 1999); Gautam Bhadra, *Nyara Battlalay Jay K'bar* (Kolkata: Chhatim, 2011); Anindita Ghosh, 'Coming of the Book', Early Print Cultures in Colonial India', *Book History* 6 (2003): 23–55.

39  Bhavanicharan Bandopadhyay, *Kalikata Kamalalaya*. ed. Bishnu Basu (1823; Kolkata: Pratibhas, 1986).
40  Ibid., 140–1.
41  Originating in the Latin *armarium* for closed cabinet in which all kinds of valuable objects would be stored, it had come down as *armoire, almery, almirah*: Petroski, *The Book on the Bookshelf*, 63.
42  The large library of the Sobhabazar Rajbari occupied the long hall of the outer courtyard, a connecting piece between the public spaces organized around the courtyard and the Natmandir (meeting hall) built as a separate structure to facilitate political and social gatherings. See Chattopadhyay, *Representing Calcutta*.
43  Nirad C. Chaudhuri describes book shelves in his upper-caste well-off family's mud-house in rural Bengal in *Aji Hote Satabarsha Aage* (Kolkata: Mitra & Ghosh, 1999), 9.
44  For a cinematic recreation of this mode of spatial connection, see *Charulata* (1964) [Film] Dir. Satyajit Ray, India: R. D. Bansal & Co., where a veranda links Charulata's private apartments and the library.
45  Sashibhusan Basu, 'Vidyasagar Smriti', *Prabasi*, (July-August 1936, Sravana 1343 BS), 584, cited in Indramitra, *Karunasagar Vidyasagar* (1969) (Kolkata; Ananda Publishers, 1997), 29.
46  Indramitra, *Karunasagar Vidyasagar*, 12.
47  Vidyasagar, when he visited friends in their *baithakkhana*, always sat on a chair.
48  Partha Chatterjee, *The Nation and Its Fragments* (Princeton: Princeton University Press, 1993).
49  He returned insulted, but penned a letter of complaint where he discussed the superstitious practices of the British regarding footwear (and their implicitly hypocritical practice, as they refused to take off their shoes when Indians did).
50  Chatterjee, *The Nation and Its Fragments*, 54.
51  Ibid., 52–3. These English terms appear in chapter headings, parentheses and footnotes, and form part of a citational apparatus that is remarkable for its bibliomigrancy.
52  Brian A. Hatcher, *Vidyasagar: The Life and After-Life of an Eminent Indian* (London: Routledge, 2014), 44.

# CHAPTER TWO

# The Power of Television in Modern Turkish Homes

## Meltem Ö. Gürel

Consideration of the television set within the home space raises several questions. How do recent developments in home technologies transform spatial practices and the way we engage with domestic spaces? What are the interconnections between the TV as an object and architectural design? And what are the implications for the creation of new home layouts? To explore the mutually informative relationship between object and architecture, this chapter examines the intrusion of television into domestic spaces in Turkey during the 1970s, when staying home and watching television with friends and family in the evenings became the norm. Focusing on the positioning of TV sets in middle-class homes, I trace the changes this development brought to the long-term practices and conceptualization of the main living room (referred to as the *salon* in Turkish) as the centre stage of the home space. Speaking generally, the salon is the most public and spacious room of the domestic realm. Frequently designed with large windows facing the front façade, it is the most visible space signifying social position to outsiders. Assigned to hosting guests, the salon is furnished with the finest belongings, conveying the residents' identity and socio-economic status. As such, it is the most prestigious space within homes, of which apartment flats constituted a major part of the urban building stock in 1970s Turkey.

The chapter first addresses the social and architectural significance of the salon, starting with ideas around modern ways of living. It then discusses how the inclusion and dissemination of televisions as the chief means of entertainment in domestic space transformed everyday life, domestic practices and ideas around a suitable home. Engaging with oral histories, relevant literature and architectural plans of middle-class apartments of the era, built in major cities, the analysis shows television's power over domestic culture and the consequent reconfiguration of salon design and practices. I will discuss specific moments that reveal how an object of home technology intervened to attain a more powerful role than permanent architectural components, such as a fireplace, as well as the changes it propelled in the way domestic space was conceptualized and domestic life was practised. The chapter addresses television's significant role in forming and informing new domestic architecture, opening a discussion for the role of technological objects in the home space. Finally, the analysis addresses the wider impact of television on cityscapes, city life and patterns of sociocultural engagement. Overall, the argument suggests that studying the changing cultural role of the TV is necessary to understand the evolving form of domestic architecture in this period and that assessing the shifts in architectural design, in turn, illuminates the translation of the TV, as a global technological object, into Turkish culture.

## Salon as the centre stage of the home

The materiality of domestic space – ranging from architectural traits, such as a fireplace, to furniture; from curtains on the windows to paintings on the walls; and from decorative knick-knacks to home technologies, such as the TV – plays an important role in representing community identity, social distinction and cultural capital (or socioculturally valued tastes), as referred to by Pierre Bourdieu.[1] In cultural terms, this materiality is instrumental in building and sustaining social relationships and reflecting group belonging in different classes. In the case of the Turkish salon, building/object relations historically have had strong political and ideological connotations, signifying a Western-orientated identity and a lifestyle with connotations of a higher level of civilization.[2] As the domestic centre stage, the salon of contemporary homes, furnished with Western-style furniture and accessories, came to represent modernity after the foundation of the Republic of Turkey in 1923. This symbolic connection had its roots in the elite Ottoman interiors of nineteenth-century mansions and apartments, reflecting the process of Westernization and the simultaneous rejection of traditional ways of living.[3] The materiality of a salon was enmeshed in strategies of distinction and the manifestation of social status. Such a salon was kept in mint condition, away from everyday domestic routines, and reserved for guests. The 2006 Nobel laureate, Orhan Pamuk, called this space a 'museum-salon' in his novel *Istanbul: Memories and the City* in the context of his family's apartment in the 1950s:

> ... always locked glass sideboards stuffed with Chinese porcelain, cups, silver sets, sugar bowls ... filling the living rooms of each apartment made me feel that they were displayed not for life, but for death ... When

we sat on couches with inlaid mother-of-pearl and silver strings, our grandmother warned us, 'Sit appropriately'. Living rooms were set up as little museums for some imaginary visitors whose arrival time was uncertain, rather than as comfortable spaces where the inhabitants could pass time in peace. Such was the anxiety of Westernization.[4]

A formal salon, as described by Pamuk, took its meaning from the objects on display to the extent that they appeared to be more important than any activities the room purported to house. As discussed in this chapter, TV sets in middle-income homes, from the 1970s onwards, had a great impact in altering this object-activity by cultivating informal attitudes in salon practices.

In architectural terms, a salon was consistently the most prominent room within the home, with larger windows, and its doors (of usually frosted glass) were kept closed (Figure 2.1). Both spatially and in terms of its material culture, a salon drastically differed from the family sitting room in which daily and mundane domestic activities took place. Unlike the salon, the latter was usually equipped with more simple furnishings.[5] Home schemes in the first half of the twentieth century were usually designed as a series of rooms around a central hall, reached from the front door. Either this hall or one of the rooms off it was used as the family sitting room. In

**FIGURE 2.1** *A salon with a door as the centre stage of a home, reserved only for the use of guests.* Arkitekt, no. 269-70-71-72 (1954): 59.

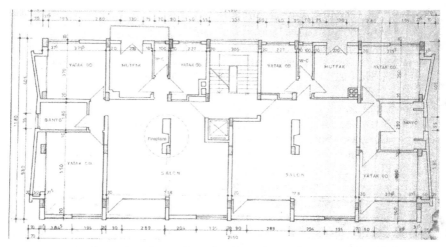

FIGURE 2.2 *Plan of a flat with a fireplace, by architect Melih Pekel (1956). Courtesy of Konak Municipality Archives.*

later plans of the 1950s and 1960s this central hall turned into a corridor, while the dining room and the salon were frequently combined into a larger space referred to as *salon salomanje*, adopted from the French words of *salon* and *salle à manger*. Here, the entrance hall directly led into this area as the centre stage of the home. This arrangement, which concealed the backstage of the family from the gaze of the visitor, was especially common in modern apartment plans with central heating, which predominated in big cities such as Istanbul, Izmir and Ankara. Whether home plans had a more open scheme with combined living and dining areas or a more closed layout of the earlier schemes, the salon remained reserved for guests.

Curiously, many stylish 1950s and 1960s flat plans for the middle and upper-middle classes included a fireplace designed as the focal point, determining the furniture layout of the salon (Figure 2.2).[6] Arguably, the existence of a fireplace in home designs suggests cross-cultural influence from the post-Second World War West, especially the United States. As an architect who had practised over this period explained, a fireplace was considered a fashionable architectural element and accordingly 'made the flat more valuable'.[7] Usually built of local black and white marble, a fireplace in a flat was scarcely utilized for its intended function of heating. In older buildings a stove was used for this purpose, whereas the more recent apartment buildings provided central heating. Arguably, a fireplace primarily served as a design element, symbolizing social distinction and a lifestyle associated with the West. Along with showcased fine furniture and accessories, a fireplace in the centre stage of a home, then, communicated codes meaningful to a culture or to a group of people who were interconnected by shared values, norms and beliefs.[8] While a notable status symbol, it was a passive element, or a background décor in a salon where socializing took place. This was very different from the role the TV set would take in regulating practices within the home. The advent of domestic television broadcasting almost immediately led to a new form of sociability supplanting the old.

Fireplaces vanished from flat plans in the 1970s while TV sets emerged as the focal point of salon designs, taking on the role of signifying social distinction by conveying the sociocultural status associated with a certain group of people, just as fireplaces, furniture and other accessories had done. A TV set was a novelty and having one in the living room was prestigious, particularly in the beginning of the 1970s when television was still not affordable to all income groups. In the case of apartments with a fireplace, a TV set challenged not only the distinctive quality of this architectural element but also its dominant function in determining furniture arrangements. That is to say, an object of home technology attained a more powerful status than a permanent architectural component in the way domestic space was conceived and practised globally. On this account, Lynn Spigel has pointed out advertisements representing television as the 'new hearth' of the home, around which the American family gathered already in the immediate post-war years, when television secured a safe place in the US home.[9] Rapidly ubiquitous, a TV set became a pervasive object, radically changing everyday life, social production and the arrangement of the domestic stage. Unlike any other material component to date, it transformed otherwise persistent salon norms and codes with regard to social distinction as well as social practices.

## Television in the middle-class salon

Television broadcasting in Turkey started through the Turkish Radio and Television Corporation (TRT) founded in 1964.[10] Until the establishment of the first private channel in 1990, the state had a monopoly over broadcasting; television programmes were censored and intended to educate the masses.[11] Initially, broadcasting was limited to a few evening hours on certain days of the week and television ownership was rare. In 1974, one-channel broadcasting was increased to seven days a week and television ownership became more widespread, with 55 per cent of people residing in Turkey watching television. This number of people watching TV in or outside the home throughout the country increased to 81.5 per cent by 1977.[12] Broadcasting was in black and white, only moving to colour in the 1980s. Audiovisually, television brought the outer world into the comfort zone of the home space. Viewers learned about the world and connected to other cultures through international TV programmes, including older Hollywood movies and American TV series, which constituted a significant portion of the media broadcast. Before television, radio had a significant role in connecting to the outside world. However, unlike a TV set, a radio did not dominate furniture layout and concepts of entertainment. A TV set, on the other hand, regulated the physical space to the extent that it dictated where each couch or chair was to be placed. As oral histories clearly indicate, every person's seating arrangement in the room was organized according to the TV screen. The TV's visibility was the foremost consideration in organizing space, its material components and occupancy:

> TV was the centrepiece of the salon ... Every chair, sofa was placed to see it ... We, as the entire family, used to sit in front of our TV set at least a couple of minutes before our favourite TV series began. Nobody was allowed to speak during a TV series.[13]

As the centrepiece of the salon, the television was not only the chief means of entertainment, it also dictated social life and interaction, having a great impact on people's everyday lives and leisure practices.[14] However, not everyone could afford a TV; they were expensive and not widely available until the mid-1970s. For those who could not afford a TV, visiting friends, neighbours, or relatives who owned one to watch a show together in the evenings became the norm. Notably, having frequent TV visitors was something that could become overwhelming for TV owners, both socially and financially, in a culture that highly valued hospitality:

> My family bought a TV set in the beginning of 1970s. I remember always having guests over to watch TV ... We could never have an evening to our own ... they were expected to arrive *before* a TV show started. The entire evening was organized according to watching TV together. Tea, pastries, fruits ... were prepared beforehand, so that there were no interruptions during the watching time.[15]

As this anecdote exemplifies, television reconfigured social interactions and the habits of hosting visitors. The transformation was in some ways similar to the long history of the adoption of European objects and the consequent changes in object-led behaviour. Like European-style furniture, television played an important role in defining the salon as the central stage of hosting and entertaining while simultaneously signifying social status. Other technological objects such as gramophones, radios and record players all contributed to this end, serving as apparatuses of contemporary lifestyles and hosting practices. However, none had the TV's pervasive impact at all levels of society. Contrastingly, television tremendously reduced communicational interaction. Before the TV dominated domestic culture, eating and drinking over conversations were the primary means of entertainment for household guests. The TV silenced the living room, with audiovisual entertainment replacing conversations. People sat quietly together in front of a TV set with eyes glued to the screen. Television visits defined the way people socialized in the 1970s:

People stopped going out to movie theatres and other sort of places and instead went to each other's homes to watch television in the evenings. There was only one channel and a few popular series that everyone followed. You could hear the sounds of TV guests arriving in our apartment building before a favourite TV series started.[16]

Although some middle-class households still preferred to place their TV in the central hall or a family sitting room,[17] television-led sociocultural dynamics altered norms and conceptions of the salon as a closed room reserved only for formal hosting. As an object of social distinction, embodying social status, the TV set secured its place inside the salon as the centrepiece of domestic staging, while also opening its doors to more informal uses and social engagement. The requirement for sight lines called

FIGURE 2.3 *A TV set dictated the furniture layout and seating arrangements in the room. Headline: 'The new toy of Istanbul's residents: Welcome Television!' Hayat, vol. 3, no. 38 (1971): 13.*

for a narrower arrangement of sitting positions – hence the close proximity of subjects in a more casual manner (Figure 2.3). As recalled in an oral history, 'people were squeezed on a sofa, and the younger members of the group, sometimes, were seated on the floor leaning against their legs in order to be able get the best view of the TV screen'.[18] This object-led behaviour produced intimate bodily contact, clustering different age groups in a tight space physically. In this respect, the television was a centre of attraction, bringing people together and simultaneously catering to the informal life of the household and hosting practices.

## Domestication of the TV set

Domestic technologies can cause social and individual anxieties for a wide range of reasons. Some of these are scientifically grounded and include fears about the effects of technological objects on health and psychology, especially of children.[19] Others entail unease about issues such as privacy, intrusion from the outside world and penetration into daily life. One notable concern about privacy and the idea of intrusion in relation to the television was fed by the rumours that home interiors could be watched from the screen of a television even when it was off:

> Some people looked at their TV with suspicion because they thought TV screens could see. They heard this somewhere. It was a rumour with no base. I even remember people covering their TV screen when not in use because they were afraid of being watched.[20]

Such discussions and fears of surveillance were already present in the 1950s, way before television entered Turkish homes.[21] Similar to the radios that preceded them and the computers that succeeded them, television embodied such anxieties and prompted low-scale individual resistance.[22] Resistance was also stimulated by the television's mechanical appearance. Despite its central role and social connotations, the TV had an alien look; it needed domestication. Many reacted to the existence of a technological object in the most visible and prominent location of their salon and sought ways of making it more suitable, bringing it into line with accustomed domestic styling. Some preferred a TV set with a built-in cabinet depending on its availability and price:

> We owned a TV set ... before any of our relatives and neighbours could have one. It was a nice brown piece of furniture that looked like a small cabinet on four legs. The front had a sliding or folding door that closed and opened the screen. I remember the door closed when the TV was not in use ... I assume the door helped to keep it clean and safe. It looked stylish with the door closed. To open and close was almost like a ceremony.[23]

When the TV did not come with its own cabinet, people preferred to place it inside a cabinet or in the centre of a wall unit, both designed for this purpose. As a more economical solution, many purchased a TV stand, often designed with wheels and bottom shelves to hold TV apparatus, such as a regulator to overcome then-common voltage fluctuation. In almost all cases, the TV was decorated with fancy doilies (with one to stand on and often one on its top) to camouflage its mechanical looks, as was the case with radios:

> My mother made laces for coffee tables, tables, and TVs. She used to gift these to friends and family. People placed a lace or fancy fabric cover of some sort on their TV set. It was almost a necessity. My mother's creations were highly appreciated as gifts.[24]

Doilies were significant objects in home decoration, commonly used on coffee tables, shelves and other such surfaces as an essential method of dressing domestic space. However, their use to adorn the TV is particularly interesting because of the treatment of the uppermost surface as a table or mantelpiece for showcasing decorative objects. In some instances, decorative doilies worked as a veil, covering the screen when not in use and opening up when in use. Notably, they were accompanied by bibelots placed on and around TVs in an attempt at domesticating their industrial look. As an anecdote reveals, people sought creative solutions to hide the mechanical appearance of the object and frame the screen inside the room:

> My mother made a hole in the wall between our sitting room and my bedroom for the TV to sit on because there was no space for an extra table [or cabinet] in the room. She then put a *frame* around the TV to decorate it.[25]

All of these decorative additions to the TV were intended to please the eye and make the set more domesticated, like other home fittings and embellishments.

## Concepts of mobility and dissolving the boundaries

Unlike a permanent spatial element, such as a fireplace, or a fixed piece of heavy furniture, TV sets were semi-portable objects conveniently adaptable to informal ways of creating space. Some of the early devices were built inside their own movable cabinets. Others were often placed on a TV stand with wheels. This mobility had implications for the way social and physical space was composed and consumed:

> My family lived in a small apartment . . . A furniture set, a dining room set and a stove were crammed into the tiny room. When the TV arrived, it was strategically placed on a TV table so that we could see it while

eating at the table and from the armchairs and couches while sitting. The TV was turned towards the table during dinnertime. In summer, it was turned towards the balcony and we watched it from there.[26]

As this anecdote explains, a TV placed on a portable stand could be moved or turned, within the reach of an electrical and antenna outlet, in order to accommodate viewing from different parts of a salon with a combined dining area of a typical apartment layout. Furthermore, during hot summer nights, it could be relocated to a salon's balcony door or window to be seen and heard from the outside. This mobility not only cultivated more casual and flexible forms of salon practice, but also blurred the boundaries between the inside and the outside of the domestic space. A flat's balcony, with people sitting and watching television, redefined concepts of domesticity and discretion, simultaneously transforming images and sounds of the streets in the city. In warmer locations and seasons, TVs were positioned to be viewed from the outdoor spaces of gardens, verandas, porches, terraces or most commonly balconies, depending on the physical traits of a home:

> We were one of the two families in our neighbourhood of 36 houses to own a TV. It came from Germany through my uncle in 1969. My mother shared our TV with neighbours as much as possible. We had a small garden, and my mother used to turn the TV towards this garden for all to watch through our salon's window during summer months. The place was filled with neighbours. My mother served tea and snacks, but neighbours also contributed by bringing snacks.[27]

Television brought the inside to the outside, and the same television programmes were seen and heard throughout the neighbourhoods. They were also viewed together in the public domain of neighbourhood coffeehouses as well as city cafes. In cultural terms, these instances of viewing (single channel) TV as a group activity interwoven into domestic habits as well as customary living patterns can be understood as a local translation of a global television-viewing culture produced by a slippage (or difference) of practices.[28]

Such translation and dissolving of boundaries was quite distant from the original reserved salon ideals embodied in a physical environment kept in mint condition for the arrival of guests. Even if the salon, with its material culture, maintained its role as a status symbol, indicating social distinction, the television as a semi-mobile object of significance redefined domestic culture by softening the hard line between the salon and family sitting rooms, as well as the dichotomy between the notions of formality and informality. Later on, when TV sets became more affordable and available in a greater range of sizes, they appeared in different rooms of the house. A small portable TV in the kitchen or in the bedroom allowed people to individually watch TV, especially in the multichannel television era from the 1990s onwards. By this time, possibilities for individual interactions with television screens widened, for example by connecting early computers to a TV or following the stock market via teletext on the TV screen.[29] In all these instances, casual TV practices had a pivotal impact on domestic culture and the consequent transformation of the formal salon concept maintained as a space distant from private family life, as discussed earlier. When, for practical reasons, the TV was moved from the salon to another location (such as a family sitting room or an outdoor space) and back, the practices surrounding it did not change. Rather, it was the design and the occupancy patterns of the salon that had to change in the ensuing home plans. With respect to building/object relations, this outcome is significant in forming and informing our understanding of the translation of design across cultures.

## Domestic designs, the city and city life

Following the Flat Ownership Law of 1965, flats became more widely available and affordable for the middle class. Apartment buildings were rapidly built in the cities, simultaneously changing domestic arrangements of the middle class as well as the cityscape more widely. This was partly because of a build-and-sell model which enabled construction of apartment buildings with little capital.[30] Government-initiated mass-housing developments and building cooperatives also contributed to the rise of the multistorey apartment block in Turkey, which was in essence the result of population growth and rapid urbanization related to government policies and economics. Domestic schemes in this hastily proliferating building type had to recognize the power of the TV set in the home space. In the comfort of a modern flat, salons were designed as more open spaces, bringing the household as well as guests together while watching TV. Acknowledging television's significant role in domestic practices and spatial arrangements, architects, designers and builders all had to consider the location of a TV set and equip the wall at this location with electrical and antenna outlet. A designated TV socket inside the salons of modern apartment buildings became standard during the 1970s.[31]

With a TV set installed in every flat, the roofs of apartment buildings and houses became extensively covered with antennas. Before the use of centralized antennas or cable, each household erected its own on the rooftop. As a result, images of red terracotta roof tiles characterizing cities were replaced by a mass of TV antennas of variant heights – clear material evidence of the TV's significance. Later on, this evidence has persisted in other forms, such as satellite dishes extending from balconies and façades, so much that they have been recognized as serious visual pollution requiring intervention at the level of the Ministry of Environment and Urbanisation (Figure 2.4).[32]

The TV set in the home not only transformed the appearance of the city, but also the rhythm of its existence. Television dramatically changed concepts of entertainment and leisure practices. Addressing these changes and the impact of television on social life in the 1970s, a Turkish novelist wrote:

FIGURE 2.4 *A recent photograph showing satellite dishes attached to buildings, following the age of TV antennas, as material evidence of TV's significance and the changes it wrought on the cityscape. Courtesy of Meltem Gürel.*

> Television changed the rhythm of life and habits were abandoned ... The number of people sitting in tea gardens, eating ice cream decreased. Evening sittings were abandoned, playing cards, which appeared when neighbours gathered, were forgotten in drawers, cinemas closed ... Black and white images of the screen completely changed slow but rich lifestyles.[33]

A major reason for television's popularity was certainly its convenience. People simply preferred to stay home in the evening and watch television shows in the comfort of the domestic environment. Another major reason was financial motives. Television provided a cheaper means of entertainment for the middle class:

> My favourite TV show in the 1970s was *Music from Italy*: Rafaella Carra, Mina, Adriano Celentano ... We could watch a variety of music

and famous Turkish singers like Ajda Pekkan and Zeki Müren. During these years people stopped going out to celebrate New Year's Eve. They preferred a (so-called) TV, pyjama and slipper party instead.[34]

While people preferred socializing at home rather going out to movies and nightclubs in the evenings, advertisements promoted television as the major means of entertainment. 'I brought the first Philips television to the neighbourhood, I am very pleased, whoever watches wants to buy one',[35] stated an ad (Figure 2.5).

In an interview, the popular magazine *Hayat* welcomed television as 'the new toy of Istanbul's residents' in 1971, picturing women watching television (see Figure 2.3).[36] Notably, this conception had consequences for women's

**FIGURE 2.5** *Television provided a cheaper means of entertainment for the middle class.* Ayfer Tunç, Bir Maniniz Yoksa Annemler Size Gelecek *(Istanbul: Can Publications, 2001/2015), 105.*

position in the domestic space, as it not only potentially limited women's time spent outside the home but also turned leisure into domestic labour.

The pervasive alteration of urban practices eventually put many cinemas, music halls and nightclubs out of business. Those who could stay in business felt the pressure to come up with new ideas and offerings to survive. Music halls increased daytime matinees, while cinemas showed porno movies during daytime to attract male audiences now that people preferred to watch television in the evening. As well as its powerful domestic presence, television also claimed a primary place in public spaces. Traditional coffeehouses, cafes and restaurants alike started to place TV sets in their premises to attract customers. The sound of football matches, news, music programmes, series and movies dominated these environments, and arguably echoed throughout the city. With regard to architectural history, and in the scope of building/object relations, this is to suggest that all these TV-related occurrences contributed to the urban environment's transformation. From the images of rooftops and façades, to closed theatres or (de)populated public spaces, an object of technology had the power to affect not only domestic practices and designs, but also the rhythm and the materiality of the built environment in its entirety.

## Conclusion

Domestic design of the post-television era had to take into consideration the power of the television in home interiors. For example, where there was a wall with a fireplace as the focal point of a salon layout in some of the 1950s home plans, this was replaced with a blank wall with an electrical and antenna outlet for the television. A TV set was at once a global code-communicating connection to the national and international community, a symbol of social distinction, an organizer of social life, a means of entertainment, a focal point of spatial design and furniture layout, and the transformer of the traditional concept of a reserved salon evoking sentiments of a museum-like environment. In cultural terms, the TV set, as a global domestic object, defined spatial arrangements while homogenizing cultures. The television has been a powerful instrument in regulating domestic life worldwide. Sitting in front of a TV set with family or friends to watch a programme as a means of entertainment became a shared domestic experience across cultures. TV programmes, ranging from popular primetime soap operas – such as the American-made series of *The Fugitive*, *Little House on the Prairie*, *Bonanza* and *Dallas* (all airing in Turkey during the single channel years of the 1970s and 1980s) – to international sports games and music shows, marked the memories of a generation globally. In this respect, the television was arguably instrumental in rendering a common domestic landscape across different geographies. However, as this chapter has shown, the television was domesticated within local culture. The presence of television in the domestic and public domains created local dynamics specific to a culture sharing common values and beliefs. Notions of hospitality, methods of socialization and spatial practices were all transformed according to these values. That is to say, television became the centre of communal life in the home, the neighbourhood, the traditional coffeehouse, as well as the modern cafe. The balcony or cafe viewing practices were precisely instances of the translation of nuclear family-based viewing practices into communal ones. In these cases, the users' performativity suggested that the local culture produced a translation of the global culture.

## Notes

1. Pierre Bourdieu, *Distinction: A Social Critique of the Judgement of Taste*, trans. Richard Nice (Cambridge: Harvard University Press, 1984).
2. See Uğur Tanyeli, 'Westernization-Modernization in the Ottoman Wohnkultur: The Evolution of a New Set of Symbols', in *Housing and Settlement in Anatolia – A Historical Perspective*, ed. Yıldız Sey (Istanbul: The History Foundation Publications, 1996), 285–8, 296–7; Sibel Bozdoğan, *Modernism and Nation Building: Turkish Architectural Culture in the Early Republic* (Seattle: University of Washington Press, 2001), Chapter 5; Meltem Ö. Gürel, 'Domestic Space, Modernity, and Identity: The Apartment in Mid-20th Century Turkey' (PhD Diss., University of Illinois at Urbana-Champaign, 2007); Meltem Ö. Gürel, 'Consumption of Modern Furniture as a Strategy of Distinction in Turkey', *Journal of Design History* 22, no. 1 (2009): 47–67.
3. Gürel, 'Consumption of Modern Furniture', 48; Meltem Ö. Gürel, 'Dolmabahçe as Liminal Space', in *Dolmabahçe Palace – 150 Years Old International Symposium*, ed. Kemal Kahraman (Ankara: TBMM Matbaası, 2007), 261–74.
4. Orhan Pamuk, *Istanbul Hatıralar ve Şehir* (Istanbul: YKM, 2003), 17–18.
5. In a 1988 study of middle-class living rooms, sociologist Sencer Ayata addressed this difference between the living and sitting rooms, explaining the former was composed of 'chandelier, glassware and crystal ashtrays, porcelain tableware, luxurious armchair, a new rug', the latter was equipped with 'a simple day bed, an old kilim, a tin ashtray, a simple lamp, a small dining table'. Sencer Ayata, 'Statü Yarışması ve Salon Kullanımı', *Toplum ve Bilim* 42 (1988): 5–25.
6. Meltem Ö. Gürel, 'Architectural Mimicry, Spaces of Modernity: The Island Casino, Izmir, Turkey', *The Journal of Architecture* 16, no.2 (2013): 181.
7. Conversations with the architect Nejat Ersin.
8. Bourdieu, *Distinction*.
9. Lynn Spigel, *Make Room for TV: Television and the Family Ideal in Postwar America* (London: University of Chicago Press, 1992), 38.
10. Initial transmission tests began on 31 January 1968, in Ankara. 'A year later, 3 hours a day, 3 days a week test transmissions were increased to 4 days a week.

In 1970 Izmir TV started its operations followed by Istanbul TV in 1971.' http://www.trtmuze.com.tr/en/about-us/trt-history (accessed 17 March 2021).

11 Hülya Uğur Tanrıöver, 'Türkiye'de televizyonun tarihsel gelişimi', in *Türkiye'de Televizyon Yayıncılığı* (Istanbul: Istanbul Chamber of Commerce Publications, 2011), 11–17.

12 Nurettin Bay, *Radyo ve Televizyon Yayıncılığı* (Istanbul: Nüve Kültür Merkezi, 2007), 44.

13 Conversations with a woman, age 50–60.

14 Meltem Ö. Gürel, 'Designing and Consuming the Modern', in *The Routledge Companion to Design Studies*, ed. Fiona Fisher and Penny Sparke (New York and London: Routledge, 2016), 457–468.

15 Conversations with a woman, age 60–70.

16 Conversations with a woman, age 60–70.

17 Mübeccel Kıray, *Toplumsal Yapı Toplumsal Değişme* (Istanbul: Bağlam Yayıncılık, 2006).

18 Conversations with a woman, age 50–60.

19 Kathryn M. Smith, 'Domesticating Television: Changing Attitudes in Postwar Britain', *Interiors* 3, no.1–2 (2012): 23–42.

20 Conversations with a woman, age 50–60.

21 See Lynn Spigel, 'Installing Television Set: Popular Discourses on Television and Domestic Space, 1948–1955', in *Private Screenings: Television and the Female Consumer*, ed. Lynn Spigel and Denise Mann (Minneapolis: University of Minnesota Press, 1992), 3–40: 26. Derek Horton, *Television's Story and Challenge* (London: Harrap, 1951), 156. Smith, 'Domesticating Television', 37–8.

22 Martin Bauer, 'Resistance to New Technology and its Effects on Nuclear Power, Information Technology and Biotechnology', in *Resistance to New Technology: Nuclear Power, Information Technology and Biotechnology*, ed. Martin Bauer (Cambridge: Cambridge University Press, 1995), 7.

23 Conversations with a woman, age 50–60.

24 Conversations with a woman, age 50–60.

25 Conversations with a woman, age 60–70.

26 Conversations with a man, age 50–60.

27 Conversations with a woman, age 60–70.

28 Homi K. Bhabha, 'Of Mimicry and Man: The Ambivalence of Colonial Discourse', in *The Location of Culture* (London, New York: Routledge, 1994). Also see Gürel, 'Architectural Mimicry', 183.

29 Conversations with a man, age 60–70.

30 In this model, the contractor took property from the owner in exchange for flats. The expenses of the construction were met by pre-selling the flats. For the development of apartments in Turkey see Gürel, 'Domestic Space', 82.

31 Conversations with architects and builders who designed and constructed apartment buildings as well as residents who moved to such apartments in 1970s in the cities of Izmir and Ankara.

32  For the visual pollution of antennas, see TRT News, 1 Şubat 2013, https://www.milliyet.com.tr/gundem/bundan-boyle-balkonlarda-canak-anten-yasak-1662317. Milliyet, 30.01.2013, https://www.trthaber.com/haber/gundem/balkondaki-canak-antenler-kaldiriliyor-73093.html (accessed 17 March 2021).
33  Ayfer Tunç, *Bir Maniniz Yoksa Annemler Size Gelecek* (Istanbul: Can Publications, 2001/2015), 103.
34  Conversations with a woman, age 50–60.
35  Tunç, *Bir Maniniz Yoksa,* 105.
36  Koray Güney, 'New toy of Istanbul's residents: Welcome television', *Hayat* 3 no.38 (1971): 13.

# CHAPTER THREE

# Bin, Bag, Box: The Architecture of Convenience

*Louisa Iarocci*

The relationship between objects and buildings is especially visible in the retail building that serves simultaneously as storage container and display unit for its contents. The convenience store, or c-store as it is known in the United States, is a prime example, emerging as a dominating retailing concept in the English-speaking world in the second half of the twentieth century. Its various names reflect both the range of products and services it offers and its physical properties – from the corner shop in the UK to the variety or milk store in Canada.[1] While these small businesses have become ubiquitous in cities throughout the world, they have drawn little scholarly attention as cultural artefacts outside of the fields of business and marketing and public health and safety.[2] But the development of this architectural type is inextricably linked to the design of objects at multiple scales – from packaged goods and display systems to personal vehicles and transportation networks. This paper examines the history of the architecture of convenience in the United States, focusing on the design of this retail type as a building/object that represents the transformation of food production, distribution and consumption in the mid-twentieth century.

Although long invoked in retailing, the idea of 'convenience' only became a recognized retailing type in the second half of the twentieth century.[3] The convenience store is defined by its form and function – typically a stand-alone, small-scale retail outlet that sells a limited range of fast-moving consumer goods and services.[4] The main selling feature is the promise of a quick, 'top-up' style of shopping where customers buy 'little and often'.[5] The 'c-store', as it is known in retailing, often has an accessible location within a manageable walk or drive and has extended hours of operation, often open seven days a week and in some cases twenty-four hours a day. This concept of convenience is thus based on the spatial and temporal distance between product and consumer, measured between the networks of movement that define the perimeter of the building site and the face-to-face contact with the individual objects inside.[6] The product range is geared towards meeting popular 'impulse' needs through the provision of a select range of consumer goods that consists largely of non-perishable groceries and snack items, soft drinks and alcohol, and some household and health and beauty items.[7] As the product of food processing and packaging techniques, this curated collection of objects forms the architecture of the store buildings from the inside out. Tracing the intersecting histories of food objects and retail buildings reveals the material and social construction of the convenience store as a nested container of things — a kind of bin, bag and box that embodies changing patterns of consumption in the twentieth century.

The small-town general store is often popularly identified as the precursor of the convenience store in the United States as a small, centrally located business selling essential staple goods to a local clientele.[8] These 'mom-and-pop' establishments serving rural communities were often only distinguishable from nearby farm buildings and houses by their painted signs and product displays. The store interior was typically laid out as a series of spatial zones that unfolded in layers; on the periphery were built-in wall cabinets and shelving that served as storage and display of packaged food products including paperboard cartons, tin cans, and glass bottles and jars.[9] The sales counter provided a horizontal working surface for exchange of objects and money and demarcated the territory of the proprietor. Food shopping was an activity that required an interactive and often protracted exchange between the clerk and customer. The interior often contained chairs and benches, reflecting its social function as a place to linger and socialize. With proprietors living above or next to their businesses, the store could take on the character of a domestic kitchen, a space of work and preparation that was 'dimly lit ... [where] aromas arose from the open packaging of bulk goods'.[10] The open floor was often cluttered with precarious arrangements of cloth bags and wooden bins and bushels that contained dry and wet goods from flour and sugar to dill pickles that were sold by weight or measure.[11] These large vessels conveyed a general sense of abundance but unlike the package goods were otherwise plain and mute, conveying few specifics about their contents — much like the building shell.

As external forces of urbanization and industry shaped the form of the architectural container, developments in food production and merchandising shaped the products it contained. The shift to a more urbanized and mobilized society altered the face of food retailing in the first half of the twentieth century. As a perishable product, the distribution of food was by nature closely tied to its place of origin and to available modes of transportation. At the end of the nineteenth century, new agricultural equipment and methods boosted yields on US farms. Advancements in the industrial processing of food further expanded the range and variety of choices available to the public. The expansion of transportation networks that included ships, railroads and trucks provided more ways and means to store and transport these products, which could be refrigerated first by ice and then mechanically.[12] These new technologies also impacted on how these consumable products made their way to the consumer through an expanding variety of retail outlets, from traditional farm stands and public markets to chain grocers and supermarkets by the 1940s. National grocery store chains like Kroeger, Safeway and AP&P arose from the massive expansion of the abundance and variety of food available in the first half of the twentieth century and the increased mobility of consumers through car ownership. The rise of industrially produced 'convenience food' that was recognizable and accessible to the consumer shaped the shopping experience in the expansive aisles of grocery stores, but also produced an assortment of other new enterprises for selling food – including what would come to be known as the convenience store.

The origin story of the largest convenience store business in the world today, 7-Eleven, reflects how this retail building type was a product of the acceleration of the mobility of people and objects.[13] Established in 1927, the Southland Ice Company in Dallas, Texas was in the business of manufacturing and selling artificial ice, with eight ice plants and twenty-one retail ice stations.[14] Company histories credit John Jefferson Green, a store employee, with coming up with the idea of adding milk, eggs and other grocery items to the block ice sold at their retail stations for home use.[15] As seen in a 1920s photograph (Figure 3.1), these stand-alone ice stations were simple one-storey wood frame boxes with either gabled or flat roofs, distinguishable from neighbouring houses and storage sheds only by their full-length veranda and painted signs.

Transactions appear to have been conducted mostly outside. The stepped platform was raised to a height to enable easy loading of heavy blocks of ice from the building onto the running boards of cars and trucks. The covered veranda was also used for displays of goods in portable wooden crates and small shelving units, illuminated by basic electrical fixtures. In some cases, the cash register was on a wheeled cart or small table, allowing it to be easily moved inside at night. The front façade of the simple building clearly communicated its function, with a series of flexible display units and painted signage identifying the company, the station number and the goods on sale. In some instances, glass-doored ice boxes recessed into the front wall were used to store and display perishable items like milk, cheese and butter, serving as their own advertisement. The block ice stored inside the building thus served the invaluable function of keeping these products chilled while

FIGURE 3.1 'The world's first convenience store. B. C. Glenn, an early store manager, stands in front of Uncle John Green's retail ice station at Twelfth and Edgefield in Oak Cliff, Texas' (c. 1928). Allen Liles, Oh Thank Heaven! The Story of the Southland Corporation (Dallas, TX: Southland Corporation, 1977), 21. Courtesy of 7-Eleven, Inc.

awaiting purchase by the public to serve the same purpose in their homes. While mechanical home refrigerators were available by the 1910s, they would not become a widespread feature of US homes until the Second World War.

The Southland Ice Stations are exemplary of how the built object was shaped by its relationship to the commodities it contained and the transportation systems with which it connected. In the late 1920s, the retail stores were renamed 'Tote'm Stores' to promote how easily people could 'tote' away their purchases. The totem pole was adopted as trademark and sign; company literature claims that a batch of these monumental carved wooden pillars were ordered from Alaskan native artists to be installed as signs at the front of the stores.[16] But more often, smaller painted versions appeared on the walls of the buildings, either on their own or forming the capital letter 'T' of the Tote'm sign. The station number and company name were clearly marked in multiple places on the buildings to be visible from different approaches from the road. The branding of these otherwise humble structures as retail space was also evident inside the stations, which now contained an assortment of food items for sale. The interior of the ice house was adapted for the purposes of exchange, with a locked desk and bench and open shelving units containing a range of dry or non-perishable items versus the fresh ones outside. Boxes of soda crackers, flaked cereals, tea and soap, along with bags of ice cream, salt and potato crisps, and even chewing gum, were all packaged and labelled to enable identification of their contents and origin.[17] Against the backdrop of the spare interior these branded food packages stood out, serving as a series of mini-buildings that gave shape and identity to their otherwise formless and anonymous contents.

The emergence of other forms of food merchandising, such as the little-known 'Motorteria', indicate how the automobile was driving the rising trend towards more convenient shopping for food.[18] This short-lived self-service grocery store on wheels launched in New Jersey was advertised as being able to deliver a complete stock of food and drug items directly to its customers. But in southwestern states like Texas, the warmer climate made the pairing of ice sales and refrigerated food at the retail stations a winning combination. The resumption of the sale of beer and liquor with the repeal of Prohibition in December 1933 helped to drive sales of beverages. An advertisement in the Fort Worth *Star Telegram* in 1931 featuring the totem pole logo promoted quick and effortless curbside service of their neighbourhood stores, noting: 'You drive in ... you give your order for ice, eggs, butter, milk, cheese, cold drinks or a hundred other products and you are quickly served while you remain behind the steering wheel.'[19] The store motto that 'time is valuable' promoted the idea that accelerating the speed of everyday food shopping was the best way to keep up with the pace of modern life.

The development of branding of consumer goods and of retail chains would continue to perpetuate this trope of time-saving convenience. Despite

FIGURE 3.2 *'Tote'm Store of the late 1930s and early 1940s' (c. 1940). Allen Liles, Oh Thank Heaven! The Story of the Southland Corporation (Dallas, TX: Southland Corporation, 1977), 54. Courtesy of 7-Eleven, Inc.*

being plunged into bankruptcy by the Great Depression, the Southland Corporation tripled its retail outlets by 1939, operating sixty Tote'm stores, mostly in the Dallas–Fort Worth area. The company continued to strengthen the connection between its brand of convenience shopping and the automobile through a pilot project to add gas kiosks at some of its stores, which were leased to oil companies. This emphasis on speed and efficiency in the shopping experience was expressed in the modernization of the design of the building as a comprehensive display system by the early 1940s. These purpose-built 'drive thru' Tote'm stores adopted the streamlined Moderne style of gas stations of the time, with flat roofs and rounded corners. Set back on front-parking lots, the oblong rectangular box was further opened up with wide accordion-style doors that covered over half the building front. The glass-fronted refrigerated vaults were neatly aligned like a series of gas station self-service bays, labelled with the name and price of the chilled products inside. Bottles of milk and beer, wrapped butter and eggs in wire bins were presented like museum artefacts in orderly rows. The open front beneath the foods' sign revealed the expanded sales area inside the store, illuminated to highlight a series of display fixtures from tall wall shelving to counter-height display cases (Figure 3.2). The store claimed it carried over a hundred different types of food items, including canned goods and breakfast cereals arranged into free-standing stepped towers along with open baskets of produce that spilled out onto the front pavement. The concealed lighting beneath the sleek canopy further emphasized the image of the building as a bright, well-ordered showcase – an open display unit that served as sales counter and sign, promoting an image of abundance and accessibility.

Developments in the construction and design of food packaging in the first decades of the twentieth century also advanced the concept of convenience. Stanley Sacharow observes that the role of the package in the nineteenth century was to protect and preserve the fragile product and ensure its safe delivery to the consumer. Paperboard cartons with waxed paper liners for cereal and crackers, tinplate cans for fruits and vegetables, and glass bottles and jars for beverages and preserves had been in use since the nineteenth century. But at the turn of the century, he argues, the food package took on an entirely new dimension as a sales agent: 'it had to be able to "protect what it sells and to sell what it protects"'.[20] Advances in technologies of packaging materials enabled the mass production of paper bags in place of canvas, aluminium plate and foil in place of tin, and lightweight glass and eventually plastic bottles.[21] Innovations in plastic materials like cellophane and polyethylene in the 1940s enabled flexible transparent packaging of fresh items that increased their shelf life and enabled them to be easily inspected for quality.[22] These advancements in packaging materials produced sealed food items that were better preserved and protected and easier to carry. The growth of this smaller 'unit-packaged food product' in the first decades of the twentieth century provided more lightweight and portable building blocks for displays in the convenience

FIGURE 3.3 'A typical 7-Eleven Store of the early 1950s' (c. 1950s). Allen Liles, Oh Thank Heaven! The Story of the Southland Corporation *(Dallas, TX: Southland Corporation, 1977), 84. Courtesy of 7-Eleven, Inc.*

store. The individual products themselves – from milk bottles to boxed crackers – became their own self-contained selling unit that could be arranged into unique architectural displays.[23] With greater structural strength, these product towers could even be liberated from their display fixtures, contained and framed only by the spare surfaces of the larger architectural envelope.

The rise of this modern convenience culture accelerated after the Second World War when automotive transportation and suburban development continued to disperse and mobilize the population.[24] The onset of the war had brought an increased demand for ice due to the cessation of the manufacture and sale of electrical refrigerators caused by the war effort. By 1945 the Southland Corporation had acquired additional ice plants and retail stations that were scattered throughout north-central Texas. The company began a major rebranding that including the renaming of all its retail outlets to 7-Eleven to reflect their long hours of operation from 7.00 am in the morning to 11.00 pm at night.[25] The campaign included the hiring of Alan Dobbs, a professional architect, who was tasked with the responsibility of extending the rebranding to the store buildings with the design of modernized stores and remodelling of existing ones. Parking lots grew five to ten times larger, reinforcing the exterior resemblance to contemporary gas stations. Dobbs was responsible for the design of the new 7-Eleven logo, which consisted of a large red number '7' with the word 'Eleven' spelled out in capital letters, creating a 'T' shape.[26] The neon sign added a vertical feature on the horizontal store exteriors, either placed on a mast on the store façade and/or on a free-standing concrete pylon in the parking lot. All of the new stores were equipped with horizontal sliding doors that slid into a pocket on the end wall, replacing the overhead industrial-type doors on older stores. Movable and sometimes branded ice boxes, like those for Coca Cola, allowed great flexibility and cleaned up the exterior by removing the more scattered array of product displays (Figure 3.3). The shifting of the refrigerated dairy vault to the back of the store also allowed for more freedom of movement for staff and customers.[27] The floor space of a typical store was doubled in area with the intensive remodelling and rebuilding campaign of over 100 stores between 1945 and 1952. The consumer experience, starting with the store sign seen at a distance to the 'artful' displays of the stacked goods to the individual branded packages were all designed to facilitate rapid identification and easy navigation.

As the supermarket moved to the periphery of cities to find the cheap space to serve its car-oriented clientele, the smaller and more agile convenience store was able to fill the gaps in city centres with a network of accessible locations.[28] The choice of store location was carefully considered, in terms of neighbourhood demographics and competition from supermarkets.[29] Even with the increase in the floor space of its redesigned stores, 7-Eleven seemed to be conscious of retaining the scale that distinguished it from the supermarket and kept goods within arm's length. An interior view of the Fort Worth store in 1951 (Figure 3.4) shows how navigation through the store continued to be defined by the products for sale displayed in a variety of store fixtures from open-tiered gondolas to refrigerated cases.

As seen in Figure 3.4, cases of Carling Ale are used to create a stacked display for a bottled drink advertised to be 'better than beer' – alcoholic beverages had become one of the chain's most popular products. The ziggurat tower of boxes is supported at its base by cardboard versions of guardian figures in the form of the store's mascots, the '7 AM Rooster' and the '11 PM Owl', who were featured in the store's first television ad in 1949.[30] On the right, a tiered stand of packages of seeds promising a 'better garden' provides a fitting endcap for the row of open display cases for produce that includes two scales for weighing items. The back wall, however, returns to the business of quick gratification and prepared food – seemingly the domain of male customers. Signs advertise prepared foods, including the store's own patented 'sharp-frozen meats' and a ready-to-eat 'breakfast with man appeal'. While a sign states that curbside service is still available, the open refrigerated unit along the back wall allowed consumers to make their own selections without any assistance. In this smaller-scale version of the

# BIN, BAG, BOX

FIGURE 3.4 'A Fort Worth 7-Eleven Store' (1951). Allen Liles, Oh Thank Heaven! The Story of the Southland Corporation *(Dallas, TX: Southland Corporation, 1977)*, 84. Courtesy of 7-Eleven, Inc.

supermarket, the layout of the aisles maps out a clear path of movement for consumers, enabling them to navigate their way through the categories of merchandise.[31]

The trend towards greater self-service in food shopping expressed in the layout of the store was closely connected to developments in trends in food marketing as well as manufacturing.[32] The 1950s have been described as a kind of golden age in food retailing when processing and advertising developed in tandem, especially with the rise of new kinds of prepared foods like frozen meals.[33] Steven Heller observes that as food became more abstract and detached from its place of production, the branded package played a greater role in forging a connection to the human psyche and inspiring devotion to a brand.[34] Earlier packages relied on distinctive typographic compositions to create a visual identity, but improved technologies of more varied non-porous surfaces made more colourful and expressive designs possible.[35] The food package was transformed from an inert receptacle into a 'silent salesman ... catching the shopper's eye, identifying what the product is and giving her all the basic information she needs about the food inside'.[36] Convenience store companies began to carry and promote their own private label products, establishing a coordinated identity that was promoted in print and television advertising and in the physical stores. With this integrated branding, packages become what Maria Fuentes calls 'active agents ... socio-material devices that play an active role in shaping the practices of food production and consumption'.[37] The role they play in 'manipulating the status of food as commodities' is evident in their embodied presence on the store shelf and their represented image in advertising. A 1970s nationwide promotion for Southland Dairies, for example, included young women dressed as milk cartons; the store's most wholesome and yet alluring products literally come to life as objects of desire.[38]

The packaging of food in the convenience store was thus not just about selling the consumable products inside but selling a larger idea about convenience as a necessary value for navigating modern life.[39] The rapid growth of the convenience store industry in the late 1960s was fuelled by the growth of the suburbs and highways and the rise in personal automobile ownership. Some stores added gas pumps to their product lines or located near gas stations, while gas stations added grocery items in order to simultaneously deliver sustenance to the driver and the car.[40] Among the numerous competitors in the convenience store industry that emerged in the early 1960s to challenge the supremacy of 7-Eleven in local markets was QuikTrip in Tulsa, Oklahoma.[41] The design of their new store in the late 1960s sought to express the chain's motto of 'fast and friendly service' in a streamlined design with an open frontage and sliding glass doors facing the parking lot. With the addition of air-conditioning, the entire store interior became a modern temperature-controlled version of the former ice house, with the coldest refrigerated sections relocated to the back for convenient access to utilities. Rather than competing with the family's weekly supermarket shopping, QuikTrip promoted a shopping experience true to its name for ready-to-go, smaller items, from dairy products to TV tubes – even the ice was now crushed to serve home entertainment needs.[42] Gleaming stainless steel and glass refrigerators were fully recessed into back walls covered in shining turquoise ceramic tiles, emphasizing cleanliness and visual order. The uniform stacks of similar branded products from food items to magazines were now firmly contained within purpose-designed display cases and shelves. The convenience store's main selling products – beer and cigarettes – continued to reflect the store's main and most loyal customers, identified as young male blue-collar workers. But with these bright, sanitary, self-service interiors, convenience stores intentionally sought to create a modern shopping environment that was suitable for middle-class women.[43] A 1966 advertisement in *Look Magazine* touts the 'park-at the-door' feature at 7-Eleven that enables a busy mother to complete her purchases without losing sight of her large brood of kids spilling out of the car (Figure 3.5). Along with the staples of milk and bread, her shopping includes a women's magazine, and she receives friendly personal service from the smiling clerk. The retail building appears to have dematerialized to enable an uninterrupted view and flow of objects and space from the interior of the store to that of the car.

This kind of efficient but personalized service was promoted by the convenience store as what distinguished it from its behemoth cousin, the

# BIN, BAG, BOX 71

FIGURE 3.5 'Leave the youngsters in the car? Why not? You can see them from anywhere in the store.' 7-Eleven, full-page advertisement, Look Magazine, 1 November (1966). Courtesy of 7-Eleven, Inc.

supermarket. While the 'big store' could 'provide a product, the little store provided a service' to the customer who wanted not only to avoid long checkout lines but to connect one-on-one with a real person in an intimate setting.[44] In the late 1970s, 7-Eleven rebranded its stores with a new design that was consistent with that being adopted by supermarkets and fast food chains, featuring a red mansard roof and a more closed brick exterior, which seemed to attempt to resurrect a (much-diminished) image of the homely general store.[45] With more stores adopting twenty-four-hour operations and gaining notoriety as the target of robberies, granting the assurance of security to the late-night customer became paramount. The simulation of the house front used a more subdued back lit 7-Eleven sign in tones of red and green set against a raised brick pylon-chimney. The idea of the store as a 'haven of rest and refreshment' conveyed the effort to create 'appealing images of attractiveness and cleanliness' to attract female customers.[46] The addition of stations where customers could prepare their own food, with freshly brewed coffee, fountain drinks and microwaves, produced a kind of simulacrum of the domestic kitchen.[47] Women frequently appeared in print and television advertising as target customers. In a 1979 TV commercial for 7-Eleven, a housewife in desperate need of milk is taken on an imaginary flight through the door of her empty refrigerator to the parking lot of the neighbourhood 7-Eleven store. There the camera pans over an abundant 'forest' of refrigerators labelled with the different names of families before entering the one labelled 'Your family' that leads the viewer to the refrigerator at the back of the store filled with cartons of milk.

The collapsing of scales in this portrayal of the shopping experience – which takes the viewer from home to retail space, from parking lot to sales counter, and from the empty to the replenished commodity – merges the image of the store building, its fixtures and food products. Experiments in reinventing the convenience store model in the last twenty-five years or so have continued to seek to blur the hard distinction between the architectural container and the objects it contains. The drive to fulfil the ideal of speed and efficiency in food shopping has led to experiments in automation that date back to the 1940s.[48] The persistent striving to create the ultimate food merchandising machine that delivers rapid and efficient exchanges resonates powerfully today in the post-COVID pandemic era.[49] Even before the crisis, economic trends seemed to suggest that the convenience store business was on a rapid decline, replaced by the instantaneous gratification of online shopping and forced out of cities by gentrification and rising real estate costs.[50] But subsequent reports suggest that these retail stores, deemed essential businesses during the pandemic, were actually preferred by consumers hesitant to re-enter large supermarkets. While fuel and food service sales and foot traffic understandably dropped, in-store sales were reported to have reached a record high in 2020.[51] Even with the widespread availability of same-day, contactless delivery, the convenience store seems to continue to offer something, perhaps more evident in the independently owned and operated versions that continue to make up the majority of these businesses in the United States today. The bodega in New York, for example, takes a more eclectic and individualized approach to the design of its building and contents, customizing its product lines and services to meet the needs of local customers, who are often immigrants and minorities.[52] Rather than striving to become the ultimate dispensing machine of plasticized food modules, these stores embrace their role as neighbourhood landmarks, returning the smells and tastes of fresh produce and prepared food to the shopping experience. The comforting clutter of objects for sale and those not for sale, from religious relics to the bodega cat, endow these businesses with the familiarity and sacredness of home.

Despite the unreliability of its gastronomic quality, ultimately the convenience store persists due to its ability to repackage the food shopping experience into a shrink-wrapped, bite-sized snack, to fufil the need for immediate gratification. As a series of nested containers, from the building envelope to packaged goods, and from the parking lot to sales counter, the convenience store makes manifest the close connection between buildings and objects, and between its living and inanimate occupants.

## Notes

1. Names vary widely even in North America from the bodega or deli in New York City, the party store in Detroit, the spa in New England and the 'depanneur' in Quebec. Dan Nosowitz, 'What Do You Call the Corner Store', atlasobscura.com (7 July 2016). https://www.atlasobscura.com/articles/what-do-you-call-the-corner-store
2. Convenience stores have been typically neglected in architectural and food histories. A distinctive exception is Steven M. Graves, 'Convenience Stores: A landscape perspective', *Yearbook of the Association of Pacific Coast Geographers* 79 (2017): 134–52.
3. Dale Southerton, 'Convenience', *Encyclopedia of Consumer Culture*, vol. 1, 1st ed. (Thousand Oaks, CA: Sage Publications Ltd, 2011), 355–8.
4. 'Convenience store', *A Dictionary of Marketing* (3rd ed.), ed. Charles Doyle (Oxford: Oxford University Press, 2011).
5. Neil Wrigley, Steve Wood, Dionysia Lambiri and Michelle Lowe, 'Corporate convenience store development effects in small towns: Convenience culture during economic and digital storms', *EPA Economy and Space* 51, no.1 (2019): 113–14.
6. Peter Jones, 'The geographical development of convenience stores in Britain', *Geography* 73, no.2 (April 1988): 146
7. Other non-consumable products are tailored to meet local needs like tobacco products, and lottery tickets as well as services like cheque cashing, photocopying and dry cleaning.
8. Janet Blackman. 'The Development of the Retail Grocery Trade in the Nineteenth Century', *Business History* 9, no.2 (1967): 110–17.
9. Gregg Steven Pearson, 'The Democratization of Food: Tin Cans and the Growth of the American Food Processing Industry, 1810–1940' (PhD Diss., Lehigh University, 2016)

10  Lisa C. Tolbert, 'The Aristocracy of the Market Basket: Self-Service Food Shopping in the New South', in *Food Chains: From Farm Yards to Shopping Cart* ed. Warren Belasco and Roger Horowitz (Philadelphia: University of Pennsylvania Press, 2010), 183.

11  John L. Stanton, 'A Brief History of Food Retail', *British Food Journal* 120, no.1 (2018): 172.

12  Helen Zoe Veit, 'American Food, Cooking , and Nutrition', *Oxford Research Encyclopedia, American History* (26 Feb. 2018) https://doi.org/10.1093/acrefore/9780199329175.013.339

13  The roots of many company-owned convenience store chains are varied and difficult to trace. Some like Circle K in Akron, Ohio (founded in 1951) and Wawa in Pennsylvania (1964) began as retail outlets added to dairies, while others like QuikTrip (1958) in Tulsa, Oklahoma began as 'bantam stores' or drive in grocers.

14  The development of the mass production of artificial ice took place in the southern United States in the second half of the nineteenth century. By 1900 Texas had 77 of the 766 documented ice plants. The decline of commercial ice houses began in the 1920s with the slow adoption of home refrigerators. Willis R. Woolrich and Charles T. Clark, 'Refrigeration', *Handbook of Texas Online*, https://www.tshaonline.org/handbook/entries/refrigeration (accessed 13 June 2021).

15  The selling of ice to the public took place in a variety of locations from docks at ice plants to wagons on the side of the road in rural locations in the United States: Walter R. Sanders, *Selling Ice* (Chicago, IL: Nickerson & Collins, c1922), 180–5. Adding groceries helped ice manufacturers maintain their business year-round, especially in winter months when ice sales normally slowed: 'History of convenience stores linked to American mobility', *National Petroleum News* 82, no. 10 (Sept. 1990): 63ff.

16  Allen Liles, *Oh Thank Heaven! The Story of the Southland Corporation* (Dallas, TX: Southland Corporation, 1977), 35–6.

17  Mudit Mittal, 'The Evolution of Packaging How innovations shaped packaging over 150 years', *https://medium.com/digital-packaging-experiences/the-evolution-of-packaging-57259054792d*, 18 December 2013.

18  'Haskin's Letter: A Grocery on Wheels', *Perth Amboy Evening News*, 13 November 1924, 6.

19  Liles, *Oh Thank Heaven!*, 55.

20  Stanley Sacharow, *The Package as a Marketing Tool* (Radnor, PA: Chilton Book Company, 1982), 1; Diana Twede, 'The Birth of Modern Packaging', *Journal of Historical Research in Marketing* 4, no.2 (2012), 245–6.

21  '100 manufacturers use new patented container to speed up sales', *New York Times*, 3 February 1921, 13.

22  Al Hisano, 'Selling food in clear packages: The development of cellophane and the expansion of self-service merchandising in the United States, 1920s–1950s', *International Journal of Food Design* 2, no. 2 (2017), 158–60.

23  *Food for Us All: The Yearbook of Agriculture*, ed. Jack Hayes (U.S. Government Printing Office, Washington, DC, 1969), 34.

24  Wrigley, Wood, Lambiri, and Lowe, 'Corporate convenience store development effects in small towns', 113–14.
25  Liles, *Oh Thank Heaven!*, 67.
26  It has been suggested that this 'T' shaped design echoed the shape of the earlier totem pole logo. Claire Nowak, 'The Real Reason the 7-Eleven Logo Looks Like That', *Reader's Digest* (rd.com), 14 June 2018. https://www.rd.com/article/7-eleven-logo/
27  Liles, *Oh Thank Heaven!*, 87.
28  John L. Scranton, 'A Brief History of Food Retailing', *British Food Journal* 120, no.1 (2018): 174.
29  Liles, *Oh Thank Heaven!*, 87.
30  Liles, *Oh Thank Heaven!*, 91. According to company histories, the first television ad for 7-Eleven came out in 1949, featuring the Rooster and the Owl who promoted the store's long hours, ease of parking and curbside service.
31  Maria Fuentes, 'Packaging', *Food Words: Essays in Culinary Culture* (London: Bloomsbury Academic, 2015), 2.
32  Fuentes, 'Packaging', 1; Carl W. Dipman and John E. O'Brien, *Self-Service and Semi-Self-Service Food Stores* (New York: The Progressive Grocer, 1940).
33  Peter Jackson, 'Convenience', *Food Words: Essays in Culinary Culture*. (London: Bloomsbury Academic, 2015), 56–9.
34  Steven Heller, 'Appetite Appeal', *Social Research* 66, no. 1 (1999): 216.
35  Mittal, 'The Evolution of Packaging'.
36  *Food for Us All*, 34.
37  Fuentes, 'Packaging', 1.
38  By the mid-1960s the Southland Corporation owned 29 dairy processing plants in 19 states and had developed a uniform 'New Look' design for their products: Liles, *Oh Thank Heaven!*, 186.
39  Southerton, 'Convenience', 357; Tim Wu, 'Rethinking the Tyranny of Convenience', *NY Times*, 16 Feb, 2018. https://www.nytimes.com/2018/02/16/opinion/sunday/tyranny-convenience.html
40  'Convenience Stores', *Encyclopedia of American Industries* (Detroit, MI: Gale, 2005), 1712. Between 1966 and 1969 convenience store sales in the United States more than tripled, with around 16,000 stores doing business to the amount of 3.5 billion dollars a year. In the same approximate time period 7-Eleven exploded from around 1,500 stores in five states to over 3,500 in 38 states, the District of Columbia and three Canadian provinces: 'Developing Critical Mass', NACS. Est. 1961, http://www.nacs50.com/decades/60s/
41  These included the Circle K Chain founded in Texas in 1951, Speedee Mart in California in 1956, and QuikTrip in Oklahoma in 1958: Jennifer Trieu, 'Convenience Stores', *The SAGE Encyclopedia of Food Issues*, ed. Ken Albala (Los Angeles: Sage, 2015), 292–3, 291–6.
42  The widespread adoption of the home refrigerator by the 1950s meant that ice sales declined and were replaced by cold drinks: Liles, *Oh Thank Heaven!*, 84;

Joe Birney, *60 Years QuikTrip Established 1958* (Fort Worth, DA: QuikTrip Corporation: 2017), 38.

43  Tolbert, 'The Aristocracy of the Market Basket', 183.

44  In 1977 Southland reported that 7-Eleven stores received an average of three million customers a day who spent an average of three and a half minutes in the store. Two-thirds of customers were identified as male, 40 per cent were between 21 and 35, 3 per cent were teenagers and children. Groceries were the single most popular category, tobacco products next, then beer and wine, and then non-food items. Liles, *Oh Thank Heaven!*, 227.

45  Liles, *Oh Thank Heaven!*, 211, 213; Graves, 'Convenience Stores: a landscape perspective', 134–52.

46  Angel Abcede, Steve Dwyer, Greg Lindenberg and Don Smith, 'New ideas in C-store design', *Petroleum News* 86, no. 10 (Sept. 1994): 50ff.

47  In the mid-1970s 7-Eleven stores added microwaves, more private label products like the Big Gulp and self-service petrol.

48  In the 1940s the 'Keedoozle' or 'Key does it all', was a grocery store in Memphis, Tennessee in which customers used a key to access merchandise displayed behind rows of glass display cabinets: Charles R. Goeldner, 'Automation in Marketing', *Journal of Marketing* 26, no.1 (1962): 53–6. More recent attempts at the automated c-store include the Robomart in California that resurrects the Motorteria now using autonomous vehicles to deliver groceries to your door: Jackson Lewis, 'How to Build an Automated C-Store', *cspdailynews.com*, 16 November 2017. https://www.cspdailynews.com/technologyservices/how-build-automated-c-store; Nick Mafi, 'Forget Amazon Go, Robomart Will Bring Groceries to Your Front Door', *Architectural Digest*, 29 January 2018. https://www.architecturaldigest.com/story/forget-amazon-go-robomart-will-bring-groceries-front-door

49  'How Food Shopping May Change After COVID-19', *Convenience.org*, 23 March, 2020; Convenience Stores, *Encyclopedia of American Industries*, 1712–13.

50  Jasmine Garsd, 'Bodegas are a lifeline in NYC ... and many are in trouble', *Marketplace.org*, 12 January 2021.

51  The National Association of Convenience Stores states that the majority of its members are small independent operators, despite having 47 of the 50 top US chains in the organization: 'Despite Pandemic, Nearly Six in 10 C-store Retailers Say In-Store Sales Grew in 2020', *Convenience Store News*, 11 January 2021. https://csnews.com/despite-pandemic-nearly-six-10-c-store-retailers-say-store-sales-grew-2020

52  Before the pandemic, the bodega (from the word for 'apothecary' in Spanish) was estimated to number over 13,000 in the five boroughs of New York City alone: Hansi Lo Wang, 'New York City Bodegas and the Generations who love them', *NPR*, 10 March 2017.

# CHAPTER FOUR

## Atmospheric Exchanges: Air-conditioning, Thermal Material Culture and Public Housing in Singapore

*Jiat-Hwee Chang*

Buildings and objects do not exist in a vacuum. Not just a social, cultural and historical vacuum but, for the purpose of this chapter, literally an atmospheric vacuum. Air constitutes the ambient environment for all entities on the terrestrial environment of this earth, both human and non-human. But because air is invisible, it receives little analytical attention, is hardly historicized, and is definitely under-theorized within design, architectural and urban histories. Furthermore, air is formless and (wrongly) regarded as non-material. It is, thus, assumed to be unrelated to the material preoccupations of design, architectural and urban historians.

The scholarship produced by the recent 'atmospheric turn' in the social sciences and humanities has begun to give greater 'visibility' and analytical attention to air.[1] Among other things, it has shown that historical attempts to regulate, modify and even govern air for public health and other social, economic and political reasons have in-built environmental implications.[2] The focus of the scholarship tends to be, however, at the larger infrastructural and urban scale, even though air exists at and shapes the smaller-scale buildings and objects. This chapter seeks to shift our attention to the material impact of air at a few smaller and more intimate scales by exploring how the introduction of air-conditioning in the public housing of Singapore affected a spectrum of things, from the scale of the building to building components and to objects of interior design (including furniture and light fixtures). Although this spectrum of things defies discipline-based distinctions and disregards other ready-made object-based distinctions, they are related to each other through the circulation of air and the exchanges of thermal energy between them and the bodies that they surround and envelope.

Conventional air-conditioning operates through a compressive-refrigeration cycle that introduces chilled and dehumidified air into an interior space and pumps out waste heat to the exterior. The earliest air-conditioning systems were first assembled at the turn of the twentieth century by a few pioneering mechanical engineers in North America – including Alfred Wolff, Stuart W. Cramer (who came up with the phrase) and, most famously, Willis Carrier – more for the 'process air conditioning' in factories than for the 'comfort cooling' of humans.[3] Air-conditioning subsequently became much more widely used for comfort cooling and the technology was soon disseminated globally, including to Singapore, by first US and then Japanese, followed most recently by Chinese and Indian, companies.[4] In the equatorial climate of Singapore, air-conditioning lowers the indoor temperature from the range of around 28–32 degrees Celsius to around 18–22 degrees Celsius and the indoor relative humidity level from the range of 70–90 per cent to the range of 30–50 per cent, following the recommendations of various international standards. In the words of sociologist Elizabeth Shove and colleagues, air-conditioning 'reconfigure[s] patterns of thermal exchange'[5] and affects not just bodily sensations and comfort, but also influences thermal exchanges and flows of energy between bodies, atmosphere and objects, creating a new thermal material culture that affects, albeit unevenly, a spectrum of things across different scales in the environment.

Called an 'air-conditioned nation' by both political commentators and urban studies scholars, Singapore is known to be heavily dependent on air-conditioning for keeping its population comfortable and productive.[6] The ubiquitous deployment of air-conditioning in Singapore was also inextricably entangled with the underlying technopolitics and socio-economic imperatives of the developmental city-state.[7] Singapore is, however, unevenly and only very recently air-conditioned. Commercial buildings like shopping malls, office towers and hotels were widely installed with central air-conditioning from the 1970s. But the spread of air-conditioning in residential buildings, particularly the public housing flats in which around 80 per cent of the Singaporean population live, was much more gradual. The post-independence public housing programme started in 1960, one year after Singapore achieved self-government. It took more than three decades – that is, until the 1990s – for more than 20 per cent of the households living in public housing to own an air-conditioner.

Despite the underlying social, economic and political differences, the introduction of centralized air-conditioning in these commercial buildings in Singapore brought about architectural and other material cultural changes that were not dissimilar to those elsewhere in the world. For instance, in terms of architectural typology, there was the emergence of hermetically sealed office towers with deep floor plans clad in glass curtain walls in Singapore that were based on well-documented precedents in the West.[8] In comparison, the transformations of public housing were less straightforward. The early public housing typologies were planned and designed to be passively cooled – that is, well shaded and naturally ventilated – to keep their inhabitants comfortable. As air-conditioning became more popular, design adjustments in the housing layout and exterior configuration were made by the public housing authority Housing and Development Board (HDB) to accommodate the appliance. Alongside these changes were broader changes to the interior furnishing that modified the thermal transfer in the interior and around the bodies of the inhabitants. Following Elizabeth Shove and her colleagues, I call this spectrum of things across different scales connected by thermal exchanges – and radically altered by air-conditioning – thermal material culture.[9] This chapter traces the gradual and contingent formation of the domestic thermal material culture of public housing between 1960 and 2000.

The chapter therefore documents transformations across different scales that were both centrally implemented by a single housing agency and introduced in a diffused manner by an array of actors that included owners and inhabitants of public housing, interior designers, building contractors and air-conditioning salespersons and installers. Given such a wide array of actors and agencies spread across many different households, I will utilize numerous types of sources, including unconventional ones.[10] As a result, the chapter draws on a mix of official household surveys and statistics, HDB regulations and guides, newspaper and magazine articles. Interior design magazine articles, in particular, are an important source for understanding changes in interior thermal material culture.

## Accommodating air-conditioning

Singapore is known for its large-scale public housing programme that houses around 80 per cent of the Singaporean population. For many years, the public housing authority HDB, established in 1960, was the largest developer in the country, responsible for one-third to half of the total construction investment in Singapore.[11] As a large developer and builder, the HDB was, until the late 1970s, driven by a policy of pragmatism that, according to its 1970s chief architect Liu Thai Ker, centred on maximization of floor area at a given cost, standardization and land optimization. It focused on building low-cost housing based on standardized types, providing living conditions that improved on those in the ubiquitous slums and squats in colonial Singapore. In this basic housing provision, the 'comfort and convenience' of the inhabitants were regarded as two of the main planning

FIGURE 4.1 *View of an access corridor in an HDB slab block, which also shades the interior of the flats. Note the louvred windows of the flats next to the corridor and an exterior view of a similar slab block in the background. Courtesy of Tan Wei Ming.*

and design considerations. Influenced by mid-twentieth-century discourse of climatic design, the public housing flats were planned and designed to provide passive cooling for the comfort of their inhabitants. The early slab blocks were oriented such that the longer sides faced north or south, minimizing their exposure to solar radiation. In addition, access corridors were placed in front of the individual flats to further shade them from the sun. The layouts of the flats were also planned to facilitate cross-ventilation.[12] Different smaller-scale building features – such as louvred windows, timber doors with louvres and ventilation holes above doors – were incorporated into the interior to further enable the movement of air (Figure 4.1).

Liu expected public housing residents to complement the architectural features of passive design with furnishing and electrical appliances like fans and refrigerators to 'add further to the convenience and comfort of flat living'.[13] The frequent appearance of advertisements for fans and refrigerators selling the promise of cool comfort in *Our Home*, a monthly magazine published by HDB between 1972 and 1989 and issued free of charge to all households living in public housing, suggests that this consumerist idea of comfort augmented by appliances was widely promoted. The 1981 HDB household survey also shows that 94.9 per cent and 85.2 per cent of the HDB households owned a refrigerator and an electric fan respectively, therefore confirming the popularity of these comfort-enhancing appliances.[14] The air-conditioner was, however, one household appliance explicitly discouraged by the HDB for two reasons: the electrical infrastructure of the early HDB flats was not designed to carry the large electrical load necessary for the operation of air-conditioners, and the energy crisis in the 1970s meant that saving energy was a national priority.[15] During the 1970s, any household that wanted to install an air-conditioner needed to apply for special permission from HDB, which would only be granted on medical grounds.[16] Even if approval was given, only one air-conditioner could be installed per HDB flat, the power of which was limited to 1 horsepower or 746 watts. Furthermore, a non-refundable installation fee of 150 Singapore dollars was levied per installation.[17] Even then, air-conditioners were not allowed in the smaller one- and two-room flats. Not surprisingly, very few households living in public housing owned an air-conditioner. In 1972, the number was regarded as negligible, so statistically insignificant that it was not even listed.[18] By 1981, the percentage of HDB households with air-conditioning was 3.2, most of which were concentrated among the larger four- and five-room flats.[19] At that time, the same rule as the 1970s applied, except that the instruction issued by HDB added that the air-conditioner 'must be installed at the air-conditioner opening provided by HDB' (Figure 4.2).[20]

Measuring approximately 900mm by 600mm (3ft by 2 ft), the opening was typically placed under the windows of the master bedroom. The 1 horsepower restriction and the design of the opening meant that it was intended for the installation of a window unit air-conditioner,[21] which could be installed without blocking any existing window. This accommodation for the air-conditioner was introduced sometime before 1978. It was selectively implemented in the bigger five-room flats, but apparently only in five-room flats located in a point block and not those in a slab block.[22] By the mid-1980s, the opening, which was regarded as a provision for one air-conditioner unit per flat, was implemented in almost half the new HDB flats, primarily the larger four-room, five-room and Housing and Urban Development Company (HUDC) flats.[23] In the mid-1980s the HDB relaxed this policy, and this contributed to the rise in HDB households with an air-conditioner to 14.4 per cent in 1987–8, a four-and-a-half times increase from 1981.[24] In the 1990s, the percentage of HDB households owning an air-conditioner would continue to rise, from 28 in 1992–3[25] to 33.7 in 1995[26] and 57.6 in 2000.[27]

The statistics in the 1990s also began to differentiate the air-conditioners into two types: the window unit and the split unit. In 1995, window units made up 25.1 per cent while split units constituted 8.6 per cent. In 2000, they were 26.8 per cent and 30.8 per cent respectively. The increasing prevalence of the split unit within five short years would have implications on how air-conditioning affected both the design of HDB flats and their interior furnishing.

In the United States, the major expansion of the air-conditioning market in the post-Second World War years was attributed to the fact that air-

FIGURE 4.2 A 1986 advertisement for Daikin split unit system that highlights the air-conditioner opening provided by HDB for the flats built in the 1980s. It also simultaneously proposes that the outdoor condensing unit could be installed at the 'aircon hole'. Our Home (1986). Courtesy of Daikin Air-conditioning Singapore.

conditioning was 'sold as appliance rather than equipment to be installed by contractors'.[28] This distinction between equipment and appliance is articulated by historian Gail Cooper as that between 'a controlled and rational system' designed by engineers and architects and a 'flexible and responsive' technology chosen by occupants according to their needs (and wants).[29] The former is specially customized and deeply integrated as mechanical services into a building, while the latter is a standard readymade that can be flexibly added to any building. The main form of the appliance in the mid-twentieth century was the window unit air-conditioner, which was a result of the miniaturization of air-conditioning over the decades – with the typical room air-conditioner being more than halved in size between 1936 and 1956. The small window unit air-conditioner was an easy-to-install package unit. It was sold as an appliance that any homeowner could purchase and install, so they could easily convert rooms in their non-air-conditioned residence into air-conditioned ones. Unlike the installation of the equipment in an air-conditioning system that required deep integration and major modifications to accommodate air ducts and other related services, the installation of an air-conditioning appliance only necessitated minor changes. In the case of a window unit air-conditioner, all that was needed was an opening to the outside that could be found on any exterior-facing wall or, as the name suggests, the window.[30] In Singapore's public housing, the window unit air-conditioner was also the main type of air-conditioner installed in the 1970s, but it was soon taken over by the split unit system.

The split unit was named as such because of the separation between an outdoor condensing unit, which housed the compressor and condenser, and the indoor fan coil unit, which blew out chilled and dehumidified air.[31] The split unit system was also known variously as the ductless split unit system or the multi-room fan coil system.[32] These names hint at the various advantages of the system over both the window unit air-conditioner and the central air-conditioning. First, a single outdoor condensing unit could be connected to up to four fan coil units to cool four separate rooms. Each of these fan coil units could be independently controlled, that is, turned on and off and set to different air temperatures and fan speeds. Second, as a fan coil unit houses only the evaporator, fan and filter, it is small, visually unobtrusive, and could easily be accommodated in even small interiors. Third, the system does not require any air duct, as only the refrigerant is moved between the outdoor condensing and the indoor fan coil units. Unlike central air-conditioning that has air ducts taking up significant amount of space – typically in the false ceiling – the split system could be installed in small apartments with low ceilings, like those in HDB housing. Only small holes needed to be bored into the walls to accommodate the refrigerant piping.[33] And fourth, the different split unit systems first introduced to Singapore in the 1970s were power-efficient and they operated within the electrical power constraints imposed by HDB.[34] As such, the split unit system combined all the advantages of central air-conditioning (or equipment) and the window unit air-conditioner (or appliance) without being afflicted by any of their major limitations and inconveniences.

In the late 1970s, the air-conditioning companies recommended that the outdoor condensing unit of the split unit system be placed in the balcony or the kitchen of a residence. As many HDB flats did not have balconies and only had small kitchens, the recommended location for the outdoor condensing unit changed in the 1980s. A 1986 advertisement by Daikin, the Japanese manufacturer of air-conditioners that was the leader in Singapore's air-conditioning market at that time, suggested that the outdoor condensing unit could be installed at the 'aircon hole', that is, the aforementioned opening that was created below the master bedroom's windows of a HDB flat (see Figure 4.2).[35] By installing at the aircon hole, it meant the outdoor condensing unit was placed just outside the hole and held in place by wooden brackets. Years of exposure to the hot and wet equatorial weather of Singapore would later cause some of these wooden brackets to rot and lose their structural integrity, leading to cases of the outdoor condensing units crashing down from high-rises. These incidents led to new regulations passed in 1999 that mandated the use of stainless-steel brackets to support these outdoor units.[36] Despite being part of an appliance that has purportedly a loose fit with architecture, the outdoor condensing unit began to gradually transform the spatial organization and fabric of HDB flats.

It was around the same time that HDB introduced a new building feature to properly accommodate the outdoor condensing unit: the aircon ledge.[37] Early forms of this feature began to appear in the HDB housing completed between 1997 and 1999. It took the form of either an enlarged cantilevered sun-shading concrete fin that doubled as a ledge for the outdoor condensing unit, or a separate ledge specially designed for the outdoor unit (Figure 4.3). In the latter case, a vertical perforated metal sheet was sometimes added to screen the outdoor unit. By 1999, the aircon ledge had become an essential component of the utility corner found in every single HDB flat, regardless of size, built from then onwards.[38]

The utility corner consists of two traditional utility spaces – the bathroom and the kitchen – that were always paired in the older HDB flats. Although conventionally regarded as 'unsightly', both 'back-of-the-house' spaces are required by building code, health considerations and functional requirements to face the exterior so that they can be naturally ventilated. Natural ventilation of the bathroom helps to remove odour and keeps it dry. For the kitchen, natural ventilation helps to remove the cooking fumes. Furthermore, both spaces are also used for laundry. In the past, households without a washing machine would do their hand washing in the bathroom. When the washing machine became a ubiquitous household appliance, it was usually placed in the kitchen. The washed clothes are typically hung outside the kitchen window to dry using bamboo and/or metallic poles as the dryer was not and still is not common.

FIGURE 4.3 *Exterior view of the vertical stack of utility corners (as indicated by a dotted rectangle) on a block of recently built HDB flats. Courtesy of Jiat-Hwee Chang.*

The aircon ledge was appended to these two older utility spaces, reconfiguring them in the process. Following the placement logic of the aircon hole, the aircon ledge continued to be positioned next to the master bedroom. With the addition of the aircon ledge and the master bedroom that it was paired with, the utility corner became a small exterior area recessed from the elevation, thus making the 'unsightly' service spaces less visible. The top railing around the aircon ledge also doubled as support for the poles used for hanging the clothes out to dry. Although one could say that the humble air-conditioner has come a long way from being disregarded and unaccounted for in the design of early HDB flats to being seen as an essential component to be accommodated in the post-1999 HDB flats, the external changes introduced to accommodate air-conditioning were relatively minor when compared to the internal transformations discussed next.

## Thermal exchanges and interior transformations

The vernacular architecture of Singapore and the hot and humid tropics is characterized by sharing what Reyner Banham called the 'selective mode' of environmental modulation.[39] The building fabric selectively admits the

FIGURE 4.4 HDB *interior featured in the May/June issue of* Our Home *(1973): 20–1. Courtesy of the Housing & Development Board.*

external environment – keeping the sun and its radiant heat out while admitting breezes to carry away the moisture in the air and lower the relative humidity of the interior. The vernacular architecture of Singapore – whether the traditional Malay house, the terraced shophouse, or the colonial bungalow – is characterized by the porosity and lightness of the internal and external building features.[40] These features include louvred windows, bamboo chick blinds, ventilation holes and bricks. As noted above, the early HDB flats shared these porous built features to facilitate cross-ventilation. But the porosity was not restricted to the building features, it permeated smaller-scale interior decorative features, furniture and even clothing. In other words, these things across different scales mediate the thermal exchanges between the body and the environment. Both environmental design and material culture scholars have seen these artefacts as extensions of the body and understood them in continuum.[41] Indeed, as Ian Hodder argues, things are neither isolated nor inert; things depend on other things. Things are connected in different ways, and in the case of the naturally ventilated interior, the various things across different scales are held together by 'flows of inter-linked bundles of [aerial] matter, [thermal] energy, and information [about keeping cool]'.[42]

During the 1970s and 1980s, at a time when only a very small proportion of HDB flats were air-conditioned, the interior furnishing of HDB flats had a few common features that can be gleaned from an examination of such interiors featured in several magazines from that era (Figure 4.4).[43] In these well-shaded interiors, almost all furniture was lightweight and porous, made with rattan or slender timber members with thin upholstery, if any. The fabrics used for curtains, bed sheets and even blankets were also thin and breathable. When the flat dwellers were photographed, they invariably wore loose-fitting clothes, short-sleeved tops and/or shorts that let their skin come into contact with moving air.[44] Furthermore, the concrete floor of the HDB flats was often either covered with ceramic or marble tiles, or simply left bare. As most HDB flat dwellers did not wear any footwear at home, the contact between their bare feet and these thermally effusive surfaces helped to give a sensation of coolness as heat was conducted away. Taken together, the thermal properties distributed among the array of interior objects reduced heat gain through radiation by providing shade and promoted heat loss through convection and conduction by exposing the body to moving air and cool surfaces. For the purposes of this chapter, let us focus on a ubiquitous interior object of that era: the rattan chair.

Rattan, derived from the Malay word *rotan*, is the common name of a large group of climbing palms found in parts of India and China and throughout Southeast Asia. It is regarded as one of the world's most important non-timber forest products and it is used for furniture, basketry, mat making, home construction, food, medicine, and so on.[45] Rattan from Southeast Asia has been exported to Europe and, later, the United States since the sixteenth century after the Portuguese started trading in the region. Rattan furniture gained popularity not just in Portugal and Spain, but also in Britain and, later, in the United States. The strong, lightweight, porous and breathable rattan chairs were more comfortable and preferred over upholstered chairs during the sweltering summers in the Iberian Peninsula and the southern United States, and all year round in the European tropical colonies. The peak of the popularity of rattan furniture was probably in the late nineteenth and early twentieth centuries, when it was found in airy houses and breezy verandas throughout the tropics, including in many colonial houses in Singapore.[46] While its popularity declined in the mid-twentieth century, rattan furniture enjoyed a revival in the 1970s and 1980s, when it became a countercultural icon in the West.[47]

In Singapore, rattan furniture has a long history, and its demand did not peak and decline like in the United States and Europe. Singapore has been a major centre for the import and export of rattan since the early twentieth century.[48] It was also a key node in the manufacturing of rattan furniture, with many factories and workshops of different scales. By the 1980s, Singapore still had an estimated forty to fifty factories producing it.[49] Since the early twentieth century, low-cost rattan furniture had been commonly found in the homes of Singapore. It was valued for its affordability, lightness, strength and comfort. Alongside bamboo and straw, rattan was traditionally used in the making of a series of household items considered as cooling by the Chinese (including the overseas Chinese population in Singapore) because of their porosity and airiness. These included the cooling chair (*liangyi*, 涼椅), cooling bed (*liangban*, 涼板) and cooling mat (*liangxi*, 涼席).[50] The tradition continued as Singaporeans were resettled into HDB flats, where rattan furniture remained ubiquitous. The 1970s revival of rattan furniture in the West had an impact on Singapore too. New and more upmarket designs of rattan furniture influenced by European and North American trends were introduced from the region – particularly Indonesia and the Philippines – and sold.[51] As the population moved into modern housing, the designs of rattan furniture were also modified, as one commentator noted:

> Once found on the verandas – as well as in the large rooms – of colonial bungalows, the designs were chunky and sturdy to weather the elements. With verandas and large rooms more a thing of the past, cane furniture is now taking on a clean, contemporary look.[52]

Not only did the slimmer and lighter rattan furniture fit the smaller HDB flats better, it continued to be regarded as providing better ventilation and was recommended as such in interior decoration guides.[53] Rattan furniture was seen as an extension of the architecture's selective mode that let air through, in the process mitigating the heat and humidity.

As air-conditioning became more common in HDB flats, the mode of environmental control also correspondingly changed. Instead of the previous selective mode when the porous building components and furnishing would admit breezes to naturally ventilate the interior and cool the body, air-conditioning introduced what Banham calls the 'conservative mode' of environmental control. For air-conditioning to work, all openings – including windows, doors and louvres – must be shut to keep the chilled and dehumidified air inside. Instead of being an asset, porosity becomes a liability. Furthermore, as the interior air is chilled and dehumidified by mechanical cooling, having one's skin exposed to moving air becomes a source of discomfort. The cooling breeze in a non-air-conditioned space becomes a chilling draft in an air-conditioned space. Similar changes in sensation apply to what one comes into contact with. While our bodies value coming into contact with breathable and thermal conductive materials in non-air-conditioned spaces, our bodies prefer less permeable and thermally insulating materials in air-conditioned spaces. As such, we see distinct changes in the thermal material culture in the interior of the HDB flats from the 1980s and 1990s onwards (Figure 4.5).

For example, in place of light, porous rattan chairs that one sits on, there are thickly cushioned upholstered sofas that one sinks into. Instead of thermally effusive concrete or tiled floors, we find more HDB interiors with wall-to-wall carpeting or rugs strewn around.[54] And taking the place of light curtains, breathable bed sheets and thin blankets, are 'luxuriously draped windows and bed' with duvets and double-layered curtains to insulate and conserve the heat within bodies and interior spaces.[55] Cosiness seems to

FIGURE 4.5 *Interior of a HUDC flat from 1992 showing a sofa with thick cushioning, carpeted flooring, shelves with accent halogen lighting, double-layered curtains, and indoor air-handling unit of a split system air-conditioning. Image courtesy of* HOMESTYLE *magazine 1992 Jan/Feb issue.*

have displaced airiness as a new keyword associated with thermal comfort in the air-conditioned domestic interior. In addition to cosiness, another oft-mentioned keyword was 'warmth', especially in relation to lighting. Fluorescent light fixtures, which were very common in HDB interiors since the 1970s, began to be regarded as emitting harsh lighting by interior designers and lighting consultants in the 1990s. In place of fluorescent light, they advocated the use of halogen lights, as they were 'bright, look attractive and create a warm ambience'.[56] Halogen lights are not unlike incandescent lights as they both create light by heating the filaments. Therefore, the warmness is not just connected to the colour temperature of halogen lights but also the large amount of energy that is converted to waste heat in the process. Halogen lights are literally warm and the cold interior atmosphere produced by air-conditioning certainly made them more feasible in the hot and humid climate of Singapore. This emphasis on lighting and ambience from the 1990s could also be attributed to the increasing separation of the interior from the exterior brought about by air-conditioning. Not only were windows shut due to air-conditioning, they were also tinted or had sun-control films applied to them to further eliminate solar heat gain and minimize glare. The elimination of solar heat gain was frequently accompanied by the reduced entry of daylight, creating dimmer interiors during the day. All sorts of blinds – such as vertical, venetian and roller – also became popular at around the same time, further darkening the interior.[57] Artificial lighting thus became necessary, even during the day, for many air-conditioned interiors. Taken together, one can argue that air-conditioning has brought about an inversion in the keywords associated with interior furnishing. Instead of airiness and cool that were connected to comfort in non-air-conditioned spaces, we have cosiness and warmth, very much temperate ideas of comfort that were made possible through mechanical cooling.

## Conclusion

The direct material transformations brought about by the air-conditioner in HDB flats were not very substantial, perhaps more than most household appliances but not significantly so. HDB introduced the air-conditioner opening in the late 1970s to accommodate the window unit air-conditioner and then the air-con ledge situated within the utility corner in the late 1990s. But these direct changes, mostly to the exterior of the HDB flats, were rather minor when compared to the *indirect* changes air-conditioning introduced by altering the patterns of thermal exchanges in the interiors of HDB flats. By modifying the flows of thermal energy in the interior, air-conditioning did not just change the bodily sensations of comfort, it also reconfigured the entanglements between bodies and things, things with other things.

John Crowley has argued that the modern concept of comfort is about the 'self-conscious satisfaction with the relationship between one's body and its immediate physical environment'.[58] According to Witold Rybczynski's 'onion theory of comfort', comfort is a multilayered concept with different physical and psychological attributes that depend on bodily interactions with an array of different types of material cultural elements, from furniture to furnishings. A comfortable body is thus an inextricable part of a larger thermal assemblage of heterogeneous entities across scales and boundaries. Marcel Mauss and others after him have argued that the body is a cog in, not a cause of, the interplay of the biological, psychological, social and material in the assemblage, which in turn is connected to other assemblages.[59] What air-conditioning did was to alter the atmospheric background for this assemblage by creating chilled and dehumidified air. The mechanically conditioned air, in turn, mediated the thermal relations of the bio-psycho-socio-material interplay differently from the previously un-conditioned air. Historians of air-conditioning and the built environment have frequently and reasonably argued that air-conditioning led to separation and isolation between things, spaces and people.[60] But air-conditioning also creates new relations of connections and dependencies, as this chapter has shown. These connections and dependencies link up an array of things across different scales, leading us to question not just building/object distinctions but also other forms of categorization.

## Acknowledgements

Research for this chapter is supported by a Ministry of Education, Singapore, Tier 2 Research Grant 'Heat in Urban Asia: Past, Present and Future' (MOE2018-T2-2-120). The author is also grateful for the research assistance rendered by Jason Ng Chih Sien and the suggestions by the editors and Gregory Clancey.

## Notes

1. Matthew Gandy, 'Urban Atmospheres', *Cultural Geographies* 24, no. 3 (2017): 353–74; Stephen Graham, 'Life Support: The Political Ecology of Urban Air', *City* 19, no. 2–3 (April 2015): 192–215.
2. See, for example, Simon Marvin and Jonathan Rutherford, 'Controlled Environments: An Urban Research Agenda on Microclimatic Enclosure', *Urban Studies* 55, no. 6 (May 2018): 1143–62; Peter Sloterdijk, *Spheres: Plural Spherology*, trans. Wieland Hoban (South Pasadena, CA: Semiotext(e), 2016); David Gissen, 'Thermopolis: Conceptualizing Environmental Technologies in the Urban Sphere', *Journal of Architectural Education* 60, no. 1 (2006): 43–53.
3. This distinction is based on Gail Cooper, *Air-Conditioning America: Engineers and the Controlled Environment, 1900–1960* (Baltimore: Johns Hopkins University Press, 1998). The most comprehensive history of air-conditioning and architecture is Joseph Siry, *Air-Conditioning in Modern American Architecture, 1890–1970* (University Park, PA: Penn State University Press, 2021).
4. The global history of air-conditioning – even as a technological history – has yet to be written. From existing accounts, US companies like Carrier and York were, and still are, major players with large market share. Carrier, in particular, established partnerships with local manufacturers in different parts of the world – such as Japan, India, and the Philippines – and became market leaders in these countries. In the post-war era, Japanese companies – notably, Daikin – became major global manufacturers. And that was, in turn, followed by Indian and especially Chinese manufactures – like Gree and Midea – more

recently. See Eric B. Schultz, *Weathermakers to the World: The Story of a Company, the Standard of an Industry* (Syracuse, NY: Carrier Engineering, 2012); Mariko Tatsuki, *Shaping theFuture: the 90-year history of Daikin Industries 1924–2014*, trans. Thomas I. Elliot (Tokyo: Daikin Industries, 2015); International Energy Agency, *The Future of Cooling: Opportunities for Energy-Efficient Air-Conditioning* (Paris: IEA Publications, 2018).

5  Elizabeth Shove, Gordon Walker, and Sam Brown, 'Material Culture, Room Temperature and the Social Organisation of Thermal Energy', *Journal of Material Culture* 19, no. 2 (2014): 118.

6  Cherian George, *Singapore, the Air-Conditioned Nation: Essays on the Politics of Comfort and Control, 1990–2000* (Singapore: Landmark Books, 2000); Peter James Rimmer and Howard W. Dick, *The City in Southeast Asia: Patterns, Processes and Policy* (Singapore: NUS Press, 2009).

7  I have discussed this elsewhere. See Jiat-Hwee Chang and Tim Winter, 'Thermal Modernity and Architecture', *The Journal of Architecture* 20, no. 1 (2015): 92–121.

8  Thomas Leslie et al., 'Deep Space, Thin Walls: Environmental and Material Precursors to the Postwar Skyscraper', *Journal of the Society of Architectural Historians* 77 (1 March 2018): 77–96; Meredith L. Clausen, 'Belluschi and the Equitable Building in History', *Journal of the Society of Architectural Historians* 50, no. 2 (1991): 109–29; Alexandra Louise Quantrill, 'The Aesthetics of Precision: Environmental Management and Technique in the Architecture of Enclosure, 1946–1986' (PhD dissertation, New York City, Columbia University, 2017).

9  Shove, Walker, and Brown, 'Material Culture, Room Temperature and the Social Organisation of Thermal Energy.'

10  This is especially so in view of the fact that HDB does not grant researchers access its archives.

11  The figures are from the 1970s. See Thai Ker Liu, 'Design for Better Living Conditions', in *Public Housing in Singapore: A Multi-Disciplinary Study*, ed. Stephen H. K. Yeh (Singapore: Singapore University Press for Housing and Development Board, 1975), 117–84.

12  Liu, 'Design for Better Living Conditions', 178; Aline K. Wong and Stephen H. K. Yeh, eds., *Housing a Nation: 25 Years of Public Housing in Singapore* (Singapore: Maruzen Asia for Housing & Development Board, 1985), 86–87.

13  Liu, 'Design for Better Living Conditions', 177.

14  Systems and Research Department, *HDB 1981 Sample Household Survey Report* (Singapore: Housing Development Board, 1982), 75.

15  Owners of HDB flats were advised to consider installing an electric fan before the air-conditioner as the latter 'consumes 20 times more power than the fan' and they were also given tips to operate the air-conditioner in an energy-efficient manner. 'How to Save Electricity in Our Homes', *Our Home*, June (1981): 8. I am grateful to Caitlin Celestine Fernandez for sharing this with me.

16  Stephen H. K. Yeh and Statistics and Research Department, HDB, *Homes for the People: A Study of Tenants' Views on Public Housing in Singapore* (Singapore: HDB and Economic Research Centre, University of Singapore, 1972), 43.

17 Public Relations Unit and the Estates Department, HDB, *Residents' Guide Handbook* (Singapore: Housing and Development Board, 1973); Housing & Development Board, *Residents' Handbook*, second edition (Singapore: Housing and Development Board, 1975).
18 Yeh and Statistics and Research Department, HDB, *Homes for the People*.
19 Systems and Research Department, *HDB 1981 Sample Household Survey Report*, 75, 76, 87.
20 Housing & Development Board, *Residents' Handbook* (Singapore: Housing and Development Board, 1980), 16.
21 'Window Unit Air-Conditioners to Suit Many Low-Cost Flats', *The Straits Times*, 5 March 1978.
22 'HDB Asked to Ease Policy on Air-Con Units', *The Straits Times*, 23 May 1978.
23 HUDC flats were the largest category of flats built between 1974 and 1987 for the so-called 'sandwiched' class of Singaporeans who could afford and prefer something better than the typical public housing but who could not afford private housing. Wong and Yeh, *Housing a Nation*, 136.
24 Department of Statistics, *Report on Household Expenditure Survey 1987/88* (Singapore: Dept. of Statistics, 1989), 31, 33.
25 Department of Statistics, *Report on Household Expenditure Survey 1992/93* (Singapore: Dept. of Statistics, 1994), 24–26.
26 Research section, research and planning department, HDB, *Profile of Residents Living in HDB Flats* (Singapore: Housing and Development Board, 1995), 58.
27 Research section, research and planning department, HDB, *Profile of Residents Living in HDB Flats* (Singapore: Housing and Development Board, 2000).
28 Robert Friedman, 'How Air Conditioning Changed Everything', *American Heritage* August/September (1984): 32. In ASHRAE Archives 91–315, *Air Conditioning – History*, n.d.
29 Cooper, *Air-Conditioning America*, 3.
30 Walter A. Grant, 'From '36 to '56, Air Conditioning Comes of Age', *ASHAE Journal* Jan., Feb., Mar. (1957). In ASHRAE Archives 94-2593, *Air Conditioning – History*, n.d. See also Reyner Banham, *The Architecture of the Well-tempered Environment*, 2nd ed. (London: Architectural Press, 1984), 171–94.
31 'Cool Living in HDB Flats . . .', *New Nation*, 24 April 1978.
32 Yew Meng Lee, 'Aircons: Not Case of Prestige', *New Nation*, 30 October 1979; 'Who's Going to Be Left out of the Cold Tonight?', *Homestyle*, Sep/Oct (1990): 82–3.
33 This was also why the split unit was the most common air-conditioning system installed in Japanese residences. See Haruyuki Fujii and Loren Lutzenhiser, 'Japanese Residential Air-Conditioning: Natural Cooling and Intelligent Systems', *Energy and Buildings* 18 (1992): 221–33.
34 'Cool Living in HDB Flats . . .'; 'Benefits of "Free Blow" Air Distribution', *The Straits Times*, 5 March 1978; 'Window Unit Air-Conditioners to Suit Many Low-Cost Flats.'

35  Daikin first introduced the split system in 1972 and the system was first mentioned in Singapore's reports in the late 1970s: Tatsuki, *Shaping the Future*, 60.

36  Cindy Lim, 'Out with Wooden Aircon Brackets', *The Straits Times*, 2 March 2000. See also https://www.bca.gov.sg/builditright/ss2-aircon.html

37  Information in this section is gathered from a careful study of the plans and photographs of public housing flats provided by HDB and, more importantly, on property websites like www.propertyguru.com.sg. Darren Soh, a local photographer and expert on the history of HDB housing, and Athanasios Tsakonas, an architect who previously worked for HDB, provided valuable insider information.

38  Yuet Fah Ong, Chee Hoong Shum, and Thomas Seow, eds., *Public Housing Design Guide* (Singapore: Building Group, Housing and Development Board, 2005), 13.

39  Banham, *The Architecture of the Well-tempered Environment*, 24.

40  Jee Yuan Lim, *The Malay House: Rediscovering Malaysia's Indigenous Shelter System* (Pulau Pinang: Institut Masyarakat, 1987); Julian Davison, *Black and White: The Singapore House, 1898–1941* (Singapore: Talisman Publishing, 2006).

41  See, for example, James Marston Fitch, *American Building 2: The Environmental Forces That Shape It* (Boston: Houghton Mifflin, 1972); Catherine Allerton, 'The Secret Life of Sarongs: Manggarai Textiles as Super-Skins', *Journal of Material Culture* 12, no. 1 (1 March 2007): 22–46.

42  Ian Hodder, *Entangled: An Archaelogy of the Relationships between Humans and Things* (Malden, MA: Wiley-Blackwell, 2012), 48. See also Tim Winter, 'Active Cooling and Low Carbon Comfort', *The Journal of Architecture* 21, no. 3 (2 April 2016): 418–32.

43  These magazines include *Our Homes, Her World*, and *Beautiful Homes*.

44  'Bliss on a Budget', *Our Home*, December (1972); Su-Ann, 'Interior of a Decorator's Flat', *Our Home*, May/June (1973): 20–21; 'Down to Earth 25 Storeys Up!', *Our Home*, Feb (1979): 12–13; 'Black Is Beautiful', *Our Home*, Oct (1979): 12–13.

45  D. A. Jordon, 'The Rattan Industry: A Survey Conducted between 1961 and 1964' (New York: United Nations, 1964); Stephen F. Siebert, *The Nature and Culture of Rattan: Reflections on Vanishing Life in the Forests of Southeast Asia* (Honolulu: University of Hawai'i Press, 2012).

46  Jeremy Adamson, *American Wicker: Woven Furniture from 1850 to 1930* (New York: Rizzoli, 1993); Emily A. Morris, 'The Development and Effects of the Twentieth-Century Wicker Revival' (Masters of Arts in the History of Decorative Arts, Washington D.C., The Smithsonian Associates and Corcoran College of Art and Design, 2012).

47  Morris, 'The Development and Effects of the Twentieth-Century Wicker Revival.' See also Estelle Caswell, 'How This Chair Became a Pop Culture Icon', *Vox*, 4 October 2019, https://www.vox.com/2019/10/4/20897269/peacock-chair-album-cover.

48 Edward M. Groth, 'The Rattan of Celebes', *Commerce Reports* 4, no. 43 (1929): 231–32.

49 These range from small workshops in Watten Estate, Holland Village, Bukit Timah and Farrer Road, to large factories in Sugei Kadut and Pasir Panjang. Suna Kanga, 'New Twists to Staid Old Cane', *The Straits Times*, 12 October 1986. See also Wanli Pan, '70 Nián Lǎozìhao Shǎugōng Zhì Téng Jiājù Lǎobǎn: Yào Zuò Dào Zuìhòu Yī Kǎuqì', *Shin Min Daily News*, 15 June 2018; Jae Chia, 'How This Third-Gen Entrepreneur Is Keeping S'pore's Last Rattan Weaving Biz Alive', *Vulcan Post* (blog), https://vulcanpost.com/709755/singapore-last-rattan-weaver-hak-sheng-co/. (August 27, 2020)

50 I learned about these terms from the conference presentations of Christopher Courtney and Madlen Kobi, on historical Chinese practices of keeping cool, at the 'Heat in Urban Asia: Past, Present, and Future' workshop organized by the Asia Research Institute, National University of Singapore, 21–23 April 2021.

51 'Casual, Charming, Comfy Cane', *Singapore Monitor*, 15 June 1985; 'Cane with Class', *Singapore Monitor*, 17 November 1984.

52 Cane is a type of rattan and the word is often used interchangeably with rattan. Kanga, 'New Twists to Staid Old Cane.'

53 *HDB & HUDC Flats: A Decorating Guide* (Singapore: MPH Magazines, 1982), 9.

54 Violet Oon, 'The Mood of a Bygone Age', *Her World*, March (1979): 133.

55 'With Modernity and Drama', *Homestyle*, May/June (1992): 61.

56 Elizabeth Gwee, 'Turn Me on, Put Me in a Romantic Light', *The Straits Times*, 26 September 1998. See also Joy Tan, 'Inside Out', *Today*, 13 November 2004; 'With Modernity and Drama.'

57 Peter Gwee, 'Make It a Cooler Haven', *New Nation*, August 30, 1981.

58 John E. Crowley, *The Invention of Comfort: Sensibility and Design in Early Modern Britain and Early America* (Baltimore: Johns Hopkins University Press, 2001), ix. See also Joan E. DeJean, *The Age of Comfort: When Paris Discovered Casual and the Modern Home Began* (New York: Bloomsbury, 2013).

59 Marcel Mauss, 'Techniques of the Body', *Economy and Society* 2, no. 1 (1 February 1973): 70–88; Elspeth Probyn, *Carnal Appetites: Foodsexidentities* (London and New York: Routledge, 2000); Gordon Waitt, 'Bodies That Sweat: The Affective Responses of Young Women in Wollongong, New South Wales, Australia', *Gender, Place and Culture* 21, no. 6 (3 July 2014): 666–82. See also Tomas Maldonado, 'The Idea of Comfort', trans. John Cullars, *Design Issues* 8, no. 1 (1991): 35–43.

60 See, for example, Raymond Arsenault, 'The End of the Long Hot Summer: The Air Conditioner and Southern Culture', *The Journal of Southern History* 50, no. 4 (1984): 597–628.

## CHAPTER FIVE

# Beyond Buildings and Objects: Reyner Banham's Freeway Ecology

*Richard J. Williams*

What can the experience of driving a car tell us about building/object relations? For many architects and critics of architecture in the 1950s and 1960s, that everyday but complex experience prompted questions both about objects and about buildings. Driving, especially urban driving on properly engineered highways, meant experiencing the world at high speed through buildings and objects simultaneously. A qualitatively new experience, it involved both building (the highway) and object (the car) but it stretched existing architectural-historical vocabularies and categorizations to produce an understanding of the built environment that extended beyond either, to a new kind of landscape, although one that is now so familiar that it appears natural. In the Anglophone world, among those to recognize the profound nature of the experience were Robert Venturi and Denise Scott Brown, in their book *Learning From Las Vegas*, as well as Alison and Peter Smithson in projects such as *AS in DS*.[1] Others important here include the urbanist Melvin Webber, the planner Peter Hall, and the subject of this chapter, the British architectural historian and critic Reyner Banham. For Banham, learning to drive a car was the starting point for a series of public and sometimes popular reflections on the topic, reflections that in many respects defined the latter half of his career. In the car-oriented city he found in Los Angeles, Banham discovered challenges to many of his existing perceptions about what constituted appropriate objects of architectural-historical attention. Before 1966, the year he learned to drive, Banham's critical world largely consisted of discrete objects and buildings. He had written about American cars and Brutalist buildings, in each case deploying iconographic methods drawing on his art-historical training at the Courtauld Institute. Banham was an original and inventive thinker, but the innovations in the early part of his career lay mostly in his choice of subject; methodologically, his art history was straightforwardly iconographical, even if its objects were not. After 1966, his interests became markedly more environmental, often preoccupied with experiences that could not be located securely in either objects or buildings. That shift, from object to environment – or ecology, to use his term – was a trend in Banham's work represented by learning to drive, rather than caused by it, but its effects were considerable. As he put it in perhaps his best-known statement on the question, 'I learned to drive in order to read Los Angeles in the original'.[2] Driving was a tool that allowed the exploration of new material.

The shift was first widely apparent in the four radio talks he did for the BBC in 1968 on Los Angeles, talks which would later be adapted to become the book *Los Angeles: The Architecture of Four Ecologies*.[3] In those accounts Banham described a city whose distinctiveness derived in large part from moving through it at high speed in a vehicle. It could be a profound aesthetic experience, but of itself it transcended traditional art-historical objects of attention. Temporal, dynamic and bodily, it was defined in his writing above all by the freeway, the environment that structured both the book and Banham's understanding of the city. That experience would go on to inform the approach of what was probably Banham's most radical book, *The Architecture of the Well-tempered Environment*, as well as the study of the desert landscape, *Scenes in America Deserta*.[4] Along with the Los Angeles material, these studies suggest approaches in which architectural history's traditional disciplinary objects have been replaced by landscapes of different kinds, the experience of which is necessarily understood to be dynamic. As a critic or historian in this new world, one was no longer so much describing looking at bounded objects, but describing movement through unbounded space. The experience of driving a car might not have been the only way to access this modern experience, but it was a readily available and – in Banham's accounts of it – an often dramatic one.

In this chapter I focus on freeway driving because (as Banham showed) it represented a new and peculiarly modern kind of aesthetic experience that because of its nature – temporal, bodily, and so on – required new means of description. Banham had had to learn the language of driving itself – equivalent, he thought, to eighteenth-century Grand Tourists learning Italian – but it also meant finding new vocabulary to put those experiences into words. Banham's case is a particularly rich one because his reflections on driving extend over a long period, and they embody the kind of disciplinary reflection explored in the present book. As Banham showed when he transitioned from non-driver to driver, driving was not just a practical skill, it was also a critical tool: it allowed one to read and experience the modern metropolis in new ways, sometimes against the grain. It was the 'freeway model of history', as the architectural historian Anthony Vidler put it much later on: urbanism understood through the rear-view mirror.[5] What that meant was clear enough from a glance at the contents page to *Los Angeles*, where the traditional objects of art-historical attention were mere fragments in a history built around big landscapes and systems of circulation.

If Banham is often associated with cars, and car culture in general, his writings on the topic are – by his own prolific standards – relatively infrequent. Out of the 800 or so articles he wrote, no more than thirty are directly about cars, or driving, and even the most car-oriented book, *Los Angeles: The Architecture of Four Ecologies*, is only intermittently about the topic.[6] Banham's automotive writings nevertheless have had a disproportionate impact, perhaps because so few of his disciplinary contemporaries wrote anything of the sort, and on the rare occasions they did, it was not always especially serious. Erwin Panofsky's essay on the iconography of the Rolls-Royce radiator grille from 1968 reads more as light-hearted speculation than a suggestion for in-depth study.[7]

Banham's first writing about cars treated them as objects, and his writings in this mode can be found throughout his career. Written in a broadly iconographic mode, they include discussions of the Cadillac Eldorado (the subject of the celebrated essay 'Vehicles of Desire'), the Jaguar Mark 10 saloon, the first iteration of the Ford Mustang, the Chevrolet Blazer, and the design philosophy of General Motors under Harley Earl.[8] Banham occasionally reported on motor shows too, and he was undoubtedly knowledgeable and enthusiastic about car design, in common with several colleagues from the Independent Group, including the Smithsons and the artist Richard Hamilton (Banham in fact had contributed to Hamilton's curated 1955 exhibition of largely automotive imagery).[9] Car design per se, however, appears in only a handful of essays and is scarcely present at all in what he regarded as his serious works, with the exception of his first book, *Theory and Design in the First Machine Age* (1960). There, in the chapter on Le Corbusier, Banham discussed the comparison the architect had made between evolving car design and Greek temple architecture.[10] Later Banham briefly described Buckminster Fuller's rear-steering Dymaxion car, a suicidally unstable design, albeit an interesting one.[11] Neither part of the book had anything of the detailed exegesis of 'Vehicles of Desire', however, and Banham as a result should really be thought of as only an intermittent historian of car design, although he undoubtedly knew a great deal about it. At home he was a part-time enthusiast – he subscribed to *Autosport*, a weekly motor racing journal – but he was never really a motoring connoisseur, and certainly never in a position to own cars for pleasure.[12] His own cars were decidedly ordinary, and the ones that appeared in the later writings as transport were rarely identified by name.[13]

Banham's work on the iconography of cars as objects, important though it is, is less the focus here than his account of the driving experience, or – to use the term Banham employed in *Los Angeles* – its 'ecology'. An ecology was implicitly a mode in which humans and machines were understood as parts of a larger, regulated (sometimes self-regulating) system. In the case of driving, this system included simultaneously engineering, culture and driver psychology. 'Ecology' possibly alluded to the emergent discipline of cybernetics, although this was not something Banham explored in any detail. There was nevertheless, in common with cybernetics, a fascination with systems and a world view that emphasized them rather than objects.[14] (Systems theories in vogue at the same time might also include structuralism and semiotics, while Marshall McLuhan's *Understanding Media* was published in 1964. It was a moment when it was important to show an appreciation of systems, however superficial.[15])

More concretely, Banham's understanding of driving as a system had been informed by some practical experience: he had himself learned to drive. It is said that he drove RAF vehicles on the airfield at Filton, Bristol during his period as an aircraft engineer in the Second World War, although that experience is hard to confirm.[16] But his official entry into the world of driving – and the one that matters here – was in 1966 when he was aged 44; family driving responsibilities up until that point were covered entirely by Mary Banham, his wife. As with a number of significant life events, as soon as he passed his test, Banham wrote about it. The article, in this case for the *Architects' Journal*, was 'Unlovable at Any Speed'.[17] The title ironically referred to US activist Ralph Nader's recently published book, *Unsafe at Any Speed*, about the lethal design flaws in the bestselling Chevrolet Corvair.[18] It is a short article, but an important one, because it identifies a shift in Banham's thinking about cars. Having passed his driving test, Banham – suddenly, it seemed – understood cars in new terms. No longer were they of interest as objects, but as elements in a system that included the human driver, along with a new set of rights and responsibilities in the world. Banham recognized by learning to drive that he had acquired a skill that at one level was a liberation. But, he wrote, newly part of the driving system, he had forfeited some of his right to critique. It was an ethical transformation as much as a practical one: 'Becoming a driver is to join a community', he wrote, 'and a culture whose public face has little to commend it. It adds up to an ugly mob.'[19] If it was a 'mob', Banham was nevertheless, through his existing journalism, at least a part-time member of it, and the essay raised questions about what was appropriate subject matter for an architectural historian. Driving was ethically unsettling, as the piece made clear; it wasn't something in which an architecture-oriented person was supposed to take an interest, let alone do. It is a curiously self-denying article, because Banham and his social circle (the Smithsons, Hamilton, James Stirling, Colin St John Wilson) clearly saw nothing alien in car culture, and in most cases rather liked it. The article's snobby, auto-sceptic architects may only truly have existed in Banham's head. Nevertheless, 'Unlovable at Any Speed' did something important in Banham's work, sketching out for the first time an understanding of driving in systematic terms. Cars were no longer discrete objects, but elements in a multidimensional ecology.

Banham developed his thinking much further in the four talks he did for the BBC's Third Programme in 1968 on Los Angeles, broadcast between 15 August and 3 September, published at the same time in the BBC's *Listener* magazine. The second of the talks – and the most important here – was 'Roadscape with Rusting Rails', broadcast on 19 August; the title referred to the alignment of the freeways along the ruins of the old Pacific Electric Railroad.[20] Banham used the word 'system' in the talk, meaning not only a set of automotive technologies but the human interactions with them and the new psychological experiences, and in doing so he took their complexity seriously. The freeways could be 'unalloyed pleasure', Banham wrote, freed perhaps by the experience of LA to write in these terms. The precise pleasure here seemed to involve at first sight one's total absorption by the system, conforming exactly to its rules. LA driving was 'generally so intelligent and considerate and disciplined', Banham continued, a remark seemingly designed to provoke the Third Programme audience, as well as any passing Angeleno readers.[21] But Banham seemed already to have anticipated that, because the following sentence described 'an entirely intolerant attitude to any imperfections in the system', such imperfections being, for example, congestion reducing median traffic speed to '40 miles per hour'.[22] To achieve that standard, and indeed to regard that speed as a traffic jam as he suggested Angelenos in 1968 did, was by English standards of the time miraculous. (It is worth noting too that he had recent comparative experience of genuine traffic chaos, namely Buenos Aires, on which he had reported for *New Society* at almost exactly the same time.[23])

In any case, what Banham described here, fantasy or not, was an automotive system involving the interaction with humans and technology and the production of new psychological conditions. It was here also that Banham tried out a theory that would be critical for the book *Los Angeles*, namely that the city's automotive pleasures were to do with the interaction of ostensible opposites: freedom and discipline. What freedom there was to be had, he seemed to argue, was constrained by the rules of the road. But at the same time, the experience of pleasure lay in the gap between the two. The pleasure could also be straightforwardly libidinal, the thrill of speed and centrifugal force on the intersection of the San Diego and Santa Monica freeways: 'to drive over those ramps in a high sweeping 60-mile-an-hour-trajectory is a spatial experience of a sort one does not normally associate with monuments of engineering – the nearest thing to flight on four wheels I know.'[24] A throwaway remark typical of Banham, in one sense it merely describes a system functioning as it should. But in another sense it identifies a gap in the system between the building (of a kind, the freeway intersection) and the object (the car) in which play might be possible. To hit the curve at the right speed, to produce precisely the right centrifugal force, to see the open sky at the right moment was a complex experience that exceeded both buildings and objects. Banham's account of that experience, fleeting as it was, indicated what his later ecological approach to the built environment might be.

Published in 1971, the book *Los Angeles: The Architecture of Four Ecologies* considerably elaborated the freeway analysis. The freeways were, Banham wrote, the city's 'crowning glory', as well as a conceptual framework by which the city might be understood.[25] (The opening chapter, 'In the Rearview Mirror', cited another automotive frame for the city: it was all of a piece.) The most detailed exploration of the freeway, the chapter 'Autopia' depicted the freeway as a de facto public space. It opened with a much-repeated anecdote of a woman car passenger glimpsed on the freeway adjusting her make-up and hair as the car shifted left to the offramp. The city's freeways were, Banham implied, its public realm, and the surface streets effectively indoors.[26] That public realm came with attendant rights and responsibilities and it was, like other idealized public spaces in human history, at a certain level, self-regulating.[27] It was, he elaborated, a 'spectacular paradox', simultaneously freedom and discipline. The private car as a system offered an unprecedented degree of 'freedom and convenience' in terms of what journeys could be made and when, for no other form of transportation could manage complex door-to-door journeys with no change of mode. But that freedom came at a price: 'the almost total surrender of personal freedom for most of the journey'.[28] Critically for Banham, to enter into that paradox was pleasurable, so his freeway drivers' tyres were 'singing over the diamond-cut anti-skid grooves in the concrete road surface, the selector levers of their automatic gearboxes are firmly in *Drive*, and the radio is on'. The freeway was, Banham concluded, the place where the city perhaps most found peace with itself, where Angelenos 'found the two calmest and most rewarding hours of their daily lives'.[29]

That assessment was designed to provoke, which it eventually did.[30] Banham then continued the argument in the 1972 BBC film he made with the director Julian Cooper, *Reyner Banham Loves Los Angeles*. The film opened at Los Angeles International Airport, with Banham picking up his rented Ford LTD, before entering a discussion with one of the film's cute fictions, 'Baede-Kar', a sweetly voiced prototypical sat-nav device that was, in technological form, the essence of the 'spectacular paradox'.[31] On the one hand Baede-Kar offered the keys to the city, while on the other subjecting the driver to the rules. The opening few minutes of the film neatly placed Banham at the centre of this paradox, his own desire for freedom tempered immediately by the need to grasp the rules of freeway driving (Figure 5.1).[32]

Banham's approach here was suggestive of new and often counter-intuitive ways of reading the city: could the freeway really be public space? It was also, more generally, a reading of the city that asked that it be accepted as a new form of nature, an attitude embodied in the work of the artist Ed Ruscha, who appeared in both the book and the film. The freeways were therefore an 'ecology', one of four in the book, the others being the beach,

FIGURE 5.1 *Frame grab from One Pair of Eyes, 'Reyner Banham Loves Los Angeles', directed by Julian Cooper © BBC 1972.*

the mountains to the east, and the flat plain between the two. Banham – somewhat typically – did not explain what he meant by the term 'ecology', nor where it came from, although he did acknowledge the importance of a 1935 German study of Los Angeles, *Los Angeles: Weden, Leben und Gestalt der Zweimillionenstadt in Südkalifornien* by Anton Wagner, a book that had something of the interdisciplinarity of Banham's approach.[33] For Vidler, Banham's ecology was an invention, a way of structuring the city that avoided the fixation on traditional objects. So 'ecology' allowed for an imagination of flows and traffic and interrelationships – a systemic imagination, in other words, rather than one fixed on objects.[34]

Something of that ecological imagination could be found in *Learning From Las Vegas* by Robert Venturi, Denise Scott Brown and Steven Izenour, the result of research with students done at much the same time as Banham's first visits to LA.[35] Their interests overlapped with Banham's in the treatment of roadside signage and the production of an architecture designed to grab a speeding driver's attention; like him, they were fundamentally accepting of the automotive landscape. But Venturi, Scott Brown and Izenour represented a case of parallel evolution rather than one of Banham's intellectual reference points. The most important of those, certainly for Banham's ecological mode, was the Berkeley-based urban theorist Melvin Webber. Webber was, according to Banham's friend and sometime collaborator Peter Hall, the major influence on *Los Angeles*.[36] Webber was a transportation planner who had been involved with the Bay Area Rapid Transit (BART) rail project in its design stages. He wrote and taught about cars in general, but cars were of limited interest to him as objects.[37] By the time Banham first visited Los Angeles, two of Webber's essays had become essential reading for Anglophone urbanists. Written as a pair, these were 'Order in Diversity: Community Without Propinquity' (1963) and 'The Nonplace Urban Realm' (1964, but written earlier).[38] By 1968, when Banham first published on Los Angeles, Webber had also published 'The Post-City Age' (1968) for *Daedalus*, the journal of the American Academy of Arts and Sciences, which was in effect a lay summary of his position in the two earlier articles. By this time, Webber was familiar to readers of *New Society*, the recently founded, left-leaning but non-aligned current affairs magazine. Webber himself summarized his work for its readers in 1964 in 'The City Building Game', and the same year Peter Hall wrote about him at least twice in the pages of the magazine.[39] Webber was in some ways a totemic writer for *New Society*: progressive but anti-Marxist, committed to personal freedom and autonomy, and broadly accepting of the market. Most importantly, he was a technological optimist, convinced that emerging technologies, especially those to do with transport and communications, had the capacity to transform metropolitan life for the better. One of the key technologies was the freeway, with its capacity for enabling fast, door-to-door trips on demand. Along with the telephone, the freeway was, Webber thought, capable of transforming urban space.

Webber's arguments in the 1963 and 1964 essays do not immediately suggest the aesthetic questions with which Banham was primarily concerned. There were no illustrations as such, and nothing about the visual appearance of the city. But they provided a language to describe the experience of the city, and it was an experience that appeared to make traditional architectural-historical objects redundant. Webber had little to say about buildings as such or objects – both seemed to have been replaced by the dynamic flow of automobile traffic. In 'Order in Diversity' (1963), Webber argued forcefully against the English tradition of planning, with its pathological need for a 'sharply bounded separation of city, suburb and country' – here Webber quoted directly from an *Architectural Review* 'Counter Attack' of 1955 that had railed against what it called at the time 'subtopia' or the results of introducing 'overpowering alien elements', blurring the differences between 'town and country, country and suburb, suburb and wild'.[40] That would certainly have got Banham's attention, and the deliberate, Webberian, blurring of such distinctions was a key provocation of the later 'Non Plan'. This blurred landscape – described by the *Review* in wholly negative terms – was in fact the perfect definition of Webber's, and subsequently Banham's, ecological sensibilities: a new form of nature in which traditional human/nature boundaries were redundant. It was also a scenario in which the architect or designer had no obvious place.

Webber gave his ecology a name: 'the Nonplace Urban Realm' – a zone defined less by spatial boundaries than by its capacity to gather 'interest-communities'.[41] The city's physical nature dissolved under pressure of new technologies. Instead of a traditionally bounded entity, it was a 'communications system', which by implication was free to take any form.[42] Its key characteristic, he went on, was 'flow' – of 'information, money, people and goods' (this idea anticipated the much later work of Webber's future Berkeley colleague, the Marxist urbanist Manuel Castells).[43] Within the nonplace, citizens would be, it seemed, perpetually mobile, rarely touching down for long in anything that might be regarded as a traditional place. Here Webber, in a likely extrapolation from his own existence as a senior academic, imagined an ideal citizen, a 'virus researcher', whose understanding of community might be extremely diverse, and only partially and fleetingly connected to place.[44] The research work might involve a 'worldwide' community of interest with no connection to place at all: 'the fact that his laboratory is located in a given town or metropolis may be almost irrelevant'.[45] If the commitment to community in that case might be worldwide, Webber's friend's 'art, literary and political' activities might be defined by the national spatial boundaries of the United States. Meanwhile domestic life ('his local PTA') might mean a range of much more obviously place-based obligations. But place had clearly dissolved as an overriding organizing principle: 'for the portions of his time in which he plays roles in other communities, he is *not* a member of the place-community'. (Webber put it more strongly in the 1968 essay. Again invoking the image of an academic, this time an astronomer, Webber wrote: 'the striking thing ... is how little of his attention and energy he devotes to the attentions of place based communities.'[46]) If, Webber wrote, we were to understand urbanity as defined by 'urban life' rather than physical form, then 'we might discover Los Angelenos enjoy as urbane a life as do New Yorkers'.[47] That was Banham's argument about LA prefigured in 1964: the value of a city, its life and its culture could be separated from its form. In a remark that could equally be Banham later on, Webber concluded, 'it is interaction, not place that is the essence of the city and of city life'.[48] It is in both cases an argument that is, or at least pretends to be, indifferent to both buildings and objects. Those things belong to an implicitly place-based, and therefore outmoded, understanding of the city and are therefore important only insofar as they facilitate interaction. The architect or designer has a reduced role in this phase of Banham's work; they have no presence at all in Webber's.

Webber's vision of urban life was a partial and privileged one, a city apparently determined by drivers alone.[49] It had nothing to say about the citizens of nonplace who would necessarily remain static in order to service those drivers as they pinged from one exciting attraction to another. That sunny vision caught the planner Peter Hall's imagination from the beginning, and he wrote enthusiastically of it as early as 1964 in a *New Society* review of five new planning books. Webber's thirty-two pages, he wrote, were more convincing than any of the other 1,250 under review.[50] Before he and Webber had met, Hall was already thinking along similar lines; his futuristic *London 2000*, first published in 1963, was in effect an English version of Webber's highway pastoral, although the two visions seem to have emerged independently.[51] Hall imagined a middle-class family, the Dumills, roaming the freeways of a London whose metropolitan identity stretched unencumbered for 100 miles. He pictured them moving frictionlessly between central London's cultural attractions and the Kent coast, bowling along elevated freeways that were an attraction in themselves ('the expressways of London are a brilliant sight').[52] By 1969, and the second edition of the book, Hall had gone some way to enacting the fantasy himself: he had bought himself a Ford Mustang, the American coupé popularized by Steve McQueen in *Bullitt*, to make the daily commute from London to the University of Reading on newly built sections of the M4.[53]

Part of the difficulty with this material now is the extent to which it can seem to reiterate car culture myths. It does not necessarily read as a critical tool, a way of reading the city beyond buildings and objects as I have argued here, but rather a form of advertorial for car culture, or California, or both. On Webber's death in 2006, Hall recognized something of this problem, writing that his friend's work was representative of 'the high-water mark of a certain self-created myth created [sic] by California about itself', a myth sustained amongst other things by fat defence contracts.[54] California's prodigious post-war growth and its equally prodigious programme of public works therefore permitted Webber's generous thinking about cities – they could be unconstrained as long as the money flowed. For the artist Peter Plagens, writing with some ferocity against Banham in 1972, *Los Angeles* was pure reaction, 'conventioneer bullshit', with its sunny account of the city's freeways, ignorant (he argued) of the iniquities they produced. 'In a more humane society', Plagens wrote, '. . . the author might be stood up against the wall and shot.'[55]

In the period both Hall and Banham were writing apparently in support of the automobile-oriented city, progressive voices in architecture and planning increasingly aligned themselves against it. In New York City, the city that had oriented itself towards the automobile earlier and more thoroughly than any other under the leadership of 'master builder' Robert Moses, activist resistance coordinated by Jane Jacobs in the early 1960s led to the cancellation of the Lower Manhattan Expressway, while the city itself reorganized its committee structure to shift the focus away from highway building and towards mass transit.[56] Moses – curiously never a driver himself – had been perhaps the United States's greatest single road builder, but by the time Banham was writing about Los Angeles he was a substantially discredited figure. The Pulitzer prize-winning 1974 biography by Robert Caro painted Moses as a reactionary thug, whose highway projects were profoundly destructive of the city they were meant to serve. To write about the automobile city in the terms Banham did in 1971 was therefore to invite criticism. In fact, Banham had discovered the previous year that he himself could be regarded as a political reactionary: in a bruising encounter with Jean Baudrillard at the International Design Conference in Aspen (IDCA), he was accused of representing the forces of the establishment.[57]

Banham's *Los Angeles* can certainly be read – superficially – as simple boosterism, blind to awkward realities. But I am not so sure Banham's critics are right, as his approach to the automobile-oriented city contains not only a good deal of irony, but he also constructs the automobile *driver* as an essentially critical figure – someone, like Baudelaire's nineteenth-century *flâneur*, who stands aloof from their surroundings in order to record them dispassionately. When Banham became a driver in 1966, his first reflections on his new identity drew attention to a set of uneasy implications that came with it: a new place in the world, new and not always welcome communities, and the loss of being able to stand truly outside a culture. It is an ambivalent piece, full of doubt, and its position is scarcely that of the motoring enthusiast. That attitude has something to say about the building/object relations that are the subject of this book. What Banham does is reveal the possibility of a dynamic system, including a dispassionate user/viewer that embodies the complexity of the modern city; Banham, in other words, transcends the limits of buildings and objects, through the seemingly mundane experience of driving.

'Autopia', the chapter of *Los Angeles* that deals with driving in most depth, has the ambivalent perspective of the *flaneur*: Banham is only partially of the scenes he describes, more often an observer at some critical and moral distance, writing a taxonomy of new experiences into existence. The chapter comprises accounts of new and sometimes puzzling behaviours. The 'spectacular paradox' at the heart of it, the standoff between freedom and discipline enacted daily by the Angeleno freeway driver, is neither celebrated nor disdained. For Banham, it is certainly an object of fascination, but also one from which he stands (or perhaps sits, in the driving seat) at some remove, observing it. That position, a surprisingly ambivalent one, is one reason why Banham's approach to the automobile-oriented city can be thought of in critical terms, for his distance allows observations that get beyond buildings and objects to an implicitly more authentic realm of urban experience. The modern city, Banham implies, is too dynamic to be read via bounded entities; it requires an ecological approach.

Banham's approach also – crucially – elevates the experience of the user-inhabitants of the city, its readers as it were. His imagined drivers can some of the time seem like automata, locked into the freeway's rules, the radio on, the tyres singing in the concrete grooves. But equally these drivers are exploring the limits of their strange new environment, turning into something its designers could not exactly have imagined. That 1968 account of the 405/10 intersection (Figure 5.2) is in some ways a reading against the grain, for to achieve that precise experience involves practice and play, as if freeway driving were a form of (accidental) sport.

FIGURE 5.2 *Aerial view of 405/10 junction*. Los Angeles: The Architecture of Four Ecologies *(London: Allen Lane, 1971), 89.*

The opening part of 'Autopia' involves exactly that kind of observation too: the freeway might be, Banham suggests, a new form of public space formed accidentally by its users, who have unconsciously produced a set of new and unforeseen behaviours in relation to it. These observations are so anecdotal, it must be said, that they cannot be proved one way or another. But they suggest a critical approach to the city in that they encourage us to see beyond designed objects (be they buildings, or in this case cars) to the users of environments, constructing a history around their perceptions.

Banham's approach to the automobile-oriented city was an essentially aesthetic one, and his attitude to driving not unlike that of an artist, alert to contradictions. The resulting book, *Los Angeles*, usually finds its place on architectural history bookshelves, but it is in some ways more like a piece of speculative fiction, an allegory of the near future in which disaster is never far away.[58] One of Banham's key sources for the book (cited in his 'drive-in bibliography') is in fact a work of dystopian science fiction, Ray Bradbury's *The Martian Chronicles*.[59] In *Los Angeles*, Banham retained an ironic distance to make clear that the Californian metropolis was – as the Futurist city had been for him at the beginning of his career – an object to think *with*, rather than to be uncritically accepted. Banham's Los Angeles was from the start a means for exploring cities in general as well as an object in its own right, a city whose form posed questions of other cities. Central to its peculiar form was the experience of driving, which Banham treated both as

FIGURE 5.3 *View of freeway signage*. Los Angeles: The Architecture of Four Ecologies *(London: Allen Lane, 1971), 218.*

investigative tool and as an object of inquiry in itself. *Los Angeles* was an enthusiastic exploration of the automotive experience, but it wasn't a car advertisement – certainly no more than the work of the pop artists he cited along the way, such as Ed Ruscha (Figure 5.3).[60]

Beyond Banham's own work, there are more than traces of his approach in Jean Baudrillard's travelogue, *America*, first published in 1986.[61] Despite their earlier conflict at the IDCA of 1970, Baudrillard turned to Banham explicitly at one point in the book to locate his own sense impressions of the desert. The source, though not cited, is clearly enough Banham's *Scenes in America Deserta*, not long published when Baudrillard must have been writing.[62] There is a lot about driving in *America* and its peculiarities. And like Banham, Baudrillard's fascination with driving has little to do with cars per se, but with it as a system, a vast human/machine network that is liberating and disciplining in equal measure. Baudrillard's pages on Los Angeles freeways are the natural, if somewhat paranoid, extension of Banham's 'Autopia'.[63] Baudrillard's *America* is probably the apogee of this highly aestheticized approach to driving, with roots in art from Futurism onwards, to the novels of J. G. Ballard, and in architecture the work of Robert Venturi and Denise Scott Brown and others.[64]

With all the new regulatory, environmental and technological pressures on it, driving's purchase on our imaginations is uncertain now. The myth of autonomy, central to Banham's writing on the subject, is increasingly hard to sustain. Matthew Crawford's 2020 book *Why We Drive* therefore reads as a form of requiem for driving, pictured as a rich but increasingly archaic skill. Nevertheless, as Crawford also writes, in ways that strongly recall Banham, the experience of driving remains a complex way of being in and experiencing the world, one that poses questions for architecture and design history.[65] If driving remains – for some – pleasurable, it is because it provides a structure for enacting a special kind of modern freedom, of exercising free choice within defined technological, legal and behavioural limits, all contingent and constantly changing: 'to drive is to exercise one's skill at being free', he writes.[66] The 'spectacular paradox', as Banham put it, the experience of being part of a human/machine system and of consciously exploring its limits, is uniquely characteristic of driving, and it remains, with the right attitude, a critical means of understanding the modern world.

## Notes

1   Robert Venturi, Denise Scott Brown, Steven Izenour, *Learning From Las Vegas* (Cambridge, Mass. and London: MIT Press, 1972); Alison Smithson, *AS in DS: An Eye on the Road* (Delft: Delft University Press, 1982). The 'DS' refers to the architects' Citroën car, and the book was shaped to resemble the car's shape as if seen in plan.

2   Reyner Banham, *Los Angeles: The Architecture of Four Ecologies* (London: Allen Lane, 1971), 23.
3   Banham, *Los Angeles*.
4   Reyner Banham, *Scenes in America Deserta* (Layton, Utah: Peregrine Smith Books, 1982); Reyner Banham, *The Architecture of the Well-tempered Environment*, second ed. (London: Architectural Press, 1984)
5   Anthony Vidler, *Histories of the Immediate Present: Inventing Architectural Modernism* (Cambridge, Mass. and London: MIT Press, 2008), 143.
6   Banham, *Los Angeles*, 223–4, 328.
7   Ewin Panofsky, 'The Ideological Antecedents of the Rolls-Royce Radiator', *Proceedings of the American Philosophical Society* 107, 4 (15 August 1963): 273–88.
8   See Reyner Banham, 'Vehicles of Desire', *Art* (1 September 1955): 3; 'Night Mrs Jagbag', *Architects' Journal* (29 November 1961), 1020–2; 'Horse of a Different Colour', *New Society* (3 November 1967): 436–7; 'The Four Wheel Life', *New Society* (18 August 1977): 350–1; 'Auto Dreamer', *New Society* (13 January 1984): 54–5.
9   *Man, Machine and Motion* took place first at the Hatton Gallery, Newcastle and then the Institute of Contemporary Art, London. Banham contributed the catalogue notes.
10  Reyner Banham, *Theory and Design in the First Machine Age* (London: Architectural Press, 1960).
11  Banham, *Theory and Design*, 304.
12  Author's interview with Ben Banham (8 September 2017).
13  Interview with Ben Banham.
14  Norbert Wiener, *Cybernetics: Or Control and Communication in the Animal and the Machine* (Cambridge, Mass. and London: MIT Press, 1948). There are hints at systems theory in Banham's account of freeway driving, never entirely developed.
15  Via Richard Hamilton, a close friend, Banham probably also knew of Roy Ascott's Ground Course at Newcastle University's department of Fine Arts – a course for undergraduates based on systems theories.
16  Interview with Ben Banham.
17  Reyner Banham, 'Unlovable at Any Speed', *Architect's Journal* 144 (21 December 1966): 1527.
18  Ralph Nader, *Unsafe at Any Speed: The Designed-In Dangers of the American Automobile* (New York: Grossman Publishers, 1965). It is unclear if it was Banham's title or not.
19  Banham, 'Unlovable at Any Speed'.
20  Reyner Banham, 'Roadscape with Rusting Rails', *The Listener* (29 August 1968): 267–8.
21  Peter Plagens, 'Los Angeles: The Ecology of Evil', *Artforum* 11 (December 1972): 67–76
22  Banham, 'Roadscape', 268.

23  Reyner Banham, 'Bus-Pop', *New Society* 12, no. 310 (5 September 1968): 343–4.
24  Banham, 'Roadscape', 268.
25  Banham, *Los Angeles*, 26.
26  Banham, *Los Angeles*, 213.
27  Banham was unsurprisingly critical of Jane Jacobs, but his account of the self-regulating nature of ideal public spaces is not unlike hers – and likewise his anthropological observations and extrapolation from them. See Janet Jacobs, *Death and Life of Great American Cities* (New York: Random House, 1961), 60–5. For Banham's review, see 'The Embalmed City', *New Statesman* (12 April 1963): 528–30.
28  This passage, with its obedient automata-drivers, is the one perhaps most suggestive of systems theory.
29  Banham, *Los Angeles*, 216, 222.
30  Plagens, 'Los Angeles'. See also aspects of T. S. Hines, review of Reyner Banham, *Los Angeles: The Architecture of Four Ecologies*, *Journal of the Society of Architectural Historians* 31 (March 1972): 76.
31  Thanks to Pat Roberts for help in identifying Banham's car.
32  Crawford has described this phase of discovering a city's driving culture in terms of discovering the rules of a contact sport. Matthew Crawford, *Why We Drive: On Freedom, Risk and Taking Back Control* (London: Bodley Head, 2020), 163–78, and elsewhere.
33  Anton Wagner, *Los Angeles: Weden, Leben und Gestalt der Zweimillionenstadt in Südkalifornien* (Leipzig: Bibliographisches Institut, 1935).
34  See also discussion in Richard J. Williams, *Reyner Banham Revisited* (London: Reaktion Books, 2021), 161.
35  Venturi et al., *Learning From Las Vegas*.
36  Peter Hall, 'Melvin M. Webber', *Access* (Winter 2006–7): 20. By the time of its publication in 1971, Banham and Hall, together with the editor of *New Society*, Paul Barker and the architect Cedric Price, had jointly written 'Non-Plan', a polemical essay much informed by Webber, whom they cited on the first page. See Reyner Banham, Paul Barker, Peter Hall, Cedric Price, 'Non Plan: An Experiment in Freedom', *New Society* (20 March 1969): 435–43.
37  In common with Banham, Webber's own cars were often clunkers. He ran an elderly Volvo before being persuaded to replace it on grounds of efficiency: Elizabeth Deakin, 'Teaching with Mel', *Access* (Winter 2006–7): 24.
38  Melvin Webber, 'Order in Diversity: Community Without Propinquity', in Lowdon Wingo (ed.) *Cities and Space* (Baltimore: Johns Hopkins University Press, 1963), 23–56; 'The Urban Place and the Nonplace Urban Realm' in Melvin Webber (ed.) *Explorations into Urban Structure* (Philadelphia: University of Pennsylvania Press, 1964), 79–153; 'The Post-City Age', *Daedalus* 97, 4 (Fall 1968): 1091–110.

39  Melvin Webber, 'The City Building Game', *New Society* (8 October 1964), 26–7; Peter Hall, 'A Long Road to Hardly Anywhere', *New Society* (23 April 1964), and 'America's Grand Tradition', *New Society* (3 September 1964).
40  Webber, 'Order in Diversity', 34.
41  Webber, 'Urban Place', 108–14.
42  Webber, 'Urban Place', 84–7.
43  Manuel Castells, *The Rise of the Network Society* (New York: Wiley, 1996). See Peter Hall's acerbic commentary in this in Hall, 'Melvin. M. Webber', 22.
44  A no doubt intentional conceit, given the tendency of viruses to exponential, polycentric growth.
45  Webber, 'Urban Place', 113.
46  Webber, 'The Post-City Age', 1099.
47  Webber, 'Urban Place', 132.
48  Webber, 'Urban Place', 147.
49  To be fair, Webber's subsequent work envisaged collective transportation, albeit road-based. See Melvin Webber, 'The Joys of Automobility', in *The Car and the City*, eds Martin Wachs and Margaret Crawford (Ann Arbor: University of Michigan Press, 1991), 274–84.
50  Peter Hall, 'A Long Road to Hardly Anywhere', *New Society* (23 April 1964): 29.
51  Peter Hall, *London 2000* (London: Faber and Faber, 1963). Hall and Webber were first in contact in 1964, after the publication of *London 2000*, and Webber isn't cited in it. Their pastoral visions were consistent with wider trends, however. See for example Colin Buchanan, *Traffic in Towns* (London: HMSO, 1963)
52  Hall, *London 2000*, 271.
53  Reyner Banham, 'Horse of a Different Colour', *New Society* (3 November 1967): 436–7.
54  Hall, 'Melvin M. Webber', 18.
55  Plagens, 'Los Angeles', 67.
56  Robert Caro, *The Power Broker: Robert Moses and the Fall of New York* (New York: Knopf, 1974), especially 961–1162.
57  'The Environmental Witch-Hunt', in Reyner Banham (ed.), *The Aspen Papers: Twenty Years of Design Theory from the International Design Conference in Aspen* (London: Pall Mall, 1974), 208–10. For a fuller account of IDCA 1970 and the Banham/Baudrillard conflict, see also Williams, *Reyner Banham*, 140–3.
58  The film, *Reyner Banham Loves Los Angeles*, took the argument further away from architecture, to encompass a wide range of material cultural artefacts.
59  Banham, *Los Angeles*, 240–2, 251. *The Silver Locusts* is the original British title of the anthology *The Martian Chronicles*, the title referring to 'The Locusts', one of the stories.

60 Mike Davis cites Banham approvingly in his highly critical account of LA, *City of Quartz*; arguably, he wouldn't have if Banham's book wasn't legible at some level as critique. Mike Davis, *City of Quartz: Excavating the Future in Los Angeles* (London: Verso Books, 1990), 73–4.

61 Jean Baudrillard, *America*, second edition with an introduction by Geoff Dyer (London: Verso, 2010), 70, 72. Dyer's remarks on Banham can be found on xi–xii.

62 Reyner Banham, *Scenes in America Deserta* (Layton, Utah: Peregrine Smith Books, 1982).

63 See Baudrillard, *America*, 55–6, in particular his account of freeway driving and its signage.

64 I would also cite the sculptor Tony Smith's much-discussed account of driving on the unfinished New Jersey Turnpike, which for him prefigured the end of art. Samuel Wagstaff Jr., 'Talking with Tony Smith', *Artforum* 5, 4 (December 1966): 16, 19.

65 Crawford doesn't cite Banham, but his approach – as a cultural historian with technological skills – is strikingly reminiscent of him. For a geographical take on driving as culture, including some reflection on Banham, see Peter Merriman, *Driving Spaces: A Cultural-historical Geography of England's M1 Motorway* (Oxford: Blackwell, 2007).

66 Crawford, *Why We Drive*, 31.

# PART TWO
# Dissolved Distinctions

In Part Two, Dissolved Distinctions, we focus on those situations in which the building/object distinction has been intentionally dissolved or bypassed, or simply never existed in the first place. The arena for this blurring has been enabled by totalizing design solutions, enacted as much by those attempting a whole and consistent world where objects and architecture speak to the same expressive vision or utopian idea of collective life as by those who see in the contemporary commercial world a cosmos in which everything is subsumed under 'design'. Such ways of seemingly embracing all objects, including buildings, also draw attention to how the most exclusive and most all-encompassing of ventures are doomed to frustration. At the other end of the spectrum, building/object distinctions are blurred simply by the economic logic of the market or of production, the directives of regimes of economy, austerity and sumptuary control. Otherwise, the bypassing, or leaping over, has been enabled by prioritizing necessity or cultural strategy.

In Chapter Six by Panagiotis Doudesis, the example of a festive construction, part table, part sculpture, part fountain, part lighting installation, reveals the extent to which the distinction between building and object was absent in an early modern context. This chapter serves to remind us that the professional categories of designer or architect are recent constructions only. These categories dissolve in the face of the evidence presented here of a practice of making that drew freely on forms, techniques and references from a diverse range of sources. Many such sources, like funerary monuments and other examples of ephemeral architecture, similarly elude building/object categorization. The picture of a professional practice, one that drew on wide-ranging knowledge and visual and technical fluencies across many different spheres, is one that would be recognized by many pre-modern and modern practitioners and yet remains one which our histories struggle with.

In Chapter Seven by Anne Hultzsch, we move forward into the nineteenth century and the early decades of the professionalization of architectural practice. Through the pages of Britain's first dedicated magazine for architecture, Hultzsch presents an intriguing glimpse of an alternative vision for modern design culture, one in which all participants, from the carpenter and artisan to the architect and (often female) client, are treated as equally capable of engaged and informed participation. The inclusion, on equal terms, of both architecture and ready-made objects – as well as enthusiasm for new, economical, substitute materials, such as artificial stone – reveals the invented character of the formal hierarchies and distinctions between the professions and trades, experts and laypeople, established later in the century.

Chapter Eight by Fredie Floré explores the evolving relationship between furniture and architecture in the dissemination of modernism to the general public in the 1950s and 1960s. This case study of how the furniture company Knoll integrated into the Belgian market allows Floré to reveal the interchange between architects and designers within the wider context of international commercial practice and soft power politics. The presence of the Knoll chair was used to convey multiple different meanings. It served to signal the modernity of a project, the reform of a manufacturing company tainted by its wartime activities, and the appeal of living and working in a capitalist society. As with a number of the chapters in this volume, Chapter Eight also underlines the integral importance of photographic representations of architecture and design, without which these meanings could not be so readily fixed and disseminated.

In Chapter Nine by Tania Messell and Lilián Sánchez-Moreno, we encounter another building/object that defies established categories. Experiments in the 1970s into the development of prefabricated, mass-produced emergency shelters were based on collaborations between architects, designers and humanitarian experts. The Oxfam Emergency House project attempted to bring together new technologies and utopian, modernist design forms to create a universal solution to post-disaster housing for the rapidly expanding humanitarian aid sector. The ultimate failure of the Emergency House rested on the top-down application of expertise from across the aid agencies, industrial designers, architects and engineers, which privileged technologically innovative design over an understanding of diverse local contexts in the Global South where such shelters were to be deployed.

The chapters in this section draw attention to examples of professional practice in which medial and professional distinctions are dissolved. In terms of academic disciplines also, these case studies all function as examples that demand disciplinary flexibility if they are to be adequately addressed. They cannot be understood without an ability to breach the conceptual boundaries between building and object and between architecture and design practice, the media, the market and the multiple different stakeholders in each design and manufacturing context.

# CHAPTER SIX

## Designing for a Nocturnal Banquet, Versailles 1674

*Panagiotis Doudesis*

On the night of 28 July 1674 a festive supper took place at the centre of the *Cour de Marbre*, the inner courtyard of the palace of Versailles. This event occurred in the middle of a festival held to celebrate the latest great victory of Louis XIV: the second conquest of the Franche-Comté region and the consequent expansion of French territory over those ruled by the Spanish crown.[1] After a buffet-type banquet at the *Théâtre d'Eau* during the afternoon, a theatrical performance at the *Allée du Dragon*, and a fireworks display at the central canal, the fourth and final festivity was a *medianoche*, namely a meal served after midnight, which was an event of Spanish origin introduced to the French court by Anne of Austria, Louis XIV's mother.[2]

It was customary in court festivities of the time for the spaces in which such events unfolded to feature prominent ephemeral structures, or *machines* as they were then called, and the inner courtyard at Versailles was no exception. In the centre of this permanent location, an unusually high *machine* was erected to serve as the centrepiece of the meal, using the whole courtyard as a setting for this temporary display (Figure 6.1). An octagonal table, 83 feet in perimeter, was placed around the court's marble fountain and laden with delicacies for the king and his thirty-nine invited ladies. An astonishing illuminated structure stood in the inner octagon created by this table, ascending above the fountain's water jets. This structure consisted of eight adorned scrolls, each 14 feet high, and a central cornice, on top of which stood a translucent triumphal column, 18 feet high, itself illuminated by six hundred candles. This highly artful 'object' was designed by Carlo Vigarani, an Italian from Modena who had been employed by the French court for more than fifteen years as a *machiniste* and *intendant des plaisirs de Louis XIV*.

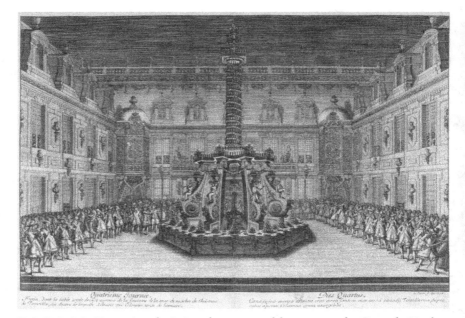

FIGURE 6.1 *Engraving depicting the nocturnal banquet at the Cour de Marbre, Versailles, Jean Le Pautre (1676). Courtesy of National Library of France/BnF.*

Vigarani's task was not to create a passive centrepiece for a formal table, but to engineer a rich experience or *divertissement*, as it was then called. At that time, the term meant 'the pleasure that heals boredom' and its purpose, as Peter Burke notes, was to distract people from the exercise of real politics and the consideration of current events.[3] The designer of such a diversion had to have the king's intentions clear in his mind. 'One must organize this court with such pleasures, which give to the persons an honest familiarity with their sovereign, touch them and charm them more than can be said', wrote Louis XIV in his *Mémoires pour l'instruction du Dauphin*.[4] The *instruction* should not be taken lightly, but rather as a strong indicator of one of the crucial aims of these *divertissements* that is particularly relevant to the discussion here. In the above passage, the king tells his son of the function of court festivities and the structures erected for them: to be a constant reminder of the glory and the presence of the crown. As such, these structures served essentially the same function as the public and royal architectural projects of the time. In other words, no matter how permanent or ephemeral the final design product was intended to be, its purpose was the same.

No part of Vigarani's construction for this event survives today, but we have many details of the event and the structure from a description written by André Félibien, the appointed court historiographer of Louis XIV, and a detailed illustration that accompanied the description, both of which can be found in the lavish festival book published two years after the event (see Figure 6.1).[5]

FIGURE 6.2 *Drawing for the* medianoche *machine, Carlo Vigarani or his atelier (1674). Courtesy of National Museum of Fine Arts, Stockholm.*

First appearing in the year of the festivity, the original version was text-only and divided into six chapters corresponding to the six days of festive events that took place in July and August 1674. The illustrated publication followed in 1676 and included rich full-page engravings signed by the court engraver Jean Le Pautre (1618–82), who chose to depict one highlight from each of the six days.[6] The fact that the *medianoche* was chosen to feature as the highlight of one whole day shows the significance and success, in visual terms at least, of Vigarani's creation.

The veracity and precision of presenting a court festivity – in this case the *medianoche* of 1674 – in textual and visual form for a royal publication aimed to glorify a ruler should be established before attempting a discussion of the nature of the 'object'. Luckily, both the text and the image can be corroborated here.[7] A sketch for a *medianoche machine* from the National Museum of Fine Arts in Stockholm (Figure 6.2), attributed to Vigarani's atelier, lends credibility to what was illustrated and described in the court publication.

Glory and memory were the driving concepts behind publications such as Félibien's *Les Divertissemens de Versailles*, argues Peter Fuhring.[8] And they surely were. In 1666, Félibien wrote that 'the engraved plates rank very high; through them posterity will one day perceive the history of the great actions of this illustrious monarch in pleasing forms'.[9] Helen Watanabe-O'Kelly's writing on festival books is very enlightening here, as she argues that such books aimed to function as historical record but were often biased and fabricated, much like early modern court historiography.[10] Accounts such as that of the 1674 *medianoche* praised the princely host of the event. In contemporary discourse, this figure of the host was not an individual human being but a representative figure playing a vital role on earth within the divinely ordained system of the universe.[11] In this regard, all the design elements for the ephemeral constructions used in the festivities needed to allude to this idea – particularly since the elements, though ephemeral in themselves, were intended to be immortalized in the court publications.

The relative neglect by scholarship and the consequent lack of insightful analyses of the *machine* from the point of view of an art or architectural historian can be explained neither by low-quality research nor by a dearth of available sources.[12] On the contrary, this lacuna can be explained by modern disciplinary practices, definitions and perceptions that make it difficult to categorize an early modern ephemeral creation that could simultaneously be art, architecture, craft, or even a (previously non-existent) category of its own. If fine arts, decorative arts and architecture historians nowadays demarcate differentiated practices that were once unified, and were treated as such during the early modern period, then early modern festival architecture and ephemeral constructions constitute a fully elusive category. As an amalgam of elements taken from diverse – at least in contemporary terms – fields of practice, to create an ensemble that is neither a building nor simply an object, Vigarani's *machine* offers a fine opportunity to discuss anew such topics as the process of amalgamation, modern disciplinary boundaries, and the element of scale in making art, architecture and functional objects.

The main body of this chapter is divided into three parts. The first contains a description of the *machine*, as found in Félibien's *Les Divertissemens de Versailles*, and a discussion of the professional and biographical background of its creator. This is followed by an analysis of the main compositional elements via a sequence of resemblances and references to other contemporaneous and earlier design products from various fields that have become separated from each other and been treated separately in modern scholarship. The third part is a discussion and critical assessment of the major historiographical issues involved in the evaluation of Vigarani's creation, such as artistic transfer and the idea of *disegno*. This leads to the conclusion that the object of our attention is a vivid reminder of widespread pre-modern practices that should change the way we think about such pieces; art, architecture and design were not distinct practices in the pre-modern period, and, for this reason, the maintenance of such distinctions today distorts our understanding and risks excluding works that cannot be accommodated within one or the other category.

## The *machine* and its creator

The original inner court of Louis XIII's hunting lodge, with its distinctive black-and-white marble floor tiles and the surrounding façade made of brick and stone, was chosen to serve as the background for the banquet. The centre of this courtyard featured a newly installed and fully functioning black marble fountain, most probably octagonal in shape, and adorned with a group of gilded figures.[13] The pillars, cornices and roofs of the walls overlooking the courtyard were probably illuminated by cords of light, made of numerous tubes filled with tallow, designed to withstand winds.[14] This was the setting in which Vigarani's creation was placed. Three distinctive parts comprised the unified appearance of the structure: the octagonal table laden with delicacies, a superstructure incorporating the marble fountain, and a triumphal column on top of this superstructure.

Félibien vividly describes the complex design: 'In the surrounding of the fountain one could see a large octagonal table, covered with the *medianoche* supper; this was surrounded by festoons of orange flowers, roses and carnations, and adorned in an extraordinary manner.'[15] With a perimeter measuring at least 83 feet, more than forty *couverts*, or place settings, were placed on top of the table, five on each of the eight sides, to serve an equal number of selected guests.[16]

Inside the space of the octagon's internal circumference stood 'eight consoles of lapis enriched with gold, which, resting on the eight corners, rose to a height of fourteen feet, and carried a ceiling of the same octagonal shape ... On the ramp of each console there was another one, smaller, made of gold, and which carried a crystal candelabrum illuminated by several candles. Lower, and in the place where the brackets sprung ... eight figures of silver, draped in gold ... carrying ... country instruments ... appearing to play'. Below each figure was 'another small bracket, in the shape of a rose, which advanced on the table, and carried a candelabrum', while in the space between each of the bigger consoles festoons of fruits and flowers were hanging.[17]

The upper part of the consoles 'consisted of eight protruding elements between the eight half-circles that comprised their shape. The ceiling that was placed on the consoles was divided into various panels of gold and azure, in the middle of which and between each abacus there was a gold rose carrying a crystal chandelier.'[18] Furthermore, this ceiling 'had an opening of three feet and one-half in diameter over the fountain'.[19] The entire cornice and all the edges were surrounded by candles, and a candelabrum stood at each of these eight edges.

On top of this construction was positioned a Tuscan column 18 feet high, 'with its basis placed on a base of marble enriched with gold' and its pedestal and capital translucent, while the only element that adorned the hollow shaft was a continuous festoon of gold flowers that spiralled until it reached the capital and carried six hundred candles along its height. Candles were also arranged all along the edges of the capital's contours. On top of the column was a large vase with crown on top of it, so 'this . . . column of light, was supporting itself in the air over the fountain, from which the water sprung through a ceiling of an extraordinary height'. The diameter of the column must have been similar to the diameter of the cornice's hole for the fountain, which was 1.06 metres (3.5 feet).[20]

Félibien concludes his description by writing that the diners 'supped to the sound of the waters of the fountain, while on the other side the *violons* and *hautbois* filled this place with an agreeable harmony, which lasted until two am, when the King and his entire Court withdrew'.[21]

The sheer pleasure the entire scene must have evoked for both diners and spectators (because of course it was the custom of the court for spectators to watch as the guests dined) is beyond questioning. But if this pleasure-triggering effect is unquestionable, then two crucial questions do arise: How best to approach this complex creation in historiographical terms, and which discipline would be the most fitting for this discussion? It is evident from both the surviving images and Félibien's description that this was no ordinary design, as it incorporated some large-scale architectural elements broadly belonging to the category of ornament, such as the column and the consoles; some other elements that triggered multiple senses, such as the water jets and the food on the dishes; elements that could be categorized as sculpture, such as the eight female figures leaning towards the brackets; some elements that appeared in their natural form, such as flowers; other elements in which specific natural forms were imitated and rendered in other materials, such as flowers made out of gold; and, finally, elements that clearly belonged to the category of singular objects, such as the chandeliers and candelabra, that were hung or placed on the larger elements as if these larger elements were a permanent architectural setting. So, in the case of this construction, where does architecture end, and where do sculpture and the decorative arts begin?[22]

It should be underlined that Vigarani's piece for the *medianoche* was not unique in its complexity. Such ephemeral constructions, greatly complex and truly spectacular, were embedded in the civic and court cultures of Europe, much in same the way that modern pavilions, booths and other similar constructions are part of our own contemporary culture of expos, fairs, music and other festivals, even wedding banquets. This broad category featured countless examples of inventive, elaborate design and extraordinary scale, often with very puzzling results. Their complex character creates extra layers of difficulty, to our modern eyes, for any attempt to approach and examine them as if they belonged to one singular distinctive typology. To understand their elusive character, though, it is useful to understand more about the craftspeople who created them, as well as about the culture of festival architecture.

To better understand the work of Carlo Vigarani in particular, it is crucial to say something about his father, the environment in which he grew up and the context of his training, as he was his father's apprentice and eventually became his partner. Carlo first came to France in 1659, together with his brother Ludovico and his father Gaspare (1588–1663) when the latter was summoned by Cardinal Mazarin, regent of France. Mazarin zealously promoted Italian artists in a wide variety of fields to the French court, and Gaspare was already renowned in Modena and beyond, holding the post of 'engineer and general superintendent of buildings' at the court of Alfonso d'Este. His main task, upon arriving in France, was to design the new *Salle des Machines* at the Palais de Tuileries in Paris – an innovative theatrical space inside the royal palace that soon became a model for theatres – and to oversee the various festivities related to the marriage of Louis XIV and the Spanish Infanta.[23]

The Vigarani family workshop is mostly known today for its ephemeral designs in France, but it produced works for many different sites and occasions, from palaces, churches and fortifications to theatrical and operatic scenography. Gaspare, in particular, designed and oversaw the completion of churches, palaces, fortifications and gardens, as well as ephemeral constructions for court and civic festivities in his native lands, often collaborating with other family members including his two sons.[24] One of Gaspare's most remarkable works related to our discussion is an unpublished series of annotated architectural drawings and sketches intended for a book on fortifications and palmistry, as bizarre as this combination may sound today.[25] As Ferrucio Canali concludes, from studying the architect's various notes, Gaspare was a very attentive reader of Vignola, but always kept Vitruvius's writings in mind, 'while, probably with clear awareness, the architect avoided any reference to the remaining modern treatises, even to the most well-known and widespread ones'.[26]

The professional title Gaspare preferred for himself must have been that of 'architetto, ed ingegnere', as this was the one he chose for the title of the above-mentioned group of drawings. Nevertheless, this title never prevented him from designing temporary monuments for funerals, stage sets for opera and theatre productions, and various apparatuses for court and civic festivities.[27] Although Gaspare's work at the court of Modena was neither underpinned by a theoretical background nor characterized by any particular innovation, he nevertheless produced compelling architectural works and ephemeral decorations for the various projects in which he was involved.[28]

This constant 'trespassing' across disciplinary boundaries as well as across professional appellations was nothing abnormal for the time, and especially for someone coming from the Italian tradition. Speaking about this fluidity, Édouard Dégans states, of Florence, that 'the sixteenth-century architects envisaged their works as a dialogue among all arts'.[29] And Dégans is not alone in this. Alina Payne's volume on materiality and crossing between the arts in the Italian Renaissance demonstrates the wider background and tradition in which the Vigarani family was situated and which influenced their overall work in multiple mediums and across multiple scales, as they produced 'objects' for various contexts, functions and purposes.[30]

Going back to Carlo, his direct involvement in royal and theatrical projects lasted almost two decades, initially as the king's appointed *ingenieur du roi*, and then *'intendant des machines et des plaisirs du Roi, inventeur et conducteur des machines, intendant des machines des théâtres, ballets et fêtes royales'*, namely the chief of all the king's festivities.[31] Much like his father, he also created designs for decorative programmes for royal apartments, palace layouts and ephemeral constructions, proving his ability in and acquaintance with all of the aforementioned design fields. With regard to the style of Carlo's works, de la Gorce comments that the creator's preference was mainly for the Italianate style, drawing inspiration from Bernini's forms and from the style of the Medici in Florence.[32] Bernini was one of the most famous artists who were, by their own assertion, interchangeably architects (so, designers of buildings) and sculptors (so, creators of objects). Furthermore, the reference to the Medici indicates Carlo's adherence to a tradition of deploying certain media-transferrable elements such as the consoles and the Tuscan order.

The juxtaposition of architecture and the arts, machinery and courtly display, at which the Vigarani family had excelled while working in Modena, was highly desired by Louis XIV, and the act of hiring Carlo aimed to boost his efforts to solidify his power during the first decades of his rule. The disseminated images of Vigarani's construction via the various royal publications played a crucial role in achieving this goal.[33]

One needs a whole array of different disciplines at hand today to examine the juxtaposition demonstrated in the 1674 *machine* properly, something that matches, to some extent, the skills of the polymath professional of Vigarani's time. Eric Monin, discussing the eighteenth-century French culture of festival architecture, eloquently draws a profile of the persons in charge of such spectacles: 'Simultaneously an architect, theatre decorator and entertainment promoter, the person in charge of these delicate, expensive, politically sensitive events needed to have exceptional qualities ... in numerous areas of competence that demanded a wide range of knowledge and experience.'[34] Moreover, they had to be familiar with theatre scenography and 'the capabilities and limitations of imitation architecture – *architecture feinte*. As an architect, they had to know how to build supporting structures and be aware of the rules governing good taste and the principles of good architecture. These skills, developed through drawings and models, allowed them to design festival projects much as they would architectural proposals.'[35]

## An amalgam of references

Vigarani's creation aimed to exude ingenuity and astonish the spectators and diners, and similarly the readers of Félibien's festival book. In examining this *machine*, one realizes that it constitutes an amalgam of references from multiple fields. The focus of our attention here will be a number of key design features, as they highlight the degree of disciplinary overlap that makes it almost impossible for the construction to be analysed in any discipline-specific way. Forms appear to have migrated from one context to the other and from one seemingly unrelated visual, structural, or compositional category to another – from a funerary monument to an object for a banquet; from a large-scale source or model into something closer to free-standing sculpture in size – changing from functional to decorative and vice versa, not to mention a strong notion of scale lurking in all parts of the design.

To take this a step further, one could argue that examination from diverse viewpoints and fields is an almost necessary process, in order to understand designs such as this *machine*. As Cammy Brothers argued in her book about Michelangelo and the mechanisms of his imagination, the architectural designs of this Renaissance creator can be best understood in terms of his experience as a painter and sculptor.[36] Taking into consideration Vigarani's transdisciplinary background and practice, one might also argue for a similar necessity here. Using the 1674 *machine* as an example, it will be demonstrated that such migrations of forms and concepts were not uncommon, and disciplinary trespassing was nothing less than the norm at the time.[37]

Upon visual inspection, one first notices the combination of a long vertical element, the illuminated triumphal column, placed on top of the eight consoles. This constituted a quasi-pedestal construction, which is a very rare combination for this type and scale of object, and one that has proved very difficult to match to designs for similar projects preceding the 1674 *divertissement*. Nevertheless, this particular arrangement can be found in another category of designs for fully portable and functional objects used mostly in interiors: lighting devices. The parallel is not so surprising given the fact that the *divertissements* took place at night. Just two years before the 1674 *divertissement*, the silversmith Claude Ballin produced a series of imposing *torchères* – free-standing pieces of furniture that supported candlesticks – for the Sun King's *grands appartements* in Versailles (Figure 6.3). Like Vigarani's construction, these *torchères* featured upward-looking brackets with figural ornament on their legs, an ascending central column and a crowning candelabrum. Vigarani, in his position as the *intendant des plaisirs du Roi*, may have had direct access to Le Brun's new creations, especially since the palaces in Paris and Versailles were quickly becoming the centre of major artistic developments in France.

Furthermore, these *torchères* were not the only lighting devices with such a composition. Around the same time, many lighting devices and other interior pieces began to feature this characteristic quasi-pedestal, with brackets or consoles on the inside and vertical elongated elements above them in the shape of a column, a statue, or any combination of the two that served to reach the desired height for the candles. Structurally speaking, an array of consoles would provide excellent stability for the *machine*, preventing the tall upright composition from overturning, and thus ensuring the safety of the device without sacrificing artistry.

FIGURE 6.3 *One of a pair of gilded limewood* torchères *produced in The Hague, design similar to Claude Ballin's* torchères, *anonymous (c. 1700). Courtesy of Rijksmuseum (CC0 1.0).*

The use of consoles to form the stable and ornate base of an upright and portable object also emerges around the third quarter of the seventeenth century, as one can see in examples such as a design for andirons – the stands for the wood in fireplaces – created by Le Brun in 1667 or, on the other side of the Channel, similar artefacts with the monogram of Charles II of England designed by the silversmith Jean Gerard around 1670.

The discourse on S-type brackets begins in the field of architectural theory with Vitruvius, who related them to the Ionian order as the supporting elements of a cornice or an entablature, ultimately stating that they were used mostly as decorative elements.[38] Giorgio Vasari, on the other hand, the sole source on brackets in the sixteenth century, created the vague term *mensola*, which referred to S-forms, applying it to both architecture and to sculpture, 'considerably enlarging the fields of application', as Dégans concludes.[39] Although a history of the bracket for the seventeenth century has yet to be traced, it is safe to say from the examples mentioned above that by the 1670s the use of this type of bracket had expanded to almost every scale and genre of artistic creation, thus constituting an example of the way pre-modern practices routinely traversed the boundaries between disciplines that were established in later centuries.

Returning to our examination of Vigarani's *machine*, one comes to another realization: the free-standing column above the consoles clearly resembled Trajan's Triumphal Column in Rome. Triumphal columns were not at all common during the time of the *divertissement*, in fact they only started to be used from the eighteenth century onwards.[40] What Vigarani does, here, is to imitate basic features of the highly imposing remnant of Roman antiquity on top of the quasi-pedestal, while changing not only the dimensions, but also transforming the shape from a massive, solid volume into an airy, translucent and illuminated one. The ornate shaft of the original, with its helical sculptural frieze, is here replaced by a helical string of golden flowers supporting lighted candles, culminating in the capital with the echinus and abacus treated similarly to the Tuscan order and those of the original column itself.

Vigarani's design was intended to celebrate a military victory of a king obsessed with role models from ancient Rome, and so this reference was far from incidental. As discussed earlier in the chapter, the function of this category of objects and installations in early modernity was to glorify the princely host, a function which is fully aligned with the forms found in Vigarani's *machine*. The Sun King himself saw Trajan as a model ruler, and he tried to associate himself directly with the ancient Roman figure in different ways and through a variety of actions, such as ordering casts of the column and incorporating the emperor's figure into the interior decorative programme at Versailles. According to Louis Hautecoeur's *Architecture Classique en France*, for example, the architect Louis Le Vau had even suggested that bas-reliefs after Trajan's Column should be installed at the *Cour de Marbre*, the place where the *divertissement* unfolded in 1674, in imitation of the example of François I in the palace of Fontainebleau a century earlier.[41] What is more, just a few months before the *divertissement*, Pietro Bellori made copper engravings after the sculptures found on Trajan's Column, dedicating his publication to Louis XIV and calling him 'Trajan de France'.[42]

Returning to Vigarani's design, direct references can also be drawn, naturally, to multiple earlier examples of ephemeral architecture in Rome and Modena. As one example, the decoration with figural sculpture and handling of the upward-looking consoles inscribed in an octagonal base closely resemble similar features used in the temporary funerary monument of Francesco d'Este, which was designed by Gaspare Vigarani at the end of 1658, just a few months before the family departed for France (Figure 6.4).[43] Additionally, the same octagonal layout of vertically positioned and colonnaded partitions, with voids

FIGURE 6.4 *Funerary monument of Francesco d'Este, designed by Gaspare Vigarani (1658). Courtesy of National Library of France/BnF.*

in between, and supporting a domed superstructure, can also be traced to the catafalque for Pope Gregory XV erected in 1623.[44]

The consoles and brackets, octagons and columns that constituted Vigarani's creation were either basic geometric shapes or elements taken from the architectural ornament of the Italian Renaissance. There is one more resemblance of note here, which comes in the form of the very definition of what architecture is perceived to be: a solid building. The referenced structure dates from the late 1400s and stands on the dome of Santa Maria del Fiore Cathedral in Florence, designed by Filippo Brunelleschi, a masterpiece that decisively influenced the course of architecture (Figure 6.5). Observing the crowning lantern of the dome, one realizes that it has an octagonal layout with eight reverse consoles acting as buttresses, with open space in between them, creating a vaulted interior. The console-shaped, quasi-circular octagonal system of buttresses was used rather ingeniously,

FIGURE 6.5 *Lantern of Florence Cathedral, Filippo Brunelleschi (mid-fifteenth century). Futureshape. Image © Alexander Baxevanis via Flickr. Courtesy of Birasuegi via Wikimedia Commons.*

just as in Carlo Vigarani's design and in the ephemeral funerary monuments above, all of them on a similar scale, to solve the structural problem of supporting the weight of the small dome of the lantern as successfully and as elegantly as possible.

## Objects, ornament and marginalization in historiography

It is well known to scholars of early modernity that multidisciplinarity in practices was nothing extraordinary, so the correspondences discussed above are not surprising. Elements and design processes travelled across time and region, being reused in new and inventive ways to create independent constructs that were neither buildings nor objects. What is surprising, however, is why we need this kind of discussion, and the reminders of earlier practices, to push us to examine Vigarani's 1674 *machine*. In other words, what obstructs us from taking an interest in Vigarani's design for its inherent value and multifaceted character?

Creating a taxonomy of distinct branches of a 'design family tree', just as the innovation specialist Bettina von Stamm does in her book on innovation design and the richness of human creativity, can prove very helpful.[45] Such simplifications, however, are often based on a linear evolutionary approach to the history of disciplines, and end up confusing relations and obscuring details, as they fail to manifest the multiple and significant overlaps among all the branches of the tree – a tree that was based on practices, principles and ideas with common roots.

Vasari argued that the visual arts and architecture shared a common basis in *disegno*, the idea in the mind of the artist that 'subsequently received material and visual form as a design drawing'.[46] *Disegno* was an idea already developed by Petrarch in the fourteenth century and taken on by Alberti in the fifteenth, incorporating not only fine arts, but also sculpture and architecture. This idea is of great relevance to our discussion, as it appears to be the one thing unifying all the heterogenous elements combined in Vigarani's *machine*, granting it the cohesion it so vividly demonstrates. One should not forget Gaspare's and Carlo's profiles: by living and working inside this culture of mobility among artistic fields, it would have been impossible for them not to have read Alberti and Vasari.

This focus of attention on the thought of a century before to solve problems of approach, taxonomy and interpretation is of course not new. The once-united general field of artistic creation instilled in the idea of *disegno* in the Renaissance started being divided gradually in later centuries. After an attempt to reunite them at the end of the nineteenth century, the many and diverse fields that once comprised *disegno* followed separate paths.[47] At the turn of that century, historians including Heinrich Wölfflin, Gottfried Semper and Alois Riegl, among others, created a discourse beyond strict divisions and watertight disciplinary boundaries and based on the assumption of an earlier unity – a discourse that was largely discontinued by the late twentieth century. According to Payne, however, there was a series of reasons for this 'suspended dialogue', as she called it, between art and architecture.[48] Among these reasons, one is the shift in the definition of architecture through the centuries, namely from a discipline closely related to painting and sculpture since the foundation of the *Accademia del Disegno* (1563), to a discipline mostly attached to science and technology and embracing the social sciences, environmental and urban planning and industry.[49] Another reason is the problem of architectural history being too closely related to professional practice, in the sense that it has been appropriated by a profession-driven discourse.[50] Additionally, the fact that art history is, and always has been, able to incorporate architecture, while architectural history does not commonly incorporate art, only adds to the aforementioned dichotomy.

The work of Heinrich Wölfflin, one of the most significant scholars of architectural history arguing beyond watertight disciplinary boundaries, is also relevant to this discussion emerging from Vigarani's composition. As Alexander Bigman summarizes in an article on architecture and objecthood, 'in his *Prolegomena zu einer Psychologie der Architectur* (1886) and later in *Renaissance und Barock* (1888), Wölfflin proposed that the perception of architectural members is essentially animistic and anthropopathic; it inheres in the beholder's projection of embodied experience onto inert constructional matter'.[51] Bigman continues by declaring that Wölfflin 'analysed architecture in terms that were not specific to itself; [he] blurred the distinction between architecture and all of the plastic arts. Indeed, in Wölfflin's account, architecture becomes a subset of sculpture (the *körperlich*, or corporeal arts) and sometimes even has painterly (*malerisch*) attributes.'[52] What derives from Wölfflin's conception of architecture is that the design of our 1674 intricate *machine* might have been much more deeply and widely understood if examined in these terms: as an embodied experience of architecture not easily distinguishable from the plastic arts.

A crucial notion in this discussion is ornament, as our *machine* literally consists of a series of elements of architectural ornament. A diachronically ambiguous and surprisingly understudied term which began in Roman antiquity in rhetoric and gradually passed on to the visual arts and mainly architectural discourse by the time of the Renaissance, ornament was abolished from architecture and its discourse with twentieth-century modernism.[53] This abolition resulted in, among many other radical consequences, the difficulty that modern scholars have had in discussing pre-modern ornament properly, and Payne's writings prove once more crucial for this train of thought.[54]

Payne argues in the introduction to her monograph, *From Ornament to Object: Genealogies of Architectural Modernism*, that in an industrial economy 'architecture had been seen as overscaled abstract sculpture both in criticism at the time and in scholarship later ... but the function of the sculptural matter *on* architecture rather than its overall *Gestalt* ... tended to be left out of discussions and remain on the periphery of scholarship to this day'.[55] What is more, according to Payne, ornament and objects have similar scale, in contrast with architecture; they are small-scale and (mostly) three-dimensional, so they 'elicit "graspability" in a very different and more direct way than architecture'.[56] Payne maintains that the realm of the small-scale and intricate has long been left at the margins of architectural scholarship.[57]

Finally, a similar marginalization and neglect has been identified for the wide field of ephemeral constructions and festival architecture. Sarah Bonnemaison and Christine Macy eloquently make this point in the introduction to their seminal work *Festival Architecture*:

The modern distinction between solid and ephemeral creates an additional difficulty for the historian of festival architecture: its marginal position in architectural historiography. When permanent is set against temporary, the opposition, as Jacques Derrida would argue, is not an equal one. Permanent architecture has long been viewed by architects and architectural historians as more significant and ultimately more central to architecture and its history ... The ephemeral works' transitory nature gives them attributes of being superficial, even fake. Yet ephemerality is the joker's card in architectural history. Often, it is used as a foil to enhance the value of more durable constructions.[58]

In the nineteenth century, architectural histories by Karl Bötticher and Gottfried Semper presented ephemeral constructions as the very origin of architecture.[59] This idea continued in the theories developed by Wölfflin, Riegl, Panofsky and Pevsner, with more recent reappraisals of the significance of ephemerality in architecture during the past few decades.[60]

## Conclusion

Just as with much early modern ephemeral architecture and construction, Vigarani's design has not yet received proper attention regarding its wider significance and impact, being part of a genre that still constitutes a marginal field to most scholars of the history of architecture and objects. Consequently, the discussion entertained in this chapter is far from complete. However, what I hope to have shown, by highlighting the liminal nature of this field, is how crucial it is for understanding material culture in general, and how a chain of problems in the various historiographies has contributed to a difficulty in initiating the proper discussion of creations such as the 1674 *machine*. This example of an early modern 'object' actively demonstrates strong and exemplary applications of a shared vocabulary among all arts, as well as the interchangeability of scales between the design of a building and an object.

Regarding this formal vocabulary, in Vigarani's design it appears that the designer borrowed elements from architecture such as the Tuscan Order, triumphal columns, dome construction and consoles. From the wider category of decorative arts, he borrowed elements from pieces such as lighting devices and temporary funerary monuments. The outcome of this varied inspiration was the production of a *machine* that today could be called a hybrid in terms of form, concept and structure. Such amalgamation is a characteristic reflection of the flexibility and versatility in the practice of a time in which artists (in the widest sense) evidently moved freely from one medium to another, from one context and order of things to another, creating ingenious constructions as a result. Ontologically speaking, and according to our current disciplinary definitions, the 1674 *machine*, like so many works and particularly early modern ones, belongs neither to the conventional objects of design, nor to the conventional objects of architecture. Away from these two categories, a bifold approach might be the option here, in fact dictated by the nature of such objects: on the one hand, to truly revisit the instructive Renaissance idea of *disegno*; on the other, to attempt a transdisciplinary analysis that incorporates fields considered fully distinct nowadays, such as scenography, sculpture, painting, architecture, rhetoric and politics.

Ultimately, there is no need to provide a definitive answer to what category Vigarani's creation belongs. This issue of categorization is a product of our time, and this kind of reflection belongs only to contemporary perceptions of the profession of the artist, designer or *machiniste*, perceptions that make no sense in the context of early modern ephemeral constructions and that cannot be applied to designs made by the professionals and within the practices that originated such constructions. Since early modern designers of one kind trespassed without hesitation into the fields of any other kind, to borrow motifs and elements and apply them to new functions and meanings, then perhaps historians of material objects can approach these interconnections and overlaps not as exceptional cases and deviations from the canon, but as the norm, possibly in more than one historical period. Failure to do so often results in trying to categorize a creative object according to certain superimposed categories and examine it using only one disciplinary lens, and this, ultimately, removes a great part of the object's value.

## Notes

1 The region changed hands multiple times before Louis XIV reconquered it, first in 1668 and, shortly after it was lost again, in 1674. It was ultimately added to French lands with the Treaty of Nijmegen in 1678.

2 La Curne de Sainte-Palaye et al., *Dictionnaire Historique de l'ancien Langage François, Ou, Glossaire de la Langue Françoise Depuis Son Origine Jusqu'au Siècle de Louis XIV* (Paris: Honoré Champion (NIORT), 1875).

3 For the first definition, see Élisabeth Caude, Jérôme de La Gorce and Béatrix Saule (eds.), *Fêtes & Divertissements à la Cour* (Paris: Gallimard, 2016), 14–15; for the second, see Peter Burke, *The Fabrication of Louis XIV* (New Haven; London: Yale University Press, 1992), 6.

4 The translation of this quotation, as all quotations taken from texts originally in French, are made by the author of this essay. Louis XIV, *Mémoires pour l'instruction du Dauphin* (Paris: Imprimerie Nationale, 1992).

5 André Félibien, *Les Divertissemens de Versailles, Donnez Par Le Roy Au Retour de La Conqueste de La Franche-Comté, En L'année 1674* (Paris: Imprimerie Royale, 1676).

6 An enlightening volume on the culture of publishing and image-making during the times of Louis XIV is Peter Fuhring et al., *A Kingdom of Images: French*

*Prints in the Age of Louis XIV, 1660–1715* (Los Angeles: Getty Publications, 2015).
7  Christian Quaeitzch, 'Die Divertissements des Sonnenkönigs: Dokumentation und Rezeption ephemerer Festkunst am Hofe Ludwigs XIV', in Erika Fischer-Lichte (ed.), *Theater Und Fest in Europa: Perspektiven von Identität Und Gemeinschaft* (Tübingen: Francke, 2012), 296.
8  Fuhring et al., *A Kingdom of Images*, 7–8.
9  Félibien, *Les Divertissemens de Versailles*, 1.
10 See Helen Watanabe-O'Kelly, 'The early modern festival book', in *Europa Triumphans: Court and Civic Festivals in Early Modern Europe*, eds. Ronnie Mulryne et al. (Aldershot: Ashgate, 2004), vol. I, 6–12.
11 Ibid.
12 In line with all scholars of early modern festival architecture, Jérôme de la Gorce argues that the artistic character of these festivities appears somewhat frivolous and unimportant to the wider public these days, resulting in them remaining largely understudied and overlooked: Caude et al., *Fêtes & Divertissements à la Cour*, 16–23. What is more, while the image and the artistic creations associated with the Sun King have been discussed exhaustively and from countless viewpoints, a substantial and detailed discourse on early modern festivals, and on how the various artistic disciplines were merged into the structures – as well as the values implied by this merging – is only very slowly and very recently taking shape. No in-depth analysis has been produced even for the *medianoche* object of 1674, despite its numerous mentions in exhibition catalogues and in books related to food studies, festival architecture, Louis XIV's public image formation, Carlo Vigarani's work, and so on. Even in one of the most recent notable mentions, in the volume accompanying the exhibition *Fêtes & Divertissements à la Cour* (see Caude et al., *Fêtes & Divertissements à la Cour*), the construction is only discussed under the category of illuminations.
13 For the adornment of the fountain, see André Félibien, *Description Sommaire Du Chasteau de Versailles* (Paris, 1674), 15. For the octagonal shape, see François Souchal, Françoise de La Moureyre and Henriette Dumuis (eds.), *French Sculptors of the 17th and 18th Centuries: The Reign of Louis XIV* (London: Faber and Faber, 1977), vol. III, 52.
14 Unfortunately, the engraving shows no illuminations on the palace walls, unlike the accompanying text where a description of these illuminations can be read. Caude et al., *Fêtes & Divertissements à la Cour*, 328.
15 For the original description, see Félibien, *Les Divertissemens de Versailles*, 13–18. As for the units used here, the *feet* correspond 1:1 to the pied (du roi), the unit used by Félibien.
16 For an additional description of the *machine*, see Jérôme de la Gorce, *Carlo Vigarani, Intendant Des Plaisirs de Louis XIV* (Paris: Perrin, 2005), 156–58.
17 Félibien, *Les Divertissemens de Versailles*, 13–18.
18 Ibid.
19 Ibid.

20 As the column was basically hollow, the spiralling festoon and the capital must have been hanging from cords attached to the exterior walls or ceilings of the château.
21 Félibien, *Les Divertissemens de Versailles*, 13–18.
22 I owe a great deal of my thinking here to Alina Payne's writings on the interconnection of the disciplines, for example Alina Payne, 'The Sculptor-Architect's Drawing and Exchanges Between the Arts', in Michael Cole (ed.), *Donatello, Michelangelo, Cellini. Sculptors' Drawings from Renaissance Italy* (Boston: Isabella Stewart Gardner Museum, 2014), 57–73; also, Alina Payne, *Architecture parmi les arts: Materialité, transferts et travail artistique dans l'Italie de la Renaissance* (Paris: Louvre Éditions, 2016).
23 Frederick Tollini, *Scene Design at the Court of Louis XIV: The Work of the Vigarani Family and Jean Berain* (Lewiston, NY: Edwin Mellen Press, 2003).
24 De la Gorce, *Carlo Vigarani*, 9–28. For a detailed analysis of the Vigarani family's works, see Walter Baricchi and Jérôme de la Gorce, *Gaspare et Carlo Vigarani: Dalla Corte Degli Este a Quella Di Luigi XIV = De La Cour D'Este À Celle De Louis XIV* (Milan: Silvana Editoriale / Centre de recherche du château de Versailles, 2009).
25 Ferrucio Canali, 'Gaspare Vigarani lettore di Vignola (e di Vitruvio). Annotazioni inedite sulla *Venustas* per un compendio di architettura: le difficoltà dell'ordine tuscanico', in Baricchi and de la Gorce, *Gaspare et Carlo Vigarani*, 34–38.
26 Ibid, 38.
27 Ibid, 34–38. Unfortunately, I was not able to determine Carlo's personal preference for his professional title in the same way as for Gaspare.
28 Baricchi and de la Gorce, *Gaspare et Carlo Vigarani*, 6–11.
29 Édouard Dégans, 'Entre ornement et sculpture – La console dans l'architecture Florentine du XVIe siècle', in Ralph Dekoninck, Caroline Heering, and Michel Lefftz (eds.), *Questions d'ornements, XVe–XVIIIe Siècles* (Turnhout: Brepols, 2013), 209.
30 Payne, *Architecture parmi les arts*.
31 On the first professional title, see Alice Jarrard, *Architecture as Performance in Seventeenth-Century Europe: Court Ritual in Modena, Rome, and Paris* (Cambridge: Cambridge University Press, 2003), 186–87; on the second one, see Daniela del Pesco, 'Gian Lorenzo Bernini e Carlo Vigarani alla corte di Luigi XIV', in Baricchi and de la Gorce, *Gaspare et Carlo Vigarani*, 205–6.
32 See de la Gorce, *Carlo Vigarani*, 145–50.
33 Jarrard, *Architecture as Performance*, 188. For the most recent discussion of the visual culture at the court of Louis XIV, see Wolf Burchard, *The Sovereign Artist: Charles Le Brun and the Image of Louis XIV* (London: Paul Holberton Publishing, 2016); see also the Introduction in Robert Wellington, *Antiquarianism and the Visual Histories of Louis XIV: Artifacts for a Future Past* (London: Routledge, 2017).

34  Eric Monin, 'Festival architecture in eighteenth-century France', in *Festival Architecture*, eds. Sarah Bonnemaison and Christine Macy (London: Routledge, 2008), 172.
35  Ibid.
36  See Cammy Brothers, *Michelangelo, Drawing, and the Invention of Architecture* (New Haven: Yale University Press, 2008). I am thankful to Caroline van Eck for directing my attention to this work.
37  Finding physical evidence to trace the exact lineage of each constituent part would be an additional path for this exploration. A thorough research around this 'object', also in the relevant archives in Paris as well as in Modena (the birthplace of the Vigarani family), would shed even more light on the design processes and decisions.
38  Dégans, 'Entre ornement et sculpture', 203.
39  Ibid.
40  For instance, the Triumphal Column seen today at the Place Vendôme was installed by Napoleon I as late as 1806, and the only contemporary example (in the Doric Order) was erected in London between 1671 and 1677, to commemorate the rebirth of the city after the Great Fire of 1666.
41  See, for example, Filippo Coarelli, *La Colonna Traiana* (Rome: Colombo, 1999), 135.
42  One could also add here that the use of the Tuscan order, and its association with power, was nothing new for the French monarchs. The Renaissance idea of the superiority of the Tuscan Order was used by the Medici family in Florence, with an extensive use of this order on both interior and exterior surfaces. The two Medici brides who entered the French royal family, Catherine de Medici in 1533 and Maria de Medici in 1600, contributed considerably to the migration of this order to the French Court.
43  De la Gorce, *Carlo Vigarani*, 157–8.
44  This ephemeral monument is discussed at length in Flavia Matitti, 'La Festa Come Laboratorio Del Barocco', in *La Festa a Roma: Dal Rinascimento Al 1870*, ed. Marcelo Fagiolo (Turin: Allemandi, 1997), vol. 1, 82–99.
45  See Bettina von Stamm, *Managing Innovation, Design and Creativity* (Hoboken: Wiley, 2008).
46  For this exact point see Caroline van Eck, 'Paper Architecture', in *Festival Architecture*, eds. Bonnemaison and Macy, 115.
47  Alina Payne, 'Architectural History and the History of Art: A Suspended Dialogue', *Journal of the Society of Architectural Historians* 58, no. 3 (1999): 292–299.
48  Ibid., 292–299.
49  Ibid.
50  Ibid. There has been a recent re-emergence of discourse trying to bring together these two disciplines and their historiographical interconnection. One of the most recent examples is Mark Crinson and Richard J. Williams, *The Architecture of Art History – A Historiography* (London: Bloomsbury, 2019).

51 Alexander R. Bigman, 'Architecture and Objecthood: Donald Judd's Renaissance Imaginary', *Oxford Art Journal* 40, no. 2 (August 2017): 263–286.

52 Ibid, 270.

53 For an informative overview of the bibliography and basic developments of the notion, see Caroline van Eck's treatment of the term 'ornament': Caroline van Eck, 'Ornament in Europe: From Antiquity to the Twentieth Century', *Oxford Bibliographies Online*. Available online: https://www.oxfordbibliographies.com/view/document/obo-9780190922467/obo-9780190922467-0042.xml (accessed 19 April 2020).

54 Alina Payne, *From Ornament to Object: Genealogies of Architectural Modernism* (New Haven: Yale University Press, 2012), 1–24.

55 Ibid., 15.

56 Ibid., 13.

57 Ibid.

58 Bonnemaison and Macy (eds.), *Festival Architecture*, 2.

59 Ibid, 3.

60 One such major work is Werner Oechslin and Anja Buschow, *Festarchitektur: Der Architekt als Ingenieurkunstler* (Stuttgart: Hatje, 1984).

# CHAPTER SEVEN

# Printed Objects and Ready-mades in the *Architectural Magazine* (1834–8)

## Anne Hultzsch

In the *Architectural Magazine* (1834–8), commonly cited as the first journal devoted to architecture in Britain, articles on designed objects often make for more entertaining reading than those on what we now more specifically refer to as architecture.[1] Reflecting the dynamic meaning of what was considered architectural in the 1830s, the *Magazine* was filled with illustrated descriptions of appliances often intended for mass production, ranging from a 'simple and effective Preventive for the Slamming of a Passage Door', a portable shower-bath, a 'fastening for a Dressing-Room Glass', as well as endless types of stoves and prefabricated – ready-made – objects. As such, the *Magazine* bears witness to the dialectics of architecture and design as they unfolded at this moment in Britain (Figure 7.1).

John Claudius Loudon (1783–1843), founder and editor of the *Architectural Magazine*, was not an architect in the strict sense, either by training or by experience. Nevertheless, he shaped the field of architecture at a crucial moment; in the decade in which the Royal Institute of British Architects was founded, it was all but clear who was an 'architect' or who should produce – and judge – the 'architectural'. Did one need to have had specific training in a college or institution? Not yet. The architectural profession was not an exclusive circle and the term 'architectural' even less so. Loudon attempted to make use of this somewhat accidental inclusivity to establish a level intellectual playing field among anyone involved with building; from the carpenter and artisan to the student, architect, amateur and client, everyone should *read* the same publication. Playing to his strengths

FIGURE 7.1 *John Loudon's* Architectural Magazine, *vol. 1 (1834). Private collection.*

as a seasoned editor and author, he employed the relatively young genre of the specialized magazine to reach new audiences. In this, Loudon could draw on his experiences with the successful *Gardener's Magazine* (1826–44), the *Magazine of Natural History* (1828–36), as well as a number of encyclopaedias, among them the often-quoted *Encyclopaedia of Cottage, Farm, and Villa Architecture and Furniture* (first edition 1832–3).[2] By the 1830s, Loudon had published, often in collaboration with his wife Jane Webb Loudon, an astonishing number of books, articles and magazines, mainly on agricultural and botanical subjects, but also of a political nature and, increasingly, on architectural matters.[3] Loudon was also a convinced republican, a follower of Jeremy Bentham, and has even been called a feminist.[4] Following these convictions, he attempted to spread knowledge about architectural forms, styles and technologies beyond those who would previously have been exposed to them, including the working classes and the female client and homemaker. He was not the first or only one in this endeavour, but his was the first attempt in Britain to facilitate an inclusive arena of building practitioners and users by means of a serial print publication.

When the *Architectural Magazine*'s first issue came out in March 1834, it addressed three reader groups. First, the expected: the architect, the architectural student, and the 'amateur' – that quintessentially eighteenth-century, white, mostly male, figure, privileged through upbringing, education, social networks and the opportunity to travel. Second, the less expected: anyone who 'occupies ... houses ... and especially the female portion of it', remarkable for the inclusion of women in an 'architectural' audience.[5] Finally there is a third group, which is perhaps least expected from today's vantage point: anyone involved with the erecting and equipping of buildings; thus, artisans and mechanics. By targeting this diverse readership, the *Magazine* attempted to create a visually literate public across all strata of society, able to recognize good design from bad and thus creating and encouraging a better built environment – preceding similar twentieth-century concerns from the likes of Herbert Read or Nikolaus Pevsner.

This chapter examines the relationship between the first and the third group, or rather, their designed outputs in print: the object – both the one-off and the ready-made – and its relationship to the designed space, the building. What role did the object play in Loudon's project of taste improvement? How could objects, perhaps more than buildings, help him in reaching his intended audience? More specifically, how could the mass-produced, ready-made ornament as discussed and represented *in print* contribute to higher standards in architectural design? Loudon's aims are directly related to the wider questions asked by the present book as a whole: What can we, as historians of architecture and/or design, learn from the free mixing of objects and buildings on the *Magazine's* pages? What were, and are, the consequences of this inclusivity, of bringing together all stakeholders of the design world – if we can call it thus – on the same page, into the same discursive space?

## Printed objects

The *Architectural Magazine* was founded in precisely the same year, 1834, as the Royal Institute of British Architects (RIBA), until today the arbiter of architectural taste, judging with an array of awards, medals and guidelines what constitutes the 'good' building. Both institute and magazine were born from the loose definitions of what it meant to be an architect in Britain at the time, but they reflected this vacuum in very different ways. While the RIBA mirrored the contemporary struggle over the need for clearer professional definitions alongside educational specialization, Loudon's *Magazine* exploited and expanded the space opened up by the vague meaning of 'architectural'. However, there were differences and contradictions between these two positions. Loudon did not antagonize proponents of professionalization – indeed, the *Magazine* regularly printed reports of the RIBA's meetings; clearly they had to be part of the conversation. But Loudon's was a larger conversation, with space for both a larger architectural audience as well as a wider range of architectural objects and buildings. Thus, the RIBA – as an institute of architecture – and the magazine – the architectural in print – simply served different purposes and audiences. As such, the *Magazine* is neither pioneer nor latecomer, but reflects a particular moment in which building and object could operate in the same sphere.

At the time, print cultures put a spotlight on contemporary paradigms of professional exclusivity as well as more diverse, inclusive approaches. While, as Richard Wittmann has shown, in eighteenth-century France print empowered architectural debate among the bourgeoisie,[6] in early nineteenth-century Britain it led to an even wider expansion of audiences, accompanied by increasing fragmentation. As printing became cheaper, faster and more varied in terms of word–image relationships, new print genres sprang up, enticing all strata of society to engage with the world of buildings and objects.[7] Literacy rates improved, but even the illiterate or those with low reading skills participated through illustrated broadsides, pamphlets and posters. Much of this was market-driven. There was money to be made with cheap periodicals and serial fiction, especially given the gradually reduced taxes on paper and print products.[8]

Loudon's unique contribution to this shifting arena of design practices lay in formalizing a status quo in print and turning it into a project of increasing equality. Knowledge about architectural principles, and as a consequence, taste, should be shared more widely and purposefully, and in particular with those who actually did the building. Boldly, he argued that

> taste ... is not necessarily connected with wealth: it may be possessed by the journeyman, carpenter, mason, bricklayer, or cabinet-maker in as high a degree as by the architect, surveyor, or learned and wealthy amateur. In all it must first exist naturally, and in all it must be improved by cultivation.[9]

The subtitle of the *Architectural Magazine* indicates this wide-ranging project of 'cultivation', suggesting both a didactic as well as a promotional intent: *Journal of Improvement in Architecture, Building, and Furnishing, and in the Various Arts and Trades Connected Therewith*. 'Improvement' is central here; like many British architectural writers of the early nineteenth century, Loudon's writing is characterized by a frustration with contemporary architectural production, especially in the growing fringes of the larger cities. Many were the attempts to improve matters, ranging from reforming architectural education to establishment of a builders' guild.[10] Loudon's endeavour, however, must be placed in the context of both a boom in popular educational literature and a rise of institutions for adult education, rather than in that of the emerging architectural profession. In London, the Royal Institution was founded in 1799 by leading scientists with the clear intent to spread scientific thinking (and perhaps especially mechanical innovation with the potential to increase industrial capital) beyond the walls of Oxford and Cambridge. Smaller learned societies sprang up around the country in the first decade of the nineteenth century, including the London Institution and the Russell Institution in the capital. All offered an array of lectures on the sciences, but also the arts, history, geography, and more applied subjects such as mechanics. Institutes commonly had libraries, very comprehensive in the case of the larger institutions and often located in newly erected substantial buildings, spreading the influence of new journals and books even further. And there was another link between physical lecture space and printed page: often, lectures given in these institutions were collected and published as books, such as James Elmes's *Lectures on Architecture, Comprising the History of the Art from the Earliest Times to the Present Day* (first edition 1821, second 1823). This demonstrates the close link between physical, oratorial space and the printed, read page.

In the 1820s, another movement joined this world of adult education: that of the Mechanics' Institutes, which aimed explicitly at the working classes (even if it failed eventually, reaching at best the well-situated mechanic and clerk). Again, the physical venues of education were accompanied by printed sites, by means of the weekly *Mechanics' Magazine*, a publication praised by Loudon (Figure 7.2).[11] The cheap magazine, octavo sized and sold weekly at 3 pence, transformed the dissemination of specialized information and knowledge. In an attempt to popularize knowledge from two key arenas of the period – the sciences and the colonial project of empire – among the working classes, it covered subjects ranging from air pumps and the 'ancient inhabitants' of the United States to bedchamber bolts and the effects of the imagination.[12] An equally eclectic mix of topics, yet with less emphasis on technology and more on what can be called 'culture', was present in the *Penny Magazine*, also issued weekly from 1832.[13] Both these magazines were part of a general trend in publication from the 1820s onwards, which saw whole publishing houses specialize in cheap educational literature. *Lardner's Cabinet Cyclopædia*, for instance, included treatises on optics, mechanics and chemistry, but also statistical surveys on the production and trade of silk and porcelain.[14] The Society for the Diffusion of Useful Knowledge, also responsible for the *Penny Magazine*, published biweekly titles in its *Library of Useful Knowledge*. The readers of journals and magazines were thus joined by those of surveys and textbooks targeting

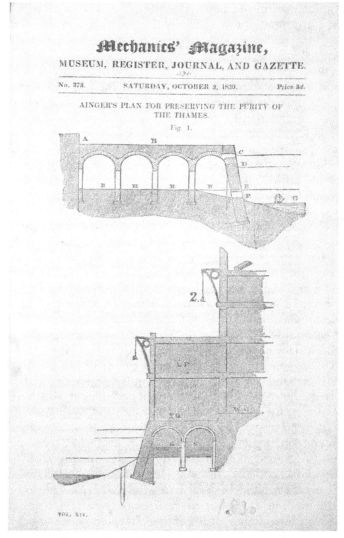

FIGURE 7.2 *Title page of* Mechanics' Magazine, *2 October (1830). Private collection.*

previously excluded groups, such as tradesmen, workers, or women. Generally, one can attest in this period not only to a 'second print revolution', as publication historians have done, but also an explosion of campaigns for educational improvement among the working and middle classes.[15]

The success of such publications was not always a given, but those that did sell often sold very well. The *Mechanics' Magazine* reached a circulation of about 16,000 copies per issue, while the *Penny Magazine* topped an unprecedented print run of 100,000. Both the specialized and the general-interest title thus maintained a very respectable readership, especially considering the sharing of copies in both private contexts as well as in libraries and coffeehouses. In comparison, the more highbrow *Athenaeum* sold only between 500 and 1,000 weekly copies in 1830, while *The Times* issued just under 6,000 copies daily.[16] While the *Athenaeum* had a more literary tone, both the *Penny* and the *Mechanics'* magazines were explicitly of an instructive nature, exploiting advances in diagrammatic representations of complex objects and processes. The image of the object had an instructional role in the acquisition of technical literacy at the same time as marketing new products. It is in this sense, of what Brian Maidment has called 'the new market-driven, commodity visual culture of the 1820s and 1830s', that building/object relationships in the *Architectural Magazine* must be examined.[17]

Even if Loudon was aware of earlier architectural journals and often quoted from German, French and other European sources, his own magazines were much closer to publications such as the *Mechanics' Magazine* and the *Penny Magazine*. He employed both the instructive tone of these magazines as well as an emphasis on using illustrations whenever he had them available (and the funds to print them). He also kept to their cheap pricing – monthly issues of the *Architectural Magazine* cost 2 pence – and their format – a slim octavo. In comparison, Loudon's *Encyclopaedia of Cottage, Farm and Villa Architecture* was sold at £3 3s, an impossible price for London bricklayers with a daily income of about 5 shilling per day or a labourer earning just over half as much.[18] Even if books were often sold in cheaper instalments, when aiming at the working classes the advantage of a magazine becomes immediately apparent. This was valid not only in terms of affordability, but also of content: a magazine did not need a stringent order, a plot with a beginning and an end. Instead, it took both the form of a storehouse of miscellanea (a magazine, literally) and of a conversation, through its seriality; a place of exchange characterized by a diversity of voices, rather than a monolithic organ. A magazine could be coherent while including a wide variety of subjects, objects of different scale, theories and histories, as well as very technical articles, promoting Loudon's project of equal access to taste and judgement. In short, it was much better suited to the 'architectural' as a non-hierarchical space of buildings and objects.

## (Un)architectural objects

The title vignette of the *Architectural Magazine*, drawn by one of its most frequent contributors, the architect Edward Buckton Lamb, described the wide range of contents which Loudon intended to include as a list of practices: architecture, building, furnishing, ironmongery, cabinet making, joinery, carpentry, and so on. These linked not only to the subjects covered but also to the magazine's readers. Any one of the implied practitioners – the architect, the builder, the ironmonger, the cabinet maker, the joiner, the carpenter, up to the road maker and engineer – would find material of direct interest and benefit from all the rest too. As this list implied, the 'objects' discussed in the *Architectural Magazine* varied widely, besides architecture, and readers found articles on what we would now call interior decoration as well as furniture, ornaments, inventions and machines, tools, and much else. More often than not, such matter was addressed both to the artisan or mechanic who would execute it, as well as the architect. As one author of an article on 'Advantages of Painting and Papering the Walls of Apartments' wrote,

> One step towards the improvement of any trade or profession is, to disseminate a proper knowledge of it … for, when this point is accomplished, such a trade or profession is more likely to become a general topic of conversation, and, when improvements are made, they will thereby have a better chance of being understood and appreciated.[19]

Essentially, the magazine hoped to trigger a gathering 'conversation' in print. By exposing more and more readers to a discourse about design, Loudon hoped to raise both the quality of the discourse as well as that of its designed outcome, whether building or object. In the following, I examine four objects, presented in the magazine's pages in turn by a surveyor, an architect, a builder and an inventor, to explore both their relationship to the building as well as, more widely, the concept of the 'architectural' in the *Magazine*.

In February 1838, a somewhat regular contributor, 'W.S.', elsewhere attributed as being a surveyor, published a description of a simple, yet ingenious device: 'A Temporary Table, Or Ironing-Board, for Small Country Cottages' (see Figure 7.3).[20] The article, a little more than half a page, was accompanied by an axonometric drawing showing how the temporary table, or ironing board, doubled as a window shutter. Text and image here were closely aligned, with the text describing the contraption in some detail so that it could be easily replicated. While simple, this utilitarian piece of furniture demonstrated the fluidity between 'architecture' and 'design'. It turned the building itself into a piece of furniture, and vice versa, blurring the lines between building and object. In the end, both are united through utility and the intent to better the human condition.

In the previous issue, Edward Buckton Lamb had contributed a piece entitled 'On Furniture'. Lamb was in equal measure architect, draftsman and author, publishing almost as frequently as Loudon himself. In this article, he discussed the difficulties that arose from applying similar paradigms to both architectural and furniture design, to building and object. Lamenting 'the want of some knowledge of the styles and details of architecture by upholsterers', he pointed to 'many absurdities which we frequently discover in ornamental furniture'. His criticism was not limited to the artisan, however; architects themselves, he argued, too often looked on furniture design as 'derogatory to the art'. To counter this, Lamb called on both architects and

ART. VII. *A temporary Table, or Ironing-Board, for small country Cottages.* By W. S.

It is a matter of some little difficulty, in small cottages for the labouring classes in the country, to place the shutters to the windows on the ground floor in such a manner as to answer the purpose, and yet be out of the way. The following plan I have adopted in some buildings of that description which have been lately erected under my superintendence.

The shutters in *fig.* 29. are hung on hinges in such a manner as to fall down into a recess below the window during the daytime; and, consequently, are quite out of the way when not wanted for shutting up the house, or for the purposes hereafter described. The idea suggested itself to me, that shutters might be occasionally used as a temporary table or ironing-board; and, to effect this end, two moveable bars, as supports, were let into mortises in the floor, and made to abut against similar mortises made in the ledges on the under side of the shutters. The two cornices were slightly rounded, and the upper surface was left plain, without paint. Two swing iron or wood brackets might be used instead of the two wooden bars, as they could be folded back into the recess also.

London, Oct. 1837.

FIGURE 7.3 'A Temporary Table, Or Ironing-Board, for Small Country Cottages', Architectural Magazine, *February (1838)*. Hathi Trust.

artisans to strive for three paradigms when designing furniture: 'usefulness and comfort' first, then 'beauty of proportion', and finally 'unity with surrounding objects'. Furniture and the design of the room it was placed in had to be in harmony to entirely 'satisfy the mind'. A 'union' between object and building, Lamb demanded, could only be achieved by 'the propriety and fitness of the minor details'. It was not a matter of simply attaching decorative columns and cornices to any piece of furnishing, clearly more thorough knowledge of underlying ideas of harmony and decorum was necessary.[21]

Lamb explained these difficulties by presenting his own design for an upright piano, solving what he characterized as the 'very unarchitectural character' of the grand piano.[22] Why 'unarchitectural'? It was the form 'prescribed by its uses' and the considerable size of the instrument which

FIGURE 7.4 *Lamb's design of a piano*, Architectural Magazine, *January (1838)*. Hathi Trust.

preoccupied Lamb. His solution essentially stripped the instrument of its recognizable appearance, turning the mechanism and strings not only upright (from horizontal in the grand piano), as had been devised as recently as 1826 by Robert Wornum in London, but also downwards, in order to keep the space above the keyboard free for a singing voice to spread easily – or perhaps more to hide its original form.[23] In the illustration (see Figure 7.4), we find an object perhaps more akin to a mantelpiece, complete with vases on pedestals flanking a framed painting or mirror above. The only distinctions are a closed console, containing the keyboard (but rather short-looking), two pedals (awkwardly hovering at its bottom edge without a clear connection to the inside of the instrument) and a stool placed in front. No columns are applied anywhere; instead the mantelpiece-turned-piano is treated as part of the wall, with panels and decorative inlays and a hint of a cornice from which the keyboard projects. Although a lot more carefully designed than the ironing table by 'W.S.', the object here is equally made 'architectural'. While the ironing board emphasized its utility through its plainness, both it and Lamb's piano were multifunctional, disguising one potential use (shutter or instrument) while being employed for another (table or mantelpiece). At the same time, neither building nor object are sovereign, physically attached to each other, conditioning each other's appearance and use, united by an 'architectural' character.

As utility, beauty and context were crucial to the design of building and object, so were the technologies and materials dominant at the time. It was in the latter that the most obvious change occurred in the course of the Industrial Revolution during the late eighteenth and early nineteenth centuries, discussed at length in the *Magazine*. An article in the very first issue in March 1834, signed by 'Mr. William Rose, Builder', proposed slate to replace marble in the furniture for 'the middling classes and the poor'; tabletops could be made out of slate 'with or without margins of wood, or, in some cases, of cast iron or copper ... or even zinc' and supports 'might be cast iron bronzed'. As with many other

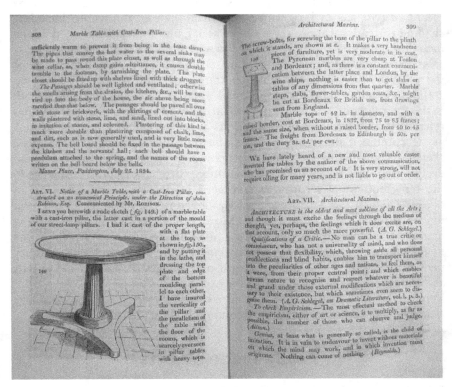

**FIGURE 7.5** 'Marble Table, with a Cast-Iron Pillar, Constructed on an Economical Principle', Architectural Magazine, October (1834). Private collection.

articles, Rose gave the cost for such a table (slate 15s, joiners work 2l, painting 12s, plus 20 per cent as these were, he adds, 'trade prices'), concluding that, in the end, 'you have... a very cheap, durable, and, as I think, handsome sideboard'. As was his habit, Loudon added a comment to the article applauding Rose's proposal as both practical, thus useful, and handsome, thus pleasant.[24]

A very similar design was presented in the *Magazine* again just a few months later, in October 1834, by John Robison, a Scottish inventor and scientific administrator. He became a regular contributor and later published proposals for other inventions, such as a lamp post which included a water fountain for dogs or a heating and ventilation system for public buildings.[25] His 'Marble Table, with a Cast-Iron Pillar, Constructed on an Economical Principle' (Figure 7.5) was praised for its reproducibility, its appearance, as well as, so the title indicated, its economy: 'It makes a very handsome piece of furniture, yet is very moderate in its cost.'[26] Going as far as including prices for marble in France as well as the cost for freight from there to Edinburgh, the article reinforced the fundamental categories of judgement: utility, economy and aesthetics. In the *Architectural Magazine*, both building and object had to adhere to this paradigmatic triad, again blurring distinctions between the two categories.

As with Rose's slate table, Robison's marble table was presented by means of two sets of images: a perspective view of the whole, including shading to render it more three-dimensional, and a diagrammatic drawing including letters indicating specific parts with the accompanying text serving as an extended legend, noting that 'the screw-bolts, for screwing the base of the pillar to the plinth on which it stands, are shown at *a*'.[27] This was common practice in books and journals and one perfected by Loudon both in the *Encyclopaedia* as well as in his *Gardener's Magazine*. Sarah Dewis has referred to Loudon's use of illustrations as an 'epistemology of the image', as he combined diagrams, such as the one by Robison, with pictures, sketches, vignettes, maps, plans, or other image types, training his readers in deciphering their meaning.[28] In this context, there is very little difference in the representational techniques employed in depicting a building or an object. The fact that such emphasis was given to the image in its different modes was, however, remarkable. More expensive and more highbrow literary magazines often purposefully avoided including more than one image on the title page. As Dewis has remarked, in early nineteenth-century periodicals 'written text was privileged over images because of the latter's associations with the less literate culture of the poor, women and children'.[29] Loudon included images both to render complex matters clearer as well as to provide an inclusive space for object and buildings to mingle.

## Ready-made objects

Evidently, reproducibility played an increasing role in many aspects of design over the first decades of the nineteenth century. One much discussed, and applied, material was artificial stone, and Loudon was a particular proponent of it. Already in the *Encyclopaedia* as well as *Gardener's Magazine*, he had drawn his readers' attention to the products of Austin & Seeley, one of the leaders in the field of architectural and garden ornaments supplying everyone from the suburban middle classes to Queen Victoria herself. The company kept a show yard on what is now Euston Road, referred to by Loudon as 'Mr. Austin's very interesting museum'.[30] Loudon's use of the term museum presents the commercial space of the sales shop as a collection with scientific, artistic and cultural aspirations. Without the concern for truth in materiality, which would later concern the Arts and Crafts movement, Loudon regarded artificial stone as a tool in his project of widening access to the cultural good of decorations and ornaments.

Austin & Seeley's products were the subject of repeated articles in the *Architectural Magazine* and their designs are found in advertisements across the contemporary press, from the *Morning Chronicle* to the *Civil Engineer and Architect's Journal*. In October 1834, Loudon declared that the demand for artificial stone as well as its durability was now unquestioned, yet what

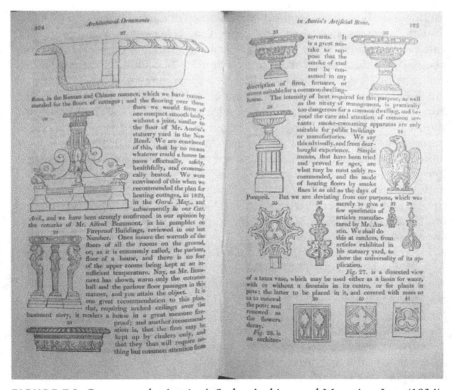

**FIGURE 7.6** *Ornaments by Austin & Seeley,* Architectural Magazine, *June (1834). Private collection.*

'appears to be wanting is, to make known generally to architects, and to amateurs of architecture and garden scenery, what can be effected in this material, at a price . . . extremely moderate when compared with that of real stone'.[31] Ornaments such as those reproduced on the pages of the *Architectural Magazine* (Figure 7.6) could do for outdoor decoration, both as parts of buildings as well as in gardens and parks, what Lamb had done for the piano (even if Lamb might not have agreed with this).

Harmony, in this sense, was however not equivalent to homogeneity. Influenced not least by ideas of the Picturesque as developed by Price and Knight, Loudon fervently argued for greater variety and less regularity, extending this to the design of the new suburbs.[32] This was not the same kind of variety that Ruskin would, just over a decade later, seek in *The Stones of Venice* (1851). Ruskin, with a focus on the distinct contribution by the individual worker, contested variety, or 'changefulness', as one of the 'characteristics or moral elements' of the Gothic, praising 'that strange *disquietude* of the Gothic spirit that is its greatness'.[33] In direct opposition, the variety that Loudon hoped to encourage by promoting artificial stone ignored any such concerns of artistic individuality. Instead, he pointed to the mix-and-match possibilities of the ornaments available in Austin's catalogues. Thus, the mass-produced chimney pot could be used in a variety of ways: perhaps as a 'shaft of a sundial', as a 'pedestal to an ornamental vase', or 'as a support for a . . . stone basin to contain gold-fish or a curious plant' – even for a 'baptismal font in a church'.[34] Loudon also alluded to the circumstance that chimney shafts, in their original use, were ideally of different patterns in the same stack, following historical precedent. Previously, this made them very expensive.[35] Now, house builders could choose from a variety of types of ready-made elements, creating a picturesque impression without spending more on variety than they would on uniformity.[36] Crucially, Loudon gave not only the seal of aesthetic approval to one of the chimney stacks, describing it as 'handsome', but also that of usefulness, pointing to features increasing the chimney's efficiency to expel smoke and thus ascribing it with the 'double purpose of ornament and utility'. Again, the triad of utility, economy and aesthetics sealed Loudon's approval.

Interestingly, variety in the object is here provided by means of universality. As with a set of building blocks, Loudon wrote, 'Mr. Austin can compose a great many different kinds of . . . [ornaments] out of a given number of what may be called elementary parts'.[37] If different parts could be arranged to form different wholes, he argued, this 'contributes . . . both to variety and cheapness'.[38] Tazza vases, pedestals, eagles, Gothic ornaments – all demonstrated a 'universality of . . . application', not only in terms of the materiality of the cast stone itself, mouldable as it was to most shapes and forms, but also regarding the finished ornament-object. Its universality implied that it did not quite matter which one was chosen and where it was placed – the key being that it was there.[39] Being universal in application indicated both an increase of its reproducibility – the same ornament could be used in a multitude of situations – as well as its commodification. While this increased visual variety – which, in Loudon's mind, would improve many suburban homes – it would ultimately be precisely what Ruskin revolted against: the loss of individual expression in the ready-made, stripped of the link to the worker.[40] If Ruskin looked for variety in parts to unite into a truly whole work of art – the building – Loudon regarded the parts as single, replaceable objects, to be arranged in myriad ways with much less concern for the concept of an artistic whole.

Loudon was confident in the success of his mission, writing that if the *Magazine*'s promotion would lead to 'only one or two' of Austin & Seeley's ornaments being placed 'in the gardens of those long rows of houses lining the New Road, the Kent Road and other suburban roads, we shall be satisfied with the beginning'.[41] Increasing variety was his way to instil a basic awareness for the aesthetically pleasing in design among builders and house owners. Every reader counted, as did every improved building, every ornament and every piece of furniture. There is a focus here on atomized parts, whether ornaments or people, rather than the spirit that lies in the whole of a work or art, or in the genius of the artist.

At times, Loudon seemed rather unconcerned with the quality of the ornament itself, going as far as proposing that there was merit simply in the circumstance of more people engaging with the 'advancement of the decorative part of architecture'.[42] While the chimney pots and shafts are for the most part 'handsome', 'elegant' and 'look remarkably well',[43] he was, however, critical of stylistic clashes in some of them. He admitted that many of Austin's products constituted 'a compound of forms, some of them of the Grecian class, and others belonging to Gothic architecture'. But, he contests, the object in question 'is not introduced here on account of its beauty, but as aiding to form a variety'.[44] Ready-made architectural decoration is multifunctional, multi-style and combinable in endless variations. In the end, Loudon added a disclaimer: 'we are not responsible for the taste displayed in them' (that is, in Austin's products).[45] His aesthetic, then, is one of pragmatism: better to engage as great a number of people as possible in matters of aesthetic appreciation rather than being limited to an elite by using words and objects that would be impenetrable to the many. By judging both object and building according to their utility, economy and aesthetics (often in this order), Loudon stood at a turning point in British architectural discourse: his pragmatism would not last, at least not in the world of print. The *Builder*, often posited as successor to the *Architectural Magazine*, at first followed in its tracks, addressing in its subtitle anyone in the *Drawing Room, the Studio, the Office, the Workshop, and the Cottage*, so matching Loudon's intended audience. But by the fourth volume and under different editorship, the *Builder* changed tactic, now focusing on the *Architect, Engineer, Operative and Artist*, targeting the professional elite rather than the populace at large.[46] For the magazine format, the architect and building won, the public and the object lost. This would only shift again with the Arts and Crafts movement later in the century and then with a renewed, and fervent, link established between the craftsperson and the work of art.

## Building and object in the *Magazine*

As historians, we now mark the *Architectural Magazine* as the first of a new genre, one that is strong still today. Yet, Loudon himself did not once remark on such novelty (which is noteworthy in a period obsessed with novelty). For him, this was not an architectural magazine for architects, or even for architectural circles, including critics and other stakeholders, but excluding workers, artisans and the wider public. Instead, it was a magazine, a storehouse, for useful knowledge on forms and lines, of objects and buildings, for making space and making place, and for conversations and debates about all of this. For him, the magazine was a natural continuation of the encyclopaedia, and thus of the existing field of educational literature generally. Architects, ladies and amateurs, as well as masons, cabinetmakers and ironmongers should know about 'the Elements and Principles of Gothic Architecture', but also about 'a simple and effective Preventive for the Slamming of a Passage Door' or 'Dovetailed Caps for Wooden Fences', all of which were discussed in the first year of the *Magazine*. Beyond this, however, the *Architectural Magazine* was, for Loudon, also one thing: a means to earn a living, and to pay for his more costly undertakings, such as the *Arboretum*. Addressing a wide readership was simultaneously a marketing strategy to sell more issues as well as an expression of his belief in equity between architect and mechanic. It is likely that the latter was, in the short term, more successful than the former.

There is little difference indicated in the *Magazine* between the building and the object – and indeed also between the one-off design and the ready-made, mass-produced design. Loudon provided what was, at times, a simplified, intellectual reasoning to place building and object into one discursive space. He commented and explained and critiqued, but the latter was not the main purpose of his endeavours. He was concerned with exposure to and dissemination among as many readers as possible, but he was not working on behalf of any one group. His aim was neither the furthering of an elite high culture nor the advancement of or increase in business for the architectural profession.

I have argued elsewhere that the *Architectural Magazine* is evidence for a short-lived democratization of architectural production and reception, an episode that receded with increasing professionalization and the rise of the much more 'architectural' type of magazine, in the form of the *Builder* (from 1843) or, later, the *Architectural Review* (from 1896), both of which are still published today.[47] In Loudon's *Magazine*, the 'architectural' stood not for the building, nor for the remit of the architect, and least of all did it signify exclusivity. Instead, it provided a non-hierarchical collection of objects and buildings, copies and originals, more akin to a *Wunderkammer* than to the modern museum.

## Notes

1  While Loudon's magazine was the first of its kind in the English language, there had been periodicals on architectural matters in both the German states as well as in France as early as in the 1780s. See Anne Hultzsch, 'Sharing Knowledge, Promoting the Built: The Origins of the Architectural Magazine in Nineteenth-Century Europe', *The Journal of Architecture* 25, no. 7 (2 October 2020): 799–808, https://doi.org/10.1080/13602365.2020.1841940. For an overview of the development of the early architectural magazine, see also Marc Saboya, *Presse et Architecture Au XIXe Siècle: César Daly et La Revue Générale de l'architecture et Des Travaux Publics* (Paris: Picard, 1991); and Rolf Fuhlrott, *Deutschsprachige Architektur-Zeitschriften: Entstehung und Entwicklung der Fachzeitschriften für Architektur in der Zeit von 1789–1918* (Munich: Verlag Dokumentation, 1975).

2  See Sarah Dewis, *The Loudons and the Gardening Press: A Victorian Cultural Industry* (Aldershot: Ashgate, 2014). For the relationship between encyclopaedia and the magazine, see Anne Hultzsch, 'From Encyclopaedia to Magazine: The Loudons, the Public, and the Architect in 1830s Britain', *The Journal of Architecture* 25, no. 7 (2 October 2020): 844–72, https://doi.org/10.1080/13602365.2020.1833962.

3  For Webb Loudon's role, see Chapter 6 in Dewis, *The Loudons and the Gardening Press*; as well as Bea Howe, *Lady with Green Fingers: The Life of Jane Loudon* (London: Country Life, 1961).

4  See Isobel Armstrong, *Victorian Glassworlds: Glass Culture and the Imagination 1830–1880* (Oxford: Oxford University Press, 2008), 170.

5  While remarkable, this was not meant to encourage women to actually become architects. Rather, they were encouraged to take a share in improving homes, as homemakers, clients and patrons, given adequate education and knowledge. In this sense, it is another demonstration of the unspecific and inclusive concept of the architectural world, rather than a call for wider access to the architectural profession. See John C. Loudon, 'Introduction', *The Architectural Magazine* 1 (March 1834): 4.

6  Richard Wittman, *Architecture, Print Culture and the Public Sphere* (Aldershot: Ashgate, 2007).

7  For the dynamics between print and architecture in the nineteenth century, see Mari Hvattum and Anne Hultzsch, eds., *The Printed and the Built: Architecture, Print Culture, and Public Debate in the Nineteenth Century* (London: Bloomsbury, 2018). For the evolving tensions between words, images, and buildings, see Anne Hultzsch, '"To the Great Public": The Architectural Image in the Early *Illustrated London News*', *Architectural Histories* 5, no. 1 (28 December 2017), https://doi.org/10.5334/ah.268.

8   See Patricia J. Anderson, *The Printed Image and the Transformation of Popular Culture, 1790–1860* (Oxford: Clarendon Press, 1991), 192.

9   Loudon, 'Introduction', 4.

10  For other attempts, such as John Blyth's plans for reforming the Royal Academy, C.R. Cockerell's Government Schools for Design, or George Godwin's ideas for a new university curriculum, see J. Mordaunt Crook, 'The Pre-Victorian Architect: Professionalism & Patronage', *Architectural History* 12 (1969): 62–78, https://doi.org/10.2307/1568337. For Joseph Hansom's Grand National Guild of Builders (1833) and Alfred Bartholomew's National Architectural College (1831), see Mark Crinson and Jules Lubbock, *Architecture – Art or Profession? Three Hundred Years of Architectural Education in Britain* (Manchester: Manchester University Press, 1994), 52–3.

11  Loudon, 'Introduction', 11.

12  *Mechanics' Magazine, Museum, Register, Journal, and Gazette*, vol. 9 (London: Knight & Lacey, 1828), 193, 279, 364, and 15, and 344, 428, and 16.

13  Barry Bergdoll rightly argues that the *Penny Magazine* should occupy a more important role in the historiography of early nineteenth-century British architecture. See Barry Bergdoll, '"The Public Square of the Modern Age": Architecture and the Rise of the Illustrated Press in the Early Nineteenth Century', in *The Printed and the Built: Architecture, Print Culture, and Public Debate in the Nineteenth Century*, ed. Mari Hvattum and Anne Hultzsch (London: Bloomsbury, 2018), 27–49.

14  Dionysius Lardner, *Catalogue of the Cabinet Cyclopædia* (London: Longman, Rees, Orme, Brown, Green & Longman, 1835).

15  See Anderson, *The Printed Image and the Transformation of Popular Culture*. On the expansion of popular education, see Jon Klancher, *Transfiguring the Arts and Sciences: Knowledge and Cultural Institutions in the Romantic Age* (Cambridge and New York: Cambridge University Press, 2013).

16  Unless otherwise stated, all figures quoted here on print runs are taken from Richard D. Altick, *The English Common Reader: A Social History of the Mass Reading Public, 1800–1900* (Ohio State University Press, 1998), 393–5.

17  Brian Maidment, 'Scraps and Sketches: Miscellaneity, Commodity Culture and Comic Prints, 1820–40', *19: Interdisciplinary Studies in the Long Nineteenth Century* 0, no. 5 (10 January 2007): 15, https://doi.org/10.16995/ntn.462. For a veritable 'commerce of images', in which plates and blocks were sold and reused in several publications across national borders, see Paul Jobling and David Crowley, *Graphic Design: Reproduction and Representation Since 1800* (Manchester: Manchester University Press, 1996), 25; and Thomas Smits, *The European Illustrated Press and the Emergence of a Transnational Visual Culture of the News, 1842–1870* (London: Routledge, 2020).

18  See A. L. Bowley, *Wages in the United Kingdom in the Nineteenth Century* (Cambridge: Cambridge University Press, 1900), 83.

19  D. R. Hay, 'On the Comparative Advantages of Painting and Papering the Walls of Apartments in Dwelling-Houses', *Architectural Magazine* 2, no. 18 (August 1835): 363.

20  S. W., 'A Temporary Table, Or Ironing-Board, for Small Country Cottages', *Architectural Magazine* 5, no. 28 (February 1838): 75.
21  Edward B. Lamb, 'On Furniture', *Architectural Magazine* 5, no. 47 (January 1838): 27–8.
22  Lamb, 'On Furniture', 27.
23  For development of the upright piano, see Robert Palmieri, ed., *Piano: An Encyclopedia*, 2nd ed. (New York: Routledge, 2003).
24  W. Rose, 'On the Use of Slate and Cast Iron in Household Furniture', *Architectural Magazine* 1, no. 1 (March 1834): 41–42.
25  John Robison, 'Modes of Warming and Ventilating Public and Other Buildings', *Architectural Magazine* 4 (July 1837): 326.
26  John Robison, 'Notice of a Marble Table, with a Cast-Iron Pillar, Constructed on an Economical Principle, Under the Direction of John Robison, Esq.', *Architectural Magazine* 1, no. 8 (October 1834): 308–9.
27  Ibid.
28  Dewis, *The Loudons and the Gardening Press*, 81.
29  Ibid.
30  John Loudon, 'Notice of Some Designs for Architectural Fountains, Manufactured in Artificial Stone by Mr. Austin of London', *Architectural Magazine* 1, no. 8 (October 1834): 295–302. Loudon explicitly encouraged 'all architects and architectural amateurs' to visit Austin's premises quite like a museum or exhibition, not only to shop. John Loudon, 'Notice of Some of the Ornamental Chimney Pots and Shafts Manufactured of Artificial Stone by Mr. Austin of London', *Architectural Magazine* 1, no. 4 (June 1834): 160.
31  Loudon, 'Notice of Some Designs for Architectural Fountains'.
32  See Melanie L. Simo, *Loudon and the Landscape: From Country Seat to Metropolis, 1783–1843* (New Haven, London: Yale University Press, 1989), 171–5.
33  John Ruskin, *The Stones of Venice, Volume II. The Works of John Ruskin, Library Edition*, ed. E. T. Cook and Alexander Wedderburn, vol. 10 (London: George Allen, 1904), 184, 214.
34  Loudon, 'Notice of Some of the Ornamental Chimney Pots and Shafts Manufactured of Artificial Stone by Mr. Austin of London'.
35  Ibid.
36  Ibid.
37  Loudon, 'Notice of Some Designs for Architectural Fountains, Manufactured in Artificial Stone by Mr. Austin of London'.
38  Ibid.
39  John Loudon, 'Notice of Architectural Ornaments Manufactured in Artificial Stone by Mr. Austin', *Architectural Magazine* 2, no. 13 (March 1835): 123–6.
40  Ruskin, unsurprisingly, was strictly against the use of artificial stone (or cast iron) arguing that all natural stone had to be carved. John Ruskin, *The Seven Lamps of Architecture. The Works of John Ruskin, Library Edition*, ed. E. T. Cook and Alexander Wedderburn, vol. 7 (London: George Allen, 1903), 85.

41 Loudon, 'Notice of Some Designs for Architectural Fountains'.
42 Loudon, 'Notice of Some of the Ornamental Chimney Pots and Shafts Manufactured of Artificial Stone by Mr. Austin of London'.
43 Ibid.
44 Ibid.
45 Ibid.
46 See Michael Brooks, '"*The Builder*" in the 1840s: The Making of a Magazine, the Shaping of a Profession', *Victorian Periodicals Review* 14, no. 3 (1 October 1981): 86–93.
47 Hultzsch, 'From Encyclopaedia to Magazine' *The Builder* was later renamed *Building*.

# CHAPTER EIGHT

# Entangled Histories of Buildings and Furniture:

# Knoll International and the Production and Mediation of Modern Architecture in Post-war Belgium

*Fredie Floré*

Furniture design is, quite obviously, a well-established branch of object design. At the same time, it is still considered by many to be a sub-discipline of architecture – seen especially by architects as a means of extending their authorship. There are countless examples of architects who designed furniture to match their building projects. The topic of architect-designers was addressed in the exhibition, *From Aalto to Zumthor: Furniture by Architects*, held at the Museum für Angewandte Kunst Köln in 2012. Reflecting on the contemporary situation, the curator, Gabrielle Lueg states: 'for architects, design has now also become an image factor and vehicle for increasing media presence. In reverse, a number of designers aspire to play a part in the world of architecture, which is somewhat higher up in the hierarchy.'[1] While they may seem self-evident, this citation contains two observations on recent architecture and design practices that are worth taking note of. On the one hand, many architects are interested in (furniture) design as part of their self-representation or image building. On the other hand, a significant number of (furniture) designers – and I would add design companies – aspire to enter the realm of architecture. These tendencies, which are closely related to how we perceive, mediate and consume buildings and objects, are, of course, not entirely new. This chapter sets out to illustrate, discuss and relate similar mechanisms within the world of architecture and design in the 1950s and 1960s, a key period in the rise of Western consumer society, and, as this chapter suggests, in the evolving position of furniture in relation to architecture. It focuses on how the production and mediation of modern architecture in Belgium was impacted by the arrival of the United States-based furniture brand Knoll on the Belgian market. Comparable to other episodes of the twentieth and twenty-first centuries, in the 1950s and 1960s several Belgian architects explored furniture design as part of their practice, but, as this chapter shows, many of them and/or their clients also integrated existing products, in particular Knoll products, in the visuals of their architectural projects. In some cases, these objects, including designs by Eero Saarinen, Harry Bertoia and Ludwig Mies van der Rohe produced by Knoll, became an integral part of the visual and spatial language of a building interior. It must be kept in mind that the integration of furniture elements available on the market as valuable ingredients of the expression of modern architecture was not uncommon at the time. As architectural historian Alina Payne explains, such practices had gained self-consciousness with the arrival of architectural modernism, as the eloquence of architectural ornamentation was taken over by objects of daily use.[2] However, in the 1950s and 1960s, the range of available objects to choose from markedly diversified and increased. Moreover, furniture designers and manufacturers like Knoll, stimulated by post-war political and economic developments, saw an opportunity to invade the global world of architecture. As the Belgian case illustrates, this sometimes significantly impacted the visual expression of local productions of modern architecture.

Combining architectural history and design history perspectives, this chapter argues that the prominent presence of Knoll in the visual representation of modern architecture in Belgium did not happen by accident. It was part of the policy of Knoll International – the legal entity, established in 1951, which oversaw the overseas licensing of the manufacture and sale of its products – to actively approach networks of modern architects as a way to quickly integrate within local cultural scenes. This in turn was stimulated by the general context of post-war reconstruction and the subsequent Cold War. The Marshall Plan aid programme had provided the necessary financial basis for the European expansion of Knoll and the company directly profited from the post-war cultural propaganda campaign orchestrated by the US State Department. By integrating Knoll products in their work, Belgian architects and/or their clients contributed to the visibility of the US brand, but also used it as a means to underline the modern or international character of their projects and to consciously link them with the progressive aesthetic language Knoll was exporting and cultivating around the world. While Knoll strategically sought connections with local modernist scenes, architects also aspired to be associated with the world of Knoll.[3] As such, the disciplinary hierarchy between the world of architecture and that of design, as referenced by Lueg, was in this case far less evident or perhaps even non-existent.

## Post-war architecture in Belgium and the arrival of Knoll

Several architects working in post-war Belgium experimented with furniture design as part of their practice. An important driver for explorations in the 1950s was dissatisfaction with what the contemporary Belgian market had to offer by way of affordable home furnishings. Willy Van Der Meeren (1923–2002), one of the architects frustrated by the situation, responded by designing tubular furniture, which was produced by the Belgian Tubax company. Architectural historian Mil De Kooning explains that Van Der Meeren designed furniture much as he designed architecture, focusing on rational conception, affordability and exploiting the possibilities offered by industrial production.[4] In published photographs, his architectural work is often combined with his furniture designs – the chairs, tables, cupboards and lamps carefully positioned to form an integrated yet flexible and adjustable whole. A telling example is that of the European Coal and Steel Community (ECSC) house, a minimum prefabricated workman's dwelling, which Van Der Meeren designed along with his colleague Léon Palm in 1954 (Figure 8.1).

The house referred to the ECSC, which was established two years earlier to create a common market for coal and steel and, among other things, promoted the use of steel in housing for miners and steelworkers. Van Der Meeren and Palm's ECSC house was presented in full scale at the international Annual Fairs in Liège and Charleroi in 1954.[5] The living room most prominently featured the F1 armchair and several boomerang tables designed by the architect. Through these and other furniture designs Van Der Meeren became one of the protagonists of what has been termed the post-war movement for 'modern social furniture' in Belgium, with the term 'social' directly referring to affordability.[6] Like the ECSC house, the Tubax furniture promoted the use of steel and shared the same formal and structural language of the architecture.

As the European economy gradually liberalized and more furniture with a contemporary look became available in the 1950s, other examples of post-war modern architecture in Belgium – often less connected with the pressing housing problems of that time – were photographed and displayed with carefully selected furniture available on the market. A remarkable newcomer in that respect was Knoll. The company's productions became available in

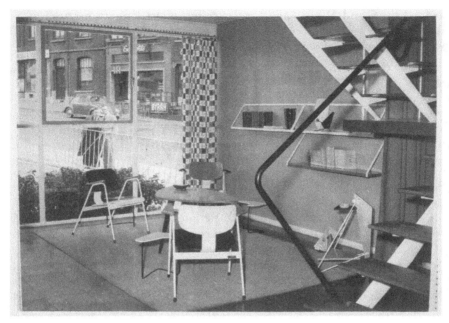

FIGURE 8.1 Architects Willy Van Der Meeren and Léon Palm, ECSC house with Tubax furniture designed by Van Der Meeren, International Annual Fair, Charleroi (1954). Unknown photographer. Courtesy of WVDM Archives/coll. A&D 50, Mechelen.

Belgium from 1954 onwards as the result of a production and sales contract between the renowned Flemish family business De Coene and the US firm.[7] It was one of many overseas licensee contracts Knoll International entered into in the post-war decades. The company also established subsidiaries; the doors of the first two European showrooms opened in Paris and Stuttgart in 1951.[8] By the end of the decade, rapid growth of the company's international arm led to more subsidiaries, licences and factories as well as showrooms in cities on every continent. One of the key selling points was that Knoll's furniture provided an appropriate response to modern life and the aesthetics of modern architecture, in particular the new office buildings and middle- to upper-class housing projects emerging in many different parts of the world. Furniture was staged as a professional partner in the creation and communication of a contemporary spatial setting.

Knoll's global expansion was politically charged and directly linked to strategies aimed at promoting and exporting the US example. After all, the company's move into Europe had been motivated by the US State Department's plans to use blocked European assets for war reparation and the rebuilding of local economies. In 1951, Hans Knoll, founder and president of the New York-based Knoll Associates, negotiated a large contract for furniture for US

State Department employee housing in Europe.[9] As architectural historian Greg Castillo points out, 'Knoll was the perfect Marshall Plan partner: a charismatic entrepreneur, familiar to officials in Washington through its firm's design commissions for federal office buildings, and endowed with business contacts across Europe'.[10] Knoll products were also displayed in several pro-American exhibitions that were part of US 'soft power' diplomatic efforts in West Germany.[11] They were likewise included in several editions of the 'American Design for Home and Decorative Use' exhibition, the first of which was held in 1953 in Helsinki.[12] Sponsored by the newly formed United States Information Agency (USIA), the exhibition presented over 300 US domestic commodities selected by curators of the Museum of Modern Art in New York and travelled to many other European venues, including the Casino in Ostend and the Ghent Museum of Decorative Arts in 1954.[13]

The Belgian company De Coene's decision to sign an agreement with Knoll was also informed by politics. Before the war the company was internationally known for its high-quality Art Deco furniture, but its reputation was severely damaged when its directors were convicted of economic collaboration during the Second World War. De Coene had produced barracks, emergency housing and furniture for the German military and civilian services, as well as a number of fake wooden airplanes meant to mislead the Allied Air Force. After Liberation, the company was sequestered by the government. It was not until 1952 that members of the De Coene family and their close allies were back in charge. Because in the 1950s the company still risked having its profits confiscated, Pol Provost, the new general director, decided to reinvest as much capital as possible into new technologies and in particular into developing new branches of the timber and furniture industries. At the same time, both furniture and interior design departments were reformed. This process was marked by the 1954 acquisition of the production and sale licences of Knoll furniture for the Benelux and the Belgian Congo and the opening in the same year of a Knoll showroom in Brussels. For De Coene, producing and selling this furniture signalled an important step in the modernization of its product range and in distancing itself from its wartime activities. In collaborating with a US-based company, De Coene was clearly taking the side of one of the former allied forces.

From 1954 onwards, Knoll regularly appears in Belgian architectural journals. As might be expected, the furniture prominently featured in publications on architectural projects in which De Coene was directly involved, such as the European House, a full-scale model house presented at the 1957 International Fair in Ghent, designed by architect Henri Guchez and constructed by De Coene, and the prefabricated De Coene model home at the 1958 Brussels World's Fair.[14] In a different way from Van Der Meeren's ECSC house, these houses explored the possibilities of the liberalizing European market for the production of architecture and furniture design. After all, in the 1950s De Coene not only started a collaboration with Knoll

FIGURE 8.2 *De Coene model home furnished with Knoll designs, Expo 58, Brussels (1958). Unknown photographer. Courtesy of Archive Stichting De Coene, Collection Verzameling De Coene nv., Rijksarchief Kortrijk, no. 179.*

and modernized its own furniture lines in order to strengthen their market value in relation to foreign products, it also quickly made a name for itself in the architectural construction world as a producer of wood-based building elements, industrialized building systems and prefabricated buildings, several of which were intended for local markets and export.[15] The De Coene model home at Expo 58 was clearly conceived and presented as a commodity. 'A house for you! Take your pick', the accompanying brochure was titled, proposing a series of options.[16] At the same time the house served as a spatial setting for the display of other products of the company. One of the interior views shows the living room furnished with, among others, executive chairs and a Womb chair by Eero Saarinen from the Knoll collection (Figure 8.2). Other spaces were equipped with furniture designed by De Coene collaborators and curtains made from Knoll textiles. Building and furnishings were thus staged as purchasable and reproducible products, which supported each other in expressing a modern and Western way of life.

Knoll's presence in Belgian architectural journals was not limited to projects in which De Coene was involved as the main contractor. In many cases the furniture was meant to support the modern character of the project under discussion. A telling example is that of the Brussels Résidence, designed in 1958 by the functionalist architect René Stapels (1922–2012). *Rythme*, the journal of the Société Centrale d'Architecture de Belgique (SCAB), described the project as a 'new housing formula, situated halfway between a hotel and an apartment'.[17] Located on the Avenue Louise, one of the city's most prestigious nineteenth-century boulevards, the modern apartment block was designed to provide its residents with the comfort of a hotel thanks to, among other amenities, the daily presence of housekeeping staff, a restaurant and bar on the ground floor, and an integrated radio distribution system. The private apartments in the building were rented fully furnished with Knoll furniture. Photographs in *Architecture*, the Belgian journal in which Van Der Meeren was also involved, show that the restaurant was equipped with executive chairs by Saarinen and side chairs by Harry Bertoia.[18] A Bertoia Bird armchair and ottoman and a Florence Knoll table and sofa feature prominently in photographs of the duplex apartments (Figure 8.3).

While the emphasis in the De Coene model homes was on the building as a modern industrial product, purchasable from a catalogue just like the furniture, in the case of the Brussels Résidence, the modern character of the project to a significant extent was realized through the building's programme – a contemporary variation on the typology of the US residential hotel, which was far less common in Belgium.[19] Knoll was a valuable partner in visualizing what the building could offer, particularly in terms of services, and as a stage for modern life. While the Brussels Résidence at the time was a quite experimental manifestation of modernity, many other projects, especially modern houses directed towards a middle- to upper-class clientele and new corporate buildings, were published with Knoll furnishings in the late 1950s and 1960s.[20] Overall in the Belgian architectural press Knoll furniture repeatedly appeared as a reliable ally in architectural expressions of modern living and work in a Western capitalist society.

## Building relations with the local architectural community

The appearance of Knoll in Belgian architectural journals and its arrival on the country's architectural scene was cleverly planned and subsequently managed. As was the case in France, Knoll strongly invested in building strategic relations with local designers and architects.[21] But, while in Paris emphasis was placed on finding an entry into the quite conservative world of the French bourgeoisie, Knoll International Brussels mostly focused on connecting with the local network of modernist architects and artists. Opened in 1954 on the Rue Royale 145 and managed by the new licensee De Coene, the Knoll showroom played a key role in establishing and fostering these contacts.

Florence Knoll (1917–2019), the business partner and wife of Hans Knoll, in collaboration with her Knoll Planning Unit, designed many of the company's showrooms. In a series of her designs for US showrooms, she

FIGURE 8.3 *Florence Knoll, Knoll Planning Unit, architects Marcel Breuer, Constantin Brodzki and De Coene, Knoll International Brussels showroom, Brussels (1954). Photograph by Serge Vandercam.* Bouwen en Wonen, *no. 12 (1958), 133.*

created the so-called 'Knoll look', which was characterized by, among other things, the careful positioning of iconic furniture pieces and textile samples, and the bold use of primary colours in combination with black, white and beige.[22] However, for the Brussels showroom the company chose to bring in outside designers; Marcel Breuer, who was working on the UNESCO project in Paris at the time, acted as the architect of the Brussels project, and the young Belgian-Polish modernist architect Constantin Brodzki (1924–2021) was asked to collaborate with Breuer and De Coene.[23]

Choosing Brodzki as a local partner was a well-considered move. Brodzki had studied architecture at the École nationale supérieure des arts visuels, also known as La Cambre, a progressive design school established in Brussels in 1926 by the architect Henry van de Velde. Looking back, however, Brodzki first and foremost acknowledged the importance of what he learned afterwards. Shortly after his graduation in 1948, he had travelled to the United States. Thanks to the network of his father, a Polish diplomat, he was able to work for several months as a sort of trainee in the office of Harrison & Abramovitz, which at the time was coordinating the construction of the United Nations Headquarters in New York.[24] In 1952, Brodzki started his own architectural office in Brussels. According to him, it was Hans Knoll, who, following a visit to La Librairie de l'Edition Universelle, a bookshop located on the same street, the interior of which Brodzki had designed with the decorator and artist Corneille Hannoset (1926–97), invited him to collaborate (with Breuer) on the Brussels showroom.[25] In addition to the quality of his work, Brodzki's experience at Harrison & Abramovitz, from which the Knoll Planning Unit received its first commission in 1943, must have given him the right profile to become a local Knoll partner.[26]

Brodzki also provided Knoll with a direct entry into Belgian modernist circles. He was a member of the Société Belge des Urbanistes et Architectes Modernistes (SBUAM), which was established in 1923.[27] In 1953, Brodzki was involved in an exhibition project set up by SBUAM. Along with several colleagues, he designed a SBUAM model house for the Salon de l'Enfance et de la Famille (Childhood and Family Exposition) in the Brussels Palais des Beaux Arts.[28] Already working with Hans Knoll and Breuer on the Knoll showroom in Brussels, Brodzki arranged for the model house to be furnished with Knoll products.[29] 'What really interested me on that occasion', Brodzki recalled in 2004, 'was to show the Knoll furniture, which was for the first time on display in Europe. Then, as today, it stood for the *nec plus ultra* of contemporary design.'[30]

Shortly after the exhibition in the Palais des Beaux Arts, the Knoll showroom in Brussels was inaugurated. Consistent with the company's showrooms in the United States, it was conceived as an environment where the professional design community as well as consumers could explore new ideas about modern interiors, furniture and modes of living. 'Utilizing open-plan arrangements and flexible partitioning systems, the furniture showroom provided an unencumbered landscape ideally suited to the exploration of the new directions and attitudes towards American interiors and lifestyles', design historian Margaret Maile Petty states in her article on the mid-century showroom.[31] The Brussels showroom similarly offered such an immersive environment, aimed not at a US audience but at a local network of modern architects and other clients. To ensure a good start, special attention was given to clients who had already shown interest in US architecture with a modernist idiom. Jan Saverys (1924–2017), the first manager of the Brussels showroom, remembered how he was advised by the company to collect the names and addresses of architects in the Benelux who subscribed to *Progressive Architecture* or *Architectural Forum* – US journals which at the time also regularly published showroom reports including, among others, floor plans, details of the display architecture, and descriptions of the materials, colours and lighting employed.[32] The contact details of the subscribers were meant to serve as a basis for the new showroom's network.

At the same time, alliances with the local artistic scene were fostered. While the showroom's interior design presented key features of the Knoll look and was primarily focused on the display of furniture, from the very beginning it seemed clear that room would also be made for a dialogue with the fine arts. One of Marcel Breuer's 1953 drawings of the project contains a detailed description of a photomural of his hand depicting the reclining figure of Adam from the Sistine Chapel in combination with a variety of animals, including an octopus, a goat and a cobra.[33] It remains unclear how this drawing related to Knoll, but we do know that Saverys, an artist himself, quite early on started using the Knoll showroom as an exhibition space for the work of Belgian artists, including the painter Bram Bogart (1921–2012) and the sculptor Pierre Caille (1911–96).[34] One of Saverys's former collaborators, the interior designer Jacques Vernest, remembers that the artists he invited to exhibit in the showroom often installed their work themselves. He also recalls that for one of the opening events, he, in consultation with Saverys, took the initiative to play experimental electronic music by the Belgian composers Louis de Meester (1904–87) and Lucien Goethals (1931–2006), using his own sound installation.[35] The showroom quickly became a progressive cultural hub where different design and art disciplines met and was frequented by leading personalities in the Belgian architecture, design and art scene, including the architects René Stapels, Roger Bastin, Henri Montois and Robert Courtois, the interior designers Jules Wabbes, Stéphane Jasinski and Emiel Veranneman, and other artists, among them Vic Gentils, Roger Raveel, Pol Mara and Hugo Claus.[36] Seemingly without much effort, what was in essence a commercial space also functioned as a place of high culture. While the integration of modern art in showrooms and interior design projects in the United States was a strategy that strengthened Knoll's image of cultural sophistication, in this case the showroom specifically functioned as a space for local artistic experiment, thereby underlining the brand's eagerness to connect. Knoll sought to relate with modern architects and designers in Belgium and convincingly did so by creating an attractive interdisciplinary and apparently transdisciplinary space where the worlds of architecture, furniture and art could freely meet and where the activities were not strictly monitored by the US headquarters. The showroom and the events it hosted created a buzz and no doubt helped convince many more architects that Knoll was the *summum bonum* of contemporary design and as such an excellent example to underline the modern character of a building.

## Knoll furniture as a rhetorical instrument

Through Brodzki's involvement in SBUAM and thanks to his close collaboration with Corneille Hannoset, Knoll also had a direct link with the journal *Architecture*, which was established in Brussels in 1952 under the patronage of SBUAM, and for which Hannoset at the time designed the layout.[37] In 1954 Knoll advertisements started to appear in *Architecture*.[38] Several ads resembled ones published in the United States, designed by graphic designer Herbert Matter, which emphasized the sculptural and graphic qualities of the furniture elements. Others were 'local' interpretations of the US Knoll ad campaigns. A Knoll International Brussels advertisement

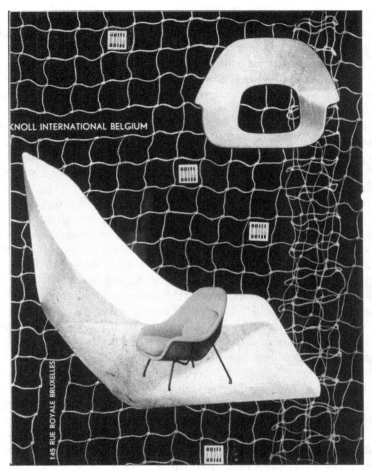

FIGURE 8.4 *Knoll International Brussels advertisement, signed by Corneille Hannoset and Serge Vandercam*. Architecture, vol. 54, no. 10 (1954). Courtesy of Knoll, Inc.

in the October 1954 issue depicting Eero Saarinen's Womb chair was signed by Hannoset and his colleague, the artist-photographer Serge Vandercam (Figure 8.4).[39] A former member of the COBRA art movement, Vandercam may have been responsible for the selection of Knoll's 'Fishnet' textile – a knotted linen netting that was used in many of the firm's early showrooms – for the dramatic backdrop.[40]

Advertisements from the late 1950s onwards emphasized Knoll's relations with modern architecture as if it was a next step in the brand's attempts to intensify its connections with the local world of building. First of all, explicit references were made to foreign projects, such as the Connecticut General

Insurance Headquarters (1953–7) in Bloomfield, Connecticut, by Skidmore, Owings & Merrill. The interior arrangements, designed by the Knoll Planning Unit, had received much attention in the international architectural press.[41] A black-and-white photograph of the restaurant by Ezra Stoller formed the centre of a rather simple Knoll ad published in a 1959 issue of *Architecture*.[42] The text copy presented Knoll International Brussels as a solid partner or ally of architecture, implicitly suggesting that the local branch fulfilled a similar role as the Knoll Planning Unit in the United States: 'Knoll International Brussels closely collaborates with the architect for the furnishing of diverse constructions.'[43] The association with the US example was strengthened in the next issue of *Architecture*, which was entirely focused on office architecture and included an article on Connecticut General.[44]

A few years later, the Knoll ads in *Architecture* started to depict a new category of buildings: prestigious architectural projects in Belgium designed by foreign architects and commissioned by successful Belgian enterprises. Readers were encouraged to become acquainted with 'good' examples of modern architecture, built close to home, with skilfully integrated Knoll designs that strengthened the building's expressive or rhetorical qualities. A revealing example is the Administrative Centre of the Union Cotonnière textile company in Ghent, designed in 1958–9 by the German architect Theodor Kelter (1907–82).[45] The decision to build a modern office tower was a clear demonstration of the company's international ambitions in the context of the liberalizing market. The headquarters' interiors, furnished by the Brussels-based interior design firms Ateliers Stéphane Jasinski, Knoll International Brussels and l'Art Décoratif Céline Dangotte, served to emphasize this.[46] Several Belgian architectural journals covered the project and published advertisements of different construction firms and other companies involved – at the time a common practice, which helped to finance their operations. A Knoll International Brussels ad in a 1961 issue of *Architecture* featured a photograph of the new boardroom of the Union Cotonnière. The striking concentric arrangement of the furniture showed a resemblance, according to another architectural journal, *La Maison*, with one of the halls in the new UNESCO headquarters in Paris.[47] The similarity might have been stimulated by the fact that De Coene, which produced the Knoll International furniture for the Union Cotonnière, also was involved in some of the UNESCO furnishings. In any case, for architects who were getting acquainted with the products and spatial language of Knoll, examples like this showed the power of association. Integrating Knoll furniture in a building implied the possibility of connecting it with an international world of modern architecture, published in journals that many colleagues in different parts of the world were reading. The furniture elements served as sophisticated, mobile and reproducible connectors between different architectural projects, but also between image and reality.

Other Knoll International Brussels ads depicting this category of buildings were slightly more playful in their visual references. For example, a 1964 ad in *Architecture* referred to the Banque Lambert (1961–3) in Brussels, the first

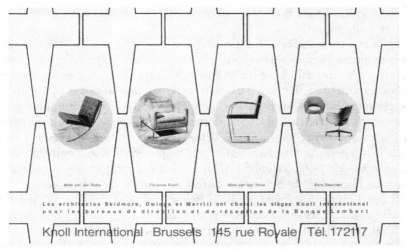

FIGURE 8.5 *Knoll International Brussels advertisement, referencing the façade of the Banque Lambert.* Architecture, vol. 64, no. 61 (1964). *Courtesy of Knoll, Inc.*

commercial building by Skidmore, Owings & Merrill in Europe (Figure 8.5).[48] The building has a façade consisting of a geometric structure of precast concrete, a material which, according to its designer Gordon Bunshaft, responded to the historical context of Belgium's capital. The Knoll ad combined the graphic pattern of the façade with circular photographs of several chairs that, according to the ad copy, had been selected by the architects for the lobby and executive offices of the bank. The image strengthened the visual associations between building and furniture already present in several journal articles reporting on the project. It did so not through the use of an interior photograph, as in the case of the Union Cotonnière Knoll ad, but by directly linking the brand's products with an abstraction of Banque Lambert's characteristic external appearance. This served to underline the message that the furniture was not just an important element of the project's interior, but of the architectural expression as a whole.

The affinities between Knoll and modern architecture were echoed and repeated in other Belgian architecture, design and art journals, as such extending the brand's visual presence and reinforcing and locally embedding its image. In 1955 *Bouwen en Wonen*, a Flemish journal established by the Belgian modernist architect Renaat Braem, published a four-page documentary section on Knoll International.[49] Knoll furniture also gained presence, as illustrated earlier, in photographs of new projects by Belgian architects and in advertisements of building and interior finishing products, from carpet manufacturers to brick factories, produced by Belgian companies.[50] The furniture elements often served as explicit references to a modern interior or lifestyle, but through their manifold appearances in architectural journals they also encouraged associations with a variety of modern building projects.

While as a multinational Knoll is well known for strategically investing in a strong visual identity through collaborations with graphic designers such as Herbert Matter and later on Massimo Vignelli, case studies on overseas subsidiaries indicate that the local publicity language adopted by the brand was characterized by it being to some extent open to manipulation or appropriation. In the case of Knoll International France, a series of remarkable ads began appearing in the early 1960s in the cultural magazine *L'Oeil*, which combined the international visual language of Knoll with historical and eclectic elements intended to appeal to a progressive segment of bourgeois clientele.[51] In Belgium a different strategy characterized the local Knoll ads. Less sophisticated publicity images first and foremost emphasized and stimulated associations between the company's products and services and foreign and local examples of modern architecture and building. Belgian architects who were interested in connecting with the world of architecture they read about in *Progressive Architecture* and *Architectural Forum* saw that this was possible through the use of Knoll furniture as a rhetorical element. While 'sameness' might seem a problem today, the fact that identical objects were featured in many contemporary projects around the world was seen as a positive quality, as if they were reliable and repeatable components of an international language of modern architecture. In the case of the earlier mentioned Brussels Résidence, Knoll furnishings not only helped to articulate the functions of the rooms and the sophisticated atmosphere the architect intended to create, they also implicitly connected the project to an international family of modern building projects with similar furnishings around the world. When the French periodical *L'Architecture d'Aujourd'hui* reported on the Brussels Résidence, the explicit mention of Knoll International as a partner in the interior design seems intended as an extra clue for readers on how to interpret the significance of the Belgian project.[52]

## Belgian modern architecture in an internationalizing world

Almost immediately upon its arrival on the Belgian market in the early 1950s, Knoll was quickly accepted by the local architecture culture. Reviews in the Belgian architectural and design press were almost unanimously positive and Knoll designs rapidly converted into acknowledged international symbols of modernity.[53] Only a very few critics in Belgium expressed any reservations. However, in 1962, the architecture critic Geert Bekaert wondered if 'this meticulous watching over perfection, this scrupulous attention to even the last detail' which characterized Knoll production perhaps also attached a sense of 'inaccessibility' to it.[54] A few years later, the

Flemish design critic K.-N. Elno remarked on the expensive nature of the products. He believed that because of their high cost, Knoll products tended to represent within society 'a certain "aristocracy" based on material power'.[55] This aspect, which raised some of the concerns of the earlier mentioned movement for modern social furniture, would bother him, he explained, 'if it was not so excellently integrated in a system of *values* which we, in this case "despite" certain social aspirations, *have to* defend, encourage, and bring to life'.[56] These aesthetic values included 'a subtle flair for form and for spatial poetry'.[57] Apart from guarded remarks like those expressed by Bekaert or Elno, most critics in Belgium agreed that Knoll set a good example and was an important ally of modern architecture and art.

While Knoll International worked to strengthen its visibility on the Belgian market and cultural scene, along the way supporting a particular conception of Western design, a considerable number of Belgian architects or their clients started to integrate Knoll products in their projects. While Willy Van Der Meeren chose to extend the architectural language of many of his buildings with furniture of his own design, the architects and clients who chose to work with Knoll International also employed furniture objects as important elements in the expression of architecture, but in a different way. Rather than using furniture as a tool to extend architectural authorship or wielding it as a means toward social emancipation, they turned to the cleverly promoted Knoll brand as a meaningful partner in creating their own interpretation of modern architecture. In the examples discussed in this chapter, the presence of Knoll objects can be read as references to new concepts of modern life and work – in particular, office work – but also as implicit political signifiers, as references to an up-to-date industrial production, as tokens of cultural sophistication, and as a means of connecting with a variety of international modern architectural projects. As reproducible objects, expensive but available in an increasingly number of countries, they were able to become as desirable to modern architects as the architectural world was to the booming furniture 'brand.

## Acknowledgements

I would like to thank interior architect Jacques Vernest for generously sharing his recollections of the Knoll showroom in Brussels and architectural historian Cammie McAtee for her valuable comments on a draft version of the text.

## Notes

1 Gabrielle Lueg, 'From Aalto to Zumthor – Furniture by Architects', in *From Aalto to Zumthor. Furniture by Architects*, eds. Petra Hesse and Gabrielle Lueg (Cologne: Museum für Angewandte Kunst Köln/Verlag der Buchhandlung Walther König, 2021), 28.

2   Aline Payne, *From Ornament to Object. Genealogies of Architectural Modernism* (New Haven/London: Yale University Press, 2012).

3   See also Robin D. Jones, '"Thinking" the domestic interior in Postcolonial South Asia: the home of Geoffrey Bawa in Sri Lanka, 1960 to 1999', *Interiors. Design/Architecture/Culture* 3, no. 3 (2012): 203–26.

4   Mil De Kooning, *Willy Van Der Meeren. Furniture Design* (Brussels: Atomium vzw, 2007), 7.

5   Fredie Floré, *Lessons in Modern Living. Source Book on Housing Exhibitions in Belgium 1945–1958* (Ghent: WZW Editions and Productions, 2004). The National Housing Body refused to give approval for building the ECSC house. In the end only eight were built, one of which became the family home of the architect. See De Kooning, *Willy Van Der Meeren*, 21.

6   Fredie Floré, *Lessen in goed wonen: woonvoorlichting in België 1945–1958* (Leuven: Universitaire Pers Leuven, 2010).

7   Fredie Floré, 'Serving a Double Diplomatic Mission: Strategic Alliances between Belgian and American Furniture Companies in the Postwar Era', *Design and Culture* 9, no. 2 (2017): 167–85.

8   See e.g. Brian Lutz, *Knoll: A Modernist Universe* (New York: Rizzoli, 2010), 62.

9   Cammie McAtee and Fredie Floré, 'Knolling Paris. From the "new look" to *Knoll au Louvre*', in *The Politics of Furniture. Identity, Diplomacy and Persuasion in Post-War Interiors*, eds. Fredie Floré and Cammie McAtee (Abingdon/New York: Routledge, 2017), 101 (98–118).

10  Greg Castillo, *Cold War on the Home Front. The Soft Power of Midcentury Design* (Minneapolis, MN: University of Minnesota Press, 2010).

11  See Paul Betts, *The Authority of Everyday Objects. A Cultural History of West German Industrial Design* (Berkeley, CA: University of California Press, 2004), 88.

12  Gay McDonald, 'The Modern American Home as Soft Power: Finland, MoMA and the "American Home 1953" Exhibition', *Journal of Design History* 4 (2010): 387–408.

13  Léon-Louis Sosset, 'In de kursaal van Oostende. In het Museum voor Sierkunsten te Gent. Tentoonstelling van door het Museum voor Moderne Kunst van New York uitgelezen voorwerpen', *Kunstambachten en Kunstnijverheden* 57 (1954): 1–3.

14  The European House featured on the cover of and was discussed in the Belgian architectural journal *Bouwen en Wonen*: 'Het Europees huis', *Bouwen en Wonen*, no. 10 (October 1957): 350–6. The De Coene model house on Expo 58 was designed by in-house architects Frans Vuye in collaboration with Gustave Creupelandt.

15  Rika Devos and Fredie Floré, 'Modern Wood. De Coene at Expo 58', *Construction History*, no. 24 (2009): 103–20.

16  'Nous avons construit une maison pour vous! Wij bouwden een huis voor U! A house for you! Ein Heim für Sie!', brochure on the De Coene model home at Expo 58, 1958.

17  'Le "Brussels Résidence"', *Rythme*, no. 26 (January 1959): 18 (18–21). Original quotation: 'une nouvelle formule de logement, à mi-chemin entre l'hôtel et l'appartement.'
18  'Brussels Résidence', *Architecture*, no. 58 (1958): 98–101.
19  Paul Groth, *Living Downtown. The History of the Residential Hotels in the United States* (Berkeley/Los Angeles/Oxford: University of California Press, 1994).
20  See Niké Vanderpoorten, 'First class seat to modernity. De import van het moderne Amerikaanse interieur in België en Europa (1945–1965)' (MA thesis, Ghent University, 2009).
21  McAtee and Floré, 'Knolling Paris', 98–118.
22  For a discussion of the 'Knoll look', see Bobbye Tigerman, '"I am not a decorator": Florence Knoll, the Knoll Planning Unit and the making of the modern office', *Journal of Design History* 20, no. 1 (2007): 67.
23  See Syracuse, Syracuse University Libraries, Marcel Breuer Digital Archive, Project Knoll Showroom (Brussels) Professional Papers, http://breuer.syr.edu (accessed 4 February 2021). In a recent interview Brodzki refers to Marcel Breuer as the designer of the showroom in Brussels. Thijs Demeulemeester, 'Iconisch Brussels kantoorgebouw krijgt makeover', *Sabato, De Tijd*, 9 May 2018, https://www.tijd.be/sabato/design/iconisch-brussels-kantoorgebouw-krijgt-make-over/10010377.html
24  See Geert Bekaert, *Bouwen in België 1945–1970* (Brussel: Nationale Confederatie van het Bouwbedrijf, 1971), 284; Thibaud Gauin and Arthur Wéry, 'Constantin Brodzki', *CLARA*, no. 5 (January 2018): 69–72 (68–91); Gertjan Hoste, *Constantin Brodzki, architect* (Sprimont: Mardaga, 2004), 28.
25  See Gertjan Hoste, *Constantin Brodzki, architect* (Sprimont: Mardaga, 2004), 29, 31. On the design of the bookshop: 'La Librairie de l'Édition Universelle', *Architecture 54*, no. 10 (1954): 44–5; 'Librairie à Bruxelles', *Habitat et Habitations* 15, no. 1–2 (January–February 1955): 4.
26  Tigerman, '"I am not a decorator"', 64.
27  Benoît Mihail, 'Société Belge des Urbanistes et Architectes Modernistes (SBUAM)', in *Repertorium van de architectuur in België. Van 1830 tot heden*, ed. Anne Van Loo (Antwerpen: Mercatorfonds, 2003), 512–3.
28  Floré, *Lessons in Modern Living*.
29  Letter from Hans Knoll to Constantin Brodzki mentioning the 'model house', 18 June 1953. See Syracuse, Syracuse University Libraries, Marcel Breuer Digital Archive, Project Knoll Showroom (Brussels) Professional Papers, http://breuer.syr.edu (accessed 4 February 2021).
30  Hoste, *Constantin Brodzki, architect*, 29. Original quotation: 'Mais ce qui m'a surtout intéressé à cette occasion c'était de montrer le mobilier Knoll qui était exposé pour la première fois en Europe. Il réunissait alors ce qui, encore aujourd'hui, représente le *nec plus ultra* du mobilier contemporain.'
31  Margaret Maile Petty, 'Attitudes Towards Modern Living: The Mid-century Showrooms of Herman Miller and Knoll Associates', *Journal of Design History* 29, no. 2 (2016): 181 (180–99).

32  Jan Saverys, unpublished notes on Knoll International and De Coene (private archive of Jan Saverys, s.d, accessed by the author in 2000); Maile Petty, 'Attitudes Towards Modern Living', 181.
33  Marcel Breuer, 'Photomural and details. Dwg. 3. Brussels Showroom for Knoll International Brussels' (drawing), 29 July 1953, Syracuse, Syracuse University Libraries, Marcel Breuer Digital Archive, Project Knoll Showroom (Brussels) Professional Papers, http://breuer.syr.edu (accessed 4 February 2021).
34  Interview with Jacques Vernest by the author, Sint-Martens-Latem, 9 October 2019.
35  Ibid.
36  Ibid.
37  France Vanlaethem, '*Architecture*. Tweemaandelijks tijdschrift', in *Repertorium van de architectuur in België. Van 1830 tot heden*, ed. Anne Van Loo (Antwerpen: Mercatorfonds, 2003), 122.
38  Vanderpoorten, 'First class seat to modernity.'
39  *Architecture 54*, no. 10 (1954).
40  Susan Ward, 'Making Knoll Textiles: Integrated Fabrics for Modern Interiors 1945–65', in *Knoll Textiles, 1945–2010*, ed. Earl Martin (New Haven/London: Yale University Press, 2010), 105.
41  For example: 'Grandi offici Americani', *Domus*, no. 340 (March 1958): 29–36; 'Siège d'une companie d'assurance, Bloomfield, Connecticut', *L'Architecture d'Aujourd'hui*, no. 9 (1959): 10–17.
42  *Architecture 59*, no. 26 (1959).
43  Ibid.
44  'Siège principal d'une compagnie d'assurance à Hartfort (Conn.) U.S.A.', *Architecture 59*, no. 27 (1959): 148–9.
45  'Centre administratif et commercial de la S.A. Filatures et Tissages Union Cotonnière à Ledeberg-lez-Gand', *Architecture 61*, no. 42 (1961): 840–9. Kelter designed the project with his collaborators H. Feltes and K. Hullmann. The Ghent architect Raphaël Wieme was in charge of the building site.
46  'Centre administratif et commercial de la S.A. Filatures et Tissages Union Cotonnière, à Gand', *La Maison* 17, no. 3 (March 1961): 83–94.
47  'Knoll International Brussels' (advertisement), *Architecture 61*, no. 42 (1961): 873; 'Centre administratif et commercial de la S.A. Filatures et Tissages Union Cotonnière, à Gand', 94.
48  'Knoll International Brussels' (advertisement), *Architecture 64*, no. 61 (1964).
49  'Moderne meubels. Knoll International', *Bouwen en Wonen*, no. 6 (June 1955): 19–22.
50  'Tapis Richelieu' (advertisement), *La Maison*, no. 11 (1961); 'La brique – confort. Ytong' (advertisement), *La Maison*, no. 12 (1963); 'SVK. Carraux Marbrabel' (advertisement), *La Maison*, no. 3 (1965).
51  McAtee and Floré, 'Knolling Paris', 108–9.
52  'Résidence-hotel à Bruxelles', *L'Architecture d'Aujourd'hui*, no. 86 (November 1959): 75.

53 For examples of positive reviews of Knoll products in architectural and design journals in Belgium, see Léon-Louis Sosset, 'Het meubel draagt bij tot het uitbouwen van de hedendaagse stijl. De firma Knoll', *Kunstambachten en Kunstnijverheden*, no. 80 (1956): n.p.; Jul De Roover, 'Meubelen Knoll International Brussels', *Bouwen en Wonen*, no. 1 (1959): 3.
54 Geert Bekaert, 'Tien jaar Knoll International', *De Linie* no. 695 (1962): 9.
55 K.-N. Elno, 'Ludwig Mies van der Rohe: genie en drama', *Tijdschrift voor Architectuur en Beeldende Kunst*, no. 4 (1965): 77 (77–81).
56 Elno, 'Ludwig Mies van der Rohe', 78.
57 Ibid.

# CHAPTER NINE

# Disaster Relief and 'Universal Shelters':

# Humanitarian Imaginaries and Design Interventions at Oxfam, 1971–6

*Tania Messell and Lilián Sánchez-Moreno*

Over the last decades, post-disaster sites in locations ranging from Southern Sri Lanka to New Orleans and Port-au-Prince have been subjected to experimental shelter solutions, from inflatable octagonal tents to polyurethane igloos and repurposed shipping containers.[1] A growing number of so-called innovative refugee shelter proposals have also emerged in the last few years, largely in response to the widespread media coverage of the Mediterranean migration crisis, which dramatically peaked during the summer of 2015.[2] These designs have been widely circulated and exhibited in the press, social media and in the context of museums, where they have been the subject of collective fascination.[3] Whilst implemented shelters conceived by designers and architects have resulted from collaborations with logisticians, engineers and international development agencies, some of these projects have also been celebrated by the design community and beyond. This is the case for instance with the 'Better Shelter', developed with the United Nations' refugee agency (UNHCR) with the support of the IKEA Foundation, which received the London Design Museum's 'Design of the Year' award from a unanimous jury in 2017. Humanitarian organizations have also shared an interest in such approaches, as evident in the UNHCR involvement in the project and its subsequent delivery of 50,000 housing units to refugees and internally displaced people around the world.[4]

Experimental prefabricated shelters have, however, also been reviled by both humanitarians and members of the design community. Humanitarians have condemned their overdetermined character, when processes of sheltering, as opposed to donor-led housing, have gained traction. Scepticism towards standardized solutions have allied with attempts to move beyond stand-alone, mass-produced technological fixes, through the provision of local building materials and training to rebuild safer housing. Beyond aiming at answering individual needs, these alternative solutions have been regarded as catering for the field's restricted resources and short intervention time frame. Some architects, on the other hand, have categorized prefabricated shelters as 'product design', due to their lack of adaptability and engagement with specific environments and users, and to an absence of aesthetic sensitivity and overall functionality.[5] Such critiques have aligned with the growing involvement of industrial designers in shelter conception over recent years, as reflected in humanitarian fairs where designer-led projects have become symptomatic of the widespread interest in standardized, mass-produced and so-called 'universal' humanitarian equipment.[6] Evolving across disciplinary boundaries, and either positioned as too object-oriented or too building-oriented,[7] such objects have become significant markers of specific conceptions of 'human need' amongst both humanitarians and design practitioners.

Whilst prefabricated shelters aimed at emergency responses in expanded geographies are continuously advertised as innovative, some of these can be traced back to the post-war period, in particular the 1960s and 1970s. Various developments during these decades contributed to heightened attempts to develop dispatchable 'universal shelters'.[8] These included the expansion of the international aid system, coinciding with the growing mediatization of crisis, rapid transportation, and the subsequent rise of humanitarian interventions in the so-called Global South. One of the few implemented designs was that of Oxfam's site-moulded polystyrene shelter, otherwise referred to as the Oxfam Igloo or the Emergency House. Conceived and developed between 1971 and 1976, it set out to increase the transportability, ease of construction and time efficiency of shelter technologies in the aftermath of emergencies. Initiated in response to military repression in former East Pakistan in 1971, which resulted in a mass migration of ten million refugees, the system was subsequently trialled following the 1974 floods in Pakistan, before being implemented in the aftermath of an earthquake in Lice, Turkey, which in 1975 left five thousand individuals without a home.

Grounded in a standardized and technocratic understanding of emergency housing, the Emergency House failed due to its high cost, belated implementation and lack of engagement with local social and cultural realities. In addition to these failures, the experiment was also interrupted by widespread critiques in the Western press, which condemned the fire risks associated with the moulded polystyrene and the potential for such temporary housing to turn into 'slums'.[9] As a result, the development and deficiencies of the Emergency House were associated with a rise of discourses and methods that advocated for the use of appropriate technology and place-based, participative responses to post-disaster sites. This led Oxfam to shift its understanding of disaster relief, which it increasingly envisioned as being interlinked with long-term development.

This chapter argues that the rationality of the project aligned with wider shifts within Western humanitarian circles, when ideological, technical and logistical transformations, expanded zones of interventions and aid responses were reconceived. The project also arose from modernist and countercultural experiments in predominantly Western architecture and design circles, where mobility, standardization and vernacular building typologies overlapped. Emerging from these entwined discourses and practices, and spurred by conceptions of 'distant suffering',[10] portable, standardized and easily reproducible approaches to housing became envisioned as a possible response to post-conflict and natural disasters in so-called developing countries. Indeed, from the late 1960s, humanitarian action became grounded in 'a very Western imagining of the Third World'.[11] This imaginary was often conceived in binary terms of victims and aid providers, a hierarchical division that has remained pervasive in more recent material practices of aid, as Lisa Smirl has argued.[12] Within wider calls to examine the connections between material cultures and humanitarian histories,[13] and instigations to unearth the complex histories and fraught values embedded in humanitarian design,[14] this chapter aims to shed light on the many cross-disciplinary influences and imperatives that shaped Oxfam's Emergency House within wider discourses on disaster relief and development. Whilst we recognize that a study of the materiality of aid needs to consider the agency of local communities and the historical, political and cultural specificities of each intervention and site,[15] this chapter primarily aims at examining humanitarian and practice-based worldviews as they were articulated through such standardized and experimental building/objects in the 1970s.[16] It furthermore links the latter with recent experiments and practices, which have remained tied to short- and long-term understandings of so-called 'basic needs', and to both architectural and design practices and methodologies. We argue that an artefact like the Emergency House can only be understood by such interdisciplinary enquiry.

## Domes and the search for 'universal shelters'

The late 1960s and early 1970s witnessed the development of a 'humanitarian knowledge community' following a series of devastating disasters at the turn of the decade, from the Biafra Civil War between 1967 and 1970 to the tropical cyclone Bhola in East Pakistan in November 1970.[17] For many humanitarian actors, the response to these events highlighted the shortcomings of cross-border emergency assistance, in particular with regard to the international coordination of aid. A series of shifts occurred on a variety of fronts. As Eleanor Davey, John Borton and Matthew Foley write, 'researchers analyzed past experiences; governments and intergovernmental agencies, including UN bodies, created new institutions and departments for humanitarian response [and] NGOs established new networks to improve their own effectiveness'.[18] The growing professionalization of aid took place alongside its geographical expansion in the decolonizing world, and alongside increasingly common encounters of Western audiences with distant disasters and wars through visual media and print.[19]

As part of these efforts, many leading agencies set out to pursue 'the elusive quest for a "universal shelter"', as Ian Davis, former architect and development and disaster expert from the 1970s onwards, writes.[20] Interest in such solutions resulted from logistical, economic and ideological imperatives, when for many of these organizations relief activity was still synonymous with immediate survival, as opposed to long-term development.[21] Moreover, product-oriented solutions such as pre-designed disaster housing constituted a 'high pictorial value'[22] for humanitarian organizations, for which press coverage of major disasters afforded the only occasion on which they received free publicity.[23] In this context, rendering visible their interventions through arresting designs assisted them in securing more influence and funds from the wider public. Hence a 'universal' temporary shelter which was rapidly constructed, easily transportable and low-priced became much sought after, combining a belief in technological solutions with efforts to cement an image of instant response.

Such experiments, however, cannot be grasped without considering the experiments conducted by architects and industrial designers in the realm of housing throughout the twentieth century, designs which contributed to shaping humanitarian imaginaries of aid and the resulting interventions. While the involvement of architects in the development of temporary emergency housing in the West can be traced back to the nineteenth century,[24] the need for low-cost and mass housing, in part due to the damages occasioned by the First World War, contributed to the emergence of architectural modernism.[25] From then onwards, prefabrication, standardized building components and modular systems became explored by practitioners such as the French architect and designer Charles-Édouard Jeanneret, known as Le Corbusier, the German architect Walter Gropius and the American architect and designer Frank Lloyd Wright. The meeting of modernism and humanitarianism once again prevailed following the Second World War,[26] when the French designer and architect Jean Prouvé and Finnish architect Alvar Aalto developed temporary emergency shelter concepts, in response to the millions of individuals who were left homeless or displaced by the conflict. By the 1970s, many relief agencies held filing cabinets which 'were bulging with "57 varieties" of shelter types' submitted by architects and designers, as a result of their shared preoccupations with 'social awareness; advanced technology; mobility and impermanence'.[27] Following in the footsteps of architects, industrial designers mostly based in the so-called Global North had also set out to develop standardized shelter designs.[28] Such efforts often remained ensconced in modernist design precepts, which, drawing from an imaginary of *tabula rasa*, were entirely conceived by the practitioner. In the British context, this was the case in a study commissioned by the British Overseas Development Ministry from the Department of Design Research (DDR) at the Royal College of Art to devise 'universal' emergency shelter design criteria, for instance.[29]

At the crossroads of design and architectural practice, the work of the American designer and architect Richard Buckminster Fuller, in particular his geodesic domes and concept of tensegrity, would have a lasting influence on emergency shelter designs.[30] From the 1950s onwards, Buckminster Fuller's dome concept became adopted for industrial and governmental uses, including by the US military in the wider Cold War climate. For instance, Buckminster Fuller believed that pre-assembled, airlifted domes could provide 'controlled' environments for housing and other functions in 'developing countries' in case of Communist insurgency, and the concept was also used in the Arctic to protect radars from harsh weather as part of US defence against Russian attacks.[31] Whilst by the 1960s 'mobility, flexibility, modular architecture and space-travel aesthetics' became some of the dominating themes of architecture,[32] the geodesic dome also had a particular influence on the commune movement that spread through North America and Western Europe from the end of the 1960s onwards.

Countering mainstream culture, such groups turned to alternative architectural forms, which included Buckminster Fuller's domes and traditional nomadic tents and yurts.[33] Avant-garde architects and designers also became influenced by communities ranging from Berber tribes to Iranian and Peruvian shepherds within wider preoccupations with anthropology and ethnology in the late 1960s and 1970s.[34] The formal properties of domes, allied with the widespread influence of 'dome culture' on Western society,[35] contributed to experiments conducted by relief organizations, at times in concert with product manufacturers and some under the aegis of governments. Such projects led the shelters devised to become more than prototypes, as was the case with two moulded spray-foam shelter designs. The first was the Bayer polyurethane 'igloo', which had been dispatched as part of German Red Cross interventions following earthquakes in Peru and Turkey in 1970, and in the aftermath of an earthquake in Nicaragua in 1973. The second would become Oxfam's Emergency House from 1971 onwards, a building/object which, as seen shortly, was shaped by imaginaries of humanitarian aid and conceptions of 'distant suffering', alongside technical and economic factors.

## Oxfam's 'portable building': Economic and ideological imperatives

The post-war context witnessed the rise of non-governmental organizations, of which those constituted by private or voluntary groups and dedicated to humanitarian action found a fertile ground for their pursuits, in the midst of Western, Eastern and newly independent states.[36] Established in 1942, Oxfam, formerly the Oxford Committee for Famine Relief, emerged during the Allied Blockade in Greece, where it provided aid, in particular through food supplies. While Oxfam had managed to position itself as a leading organization within the remit of humanitarian aid by the 1970s, its development agenda had not caught up with its international recognition on emergency relief. As a result, Oxfam members tended to be divided between those who did not want change and those who strived to pursue new objectives within the organization. Members of the former group believed that a shift towards long-term developmental activities risked confusing a public that had formerly supported the cause of emergency relief, whilst members of the latter held high hopes of the benefits of self-help developmental methods.[37] Moreover, while some in Oxfam aimed to engage in long-term solutions to so-called 'Third World' problems, including housing solutions in both disaster and non-disaster situations, as in the case of settlements, economic imperatives restricted the types of project the organization was able to develop. Indeed, expenditure on research and development (R&D) could only be justified in response to emergency situations, which, as stated above, received a higher mediatic coverage. One turning point was the intensive mediatization of the 1971 refugee crisis in India, which had led an estimated ten million refugees to flee from the military repression in what was then East Pakistan (Bangladesh) to India.[38] In the aftermath of this, the development of Oxfam's Emergency House was perceived as a project that was viable both financially and culturally.

However, some of the debates on emergency relief, shelter and housing raised the link between the twin issues of disaster relief and development, discourses which contributed to how Oxfam conceptualized this genre of building/object. As architectural historian Anooradha Iyer Siddiqi writes, the notion of 'dwelling' against that of 'shelter' was prevalent within architectural debates, and each term conveyed the need for expertise differently: the former by promoting a 'shared mission of architecture and humanitarianism, and the latter by reducing it to functionalist, instrumentalized science'.[39] Due to these wider concerns, what was to become Oxfam's Emergency House project remained a topic of contention until its withdrawal in 1976. The need for the provision of shelter in post-disaster sites was clear, but its argument as a long-term solution or prevention of poverty remained uncertain. As a result, the conceptualization of Oxfam's Emergency House was positioned between the permanent and the ephemeral from its inception.

On the one hand, the concept of 'shelter' as a housing solution was viewed as 'temporary', which needed to be produced within a short period of time and at an industrial scale in order to assist the most immediate needs of disaster-struck populations. On the other hand, the use of long-life reuseable construction materials and a visual typology embedded in exoticized ideas of shelter and communal living aligned it with development discourses of the time, which contradicted the notion of shelter as 'temporary'. This dual approach contributed to the positioning of the Emergency House within the realms of an object-oriented perspective to post-disaster housing.

## Design, implementation and reception of the Emergency House

As soon as the 1971 Bangladeshi Liberation War broke out, the most immediate needs that Oxfam set out to answer were shelter, food and sanitation. As part of these efforts, Oxfam commissioned a 'design study' for a temporary shelter.[40] Completed in July 1971, just four months after the start of the crisis, the study was presented to Oxfam's industrial officer, Jim Howard. Under the title 'The Site-Moulding of Refugee Shelters in Expanded Polystyrene', the design aimed at addressing issues of time, scale and cost constraints, as well as material suitability for production.[41] As the report acknowledged, the equipment, which included mobile moulding tools, needed to be built and transported to the disaster areas, together with quantities of raw expandable polystyrene beads. There, a heated mould and the application of dry steam would be used to shape a small quantity of expanded polystyrene beads into a dwelling which would 'comfortably' house four to six persons, and which was seen as being of adequate strength and insulation relative to cost.[42] However, as testified by the blueprints (Figure 9.1), the design submitted was also determined with regard to structural rigidity and associated aerodynamic and moulding considerations, leading an 'igloo' shape to be defined as being the most satisfactory.

The price of the unit and its capacity to be produced on a large scale were also of importance, with each unit planned to cost £4 each, and the production target providing shelter to 200 persons per day – an objective that was understood as well in excess of the Bayer igloo system, and at a lower expense in both labour and money.[43] Together, these specifications were understood as securing a global use of the shelter, as testified in the designers' aspiration to establish 'Stand-by Mobile Units' in strategic locations around the world, capable of being rapidly deployed to any disaster-struck area.[44] However, beyond acting as a temporary housing solution, the moulding process as well as the material used were also intended for the purpose of ensuring the durability and portability of the shelter. As the design study specified, the former would allow users to reuse

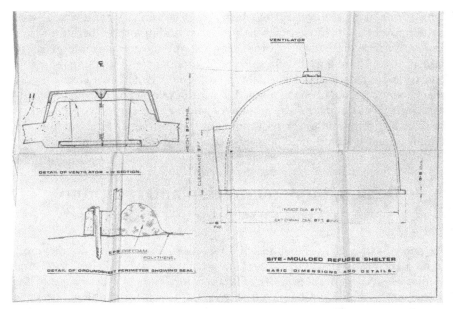

FIGURE 9.1 *Blueprints for the design study 'The Site-moulding of Refugee Shelters in Expanded Polystyrene: A Design Study Report for Oxfam', by Dante Bondonno and Brian Colleran (July 1971). Source: Oxfam Archive, Bodleian Library, University of Oxford. Courtesy of Oxfam.*

the shelter as insulation for 'permanent buildings', which could appear in the longer term. The portability and shape of the construction could furthermore convert it into a container which could 'collect and store water, and . . . provide washing facilities' when inverted (Figure 9.3).[45] These latter aspects point at the different temporalities embedded in the Emergency House, as well as to its dual function as both a building and an object that could be repurposed by users.

The 'dome' or 'igloo'[46] shape used for Oxfam's Emergency Shelter also reflected how the design and architectural specificities were far removed from the localities of intended deployment. As stated above, the popularization of Buckminster Fuller's patented geodesic dome in 1954 had led to the widespread 'dome culture' in Western society. During the 1970s, the 'dome' or 'igloo' – terms that were both used to describe Oxfam's Emergency House – acted as a cultural signifier which would have been embedded within the social imaginaries of those involved in bringing to life Oxfam's emergency shelter.[47] Nevertheless, while the early domes were applauded for their ability to be mass-produced and their lightweight modular properties (seen as one of the technical advantages of Oxfam's early Emergency House), their appropriation by the countercultures of the

FIGURE 9.2 *Visual representations for the design study, which include the depiction of the shelter as water storage unit on the lower left. 'The Site-moulding of Refugee Shelters in Expanded Polystyrene: A Design Study Report for Oxfam', by Dante Bondonno and Brian Colleran (July 1971). Source: Oxfam Archive, Bodleian Library, University of Oxford. Courtesy of Oxfam.*

late 1960s and early 1970s went beyond functionality and efficiency.[48] In this context, domes became used as 'social pivots', adopted for their emphasis on individuals working together to build them, as well as offering communal living. That is, domes were not only adopted for their potential for 'community' building, but also because their physicality, in terms of their materials, making processes and shape, embodied the countercultural discourse. The geodesic dome and its variation, when brought as a shelter strategy in post-disaster sites, thus introduced a culturally alien object, which lost its political significance as it was repurposed.

The detachment between the place of production and the specificities of sites of intervention furthermore spurred, and arguably was spurred by, an exoticized understanding of the 'Other'.[49] This process became encoded in the design of the Emergency House. On the one hand, whilst the design aligned with countercultural dome conceptions, its logic reflected early experiments in standardized mass-produced housing, which negated the need for a dialogue or even understanding of the conditions of potential occupants. This is reflected in the blueprints and visual representations of the refugee camps. On the other hand, the individuals involved in the conception and representation of the design displayed their essentializing

FIGURE 9.3 *Prototype of Oxfam's first 'igloo' Emergency House. Left: Jim Howard. (Undated) Source: Oxfam Archive, Bodleian Library, University of Oxford. Courtesy of Oxfam.*

understanding of life in refugee camps through the depiction of users in their day-to-day activities as both wearing and not wearing clothing, and the vague depiction of imagined everyday objects (see Figure 9.2). At a time when, as mentioned above, architects became interested in vernacular housing and cultures of nomadism whilst increasingly recognizing 'the cultural identities and societal needs of builder-occupiers',[50] the use of the dome typology could moreover have aimed at answering the cultural characteristics and sensitivities of disaster-struck populations. Such a strategy was also reflected in how the designers imagined the camp space where a nondescript image of rural communal living was reproduced, which further reflects their understanding of the Emergency House as an element that could function within any social fabric in so-called developing countries, in addition to its capacity to contribute to long-term development, through its reuseable and multifunctional properties.

Initially field tested in Bangladesh,[51] the trials revealed the gap that existed between Oxfam's imagined 'igloo' community and local realities. As a result, the first design of the shelter was considered unsuitable. Despite its shortcomings, the trials led to further discussions on how to engage with the design of temporary shelters within Oxfam, exchanges which incidentally would contribute to the promotion of more participatory practices, when new avenues would be explored, as examined later.[52] In the meantime, in response to the initial lack of acceptability and from lessons learnt in the field, Oxfam produced a design that would enable the houses to be united in a honeycomb plan in post-disaster sites, a set-up which it believed would assist in promoting a further sense of community in post-disaster phases. Convinced that this new design and layout would be successful, Jim Howard and Oxfam's commercial and deputy director Guy Stringer registered the design on behalf of the organization, which was granted in 1973.[53]

A first opportunity to trial the hexagonal structure was presented in 1974, following devastating floods in Pakistan, which affected between ten and twenty million people and destroyed one million homes, as estimated by the government at the time. At the request of the relief commissioner of Punjab, it was decided that Oxfam would install 100 Emergency Houses in Lyallpur, and in case of success 100 more in Kanpur, one of the worst-hit towns.[54] The team nevertheless was on repeated occasions moved to sites which had remained unaffected by the floods, in part due to local political interests.[55] Moreover, when the team set out to produce houses, technical issues resulted from the high temperatures, which rendered the moulds sticky, thereby further highlighting the gap between the design and local conditions. The constant movement of the team, which contributed to a collective 'exhaustion', alongside the lack of appropriate sites, led the mission to be halted.[56] A second trial took place in the aftermath of an earthquake in Lice, Turkey, in September 1975. A team of Oxfam volunteers was flown out three weeks after the earthquake. However once there, the team 'found it impossible to tour around the remote villages' along with some of the 'outlying villages being completely inaccessible by road'.[57] The team was therefore forced to establish a base camp at the foot of Lice, where they produced Emergency House units that would eventually be taken away, possibly due to their lack of use (Figure 9.4).[58]

After six weeks, the team returned home due to worsening weather conditions, which forced the early closure of the second trial. Despite having encountered great problems, Oxfam nevertheless remained optimistic about the future of the project. As it reported, this 'pioneering' enterprise was desirable and technically feasible, and the method, when used again in the future, would 'provide a meaningful and new way to help with disaster situations'.[59]

However, besides Oxfam's unsatisfactory results, it appears that the hexagonal shelter was not well received by its users, mainly due to cultural issues that included unease with regard to the construction material.[60] Out of the 463 igloos produced, forty-four were damaged and fewer than fifty were used, whilst the Turkish government allegedly set out to use the moulds to make chicken huts.[61] The igloos furthermore were erected sixty days after the earthquake, by which time the Turkish government had built 1,500 inhabited 'permanent' houses.[62] Besides its belated implementation, the design was also widely criticized in the media due to the high cost of the system, the risk of such units to turn into long-lasting 'slums', and fire

FIGURE 9.4 *New 'honeycomb' shaped Emergency Houses, at a house-making unit at the foot of Lice, Turkey (September 1975). Source: Oxfam Archive, Bodleian Library, University of Oxford. Courtesy of Oxfam.*

hazards, which had led the material to be considered as 'extremely dangerous' in Britain.[63] The failure of the Lice implementation, allied with these critiques, led to the withdrawal of the project by Oxfam.

## Development and self-help methods

Despite the early termination of Oxfam's disaster shelter initiative, the development of the Emergency House and its iteration contributed to the organization's shift of perspective with regard to emergency relief and the technical and cultural issues involved in the use of technology. Central to this argument was the formation of the Appropriate Technology Unit in 1974, which occurred against the backdrop of conversations regarding the Emergency House project, and which ultimately led to the organization's interest in the benefits of appropriate technology, through which it set out to address structural realities and long-term betterment and autonomy.[64] The formation of the Appropriate Technology Unit provided Oxfam with a well-established platform from which to contact and work with key figures within the realm of intermediate, alternative and appropriate technology, as evidenced in its consultation with the founder of the Intermediate Technology Development Group (ITDG), E. F. Schumacher.[65]

Oxfam set out to grow closer links with design practitioners interested in place-based and participative approaches, such as the designer Victor Papanek and architect Ian Davis.[66] Oxfam's collaborations also included joint work with Fred Cuny, a trained engineer whose methods included architectural design, and with whom the organization became involved in an educational building programme following the 1976 earthquake in Guatemala, a landmark operation which led to the setting up of similar projects in Indonesia and India.[67] In addition, the Technical Unit shifted its approach to post-disaster reconstruction, with projects such as those focusing on hybrid associations of plastic sheeting with local materials, and assistance with the production of local cement blockmaking.[68] The extent to which the Appropriate Technology Unit remained an expert-driven and methodologically standardized initiative ought to be further studied, as well as how each of these methods was received in each location. Oxfam's shift towards understanding disasters as being interlinked with development was nevertheless symptomatic of some of the debates that prevailed amongst humanitarian actors and practitioners at the time, which contributed to its changing conception of post-disaster housing and reconstruction.

## Conclusion

As this chapter has argued, the 1970s witnessed increased attempts to develop technological solutions capable of saving lives and alleviating suffering in emergency situations. In this context, many aid agencies set out to develop or to commission 'emergency shelters', propelled by the growing mediatization of disasters, technological advancements in matters of transportation, and a widening desire to assist with 'human need' amongst Western audiences. By then, experiments in the realms of industrial design and architecture had penetrated the humanitarian landscape, with widespread attempts to rethink shelter and housing for emergency. Together, these influences shaped the development of Oxfam's Emergency House, which, informed by imaginaries of 'distant suffering', was conceived as a building/object that navigated ideas of permanence and impermanence alongside attempts to create viable homes, incidentally also capable of multifunctional uses in post-disaster phases.

The shelter was developed as a result of predominantly top-down understandings of aid and an exoticized understanding of populations of the so-called Global South, which was treated as a unified and vague sociocultural entity. The gap between the conception of the project and lived realities also reflected the global ambitions of the designers and the organization. As a result of the failures and public criticism of the project, within wider discourses and practices that conceived disasters as interlinked with issues of development, Oxfam shifted its approach to post-disaster environments. These new approaches once again involved an awareness of architecture and design practices, which highlighted the shared interest in the topic across multiple professional fields by the 1970s. The examination of the Emergency House has nevertheless revealed how this typology of 'portable building'[69] was only possible in a situation in which the 'Other' was imagined and catered to, within a wider apparatus of humanitarian logistics, economic imperatives and the desire of selected actors to 'make a difference'.

Moreover, as highlighted above, the Emergency House in many ways reflects design typologies, imaginaries and methods that have remained prevalent, alongside the sustained fascination of designers and architects with standardized and 'innovative' shelter approaches. Following the release of the United Nations Disaster Relief Organization (UNDRO) guidelines, 'Shelter after Disaster' in 1982, which dismissed any attempts to design 'universal shelters to suit all cultures, climates and hazards', the practice nevertheless continued.[70] Such a situation has only become more widespread within a wider 'innovation turn' amongst humanitarian actors,[71] which has led to a heightened interest in new technologies, growing partnerships with the private sector, and rising concerns for design and design-thinking precepts. This process, which has contributed to the rise of experimentations with 'universal' shelter, has only accelerated with the heightened visibility of architectural and design initiatives, particularly Western ones, online and in the media. There, many such '"innovative designs" have become a fetish, creating a mistaken reassurance that circumstances can be controlled while obscuring a series of more serious, structural issues that remain unaddressed'.[72]

In pursuing the objective of a portable, universal shelter, the Emergency House discarded one of the predominant attributes of building – that of its relationship to site. Its enduring appeal as a media object has secured the longevity of this type, despite the known limitations of such initiatives. This chapter has contributed to lifting the veil on some of these processes, whilst bringing forth the intersections that have prevailed between design, architecture and humanitarian aid. More work, however, needs to be conducted on the local reception of such 'universal' building/objects and on how conceptual divisions have been perceived, countered and reappropriated in diverse locations.

## Notes

1   Esther Charlesworth, *Humanitarian Architecture: 15 Stories of Architects Working After Disaster* (Oxford: Routledge, 2014), 8–9.

2   Tom Scott-Smith, 'Places for People: Architecture, Building and Humanitarian Innovation', *Journal of Humanitarian Affairs* 1, no. 3 (2019): 16.

3   On the exhibition of Peter Stoutjesdijk's Shelter for Haiti (2013) at the Stedelijk Design Museum, see: Lilián Sánchez-Moreno, 'Dream Out Loud: Designing for Tomorrow's Demands', *Design and Culture* 9, no.2 (2017).

4   Better Shelter, 'Press Release: UNHCR and Better Shelter extend agreement on the provision of temporary housing for refugees', 30 July 2020, https://bettershelter.org/press-release (accessed 12 January 2021).
5   These critiques pertained to IKEA's Better Shelter. Tom Scott-Smith, 'Beyond the Boxes: Refugee Shelter and the Humanitarian Politics of Life', *American Ethnologist* 46, no.4 (2019): 513–14.
6   Scott-Smith, 'Places for People', 17.
7   Scott-Smith, 'Beyond the Boxes'.
8   Ian Davis, *Shelter After Disaster* (Oxford: Oxford Polytechnic Press, 1978), 49.
9   'Two Approaches to Scientific Aid for Disaster Areas', *Nature* 250 (16 August 1974): 527.
10  On the concept of 'distant suffering' see Luc Boltanski, *Distant Suffering: Morality, Media and Politics* (Cambridge: Cambridge University Press, 1999) and Roger Silverstone, *Media and Morality: On the Rise of the Mediapolis* (Cambridge: Polity Press, 2007).
11  Kevin O'Sullivan, 'Humanitarian Encounters: Biafra, NGOs and Imaginings of the Third World in Britain and Ireland, 1967 – 70', *Journal of Genocide Research* 16, no.2–3 (2014): 299.
12  Lisa Smirl, 'Plain Tales from the Reconstruction Site: Spatial Continuities in Contemporary Humanitarian Practice', in *Empire, Development and Colonialism: The Past in the Present*, ed. Mark Duffield and Vernon Hewitt (Martlesham: Boydell & Brewer, 2013), 90.
13  Bertrand Taithe and John Borton, 'History, Memory and "Lessons Learnt" for Humanitarian Practitioners', *European Review of History: Revue Européenne d'Histoire* 23, no.1–2 (2016); Siddiqi, 'Architecture Culture, Humanitarian Expertise'; Felicity D. Scott, *Outlaw Territories: Environments of Insecurity/Architectures of Counterinsurgency* (Cambridge, MA: MIT Press, 2016); Kate Storh, '100 Years of Humanitarian Design', in *Design Like You Give A Damn: Architectural Responses to Humanitarian Crises*, ed. Architecture for Humanity (New York, NY: Metropolis Books, 2006).
14  Tom Scott-Smith, 'The Fetishism of Humanitarian Objects and the Management of Malnutrition in Emergencies', *Third World Quarterly* 34, no.5 (2013); Tom Scott-Smith, 'Places for People Architecture, Building and Humanitarian Innovation', *Journal of Humanitarian Affairs* 1, no.3 (2019): 16.
15  Anooradha Iyer Siddiqi, 'Writing With: Togethering, Difference, and Feminist Architectural Histories of Migration', in 'Structural Instabilities', eds. Daniel Barber and Eduardo Rega, special edition of *e-flux Architecture* (2018); Daniel Bertrand Monk et al., eds, 'A Discussion on the Global and Universal', *Grey Room* 61 (October 2015): 66–127.
16  On the concept of 'politics of life', see: Didier Fassin, 'Humanitarianism as a Politics of Life', *Public Culture* 19, no. 3 (2007): 499–520.
17  Eleanor Davey, John Borton and Matthew Foley, 'A History of the Humanitarian System: Western Origins and Foundations', HPG Working Paper, Overseas Development Institute, London (June 2013): 29.

18. Ibid., 31.
19. Michael Barnett, *Empire of Humanity: A History of Humanitarianism* (New York, NY: Cornell University, 2011), 107, 132.
20. Ian Davis and David Alexander, *Recovery from Disaster* (Oxford: Routledge, 2015), 228.
21. Randolph C. Kent, *Anatomy of Disaster Relief: The International Network in Action* (London: Pinter Publishers, 1987), 46.
22. John Murlis, 'The Role of the Designer in Disaster Relief', in *ICSID, Design for Need: The Social Contribution of Design*, ed. Julian Bicknell and Liz McQuiston (London: Pergamon Press, 1977), 55.
23. Ian Davis, *Shelter After Disaster* (Oxford: Oxford Polytechnic Press, 1978), 46.
24. Andrew Herscher, 'Designs on Disaster: Humanitarianism and Contemporary Architecture', in *Routledge Companion to Critical Approaches to Contemporary Architecture*, ed. Swati Chattopadhyay and Jeremy White (London: Routledge, 2019).
25. Stohr, '100 Years of Humanitarian Design', 36.
26. On the meeting between humanitarianism and architecture historically, see: Andrew Herscher, *Displacements: Architecture and Refugee* (Berlin: Sternberg Press, 2017).
27. Davis, *Shelter After Disaster*, 49.
28. Tania Messell, 'Design and Disaster Relief: ICSID and the League of Red Cross Societies (1971–1979)', in *Design and Displacement*, ed. Sarah Lichtman and Jilly Traganou (London: Routledge, 2022).
29. For instance, this was the case with the study commissioned to the Department of Design Research (DDR) by the British Overseas Development Ministry to develop 'universal' emergency shelter design criteria. Carnegie-Mellon University/Intertect Emergency Shelter Team Reports, The 1977 International Disaster Preparedness Seminar, 1977, The Frederick C. Cuny/INTERTECT Collection, Texas A&M University Libraries.
30. Storh, '100 Years of Humanitarian Design', 37.
31. Michael John Gorman, *Buckminster Fuller: Designing for Mobility* (Milan: Skira, 2005), 125–6.
32. Simone Jeska, *Transparent Plastics: Design and Technology* (Berlin: Springer, 2007), 13.
33. David Crowley, 'Looking Down on Spaceship Earth: Cold War Landscapes', in *Cold War Modernism*, ed. David Crowley and Jane Pavitt (London: V&A Publishing, 2008), 260.
34. Silvia Bottinelli, 'The Discourse of Modern Nomadism: The Tent in Italian Art and Architecture of the 1960s and 1970s', *Art Journal* 74, no. 2 (Summer 2015): 62–80.
35. Eva Díaz, 'Dome Culture in the Twenty-first Century', *Grey Room*, 42 (Winter 2011): 80–105.
36. Davey, Borton and Foley, 'A History of the Humanitarian System', 11.

37  Maggie Black, *A Cause for Our Times* (Oxford: Oxfam, 1992).
38  Also referred to as the Bangladesh Liberation War.
39  Anooradha Iyer Siddiqi, 'Architecture Culture, Humanitarian Expertise: From the Tropics to Shelter, 1953–93', *Journal of the Society of Architectural Historians* 76, no. 3 (September 2017): 367–84.
40  Dante Bondonno and Brian Colleran, 'The Site-moulding of Refugee Shelters in Expanded Polystyrene: A Design Study Report for Oxfam', University of Oxford: Bodleian Library, Oxfam Archive, Ms. Oxfam PRG/5/5/89-Folder: 1971–1974.
41  Ibid.
42  Ibid.
43  Letter from R. B. C. Brown to Jim Howard, 7 September 1973, University of Oxford: Bodleian Library, Oxfam Archive, Ms. Oxfam PRG/5/5/89-Folder: 1971–1974.
44  Bondonno and Colleran, 'The Site-moulding of Refugee Shelters in Expanded Polystyrene', 5.
45  Ibid.
46  Terms used indiscriminately to refer to Oxfam's Emergency House throughout Oxfam documentation and media.
47  University of Oxford: Bodleian Library, Oxfam Archive ms. Oxfam PRG/5/5/89, Folder 2: 1974–1976.
48  Ibid.
49  Derek Gregory, 'Imaginative Geographies', *Progress in Human Geography* 19, no.4 (1995).
50  Paul Oliver, *Dwellings: The House Across the World* (Austin, TX: University of Texas Press, 1987).
51  Ian Davis, 'Emergency Shelter and Natural Disasters: Some Observations Based on Earthquakes in Skopje and Managua', text of a lecture sponsored by INTERTECT, given at Carnegie-Mellon University, 1975, 5.
52  See for example, architect John F.C. Turner's concept of community planning, developed in the 1970s. John F.C. Turner, *Housing by people: Towards autonomy in Building environments* (London: Marion Boyars Publishers Ltd, 1976).
53  Oxfam Disaster Emergency Housing Patents, University of Oxford: Bodleian Library, Oxfam Archive, Guy Stringer's files: Ms. Oxfam DIR/2/3/2/116-Folder: Dec 1972–Oct 1973.
54  Oxfam, 'Bulletin 5: Disaster Housing – Pakistan', Bodleian Library, Oxfam Archive DIR/2/3/2/19-Folder: Pakistan Floods, August 73–May 74.
55  Prime Minister Zulfikar Ali Bhutto's hometown was located in the Sind, where he proposed two construction sites, one being next to a statue which he was to unveil himself. Ibid.
56  Ibid.
57  Press Release, 'Oxfam Emergency House Team Return' (1975). University of Oxford: Bodleian Library, Oxfam Archive, ms. Oxfam COM/1/3/2, 1974–1975.

58 Ibid.
59 Ibid.
60 Jim Howard and Robert Mister, 'Lessons Learnt by Oxfam from their Experience of Shelter Provision 1970–1978', *Disasters* 3, no.2 (1979): 142.
61 Ian Davis, 'Charity Begins with Homes', *New Scientist* (6 July 1978): 16.
62 Phillip Knightley, 'Disasters How the Helpers Make it Worse', *The Sunday Times* (25 June 1978).
63 Adrian Greeman, 'Oxfam Building Polyurethane Foam Houses for Refugees', *New Scientist* (27 November 1975); 'Two Approaches to Scientific Aid for Disaster Areas', 527.
64 Different approaches to AT-IMG 0782. University of Oxford, Bodleian Library, Oxfam Archive.
65 Jim Howard to Guy Stringer, Memorandum, in Appropriate Technology, University of Oxford: Bodleian Library, Oxfam Archive, Guy Stringer's files: Ms. Oxfam DIR/2/3/2/67-Folder: Jan 1974–Oct 76.
66 Ibid; Siddiqi, 'Architecture Culture, Humanitarian Expertise', 374.
67 Howard and Mister, 'Lessons Learnt by Oxfam', 142.
68 Howard and Mister, 'Lessons Learnt by Oxfam', 142.
69 Robert Kronenburg, *Architecture in Motion: The History and Development of Portable Building* (London: Routledge, 2013).
70 Yasemin Aysan and Ian Davis, 'Process, Realism and Knowledge: Towards an Agenda for the International Decade for Natural Disaster Reduction', eds. Yasemin Aysan and Ian Davis *Disasters and the Small Dwelling*, second edition (Oxon: Earthscan, 2013) 12.
71 Tom Scott-Smith, 'Humanitarian Neophilia: The Innovation Turn and its Implications', *Third World Quarterly* 37, no. 12 (2016): 2229–51.
72 Scott-Smith, 'The Fetishism of Humanitarian Objects'.

# PART THREE

# Uneasy Difference

Part Three of this collection focuses on those cases in which there is friction or uneasy differences between objects and architecture. These need to be exposed if the political expediencies involved are to be understood and subsequent grounds for intervention revealed. By analysing the discomfort engendered by practices that intend to elide building and object or to transplant the qualities of one to the other, we are given the opportunity to consider the nature of the interests that seek to maintain their distinctiveness. Whose territory and privilege are being encroached on, by whom and to what end?

Chapter Ten by Alistair Cartwright explores how changes in building regulations reveal shifting conceptions of the relationship between building materials, the building and the city around it. Within the legal infrastructure, designed to regulate the urban environment and promote public safety, there is encoded an underlying understanding of what a building is and what building components are, and this understanding is the distillate of certain historical and ideological tendencies. Cartwright's research reveals the process of atomization, by which legal understanding of the building has shifted to reduce it to its constituent parts. This process of legal fragmentation turns the building from an artefact of architecture to an aggregation of commercial products, dissolving it as a social entity.

In Chapter Eleven by Ross K. Elfline, we encounter an alternative moment of engagement between architectural practice and design objects. The work of experimental architects Haus-Rucker-Co. in object design installations and exhibitions pursued an architecture of interconnectedness, beyond building. Haus-Rucker-Co. sought to intervene in people's relationships with space and their connectedness with one another, functions which had previously lain implicitly within the domain of architecture. The relational objects proposed by Haus-Rucker-Co. sought, instead, to give users the means to evade the protocols and limitations of the built world and create connections between one another on their own terms.

In Chapter Twelve by Jane Pavitt, we are again given the opportunity to consider tensions between architecture, architectural technologies and commodities. Through her analysis of the label 'High-Tech' across architecture and interior design, Pavitt reveals contradictory interpretations that coexist behind the label. In the domain of architecture, the term emphasizes celebration of advanced architectural technologies, with its roots in the ideology of the modern movement. However, as a label applied to an interior design style, High-Tech was based on the use of cheap, industrially manufactured elements in a way that mixed the playful and the practical. At the heart of this tension is the conflict between the technocratic expert and the impromptu, do-it-yourself and ad hoc. The definitional problem created by this term floating across architectural and design histories, while carrying quite different meanings, represents a gulf that is still to be bridged.

Chapter Thirteen by Livia Rezende and Tatiana Pinto invites us into a reflective dialogue that probes the uneasy persistence of divisions and occlusions marking out the territories of architecture, design and their histories. Trained respectively as a designer and design historian and as an architect and architectural historian, Rezende and Pinto consider the history of modernism and of architectural and design education in their native Brazil. They bring their insights to bear on the work still to be done to uncover and address the institutionalized inequalities that architecture and design, in both education and execution, gave substance to and continue to perpetuate.

Across all these chapters lies the long shadow of the social responsibility of architecture and design and their power to articulate relationships between people. On the one hand lies the utopian possibility to design for better futures, better communities and greater freedom; on the other hand, the persistent reality within which the focus of attention is consistently deflected away from the communal and equitable in favour of existing commercial interests and existing structures of power. Our last chapter ends with a rallying cry, echoed by the editors, for writers of architectural and design history to strive to think outside and across established boundaries and thereby contribute to making visible what those structures were established to hide or to naturalize.

# CHAPTER TEN

# Regulation by Design: Reification and Building Regulations

*Alistair Cartwright*

Designed objects and built structures – when did these two categories of 'things' enter fully into the letter of the law? When it comes to the objects of design, a rough date might be the decade or so before the French Revolution, when the first comprehensive tables for the standardized production of artillery components were adopted by the French military.[1] Craft guilds in the middle of the eighteenth century still had considerable freedom over their work but the later part of the century saw increasing moves towards standardization, driven by the demands of warfare, the scientific revolution and a burgeoning capitalist economy.[2] There is a sense in which design itself, as we understand it today, begins in this moment, born together with its standardized, legally prescribed applications. As Ken Adler notes, projective drawings, as the basic *métier* of design, achieve their standardizing effect by 'reducing the representation of objects (and their decoding) to a set of formal rules. The goal is to limit the discretion of both the person drawing the plan *and* the person interpreting it' – in other words, the worker.[3] From its beginnings, then, design is bound up with various regulatory mechanisms. It both facilitates and is a product of the capitalist division of labour.

As for built structures, Dame Judith Hackitt, in the Interim Report of her *Independent Review of Building Regulations and Fire Safety* commissioned after the Grenfell Tower disaster,[4] suggests the year 1212. After a terrible fire in Southwark that year, a council of 'reputable men' laid down a series of rules about roofing materials, distance between buildings, firefighting provisions, etc.[5] The year chosen by Hackitt fits the period that most historians of this unloved subject designate as the earliest traceable origin of our present-day system of building regulations.[6] It was around this time, five centuries before the Great Fire, that a series of devastating conflagrations razed parts of London to the ground.[7] Regulations in the wake of these fires grappled with the unruly growth of towns, the latter seen as ambiguous 'half servants . . . half parasites' upon the body politic of the feudal system.[8]

Fire fed on these half-formed conditions, and the regulations were an attempt to fight the symptom and marshal the nascent economic forces behind it. Later proclamations in the era of English absolutism that targeted tradespeople and 'substantial artisans' by strictly forbidding ad hoc construction and urban sprawl,[9] while granting licence to major developments such as Inigo Jones's Covent Garden in the 1630s, suggest the metamorphosis of an incipient urbanization (previously encouraged by landowners) into novel, frequently hostile class forces.[10] Always in the background of these proclamations lay the fear of the 'mob': the settlement of roving beggars and vagabonds thrown on the city by the break-up of the feudal land system.[11]

What these parallel histories tell us is that objects and buildings, the conventionally defined realms of design and architecture, do indeed follow different paths, at least when it comes to their writing into law and hence their meshing with powers of state and capital. If the regulation of designed objects belongs to the era of capitalism ascendant, then the regulation of buildings derives from the crisis of feudalism. The former seeks to control the production of commodities, while the latter deals with the material fabric of society's spatial organization.

And yet, as this chapter will argue, these different paths also come together at a certain point. It is this moment of convergence, formalized in the 1960s then radically overdetermined in the 1980s, that will prove critical to the nature of contemporary building regulations. If the Grenfell tragedy has laid bare the catastrophic flaws in our present-day system of building regulations, then these must be traced back to this earlier moment to truly understand them. As well as its implications for gentrification and the housing crisis, Grenfell should be understood not as an isolated accident but as the culmination of a certain logic of reification: a logic in which atomized 'things' eclipse social relations, such that the commodification of the building process – and with it the subordination of architecture's historic role in the ordering of the built environment to the priorities of design – has been embedded at the heart of the regulatory system.

This chapter presents a historical materialist account of the development of building regulations in the English context. I focus on the first national building regulations (applying to England and Wales), which became law in 1965, placing this moment in a wider historical and theoretical framework that arches backwards to the nineteenth century and flashes forwards to the 1980s and onwards. The intersecting histories of architecture and design emerge from this retelling as an outcome of reification.

## Complexity – actual and ideological

Even tentative dates of origin concerning apparently pedestrian matters like the building regulations carry political implications. The regulation of the built environment has a long history. True, there are fatal inconsistencies in the current regulations, but to portray this history as one of 'piecemeal' 'evolution' towards a state of 'complexity', or the quasi-accidental accrual of ordinances into a form of 'landscape', is an act of mystification.[12] Our current era of deregulation, heralded by the 1984 Building Act, has executed a drastic and ideologically motivated stripping out of regulations.[13]

Modern buildings may indeed be technically 'complex', but contemporary regulations display a marked abdication of responsibility to grasp that complexity, let alone master it. This chapter traces that abdication back to a process of reification dating from the nineteenth century. It is a process that has shaped the building regulations in its own image over a period of roughly a hundred years, giving rise to a notion of complexity that derives not from material reality as such, but from the artificial 'second nature' of the market; a complexity, that is, that confronts individuals and individual capitalist organizations as the evanescent effect of natural laws arising from the exchange process.[14] While the history of building regulations predates capitalism's dominance by several centuries, from the late nineteenth century onwards these regulations underwent a sea change. With the systematic incorporation of performance standards for individual components and the complementary degrading of regulations governing the building as a whole, the realm of designed and manufactured objects, of commodities, comes to dominate over that of architecture. Buildings, in effect, are reduced to agglomerations of 'objects'. And when considered from one side of the cycle of accumulation, their whole reality boils down to that of the commodity; they become giant commodities, machines for living or working.

There are several false notions of complexity that have undermined previous attempts to historicize or theorize the role of building regulations. Despite a few hopeful avenues of inquiry,[15] most dedicated studies on the subject, sparse as they are, present a litany of Acts and clauses, with asides drawn from Parliament or the industry press.[16] The approach is painstakingly 'empirical' yet frequently divorced from wider reality. One cannot help feeling that these authors have succeeded in drawing a map only slightly more compressed than the territory they describe. In a process that in fact mirrors the formalization of the law itself towards ever greater internal coherence, the reality at stake seems to disappear under the weight of legalistic detail.[17]

Existing accounts of the building regulations therefore replicate, at what appears to be a highly mediated level but is really a thoroughly disconnected plane of reflection, the fundamental process of commodification. Once the objects of production come to stand apart from the labour that went into their making, then not only do they acquire a seeming autonomy, they also become, through exchange, the only way of securing the means of survival; all social relations are mediated through this sprawling network of atomized 'objects'.[18] It is this dual social process rather than any latent material (or psychical) property that gives the elements of building – whether a vat of concrete or an air-conditioning unit – their 'animated' character.[19] For the purposes of regulating the built environment, it becomes increasingly difficult to think of buildings as anything other than a slotting together of designed components.

## Regulation and reification

The 1985 building regulations which resulted from the Act of 1984 – the template of all subsequent building regulations in England and Wales – can be seen as a forerunner of the deregulatory spirit announced that same year in the government White Paper, 'Lifting the Burden'. This key document of the Thatcher era made the case for removing what had supposedly become 'too heavy a drain on our national resources' across a whole number of areas: transport, the environment, agriculture, social security, fire safety, and more.[20] For the building regulations, this meant the final abandonment of any attempt to treat buildings holistically, as a matter of architectural inspection and intervention rather than as a codification of individually designed elements.[21]

How then did the 1985 regulations manage to shed the burden of complexity? Their overall form suggests a combination of verbal sleight of hand backed up by the incorporation of standards for proprietary products. Words like 'adequate', 'having regard to', 'workmanlike' and 'proper' condense vast areas of technical knowledge into the nudge and wink of supposedly universal conventions of competence.[22] Alongside this stand several references to performance standards published by official bodies, notably the British Board of Agrément (BBA) and British Standards Institute (BSI).[23] References like these have become absolutely integral to contemporary building regulations, particularly through 'Approved Documents', which provide an additional layer of expert but not strictly legally binding guidance.[24] The current building regulations reference over 500 standards of this kind.[25]

This combination of strategically vague descriptions with detailed product standards has been widely commented on in terms of the shift to so-called 'functional regulations'.[26] Rather than prescribing exactly what materials or methods of construction can or cannot be used, the new style of regulations would focus on the *function* that the latter should fulfil. In a kind of stylistic jump-cut, language rendered generic to the point of meaninglessness (yet overloaded with tacit understanding) contrasts with the punctilious statements of performance standards based on laboratory-controlled test conditions.

This juxtaposition is worth dwelling on. It echoes the contradiction that infuses capitalist society between detailed control at a microscopic level and widespread fragmentation at the macroscopic level, a mismatch most glaringly expressed in the way individual firms operate an extreme degree of technical control within a context of generalized market chaos. The Hungarian Marxist Georg Lukács brilliantly demonstrated how this contradiction affects the very nature of knowledge and action in capitalist society, creating a situation in which a convincing picture of the social totality seems to slip beyond our grasp at the same time as breakthroughs are won via specialized abstraction.[27] Its origins, to follow Lukács, lie in the organization of society into competing entities structured around the production and consumption of commodities. Competition sabotages any general coordination of society at the same time as commodification drives the technical control of disconnected objects.

In contemporary building regulations this contradiction takes a particular form: standards for individual building components – that is, commodities – are specified in detail while the control of the building as a whole is left to the assumed good sense of architects, engineers, contractors, surveyors, building managers, and so on, to be verified by inspectors whose role is partly privatized. This professional division of labour reiterates the historic division between architecture and design: while designers of the products deployed in buildings must conform to a testing regime of supposed rigour, architects deal mainly with the application and assemblage of those products. The regulatory regime splits itself down the middle, and in the process becomes incapable of grasping the building as a whole. The inherent blindsides of the regulatory system then persist in spite of perceptions that architects still are, or should be, sovereign over the building considered in its totality. Architecture's deference to largely unexamined regulatory regimes – for reasons to be explained shortly – is one sure sign of the illusory nature of these perceptions.

The critique outlined above hails from Marx's concept of reification. It is rarely, if ever, articulated with respect to building regulations. And yet calls following the post-Grenfell review of building regulations for a renewed focus on 'whole buildings' in many ways seem to answer precisely such a critique.[28] The demand for a 'holistic view of building safety' – one that treats each 'complex' building as 'a single coherent system' with a durational 'life cycle' – has an admirable spirit.[29] But such recommendations remain modest about trespassing into the realm of precisely those 'components' that form the basic elements of the building – that is, designed and manufactured products.[30] One of the most glaring features of the current regulations – the privatization of the product-testing regime – largely escapes direct intervention. Recommended measures introduce greater transparency but dare not consider the renationalization of testing, let alone more direct forms of intervention in production.[31] Instead, emphasis falls on the 'responsibility' of named 'dutyholders': architects, contractors, clients and building managers – the realms of construction, maintenance and architecture, but far less so that of design.[32] To the extent that 'designers' are talked about, these are 'principal designers', meaning whoever supervises the *overall* design of the building – in other words, architects. Really this response doubles down on the division between building components as commodities and the 'whole building' as a matter of tacit (but still highly technical) professional knowledge. A thorough, root-and-branch knowledge of the 'whole building' is in fact a myth. Indeed, the one measure that could straightforwardly achieve this – the planned circumscription of building components as part of, for example, a mass public housing programme – seems basically impossible within the current regulatory imagination. As long as this is the case, the wished-for status of buildings as integrated wholes must remain precisely that: a wish.

## The welfare state and the roots of deregulation

As scholars at the time pointed out, the 1980s deregulatory moment was accompanied by a great deal of 're-regulation'.[33] One of the hallmarks of neoliberalism is the role of state regulatory mechanisms in creating new 'artificial' markets and quasi-markets: markets in carbon emissions, in educational attainment, and indeed in testing regimes and building inspection. This double role of regulations does not begin with the 1980s but forms a central contradiction of advanced capitalism that becomes more and more evident throughout the twentieth century. It is, I would argue, the post-1945 welfare state that crystallizes the contradictions of capitalist regulation, bringing them to a point of clarity and tension that stands out from both earlier and later periods.

To understand the roots of the 1980s deregulatory moment it is necessary to return to this earlier, more foundational one, which ironically appears to represent the peak of regulatory control in the form of the first national building regulations of 1965. The latter replaced the panoply of local byelaws that existed up to that point and will be discussed shortly. First, however, I want to lay out some of the theoretical background that can help understand how the imperatives of a commodity society are mediated politically; how one moves from the fundamental critique of reification to an apprehension of the social totality constructed on that basis. One important way this movement takes concrete form is in the development of the welfare state, and with it the beginnings of a system of regulation by design; a form of legal code, in other words, that takes designed objects as its elementary principal.

As others in the Marxist tradition have argued, at a certain point in the history of capitalist development, depending on national conditions, something approximating the welfare state often becomes necessary for capitalism's survival.[34] The state comes to act as an essential mediator between the interests of capital and labour, maintaining a stable environment for accumulation by both regulating capital and underwriting or directly providing for the costs of labour's reproduction. Such a compromise is both a hard-won product of class struggle and a necessary adjunct to continued accumulation; it is at root contradictory. The function of building regulations in this context is clear. At the same time as they seek to prevent fires, or structural failure, or the spread of infectious diseases, they equally aim to reassure architects and contractors of the reliability and compatibility of building products, providing a coherent framework for standardization and security of contracts, as well as taking responsibility for fundamental research and development. Just as important, the very same regulations present the whole nature of building as a neutral business, obscuring any sign of political intervention.

The harmonization of these two aspects of the welfare state implies a closer and closer overlapping of the state's preventative or compensatory functions with the fundamental principles of a capitalist economy. This is what we see starting to happen in the 1965 building regulations. The latter represent a shift from principally negative, reactive responses to the harmful side effects of urbanization, towards positive, proactive measures that attempt to guide and steer the business of building and urban development. Contrary to more recent claims,[35] the systematic incorporation of performance standards or 'functional' regulations begins here, in 1965, rather than in the push to deregulation twenty years later.

This shift was well recognized at the time. The director of building management in the research and development section of the Ministry of Public Building and Works, C. E. Wooster, described the change in terms of a progression towards regulating not just safety issues but also 'matters of amenity' (e.g. thermal insulation).[36] Performance standards were central to this reorientation. Rather than simply a progression towards more 'scientific' control of buildings, as some have framed this history,[37] the building regulations sought to offer what one of their main drafters, O. H. Lawn of the Ministry of Housing and Local Government, called 'built-in flexibility' to an industry undergoing rapid technological and social change.[38] It is this focus on 'flexibility', with the possibility of rapid adjustments via updated performance standards rather than primary legislation, that constitutes the real 'positivity' of the 1965 regulations. The building regulations of 1965 are thus peppered with references to BSI standards applying to a whole range of materials and components.[39]

Contrast this with the situation roughly a century earlier. The Metropolitan Building Act of 1844 (the first major change in the building regulations since the eighteenth century and the legislative template for the next thirty years) prescribed a narrow repertoire of materials – principally brick, stone, mortar, tile and slate – that recur in various combinations regarding exterior and party walls, roof coverings, drains and hearths.[40] Innovations in iron frame construction fall completely outside the scope of the regulations and could only develop thanks to the exemption of certain dock and railway buildings.[41] But if the difference were only one of resistance to new technology it would be a matter of degree rather than quality. The real distinction lies in the generic definition of the materials. Brick is brick, stone is stone, tile is tile. There is no mention of this or that particular type of brick, which must meet this or that particular standard. The regulations at this point still regard the building as a work of combined labour by various trades (bricklayers, stonemasons, carpenters, etc.), with the materials named standing as symbols or relics of these trades.[42] The stonemason's assumed knowledge of the different capacities of stone, or the carpenter's of wood, lives on in the regulations as another feudal remnant. It is only later in the nineteenth century that a more thorough commodification of the building process would totally efface this labour.

To the extent that the regulations refrained from decomposing the building into a series of products and standards, they also tended to focus on the overall form of the building, on the dimensions and elements determining that form (exterior and party walls, chimney flues, roofs, etc.), or on spaces surrounding the building such as streets, courts, backyards, etc. – that is, on the limits and edges of the building.[43] In this way, the negative, reactive attitude to the growth of towns reasserted itself in the midst of industrialization. The threat of conflagration and plague, meaning the spread of fire *between* buildings and the spread of disease *between* households, still haunted the regulatory imagination. Yet a concern with public nuisances aligned easily here with deference to private property: the boundaries described were the boundaries of what is owned. And in this sense the regulations were in tune with the ruling ideas of the time. The interior of the building, especially the home, the 'castle' of the private citizen, represented the socio-economic space where the regulations feared to tread.[44] The inherent tension between the building as a capitalization of ground rent[45] and the building as a productive or reproductive assemblage of commodities (a machine for living or working) achieved a temporary, unstable balance in the form of regulations that privileged the whole over the part, even if that whole was itself reified as a domain of private property.

The restructuring of whole buildings around specialized components in the name of sanitation that Reyner Banham traced to the 1860s would therefore have to wait until the twentieth century for anything approaching a mass application.[46] In the meantime, the regulations continued to focus on the ways in which buildings impinged on the wider public realm, with only tentative additions over the next few decades regarding the detailed internal composition of the building.[47]

Something begins to change towards the turn of the century. The seeming paradox that Lukács identified in the relationship between the law and the material world, whereby the former pursues the same accelerating specialization as the latter, only to become increasingly fixed and rigid in the face of an ever-changing reality, now finds expression in the relationship between building regulations and the world of building.[48] By the late nineteenth century the constant revolutionizing of production, which seized on the building materials industry much more than the construction site, became an unstoppable force that jostled and fragmented the already manifold form of the regulations.

The signal developments are familiar: the invention of reinforced concrete in 1854–6 and its first serious applications in the 1880s; steel frame construction leading to the first skyscrapers around the same time; and the growth in the variety of proprietary materials, many of which resemble more or less designed *components*, from layered sheet materials such as millboard (developed in 1875) and plasterboard (1904),[49] to prefabricated window and door units, and finally mechanical components including humidity-controlled ventilators (1920s onwards).[50] Among these changes there are in fact two complementary developments: on the one hand, the perfection of the structural frame, and on the other, the proliferation of 'augmented' components. The frame both enables and makes necessary the use of such components. By freeing the walls from their load-bearing function, the frame allows the introduction of a wide variety of lightweight materials in place of traditional masonry.

Architectural history has internalized this basic move as the modern movement's original moment of genius.[51] Less often commented on is how the thinning of the exterior envelope, precisely the focus of building regulations up to this point, encourages the invention or application of a whole new range of products designed to replace or surpass the qualities previously received as inherent from heavy masonry or breathable timber. Qualities of thermal insulation and fire resistance (in the case of masonry) or solar screening and ventilation (in the case of timber) must now be supplied in the form of specifically designed components, whether of a mechanical or composite kind. Industrial design seals these qualities within the product while architecture provides the gridwork for their deployment.

This is precisely the set of problems that Banham analysed in his *Architecture of the Well-tempered Environment* (1969). Writing towards the end of the tradition that assumed the architect's professional sovereignty, Banham conceived of these problems as above all an architectural challenge: a problem specific to and resolvable within the terms of architecture, even if the latter was no longer understood as the masterly play of volumes in light (paraphrasing Le Corbusier) but rather as the spatial organization of light-emitting, heat-emitting, cooled-air-emitting components.[52] At no point does Banham acknowledge that the 'environmental' technologies around which this new architecture organizes itself are nothing but incidents in the growing flood of commodities hitting the building market.

This market had of course formed many years before. But the differentiation of 'raw' materials, themselves commodities, into a vast panoply of components, many of them marketed under specific brand names, represents a shift in gear. Moreover, what begins as a technical challenge to traditional building gradually acquires a momentum all of its own. As Marion Bowley showed regarding prefabricated wall boards, a period of genuine cost saving or technical innovation during the 1920s and 1930s led to the amalgamation

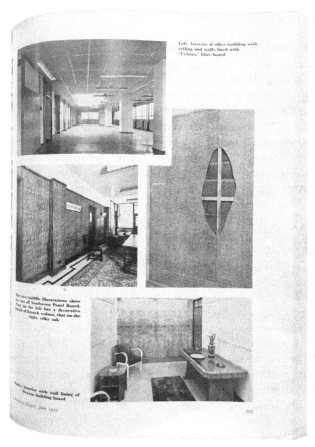

FIGURE 10.1 *Celotex fibreboard panels*, Building Digest, *June (1950): 197.*

of competing manufacturers.[53] The resulting post-war expansion of the market in building boards, resting as it did on just a handful of major companies, was the result 'not of product innovations' but rather 'of market innovations', many of them of an 'ersatz character'.[54]

Ornamentation is effectively designed into the surface appearance of components, especially lining and cladding panels. These materials have the peculiar quality of being elaborately differentiated within the market and yet designed to create a homogenous surface once installed, at which point their 'individual' character is completely effaced (see Figure 10.1). The reification of the designed product does double service in erasing not only the labour that went into its own manufacture but also the labour of architecture and construction, and even the acquired social history of a building. It is no coincidence that such products, applied as a disguising skin to council housing, have been found to be at the root of the Grenfell Tower disaster. Aesthetic, economic and political questions fuse at this point.

The question of how to regulate the vastly increased volume and variety of commodities stemming from the post-war building industry is therefore not merely architectural, as Banham would suggest. The systematic answer provided by the 1965 regulations was in fact suggested first by private enterprise. Architects, engineers and insurers increasingly felt the need for some means of assuring the quality and compatibility of a proliferating range of products. Under these conditions the first building product-testing houses were founded. BSI (originally the Engineering Standards Committee) was established in 1901 as a private organization, only to be effectively nationalized in 1942 after receiving a Royal Charter in 1929.[55] Fire safety research also encapsulates this process. A Royal Commission on the subject in 1921 trailed behind the first private testing facilities by over twenty years.[56] A looming world war then spurred on the amalgamation of private and public initiatives, leading to the first truly national fire safety organization with a 'scientific' approach, the Joint Fire Research Organisation (JFRO), in 1946.[57] Initiatives that had a somewhat later start, were, by contrast, government creations from the beginning, notably the Building Research Station (BRS), which was established on a permanent national footing in 1925.[58] By this point 'building science', or more specifically product testing, had emerged as what Mark Swenarton calls 'the talisman of the social-democratic confluence' over state housing.[59]

Swenarton's history of the BRS offers valuable insights into the relationship between 'building science' and the interwar housing programme, showing how the promotion of standardized components was used to attack trade unions by reducing contractors' reliance on skilled labour.[60] This trend was to continue in the post-war period, exemplified by lobbying centred on the Ministry of Labour carried out by the powerful Fibre Building Board Development Organisation (FIDOR).[61]

However, this must be seen within a more fundamental paradigm of reification. The welfare state's regulatory regime developed by incorporating and formalizing private initiatives, which themselves were born out of the absolute necessities of industry. But in its early stages this 'building science' was a principally economic and therefore one-sided solution. It remained for the state to incorporate a partial form of self-regulation into a totalizing system that would operate ostensibly in the interests of society as a whole. For this to happen, the services that the state renders to capital (in the form of newly nationalized regimes of testing and certification) would have to be hidden from view, divorced from the 'public' function of the building regulations and yet secretly embedded within their structure.

For this reason, the first national building regulations of 1965, as well as their immediate predecessor, the 1952 Model Building Bylaws, do not speak of national regimes of testing and inspection of products. All of that must happen within the closed loop of the testing lab. The latter's methods are subject to little or no democratic scrutiny. What leaves the lab to be absorbed into the building regulations are formalized standards labelled with unique codes. But these standards, despite state sponsorship, are themselves proprietary materials – in effect, commodities. Commentators at the time noted how architects and contractors would need to invest significant sums acquiring libraries of these standards.[62]

From there, it is easy to see how competitive interests develop within the regulatory regime itself. Powerful industry associations came to form close links with the official bodies of state-sponsored 'building science'. The intimate relationship that FIDOR maintained with both BSI and JFRO during the 1950s and 1960s, the former via leading positions on its technical committee and other divisions, the latter via the commissioning of fire safety tests, provides one example of this.[63] Such connections develop not simply on the back of direct lobbying efforts but because the technocratic, reified function of the testing regime implies a basic 'neutrality' and indeed exchangeability of scientific knowledge. As industry continues to churn out more and more products, the pressure increases on testing facilities, offering a further reason to accept private funding.[64] If the government is not prepared to expand the testing regime under state auspices, then it may look to third-sector organizations or private enterprise; indeed, it may become convinced that competition between regulatory bodies will have beneficial effects in terms of efficiency.[65] Finally, it may appear that self-certification by manufacturers is the only way forward. This is in fact exactly what happened with the 1984 Building Act.

## Towards regulation by design

We see from this history how the welfare state forms a contradictory whole with inherent tendencies to erosion and breakdown. And yet this inherently crisis-prone situation appears in the guise of its exact opposite, a system of harmonization. From this point onwards the building regulations would reflect and incorporate the latest developments in industry, while industry would be guided by the systematic framework of the regulations.

This, at least, was the idea. One of the key advocates of performance standards in the 1960s, C. E. Wooster of the Ministry of Public Buildings and Works, imagined a system of regulations that could be programmed into a computer and used to check any design, or indeed to produce a design based on the parameters of the regulations.[66] An experiment at the Industrialised Building Systems and Components Exhibition in 1964 had already demonstrated the feasibility of the idea (see Figure 10.2).[67] Here architecture was reduced to the 'discovery' of solutions within the scope of a system that emerges from the inherent properties of designed objects. Wooster even suggested that the programmability of performance standards raised the possibility of architects certifying their own work.[68]

# REGULATION BY DESIGN

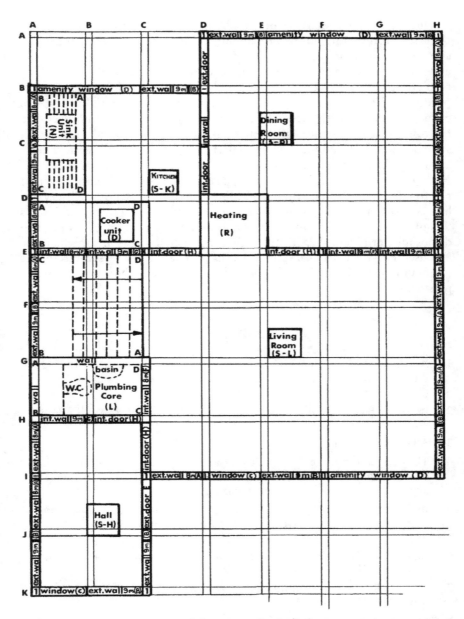

**FIGURE 10.2** *Demonstration of planning grid to be fed into computer programmed with Parker Morris standards. Reproduced in G. R. Fair et al., 'Note on the Computer as an Aid to the Architect',* Computer Journal, *vol. 9, no. 1 (1966): 16–20.*

One of the most extreme proposals, though, came from the architect Geoffrey Hutton, little known today outside his reputation as a stonework specialist. Responding to an article by O. H. Lawn at the Ministry of Housing and Local Government, Hutton envisaged the evolution of the building regulations towards a constantly updated, computer-accessible catalogue of products.[69] The supposedly inevitable standardization of buildings should be met by a policy of 'replacement' rather than maintenance or improvement. Hutton's article lays out with remarkable clarity the logical outcome of systematizing the building regulations into a set of flexible performance standards. Leaving aside the prominence given to it in the *Royal Society of Health Journal*, this position might appear the work of a fantasist, were it not for the echoes found among a curious mixture of senior civil servants like Wooster and architectural avant-gardists like Archigram. The latter's 'Plug-in City' of 1965 envisaged whole buildings themselves reduced to disposable 'products'.[70] With this new type of building – 'from which the first user tears the plastic wrapping' – industrial design and its sub-disciplines (ergonomics, market research) would finally replace architecture in all but prestige projects.[71]

## Notes

1   Ken Adler, 'Making Things the Same: Representation, Tolerance and the End of the Ancien Régime in France', *Social Studies of Science* 28, no. 4 (August 1998): 519.

2   Lawrence Bush, *Standards: Recipes for Reality* (Cambridge MA: MIT Press, 2011), 94.

3   Adler, 'Making Things the Same', 514.

4   The Grenfell Tower fire (14 June 2017) caused 72 deaths and was the worst UK residential fire since the Second World War. A British public inquiry in its aftermath involved close scrutiny of building regulations in relation to fire safety.

5   Judith Hackitt, *Building a Safer Future – Independent Review of Building Regulations and Fire Safety: Interim Report* (London: HMSO, 2017), Cm. 9551, 31.

6   C.C. Knowles and H. Pitt, *The History of Building Regulation in London 1189–1972* (London: Architectural Press, 1972), 6.

7   Anthony Ley, *A History of Building Control in England and Wales 1840–1990* (Coventry: RICS Books, 2000), 1.

8   Maurice Dobb, *Studies in the Development of Capitalism*, 2nd edn. (New York: International Publishers, 1963), 71.

9   Thomas G. Barnes, 'The Prerogative and Environmental Control of London Building in the Early Seventeenth Century: The Lost Opportunity', *California Law Review* 58, no. 6 (November 1970): 1332–63, 1338.

10  Terry R. Slater, 'Medieval Town-founding on the Estates of the Benedictine Order in England', in *Power, Profit and Urban Land: Landownership in*

*Medieval and Early Modern European Towns,* eds. Finn-Einar Eliassen and Geir Atle Ersland (Aldershot: Scolar Press, 1996), 74 and 77.

11  Dobb, *Development of Capitalism,* 12–13 and 26.

12  Hackitt, *Interim Report,* 6 and 31. For an example of how the vocabulary of complexity is used in an uncritical way see Judith Hackitt, *Building a Safer Future – Independent Review of Building Regulations and Fire Safety: Final Report* (London: HMSO, 2018), Cm. 9607, 5, 13, 41 and 87.

13  Peter Apps, 'The Paper Trail: The Failure of Building Regulations', *Inside Housing* (23 March 2018) https://www.insidehousing.co.uk/news/news/the-paper-trail-the-failure-of-building-regulations-55445 (accessed 5 March 2021).

14  Alfred Sohn-Rethel, 'The Formal Characteristics of Second Nature', trans. Daniel Spaulding, *Selva Journal* (20 July 2019) https://selvajournal.org/the-formal-characteristics-of-second-nature/ (accessed 16 June 2021).

15  Mark Swenarton, 'Houses of paper and brown cardboard: Neville Chamberlain and the establishment of the Building Research Station at Garston in 1925', *Planning Perspectives* 22, no. 3 (July 2007): 257–81; Amy Slaton, '"As near as Practicable": Precision, Ambiguity, and the Social Features of Industrial Quality Control', *Technology and Culture* 42, no. 1 (January 2001): 51–80.

16  Roger Harper, *The Evolution of the English Building Regulations 1840–1914* (PhD Diss., University of Sheffield, 1978); Ley, *History of Building Control*; Knowles and Pitt, *History of Building Regulations.*

17  Friedrich Engels cited in Georg Lukács, 'Reification and the Consciousness of the Proletariat', in *History and Class Consciousness,* trans. Rodney Livingstone (Pontypool: Merlin, 1971), 83–222, 103.

18  Lukács, 'Reification', *History and Class Consciousness,* 91.

19  *Contra* Francesca Hughes, *The Architecture of Error: Matter, Measure and the Misadventures of Precision* (Cambridge MA: MIT Press, 2014), 126–7.

20  J. Rowan Robinson and M. G. Lloyd, 'Lifting the burden of planning: A means or an end?', *Local Government Studies* 12, no. 3 (May–June 1986), 51.

21  For contrast see Alistair Cartwright, 'The Un-Ideal Home: Fire Safety, Visual Culture and the LCC (1958–63)', *The London Journal* 46, no. 1 (2021): 66–91.

22  See for example Schedule 1, Part B of The Building Regulations 1985, SI 1985/1065, 3408.

23  E.g. Section 12.3 concerning cavity walls requires a statement of proprietary materials used and their BSI or BBA conformity. Ibid., 3402.

24  Susan Bright and David Sawtell, 'The Oxford Conference: Building Regulations and Cladding', *University of Oxford: Faculty of Law* (28 October 2019) https://www.law.ox.ac.uk/housing-after-grenfell/blog/2019/10/oxford-conference-building-regs-and-cladding (accessed 17 February 2021).

25  Hackitt, *Final Report,* 95.

26  Judith Evans and Robert Wright, 'How Lax Building Rules Led to Grenfell Disaster', *Financial Times* (29 June 2017) https://www.ft.com/content/bf6bcbd0-5b35-11e7-9bc8-8055f264aa8b (accessed 17 February 2021).

27 Lukács, 'Reification', *History and Class Consciousness*, 102.
28 Hackitt, *Final Report*, 24, 45–6, 50–1 and 59.
29 Ibid., 59 and 24.
30 Ibid., 92.
31 Ibid., 95–6.
32 Ibid., 33 and 64.
33 John Kay and John Vickers, 'Regulatory Reform in Britain', *Economic Policy* 3, no. 7 (October 1988): 286.
34 Claus Offe, *Contradictions of the Welfare State*, trans. John Keane (London: Hutchinson & Co., 1984).
35 Evans and Wright, 'How Lax Building Rules', *Financial Times* and Bright and Sawtell, 'Building Regulations and Cladding', *University of Oxford: Faculty of Law*.
36 C. E. Wooster, 'Modern Building Regulation Policy', *Architect and Surveyor* 10, no. 6 (November–December 1965): 129–32, 129.
37 Ley, 'History of Building Control', 114.
38 O. H. Lawn, 'The Administration of Building Regulations: with Special Reference to Relaxations', *Architect and Surveyor* 12, no. 4 (September–October 1967): 97–9, 97.
39 C. Kennard and J. Dufton, *The Building Regulations* (London: Butterworths, 1966), for example 23–4.
40 Harper, *English Building Regulations*, vol. 1, 111–18.
41 Ibid., 72.
42 Katie Lloyd Thomas, 'Going into the Mould: Materials and Process in the Architectural Specification', *Radical Philosophy* 144 (July/August 2007): 16–17.
43 Harper, *Evolution of the English Building Regulations*, vol. 1, 78 and 80–1.
44 Ibid., vol. 1, 20.
45 Neil Smith, 'Toward a Theory of Gentrification: A Back to the City Movement by Capital, Not People', *Journal of the American Planning Association* 45, no. 4 (1979): 543–5.
46 Reyner Banham, *The Architecture of the Well-tempered Environment* (London: Architectural Press, 1969), 35–8.
47 Harper, *Evolution of the English Building Regulations*, vol. 2, 293 and 443.
48 Lukács, 'Reification', *History and Class Consciousness*, 97.
49 Marian Bowley, *Innovations in Building Materials: An Economic Study* (London: Gerald Duckworth & Co., 1960), 53–4, 118, 120.
50 Banham, *Well-tempered Environment*, 175–7.
51 Colin Rowe, 'Chicago Frame', in Colin Rowe, *The Mathematics of the Ideal Villa and Other Essays* (Cambridge MA: MIT Press, 1982), 89–117; Le Corbusier, *Towards a New Architecture*, trans. Frederick Etchells (New York: Dover, 1986), 230–3.

52  Banham, *Well-tempered Environment*, 117 and 146.
53  Bowley, *Innovations in Building Materials*, 359–60 and 335–7.
54  Ibid., 351.
55  'British Standards Institute', *Institute of Civil Engineers* https://www.ice.org.uk/what-is-civil-engineering/what-do-civil-engineers-do/british-standards-institution (accessed 17 February 2021).
56  S.B. Hamilton, *A Short History of the Structural Fire Protection of Buildings Particularly in England,* National Building Studies, Special Report no. 27 (London: HSMO, 1958), 25–6, 36, 38 and 40.
57  Ibid., 26, 36 and 40.
58  Swenarton, 'Houses of paper', 268–9.
59  Ibid., 276.
60  Ibid., 264.
61  Fibre Building Board Development Organisation Ltd: Consultations (1965–68), National Archives [henceforth NA], LAB 18/1241.
62  Edwin Williams, 'The New Building Regulations', *RIBA Journal* 73, no. 7 (July 1966), 321.
63  Organisation for Economic Co-operation and Development [OECD], *The Trend in the Fibre Building Board Market in Europe, 1955–1960* (Paris: OECD, 1962), 56 and 55.
64  Memo by Maurice Hall (Senior Fire Surveyor) to Clive Wooster (24 February 1964), Building Regulations Advisory Committee [henceforth BRAC]: Surface Spread of flame; Correspondence, NA, WORK 75/35.
65  Kay and Vickers, 'Regulatory Reform', 288.
66  Wooster, 'Modern Building Regulation Policy', 131.
67  G. R. Fair et al., 'Note on the Computer as an Aid to the Architect', *Computer Journal* 9, no. 1 (May 1966): 16–20.
68  Wooster, 'Modern Building Regulation Policy', 131.
69  Geoffrey Hutton, 'The Building Regulations: Some Suggestions', *Royal Society of Health Journal* 88, no. 3 (May/June 1968): 140.
70  Paul B. Jaskot, 'Review: Archigram: Experimental Architecture, 1961–1974', *Journal of the Society of Architectural Historians* 63, no. 1 (May 2004): 102.
71  Hutton, 'Building Regulations', 138–9.

# CHAPTER ELEVEN

# The Relational Object: Haus-Rucker-Co.'s Designs for Reshaping the Environment

*Ross K. Elfline*

A couple, one man and one woman, snuggle tightly together atop a moulded plastic seat (Figure 11.1). Its inset depressions indicate the proper positions of the two: one (in this case the male figure) centrally positioned with his legs spread slightly, the other seated off to one side with her legs lying between his. The seat obliges them to perch intimately together, to entwine themselves in an erotic clutch. Lowered atop their heads is a large, seemingly bug-eyed Plexiglas dome. This both shields them from our view and brings them closer together still. Beneath the clear dome, decorated with swathes of colour that mimic the look of circuitry, is a solid core beneath which our couple huddle. Here, we are told, they would experience an immersive light and sound environment designed to encourage their congress.

The work presented is *Mind Expander II* (1968) by the Viennese architectural group Haus-Rucker-Co., and with it we are confronted by a queer thing. As a piece of furniture, it is a great, hulking mass. It takes up a significant amount of space and would sit uncomfortably alongside other objects in a domestic interior. It creates its own discrete environment, closed off from the room around it. The suspended dome forms its own chamber, its own room, with a distinct ambience. It is thus simultaneously a scaled-up piece of furniture and a scaled-down, condensed room. It is both object and miniature 'building'; or, perhaps, it is an object playing the role of architecture.

*Mind Expander II* and other objects produced by Haus-Rucker-Co. in the late 1960s and early 1970s pose a set of intriguing questions for

FIGURE 11.1 *Haus-Rucker-Co.*, Mind Expander II *(1968). Photograph by Uli Boecker. Courtesy of Archive Zamp Kelp.*

architectural and design historians alike, as they straddle the disciplines in pointed and provocative ways. This chapter seeks to use the group's range of electrified and networked objects as case studies to investigate the architectural avant-garde's disciplinary erosion of the boundary separating architecture from design – or building from object – and to point toward the ways in which alternative mediums beyond tectonic building might be deployed toward architectural ends, especially with regard to architecture's role in fostering, enabling, or advancing ideas of communal identity and self-determination. Haus-Rucker-Co. often deployed a variety of technological media to unite disparate users into a network of participants who, through their collaborative communication, might form the kernel of a new community. While a prime architectural function remains – the ability to enclose and catalyse a corporate group of people – the medium has shifted from building to object.

This study is grounded not in the modernist ideal of the architect as master planner, which might view architecture as a sort of *grand récit* that sweeps every material or spatial practice into its wake. Such a view of the expansion of architecture's purview is a familiar one and may be epitomized by Manfredo Tafuri's view of the architectural avant-gardes of the early twentieth century discovering new technical (and technocratic) ways to solve even greater problems.[1] Here, the functionalist logic of modernist planning is mapped onto a broader disciplinary landscape that had previously been overseen by other experts, including designers, landscape architects, and so on. Indeed, by '*grand récit*', I am referring to Jean-François Lyotard's theorization of those so-called 'metanarratives' that structure a modernist notion of history, and am arguing that the idea of the architect as 'master planner' is indicative of a language of mastery that is common to the modernist condition.[2]

Instead, the current chapter approaches this generative space between architecture and design as a postmodernist case of disciplinary blurring. Though trained as architects, Haus-Rucker-Co.'s works both circulated through countercultural architecture channels and were seen in art world periodicals and galleries. This interdisciplinary space, borrowing from discourses within and beyond architecture, allowed the group to investigate how discrete objects, once networked, might serve as catalysts for community formation. For Haus-Rucker-Co., the specific medium used – whether building, furniture, inflatable environment, or ephemeral performance – mattered less than the resulting shift in group behaviour. A collective, albeit provisional, sense of 'we' could be achieved not by building a new Roman forum, a senate chamber, or a new lecture hall but rather via technological extensions to the body. And so, as with the couple nestled under the *Mind Expander II*, Haus-Rucker-Co.'s architectural users were impelled to discover newly relational modes of inhabiting our world, and this architecture of interconnectedness could be achieved by eschewing monumentality and building entirely.

## Radical architecture and the expansion of architectural media

The 1960s and 1970s saw a flourishing of activity from architects and architectural collaboratives that avoided the tectonic altogether. Often cast as a refusal to engage with the act of building – seen as a tacit collusion with capitalist accumulation and land speculation – the projects by these so-called 'Radical Architects' ran the gamut of available media at the time, from eye-popping magazine spreads to museum installations, ephemeral performances and film works.[3] Haus-Rucker-Co. and their Viennese counterparts Hans Hollein and Walter Pichler could be considered part of this broader movement that included the Italian groups Superstudio, Archizoom and Gruppo 9999, as well as the British group Archigram and the US collective Ant Farm. Subsuming the work of these European and American post-war avant-gardists under the category of 'paper architecture' does not, therefore, adequately capture the immense diversity of formal exploration witnessed in this era. Beyond the fact that drawing was only one of many mediums employed, the phrase 'paper architecture' carries with it dual senses of utopian longing and inapplicability in the present moment. It is argued that architects engage in such intangible work only when their economic prospects in built form have dried up.[4] Setting aside the financial exigencies of the Radicals, and turning toward the frankly material and formal aspects of their works from this crucial period, I am proposing that we consider the ways in which these projects sought to alter users' perceptions of space, thus offering new, liberatory forms of community and being-together. In brief, the works of the Radical Architects sought to perform a range of architectural functions by means other than building – functions that include shelter but also the infrastructure by which communal belonging might occur.

In particular, we might look to the designed object and its role in expanding the field of architecture beyond building itself.[5] The Radical Architects were by no means the first architects to design domestic goods. Indeed, following Ernesto Nathan Rogers's dictum that the architect's role is to design everything 'from the spoon to the city', modernist architects often took on furniture design as one component of an interconnected practice of the total design of a cohesive environment.[6] It remained the case, however, that despite the expanded purview of the architect under modernism, the building itself retained its place of prominence; the ancillary design arts were meant to enhance or support building as the master art. Radical design of the 1960s and 1970s approached the designed object from a different position, however, by eschewing the building as the locus of architectural research in favour of other mediums and means to address traditionally architectural questions around shelter and communal gathering. As such, the work of the Radical Architects presents us with an interesting methodological problem: if architectural history and design studies have seen the building and the designed object respectively as the subjects of their disciplinary purviews, then how might we account for the act of claiming the designed object *as architecture*? Might this be evidence of a shift from the modernist idea of architecture as the master discipline that sees everything behind its curtain wall fall under its auspices? Indeed, might the work of the Radicals point toward a postmodernist notion of design as the hydra-headed discipline that considers the multiple means, including buildings, by which lives and lifestyles are formed, ordered and regulated?[7] And, similarly, might the work of the Radical Architects also signal a shift in emphasis away from the architect as master planner to the user as co-creator of the resulting environment?

Rather than seeing the nomination of the designed object-cum-architecture as evidence of a de-disciplining of architecture in favour of design as a more general field, it is worth retaining the specifically architectural character of the Radical Architects' gestures. In all their various acts of refusal, they never abjured architecture as field of inquiry; it was building they wished to supplant while retaining the moniker 'architect'. By decoupling architecture from its stubborn adherence to building, they meant merely to expand the available mediums at the architect's disposal – to 'do architecture' differently – not to dissolve the discipline entirely. A link could be made to contemporaneous attempts on the part of conceptual artists in the 1960s to move away from medium-specific practices to those that took on the problem of art-as-such. While artists increasingly ranged over a variety of media that suited their immediate needs or goals, they retained the term 'art' as a category.[8] Similarly, the Radical Architects increasingly ventured away from building as the primary medium in favour of multiple material and dematerialized formats, all the while retaining distinct and cohesive critical projects situated within the field of architecture.[9] In what ways, then, had the designed object become a new architectural medium within this new postmodern approach to architectural practice? To respond to this question, we might turn back toward the object-based research of Haus-Rucker-Co.

## Haus-Rucker-Co.'s objects of mediation

Haus-Rucker-Co. was founded in 1967 by a group of three recent graduates of the architecture programme at the Technical University of Vienna: Laurids Ortner, Günter Zamp Kelp and Klaus Pinter. Manfred Ortner, who trained in painting at the Academy of Fine Arts in Vienna, would join the group in 1971, and Carroll Michels in 1972.[10] While the original members of the collective had trained as architects, they shared a desire to move beyond built form in favour of a range of alternative media. Within their first few years, Haus-Rucker-Co. had developed abundant objects, inflatable environments, technological prosthetics and performative interventions that functioned to provide their users with new opportunities to perceive and engage with their environment and with one another. As with many of their peers in the 1960s and 1970s architectural avant-gardes, their projects circulated primarily through architectural publications: *Casabella, Domus, Bauwelt, Architectural Design* and *Progressive Architecture,* among others. In addition, when their works were exhibited in fine art gallery or museum contexts, they were framed and presented as architectural projects or experiments.

As introduced above, one non-building medium Haus-Rucker-Co. often employed early in their careers was the design of furniture that brought couples together in erotic media surroundings. The *Mind Expander* works were consistent with their broader interest in objects that created their own distinct environmental conditions. Consider *Battleship* (1968), a low, bed-like Styrofoam wave topped by a moulded plastic canopy that integrated a rudimentary push-button electronic game (Figure 11.2). Tap the buttons on the plush faux fur console and lights on the two schematic nude figures outlined in

FIGURE 11.2 Haus-Rucker-Co., Battleship *(1970)*. *Image produced in association with the exhibition 'Haus-Rucker-Co. Live' held at the Museum of Contemporary Crafts, New York City, 1970. Courtesy of the Museum of Contemporary Crafts Archive, American Craft Council.*

the canopy lit up. As with the earlier example, the goal of this mediated engagement is a sexual (albeit heteronormative) union.[11] These works served as interventions into the interior space of the modernist interior, in line with similar projects by Haus-Rucker-Co.'s contemporaries, such as the Florentine group Superstudio, who described their aims for their future designs thus:

> ... introduce foreign bodies into the system: objects with the greatest possible number of sensory properties (chromatic, tactile, etc.), charged with symbolism and images with the aim of attracting attention, or arousing interest, of serving as a demonstration and inspiring action and behaviour. Objects in short that succeed in modifying the container unit and involving it totally together with its occupier.[12]

FIGURE 11.3 *Haus-Rucker-Co.*, Flyhead, View Atomizer *and* Drizzler *(1968)*. Courtesy of Archive Zamp Kelp.

Haus-Rucker-Co.'s designed objects for the interior did serve to inspire sybaritic behaviours through the introduction of eccentric and hip objects that, in their sci-fi appearance, would have clashed dramatically with most interior spaces.

Haus-Rucker-Co.'s new media objects were not confined to the interior. Beyond serving as interventions into the architectural surround, the group also sought to instigate new relationships with the urban environment as well. Take, for example, their *Environment Transformers* from 1968. Titled *Flyhead, View Atomizer* and *Drizzler,* (Figure 11.3) the three objects fit atop the head of the user in a manner reminiscent of the *Mind Expanders*. Now the objects were fashioned to the body, an early form of wearable technology that could be taken into the city streets in order to trigger new perceptions of the outside world. Plexiglas screens in a variety of shades and shapes were intended to distort and colour one's view of the urban landscape. Music, too, was to be piped in to the headset about the wearers' ears, providing them with a modish soundtrack to their urban wanderings. Ultimately, the users were to experience the city in a heightened state of consciousness, with a new set of stimuli layered atop the old, forcing the user to do more mental work to take in their surroundings. The name given to the suite of objects, *Environment Transformers,* elaborates on their purpose: to temporarily alter the city itself, transmuting the coolly efficient cityscape into a pulsing nightclub. As such, the wearable objects anticipate a new city to come, one teeming with turned-on inhabitants seeking pleasure and sensory wonder.[13] It should be mentioned that these works do assume a particular kind of user, one already predisposed to rock and psychedelic music as well as its attendant lifestyle. So, while the collective's works point toward a form of social liberation, those who partake in this new freedom may be hailed by the very character of the objects themselves.

An essential aspect of the *Environment Transformers* was their networked character. These prosthetic objects, produced only as a set of three prototypes, were not intended for individual use by sole urban wanderers. Rather, they would have been fitted out with microphones, receivers and wireless communication technology to allow the users to talk to one another across medium-range distances. A network of users would therefore have been able to relay to one another their perceptions of the cityscape, precipitating a discursive exploration into the relative successes and failures of the various stimuli superimposed atop the extant terrain. Importantly, the network served as a functional means to unite a provisional 'community' of users. This is to say that the *Environment Transformers*, in their ability to connect individuals and thus to form a corporate entity, gather individuals and facilitate the further cohesion of a given 'we', a role often given over to monumental architecture. Here, though, the object *is* architecture, now untethered from the building that once housed it.

From the examples above, we might approach a theory of the object as it was understood by Haus-Rucker-Co. and their Radical Architecture peers. For them, the object was a means toward new, unalienated modes of relationality. The interior furniture of Haus-Rucker-Co. was meant to unite couples in erotic assembly. Wearable prosthetics networked citizens, no longer monadic individuals forever separated from one another. To Haus-Rucker-Co.'s works, we might add the numerous projects by Archigram that similarly fit the mobile body (Michael Webb's *Suitaloon*, 1967) or linked one to information technologies (Peter Cook's *Info-Gonks*, 1968, or Warren Chalk and David Greene's *Electronic Tomato*, 1969); Ant Farm's mobile *Media Van*, 1971; Superstudio's and Archizoom's louche furniture designs (*Bazaar*, 1968, and *Safari*, 1968); as well as the media environments created by the latter groups for the groundbreaking 1972 Museum of Modern Art exhibition 'Italy: The New Domestic Landscape'.[14] In all cases, the designed object or media environment was intended for communal use rather than individual consumption, even as the 'we' assumed by such objects was highly circumscribed by class or subculture.

For the Radicals, the goal was that 'we live with objects ... not for objects', in the words of the Italian Superstudio members.[15] This is to say that the object should be a means by which we learn to live together and inhabit the world as part of a shared project. No longer should the object signify status, provide the basis for greater capital accumulation, or further the capitalist goal of heightened productivity. Instead, the user should incorporate the object into their daily lived rituals. Furthermore, the object should serve as a catalyst for communal behaviours. In a society where spectacular relations between the commodity form as well as its projection as media image onto every available public surface have rendered us alienated both from things and from one another, an alternative conception of the object as a trigger for new connections among users emerged as a project of intense urgency within avant-garde architecture and design circles.[16] For Haus-Rucker-Co., 'the city is killing itself with urban problems', as they claimed in advance of a 1971 public performance work in Minneapolis.[17] The 'urban problems' to which Haus-Rucker-Co. refer included the many ways in which urban flight and suburbanization had led to social conditions that see us increasingly disengaged from one another and from civic life in general. One solution to such alienation became the relational object that might mediate between individuals, an object that serves many functions traditionally given to architecture and urban design: community congregation, group identity and a sense of shared values. By producing objects that foreground, and even demand, direct participation from their users, Haus-Rucker-Co. put forward the recursive media circuit as one tool to address modern alienation. While such works do not address the material vicissitudes of urban decline head-on, they intended to help ameliorate one of its root causes: a declining sense of shared values. Here, if we are to follow the modernist dictum that 'form follows function', then might the function of public cohesion be met not by a building as monumental locus but by an object or a networked system?

## Toward relational mediums as architecture

While Haus-Rucker-Co. and other Radical Architects of the era sought to mine the architectural implications of objects and other media beyond building, architectural theory and criticism also engaged in an expansive debate on the ways one might do architecture by other, non-traditional means. Key among such critics was the British writer Reyner Banham, who in a series of essays published in the mid-1960s addressed the methods by which US culture has produced remarkable architectural feats while avoiding monumentality and, indeed, by avoiding building altogether. The tension between architectural form as ur-discipline and product design as a 'minor' art with far-reaching implications is similarly worked through in Haus-Rucker-Co.'s objects from the years following Banham's now-classic texts.

Famously, Banham was taken with the American fascination with the 'gizmo', an ingeniously designed object that solves a particular problem through efficient, usually portable, means. In his 1965 essay 'The Great Gizmo', originally published in *Industrial Design,* the author mused on US pioneer culture's attempts to rein in the disorder of a chaotic situation by use of a simple gadget. Some of his examples include 'the Franklin Stove, and the Stetson Hat, through the Evinrude outboard to the walkie-talkie, the spray can and the cordless shaver'.[18] Banham retains an interest not only in US entrepreneurialism and know-how but also in the wide-ranging ramifications of discrete consumer goods. He proceeds to define the gizmo as 'a small self-contained unit of high performance in relation to its size and cost, whose function is to transform some undifferentiated set of circumstances to a condition nearer human desires. The minimum of skill is required in its installation and use, and it is independent of any physical or social infrastructure.'[19] Here, I would underline Banham's emphasis on the gizmo's ability to operate free from 'physical or social infrastructure'. The gizmo, in short, is an object detached from the building. It may operate within the interior or, more frequently, out in the wilderness, but in its capacity to initiate order within disorder, it often performs functions ceded to building.

While it is the case that Banham possessed a protean ability to shift from design criticism to architectural history, it is important to note how intertwined these two disciplines were for him. He was not merely gripped by the power of objects as objects and buildings as buildings but saw in the consumer object architectural applications. For instance, in summarizing his withering criticism of Max Lerner's argument that the United States lacks great architecture because of a dearth of 'belief', Banham points to the 'under-window air-conditioner and under-sink waste-disposer' as evidence to the contrary. In brief, Banham saw in the profusion of new consumer goods a new US architectural form. He concludes by saying: 'Americans believe in technology and that is where to look for the greatness of their domestic architecture.'[20] Banham continued this line of thinking in his essay of the same year titled 'A Home is Not a House'. There, he argued that a variety of technological means, when introduced to the landscape, made it habitable without the need for built form. In a particularly evocative passage, Banham claimed:

> But a properly set-up standard-of-living package, breathing out warm air along the ground ... radiating soft light and Dionne Warwick in heartwarming stereo, with well-aged protein turning in an infrared glow in the rotisserie, and the icemaker discreetly coughing cubes into glasses in the swing-out bar – this could do something for a woodland glade or creekside rock that *Playboy* could never do for its penthouse.[21]

Once again, it is the building itself, in this case the swinging *Playboy* penthouse, that has been superseded by a variety of gadgets that provide both a newly liberatory life and a particular lifestyle as well, thus demonstrating how one might satisfy architectural ends (in this case shelter as well as accommodating a certain notion of leisure) through non-tectonic means.

In a literal sense, Haus-Rucker-Co. were in the business of making gizmos, and they did so from the position of architects. In Banham's sense, the Stetson hat, Evinrude motor and Franklin stove were all examples of accidental architecture – objects that contained architectural implications, even as they situated themselves in the consumer realm. Haus-Rucker-Co., by insisting on their position as architects, self-consciously deployed their *Environment Transformers* and furniture works as new forms of architecture, in line with Banham's expanded view of what counts as 'architectural'. In so doing, Haus-Rucker-Co. were also following in the footsteps of their fellow Viennese radical Hans Hollein, who in his renowned essay 'Alles ist Architektur' similarly nominated a number of technological phenomena as architectural works *avant la lettre*. The ability to shape the environment is all that matters for Hollein, and ditching the building in favour of other media allows for a new liberation: 'After shedding the need of any necessity of a physical shelter at all, a new freedom can be sensed. Man will now finally be the center of the creation of an individual environment.'[22] Building, therefore, represented both literal and ideological confinement for the Radical Architects. Freedom was to be found in the itinerant, portable object. The next task was to move beyond US individualism to communal togetherness.

## From relations to networks

Banham's focus on the object's ability to serve architectural ends is indeed important, though his point is often made in standard functionalist terms – that the role of architecture is, in the end, to provide shelter from the elements and to impose order on the landscape. We might, though, extend Banham's thinking, and it is his frequent references to the walkie-talkie as one architectural 'gizmo' that point the way. What does this object do in the end? It connects individuals across space in a rudimentary network of interlocutors. Here, we are talking about an architectural function that extends beyond the 'firmness, commodity, and delight' that Banham's hypothetical woodland standard-of-living package might provide. This is an architecture that helps to unite or define a community of individuals, an architecture that helps to establish a 'we' beyond the atomized basic needs of the individualized 'I'. This is to say that beyond the convenience that gizmos might provide individual users, another essential role that they might provide is the ability to network interlocutors and create the infrastructure through which one might be able to connect with others – a necessary precondition for the establishment of a provisional *polis*.

Ultimately, then, this is a communications network as architecture. As architectural historian Mark Wigley has noted, the 1960s and 1970s were a moment of focused research into the architectural ramifications of systems, to the point that one could speak of a 'network fever' within the field.[23] The Radical Architects often illustrated futuristic networks as replacements for building. Examples include Superstudio's global grid for nomads to plug into (*Supersurface*, 1971–2) and Archizoom's rhizomatic urban complex of ever-expanding retail space (*No-Stop City*, 1969). Perhaps the most elaborate and literal translation of this idea could be seen in Ant Farm's *Truckstop Network* (1971), which imagined a series of connected sites across the United States where 'media nomads' would be able to receive nourishment, petrol for their kitted-out vans and buses, and media services such as video production studios and communication links to other 'truckstops' along the media superhighway.[24] Ant Farm envisaged an alternative media network that operated outside of mainstream society's mass media systems. The physical architecture of these nodes might employ transitory inflatable domes or disused missile silos, but it was the ability of these sites to connect a renegade counterculture society that formed the basis of this architectural network.

Likewise, it is important to note the relational aspect of Hollein's expanded sense of architectural media as well. 'Architecture is a means of communication', Hollein states early on in 'Alles ist Architektur'.[25] He goes on to claim:

> An early example of the extension of buildings through media of communication is the telephone booth – a building of minimal size extended into global dimensions. Environments of this kind more directly related to the human body and even more concentrated in form are, for example, the helmets of jet pilots who, through telecommunication, expand their senses and bring vast areas into direct relation with themselves.[26]

One of architecture's primary goals, then, is uniting individuals for the purpose of exchange. Decentred and dematerialized, the communications network might accomplish what the Greek *agora* had once done in a placebound fashion. However, it is again crucial to mention the class-based nature of such technological liberation: this newly itinerant body carrying its own networked architecture may be an upwardly mobile early adopter of such technologies, while other bodies remain tethered to the phone booth.

In his pioneering 1984 book *Social Systems*, the German sociologist Niklas Luhmann analysed the formal composition of various human networks. Importantly, he devotes one chapter to the relationship between systems and their environment. Luhmann's argument that systems are coextensive with their environments while retaining a degree of autonomy helps to clarify the architectural implications of networks. At one point he states:

Every system removes itself from its environment. Therefore, the environment of each system is different. And thus, the unity of the environment is constituted by the system. 'The' environment is only a negative correlate of the system. It is not a unity capable of operations; it cannot perceive, have dealings with, or influence the system.[27]

In brief, systems hover over the environments of which they are a part, but in their relative autonomy one finds a critical distance from which to perceive the environment and establish it as a 'unity', an object of study. Systems, as modes of information distribution and communication, however, must necessarily edit and refine the available data from the environment, which retains a higher order of complexity. 'Society can never make possible communication about everything that occurs in its environment... Therefore, like every system, it must compensate for its own inferior complexity by superior order.'[28] As with Banham's gizmo, the system is, for Luhmann, a means by which the undifferentiated and chaotic environment can come under some degree of control, and in so doing it becomes knowable to its users. It is both a medium through which shared meanings of the environment might be communicated and, at the same time, the means by which the community's members achieve cohesion.

In an interesting passage, Luhmann notes the crucial role played by chance in this process of signification. As the system is coterminous with, and yet some remove from, the environment, this leads to a degree of uncertainty in terms of the information that circulates through the system from the environment. Again, systems must economize and filter out much of the 'signal noise' from the environment, but in so choosing, there is an element of unpredictability involved in what signals circulate through the network. 'No system can avoid chance, because no system possesses enough complexity to react "systematically" to everything that occurs.'[29] The relative autonomy of the system with respect to its environment, then, allows the information that circulates through it to take on a life of its own.

It is in this arbitrary relationship between the environment and the networked system that we might then consider Haus-Rucker-Co.'s *Environment Transformer* objects. While the various stimuli received by the prosthetic helmets are derived from the surrounding cityscape, they are filtered, distorted and augmented. They emerge from the surrounding field and yet circulate in changed form once they are perceived by the user and then disseminated through the system. In addition, sounds or the music from the headphones introduce other external data into the system. Ultimately, one's perception of the environment is highly selective (the helmets serve as blinkers, letting in only a restricted view of the user's surroundings) and yet novel, even revelatory. However, as with other architectural systems, the networked *Transformers* provide certain affordances to their users. They allow for a conceptual space to emerge where individuals immerse themselves into, react to and converse discursively about their environment. As such, we might say that such objects provide the means by which a discrete individual comes to practise a provisional form of citizenship. Historically, various built structures may have provided such affordances. For instance, as David Harvey has so incisively analysed, in the context of working-class agitation in the years preceding the Paris Commune of 1871, the dance hall, the cabaret and the drinking house served as the architectural loci of communal attachment, where the political effects of the Parisian social landscape could be processed.[30] One role of architecture, then, has been to provide the means by which a community comes together to debate and discover the political import of the environment, broadly defined. As such, architecture has also functioned as a social system in Luhmann's understanding of the term. Haus-Rucker-Co., along with their Radical Architecture counterparts from the era, literalized the systemic character of architecture by dematerializing architecture in the form of the network, or, to be more precise, condensing architecture in the form of the networked object.

Radical Architecture was subject to often stern criticism from historians and critics, who saw in its various utopian proposals a lack of engagement with the material vicissitudes of building and the lives of the many who continue to clamour for more just and sustainable housing solutions.[31] Utopian thought, it is supposed, represents a retreat from the everyday, its messiness, and concrete solutions to its chronic problems. Such arguments rest on a persistent equation of architecture with building and rely on a narrow definition of architecture's purview as extending primarily to shelter. One important implication of Radical Architectural thought is to broaden our understanding of architecture's various functions to include communal identity and self-determination while forcing the question: Is building the right medium by which such functions might be fulfilled? For the Radical Architects the answer to the question is a resounding 'No'.

The charge of impracticality levelled against the Radical Architects and their experimentation with alternative media loses its impact when we consider the vast array of wearable, networked technology on today's consumer market. One might justifiably quibble with the Radicals' faith in the consumer object to deliver a greater sense of individual and collective liberty. However, as much as such devices alienate us from one another and dazzle us with their sleek curves, they also contain within them the means of covert communication. Whether in the North African capitals of the Arab Spring or in the streets of Washington DC during the certification of the Electoral College votes in January of 2021, the networked bodies fomenting revolution have moved beyond the dance halls and drinking houses through the use of the great gizmo. If we are, then, to see today's relational objects as the descendants of Radical Architecture experimentation, we would be hard-pressed to say that these objects represent any sort of retreat from the materiality of our present world. In their capacity to network, to coordinate and to catalyse, they offer the means by which new forms of being-in-common might develop. For the Radicals of the 1960s and 1970s, it was precisely this form of communal activity that was thwarted by standard architectural practice and yet was made possible by new technological prostheses. Old architectures lie in ruins while new ones burgeon with sly, nomadic promise.

## Notes

1 See especially Tafuri's 'Introduction: The Political "Project"', in *The Sphere and the Labyrinth,* trans. Pellegrino d'Acierno and Robert Connolly (Cambridge, Mass.: The MIT Press, 1987), 1–21.

2 See Jean François Lyotard, *The Postmodern Condition,* trans. Geoff Bennington and Brian Massumi (Minneapolis: Univ. of Minnesota Press, 1984).

3 For more on the abstention from building, see my 'Superstudio and the "Refusal to Work"', *Design and Culture* 8, no. 1 (March 2016): 55–77. Also, the term 'Radical Architecture' was coined by the critic Germano Celant to describe the work of Italian avant-garde production in the 1960s and early 1970s. I am extending Celant's term to encompass a range of architectural groups from Europe and the United States at the same time. See Celant, 'Radical Architcture', in *Italy, The New Domestic Landscape: Achievements and Problems of Italian Design,* ed. Emilio Ambasz (New York: Museum of Modern Art, 1972), 380–7.

4 See Diane Ghirardo, 'The Architecture of Deceit', *Perspecta* 21 (1984): 110–15.

5 I am referring here to Rosalind Krauss's foundationally important essay 'Sculpture in the Expanded Field', which argued for the ways in which the term 'sculpture' could be situated logically in an expanded field of related spatial practices within the postmodern era. I am arguing that architecture's engagement with new media as architecture is evidence of a postmodern attitude. See Krauss, 'Sculpture in the Expanded Field', in *The Originality of the Avant-Garde and Other Modernist Myths* (Cambridge, Mass.: The MIT Press, 1986), 276–90.

6 Ernesto N. Rogers, 'Ricostruzione: Dall'Oggetto d'Uso alla Città', in *Domus* 215 (November 1946): 2–5. With thanks to Jonathan Mekinda for pointing me to the origin of this infamous phrase.

7 The view of design as a new 'master discipline' has been articulated by Hal Foster in a number of studies, most famously in his *Design and Crime (and Other Diatribes)* (London: Verso, 2002).

8 See Joseph Kosuth's 'Art After Philosophy', where the artist claims that the essence of modern art is to question the very nature of art as a discipline rather than investigating the core properties of the individual mediums. In *Art in Theory, 1900–2000: An Anthology of Changing Ideas,* eds. Charles Harrison and Paul Wood (Oxford: Blackwell Press, 2002), 852–61.

9 For more on the intersection of architecture and conceptual art, see my 'The Dematerialization of Architecture: Towards a Taxonomy of Conceptual

Practice', *Journal of the Society of Architectural Historians* 75, no. 2 (June 2016): 201–23.

10  For further details regarding the history of Haus-Rucker-Co.'s founding, see Katja Blomberg, ed., *Haus-Rucker-Co: Architektur–Utopie Reloaded* (Berlin: Haus am Waldsee, 2015) and Andrea Bina, ed., *Haus-Rucker-Co LIVE Again* (Linz: Lentos Kunstmuseum, 2007).

11  An issue for further study would involve the ways in which Radical Architecture, as an intermedia movement, allowed for an investigation of erotics and non-standard sexualities that had previously been sidelined or ignored within the histories of hidebound disciplines.

12  Superstudio, 'Inventory, Catalogue, Systems of Flux . . . a Statement', in *Superstudio: Life without Objects*, ed. Peter Lang and William Menking (Milan: Skira, 2003), 166.

13  My reference to drug use is intentional. As one member of Haus-Rucker-Co. stated, 'Aldous Huxley and Timothy Leary experimented with psychedelic drugs while being the leading lights of the counterculture. We wanted to expand consciousness not by drugs but rather by new, unexpected spaces, objects and utilities.' Interview with Günter Zamp Kelp in *Haus-Rucker-Co: Achitektur–Utopie*, 98.

14  See Emilio Ambasz, ed. *Italy: The New Domestic Landscape*.

15  Superstudio, 'Destruction, Metamorphosis, and Reconstruction', 120.

16  I am referring here to theories of spectacle culture developed by Guy Debord in his essential *Society of the Spectacle,* trans. Donald Nicholson-Smith (New York: Zone Books, 1994).

17  As quoted in Judith Bell, 'Edible architecture – eat up urban blight', *The Minneapolis Star*, 9 June 1971, 6C.

18  Reyner Banham, 'The Great Gizmo', in *Design By Choice,* ed. Penny Sparke (London: Academy Editions, 1981), 108.

19  Banham, 'The Great Gizmo', 110.

20  Banham, 'The Great Gizmo', 112.

21  Banham, 'A Home is Not a House', in *Design By Choice,* 58.

22  Hans Hollein, 'Everything is Architecture', *Architecture Culture, 1943–1968: A Documentary Anthology*, ed. Joan Ockman (New York: Rizzoli and Columbia Books of Architecture, 1993), 462. Originally published in as 'Alles ist Architektur', in *Bau* 1/2 (1968): 2–27.

23  Mark Wigley, 'Network Fever', in *Grey Room* 4 (Summer 2001): 82–122.

24  For more on Ant Farm's work, see Felicity Scott, *Ant Farm: Living Archive 7; Allegorical Time Warp: The Media Fallout of July 21, 1969* (New York: ACTAR and Columbia GSAPP, 2008). See also Andrew Blauvelt, ed. *Hippie Modernism: The Struggle for Utopia* (Minneapolis: Walker Art Center, 2016), especially 294–301.

25  Hollein, 'Everything is Architecture', 460.

26  Ibid., 462.

27 Niklas Luhmann, *Social Systems,* trans. John Bednartz, Jr. and Dirk Baeker (Stanford, CA: Stanford Univ. Press, 1995), 181.
28 Ibid., 182.
29 Ibid., 183
30 See David Harvey, 'The Political Economy of Public Space', in *The Politics of Public Space,* ed. Setha Low and Neil Smith (London: Routledge, 2006), 17–34.
31 Chief among such critics was Manfredo Tafuri. See especially his 'Design and Technological Utopia.' In *Italy: The New Domestic Landscape*, ed. Emilio Ambasz (New York: Museum of Modern Art), 388– 404.

CHAPTER TWELVE

# The Stylistic End-games of Modernism:

# High Tech Design in Criticism and History

*Jane Pavitt*

This chapter examines attitudes towards postmodern style in design and architectural writing in the late 1970s and 1980s as a means to explore the entanglements of architectural criticism with the emerging discipline of design history. The focus is the 'style' known as High Tech – a highly contentious term generally rejected by the architects associated with it. High Tech occupies a peculiar position in the 'end-games' of modernism and has been largely overlooked within analysis of postmodernism. It is situated simultaneously as an adherence to (or revival of) the technocentric and functionalist principles of the modern movement in the face of postmodernism or as a fashionable technological aesthetic within the variants of postmodern style, applied to products and interiors for domestic use, retail and nightclubs. In architectural criticism, specifically that of Reyner Banham and Martin Pawley, the architecture of High Tech was a means of testing the limitations and possibilities of an unfinished modernism, driven by technological advances.[1] It was largely a British phenomenon, which first emerged in the late 1960s with experiments in lightweight and 'clip-on' architecture. In design writing, High Tech was a looser term, describing an industrial aesthetic for the home, of chromed and raw steel, exposed piping and brickwork, and materials used 'as found', which originated in the United

FIGURE 12.1 *Exterior of the Centre Pompidou, Paris, France (1977). Architects: Piano + Rogers. Structural and services engineers: Ove Arup & Partners. Photograph taken in 2017. Courtesy of Suicasmo via Wikimedia Commons.*

States as a style associated with the rise of 'loft living' and was brought into the mainstream by the publication of a popular interior design book in 1978.[2] High Tech 'loft' style was eclectic and ad-hoc, combining a raw-edged industrial look with salvaged materials, pop neon lighting and industrial elements repurposed as *objets d'art*. I argue that there were essentially two High Techs – one emerging from interior design, the other from architecture; one from the United States, the other from the UK – and that the tension between the two reveals a good deal about their professional, disciplinary differences as well as about how buildings, objects and interiors are written about. High Tech was a term coined to describe a fleetingly fashionable 'industrial' style of interior design which has adhered to architecture, rather awkwardly, ever since.

The first examples of High Tech (as it became known) architecture to be built in the UK were flexible experiments in lightweight construction utilizing a high degree of prefabrication, such as the Reliance Controls electronics factory designed by Team 4 (Norman Foster, Wendy Foster, Richard Rogers, Su Rogers) in 1967. High Tech achieved international prominence in the 1970s with commissions such as Richard Rogers and Renzo Piano's Centre Pompidou, Paris (completed 1977) (Figure 12.1) and Norman Foster's Sainsbury Centre for Visual Arts, Norwich, England (1978). By the late 1980s it was a globally recognized style associated with airports, factories, cultural

FIGURE 12.2 *Exterior of Hopkins House, London, UK (1976)*. Photographer Matthew Weinrab. *Courtesy of Hopkins Architects/Anthony Hunt Associates and Matthew Weinrab.*

institutions and high finance (such as Foster's Hongkong and Shanghai Bank and Rogers' Lloyds of London, both completed 1986).

In terms of domestic design, the most celebrated example of High Tech was arguably the Hopkins House (Hampstead, London, 1976), built by Michael and Patty Hopkins as a family home and (initially) as office to their newly formed architectural practice (Figure 12.2). The Hopkins House, a two-storey steel and glass construction, used industrial materials and 'off-the-shelf' elements (such as venetian blinds as room dividers) and was built for an efficient £20,000. A clear precedent and inspiration for the house was the case-study house of 1949 by Charles and Ray Eames, in Los Angeles, an essay in flexibility, lightweight construction and the use of factory-made components. The Eames House was a key early reference point for all High Tech architects.

High Tech architecture achieved a certain notoriety in Britain during the 1980s; Prince Charles's 1984 'monstrous carbuncle' attack on the proposed extension to the National Gallery in London (by Ahrends Koralek Burton) had led to the ABK project being cancelled.[3] Yet, as postmodernism ran out of steam in the late 1980s, High Tech proved resilient and able to respond to new global markets, rising environmental concerns (Grimshaw's Eden Project, 2001) and even to the adaptation of historical buildings (Foster's British Museum Great Court, 2000, and Reichstag Dome, 1999).[4] In 2018, I co-curated (with Abraham Thomas) an architectural exhibition at the Sainsbury Centre for Visual Arts, in celebration of the fortieth anniversary of its Foster-designed building.[5] In the exhibition we explored the historical antecedents of the style, its materials, methods and iconography and the various types of building most associated with High Tech. We settled on this definition: 'High Tech is an inadequate yet usefully succinct term to describe a persistent technological Modernism which surfaced in the 1960s, laid claim to a grand engineering tradition, and produced a series of buildings which, whilst individually distinct, shared a common approach to services, structures, assembly, materials and construction methods.'[6]

This 'persistent technological Modernism' was informed by US post-war developments in industrial engineering and by the 'expendable aesthetic' of Cedric Price and Archigram in Britain. It appeared to be the logical outcome to Reyner Banham's argument, first outlined in his *Theory and Design in the First Machine Age* in 1960, that architects must 'run with technology' in order to remain relevant.[7] As Todd Gannon has shown in his study of Banham and High Tech, Banham was engaged in a (unpublished) reassessment of High Tech architecture at the time of his death in 1988. Banham's manuscript for the book's introduction, held in the Getty archives, is included in Gannon's book.[8] As Gannon argues, Banham saw in High Tech 'an architecture that paradoxically maintained close ties to the ideologies of the modern movement yet diverged from certain of its principles to suggest a manner of working which might overcome modern architecture's deficiencies to stand in staunch resistance to postmodern architecture.'[9]

Resistance to postmodernism may be an indirect reason why the term 'High Tech' was not happily received by its architects, given that it had emerged as a journalistic style label (amid a plethora of other overtly 'designer' interior style movements) and was seen on that basis as superficial, reductive and inadequate. Debates about style in the 1970s and 1980s were frequently divisive, with architects debating the legacies of modernism, the revival of Beaux-Arts or Shingle Style, the excitement of the Las Vegas Strip, and so forth. The apogee (or nadir, depending on your view) was Paolo Portoghesi's 1980 exhibition at the Venice Biennale, entitled 'The Presence of the Past', and its centrepiece, the Strada Novissima, a street of postmodern façades by twenty international architects.[10] A rejection of the High Tech label was, in a sense, a refusal to be part of this *smorgasbord* of choice (particularly as no alternative was proposed by its architects.)

Banham's planned High Tech book was an attempt at retrieval, and to address the definitional problem of style. The style of High Tech is usually defined as one that favours lightweight construction methods and flexible open spaces, employs steel and glass, often with exposed services, ducts and pipework, which may or may not be brightly coloured. Banham summarized

High Tech's distinguishing characteristics as 'structure, services and colour' and its method as 'the most recent way of bringing advanced engineering with the discipline of architecture, comparable with the achievements of Peter Behrens and Auguste Perret in the first 15 years of the present [twentieth] century'.[11] Colin Davies also provides a teleological account of High Tech's emergence, tracing its antecedents from nineteenth-century engineering via Pierre Chareau and Bernard Bijvoet's Maison de Verre (1928–32), Jean Prouvé's 1940s prototype prefabricated houses (1949–51), Buckminster Fuller's Dymaxion House (1930/45) and geodesic domes, the case-study houses of the Eameses and others (1949–), to the plug-in playfulness of Cedric Price and radical 1960s architecture.[12] Kenneth Frampton charts a 'continuing line of post-Fuller thought' through the work of Archigram to High Tech.[13] Added to the mix was a certain sort of 'Boy's Own' fascination with planes, trains and automobiles – the world of Meccano and the *Eagle* comic, discussed in Peter Buchanan's 1983 *Architectural Review* article on High Tech (subtitled 'Another British Thoroughbred'), which fixes the idea that the style was a combination of British inventiveness, an industrial aesthetic and a persistent modernist ethos.[14]

A design history of High Tech tells us a rather different story of its appearance and popularization in the 1980s to that of architectural history, given that it emerges as part of a panoply of design styles that, then and now, could be described as 'postmodern'. Its design history has been largely unexplored, although as an interior style of the 1970s and 1980s it often appeared in conjunction with other fashionable design tendencies such as salvage, pop and retro styling. In *Design after Modernism*, the collection of essays published by John Thackera in 1988 (a highly influential text in the development of design history), Thackera refers to High Tech (in passing) as part of a problematic proliferation of 'designer' goods and spaces: 'The trouble is that the quality of our experience in highly designed hypermarkets, high-tech interiors, "theme pubs" and starter homes is not demonstrably superior to life in less designed locations.'[15] Another important historiographical source is Sharon Zukin's *Loft Living: Culture and Capital in Urban Change* (1982), a sociological study of gentrification in the United States, which describes the loft aesthetic as incorporating an 'eclectic juxtaposition of seventeenth century, Art Deco and "High Tech" design'.[16] Clearly, the interior and product style of High Tech could easily be mixed and matched with historicist and revivalist styles, and displayed a degree of hybridity which was not evident in its architectural namesake. Whereas architectural High Tech was conceived as a unified and controlled aesthetic governed by a structural logic, High Tech interior design was often a fusion of industrial elements used for playful and decorative purpose. Given that High Tech architects saw this kind of postmodern hybridity as anathema, there was no reconciling the different uses of the terms.

Part of the issue lay with a popular interior style guide published in the United States in 1978, entitled *High Tech: Industrial Style and Source Book for the Home,* by design journalists Joan Kron and Suzanne Slesin. This was the first published use of the term High Tech as a style to achieve widespread recognition.[17] The book was a hefty and lavishly illustrated guide to an 'industrial aesthetic' in interior design, which combined a little design history with detailed description and instruction on how to 'get the look' (a large portion of the book functioned as a source guide to materials, brands and suppliers). The principal focus of the book was 'the use of utilitarian, industrial equipment and materials, out of context, as home furnishings'.[18]

> Gym lockers in the bedroom, factory lamps over the dining table, detection mirrors over the dressing table, movers' pads for upholstery, Con Ed guardrails for towel racks, I-beams for end tables, steno chairs for dining chairs, supermarket doors swinging into the kitchen, warehouse shelving in the living room, scaffolding beds, test tubes for bud vases – something exciting is happening in home furnishings and it's called high-tech. If you haven't heard about it yet, you will soon. And its meaning will become as familiar as art deco and art nouveau.[19]

The style, they argued, had its roots in 'the nostalgia of a postindustrial society' and was perhaps 'a throwback to the Bauhaus' given its celebration of functional, anonymous design. It was also 'the logical follow-up to such things as the antimaterialism of the 1960s and the do-it-yourself and back-to-nature movements'.[20] In other words, it was both a form of US industrial vernacular and a fashionable tendency in contemporary design combining a host of alternative lifestyle influences, which found a new beauty and inventiveness in industrial materials and the sorts of things found in hardware stores, and which put them to novel use in the furnishing of domestic spaces (Figure 12.3).

In the book, the products, rather than designers and architects, take centre stage throughout. Kron and Slesin acknowledge the parallel architectural trend at the outset, with reference to three key buildings: Rogers and Piano's 1977 Centre Pompidou ('a cultural centre that has been likened to an oil refinery'), Foster Associates' 1978 Sainsbury Centre for Visual Arts ('a cultural centre that has been compared to an aircraft hangar') and Hardy Holzman Pfeiffer Associates' 1973 Columbus Occupational Health Center ('looking like a boiler room').[21] A prefatory essay establishes the architectural precedents of an 'industrial aesthetic' including Paxton's Crystal Palace (1851), the Eiffel Tower (1889), Chareau's Maison de Verre (1932), the Eames House (1949) and the Hopkins House (1976) ('sometimes mistaken for a filling station').[22] In his 1987 essay on High Tech, Banham swipes at Kron and Slesin's book on several fronts: first, for misusing the term High Tech to describe a (merely) fashionable trend for using industrial products; secondly, for 'invoking the whole mythology of the Modern Movement in architecture' in their determination that the Crystal Palace marks the beginning of an industrial aesthetic; and thirdly, for their claim that the Centre Pompidou 'looks like an oil refinery' when clearly (as

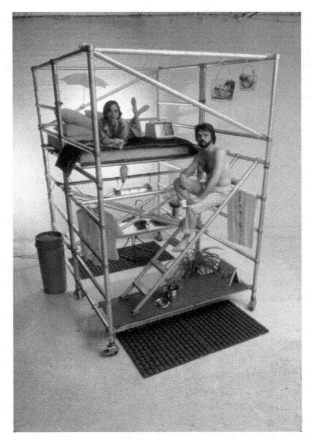

FIGURE 12.3 *Loft bed by Morsa design team (Antonio Morello and Donato Savoie), made of about $1,700-worth of standard Up-Right Aluminum Span Scaffold Parts. Featured in Kron and Slesin,* High Tech: Industrial Style and Source Book for the Home *(London: Allen Lane, Penguin Books Ltd, 1978), 56–7. Courtesy of Donato Savoie/Morsa.*

Banham says) it is better likened to a 'particular type of steam-powered electrical generating station that is favoured in California'.[23] But Kron and Slesin's journalistic analysis was not really an attempt to 'do' architectural history. Rather, it was an advice manual on how to utilize industrial products for home furnishings. In an unusual reversal, the architecture of High Tech is used as a sideshow to everyday design. In the book, design agency lies primarily with the user-consumer. The majority of architects and interior designers are included mainly for the products they choose, such as: 'architect James Rossant built a loft bed/study for his son ... with plumbing pipe and Nu-Rail clamps (about $5 each)', and 'designer Ward Bennett had a roomy hospital tub installed in his summer home'.[24]

Whilst there are numerous colour images of high-end interiors for named clients by fashionable interior designers, the bulk of the book is dedicated to black-and-white photographs of anonymous goods from manufacturers' catalogues. The book's directory gives contact details for around two thousand retailers, wholesalers and manufacturers, ranging from Herman Miller and the Sears Roebuck *Farm and Ranch Catalog* to suppliers of door-opening hardware, glass block and silo domes. The emphasis is on do-it-yourself, and on adapting simple mass-produced industrial systems (such as shelving and scaffolding) for furniture and interior structures in much the same way as the Eameses did, so that 'the end product can make a structural incompetent feel like R. Buckminster Fuller'.[25]

So, who was the intended reader of the High Tech source book? Primarily aimed at a North American readership, the book was published in the UK a year later, and its listings include suppliers in the UK, France and Italy. The majority of goods were from US manufacturers: metal furniture and electrical appliances, laboratory glass, restaurant utensils, sanitary ware and architectural elements such as railings, staircases, steel dock plate and subway gratings, wire racking and glass block walls. Although there are a few listings for antiques dealers, this is not a book about architectural salvage or restoration. It is a celebration of everyday US industrial goods raised to the status of 'good design', which the authors argue is in the tradition of the Museum of Modern Art's design exhibitions, which began with *Machine Art* in 1934, where laboratory glass and industrial components were exhibited in the manner of modern art.[26]

The book described a national network of manufacture and supply, reminding readers that they can order by mail, or contact a manufacturer to find a local dealer. Amongst the lists of retailers are several high-end design stores associated with the High Tech look (such as Manhattan Ad Hoc Housewares and the gallery Art et Industrie). However, Kron and Slesin generally encouraged readers to bypass high street retailers and seek out wholesale suppliers just as designers and architects do, saying that 'high-tech can also be more black turtleneck than blue collar'.[27] Whilst *Machine Art* was an acknowledged source of inspiration, the directory style of the book suggests that one of its precedents might also have been Stewart Brand's *Whole Earth Catalog*, the countercultural magazine and hippie bible, which ran from 1968 to 1972. Subtitled 'access to tools', the *Whole Earth Catalog* planned to equip a new generation with the means to lead a self-sufficient, alternative lifestyle and gave listings, prices, reviews and use-advice on products ranging from geodesic domes to seed drills. Brand's early ethos was inspired by the technological philosophy of Buckminster Fuller, whose influence features liberally in early issues of the *Catalog*. This was not, on the whole, a back-to-the-land philosophy that rejected the products of industry; rather, it embraced the possibilities of technology whilst seeking a means of renouncing consumerism and circumventing the market. This ethos included buying direct from wholesalers, experimenting with DIY and

THE STYLISTIC END-GAMES OF MODERNISM

FIGURE 12.4 *'The Look of the 1980s: Your House Will Never Be the Same'*: cover of *Esquire US, 29 August (1978)*. *Courtesy of Carl Fischer and* Esquire, *Herst Communications, Inc.*

self-assembly and repurposing products in ad-hoc ways. The *Whole Earth Catalog* influenced alternative design practices in the 1970s, from Italy's Global Tools to Victor Papanek's *Design for the Real World*.[28] Kron and Slesin's book adapts some of these strategies for the yuppie generation, whereby anonymous machine-made goods and industrial materials are assimilated into a system of art, taste and cultural capital.

The book's reception was also mediated by its serialized appearance, in the same year, in *Esquire* magazine. Kron and Slesin's High Tech feature was given cover status in August 1978 and dubbed 'The Look of the 1980s: Your House Will Never Be the Same' (Figure 12.4). *Esquire*, then fortnightly, was a high-end men's magazine that combined politics, business, celebrity, sport and lifestyle. High Tech was the only design-led cover feature that year; other issues featured cowboys, cars, actors, politicians and sportsmen. (Only two of the year's twenty-six covers featured women: one titled 'The Year of the Lusty Woman (It's All Right to Be A Sex Object Again)' and the other titled 'When a Woman is Boss (How Men Deal With Them)'. Although it did not often feature interior design, the magazine's readership was an important constituency for High Tech: male, educated, professional and affluent. Kron and Slesin's *Esquire* articles (and the book itself) described an interior aesthetic that was ideal for a young urban elite furnishing apartments and lofts in newly gentrified inner-city areas.

In the United States, the loft (the generic term for former factory and warehouse spaces converted to residential use) was fundamental to the development of High Tech style. Through the 1960s, low rents and large spaces attracted artists to the downtown districts of major cities, where they created live/work spaces, formed communities and were often instrumental in the preservation of industrial buildings. Gradually, through an urban resurgence in the 1970s, these districts became fashionable, developers moved in (the artists often moved out due to rising rents) and loft rents rose to the level of conventional apartments. This trend was the subject of Sharon Zukin's 1982 book *Loft Living*, which examined the sociological and economic effects of inner-city deindustrialization and the conversion of manufacturing spaces to residential use. Zukin critiques the growth of 'regeneration' schemes and what she terms 'the reconquest of the downtown by high-rent, high-class uses, the re-creation of an urban middle class, and the use of art and culture to further these ends'. The Manhattan variant of aspirational loft living, she says, became a standard for urban development in US cities and also in Europe, in cities such as London and Paris. Zukin makes clear that it was not simply the availability of loft space that made loft living desirable – it was a combination of political, economic and social factors. It was also an 'aesthetic conjuncture', which made the idea of living in a disused factory both feasible and attractive – drawing together the preoccupations such as concern for architectural preservation, the cultural status of artists (early loft adopters), a certain sort of nostalgia for an industrial past, all driven by 'the taste-setting mass media'. In order to sell lofts, the idea of a 'loft lifestyle' emerged. The vast amount of floor space, the lack of conventional room delineation, the exposed ducts, pipe and brickwork required a new design vocabulary, which was provided by a small number of interior designers who became known for their loft styling, and who feature in Kron and Slesin's book. As Zukin said: 'Loft living has played an important role in "domesticating" the industrial aesthetic ... The exaggerated scale of a loft provides a natural setting for the new cult of domesticity that worships restaurant and supermarket equipment, industrial carpeting and Pirelli rubber tiles.'[29] Artists and other 'fashionable' loft-dwellers were often featured in the press, Zukin observed, 'discoursing knowledgeably about the merits of the Cuisinart or metal wall studs and plasterboard, these people became both part of the mainstream, home-oriented public and arbiters of home style'. Zukin makes a link between the dissolving of traditional gender boundaries and the blurring of home/work and domestic/industrial distinctions, observing that a number of first-generation loft-livers in SoHo who also featured in the lifestyle press were 'men and women who lived alone or gay (primarily male) couples'.[30]

In New York, designers associated with the High Tech style were also among these first loft-dwellers, and used the style of their own homes as promotion for their business. High Tech was also sold as an affordable solution to a constrained budget. The designer Michael Schiable (of Bray and Schiable, one of the first firms associated with High Tech) observed that a good deal of the allotted budget would be required for restructuring work given the state of the buildings, and 'we didn't have much experience and our clients didn't have very much money'.[31] A degree of improvisation and ingenuity combined with the use of at-hand materials was required. A number of interior designers built their careers on the success of their High Tech experimentation, as the style crossed over into retail, restaurant, nightclub and office design, and began to attract more upmarket clients. This history of High Tech design has been largely forgotten, however, eclipsed by its architectural other (which, ironically, refused the label anyway). There are several reasons for this: the hierarchy of architecture over design; the more temporal nature of designed interiors; and the mediatization of design as 'lifestyle', often through celebrity, so that its media presence is usually more about client than designer. In addition, designers who championed High Tech in the late 1970s and early 1980s often also worked in other design styles and idioms depending on the commission and, by the mid-1980s, had simply moved on to other 'looks'. Designers such as Alan Buchsbaum, Bray and Schiable, Ward Bennett and Joseph Paul D'Urso featured regularly in the design and lifestyle press at the time as purveyors of the style. Buchsbaum, the interior designer chiefly associated with the rise of New York loft living, had invested in a disused cord factory in Greene Street in the mid-1970s, creating live/work spaces for himself and also for the art critic and editor of *October*, Rosalind Krauss. The artist Robert Morris had a studio on another floor. Buchsbaum's eclectic style made reference to New York restaurants, nightclubs and bathhouses. As Frederic Schwartz (who worked with Buchsbaum) says: 'the pre-AIDS seventies – free love, open sex, gay discos, the New York baths scene – was the context for Buchsbaum's own laboratory-for-design-lofts and their programs for almost-public baths in private spaces.'[32] Buchsbaum's own apartments (he renovated two in the same building) combine High Tech elements with the raw features of the original building, such as stamped-tin ceilings and rough timber supports. There are factory lamps with exposed cabling, industrial-scale kitchens with open wire shelving, and clinical white tiling not confined to kitchen and bathroom. The bathroom itself was an open-plan space with hot tub. Buchsbaum's partner in his company Design Coalition, Stephen Tilly, said of this approach:

> [T]he tech was not really that high at all ... Ours was the tech of the factory purchasing agent's catalogs, of building and restaurant supply

stores on Canal Street and the Bowery; it required connoisseurship but not complex technical chops. It was *not* the tech of Ove Arup, Norman Foster, Bucky Fuller or the space shuttle.[33]

Buchsbaum's client list included celebrities such as Bette Midler, Diane Keaton, Ellen Barkin, Billy Joel and Christie Brinkley. As the 1980s progressed, the style moved uptown, Buchsbaum's work became more sumptuous and was combined with increasingly playful postmodern elements (a Robert Adam-style television cabinet, polished marble fragments used as tabletops and fireplaces, and a 'japanese-tudor' house designed with Charles Moore).[34] Buchsbaum died of AIDS, in 1987, at the age of 51.

By the late 1980s, the High Tech aesthetic associated with loft living had successfully permeated the mainstream to such an extent that the fashion for factory lights and restaurant-style utensils was evident on the high street and in major chain stores. The loft had become simply another lifestyle trope, as well as a regular plot device in movies. Take, for example, Adrian Lyne's 1987 erotic thriller *Fatal Attraction*. In the film, Glenn Close's obsessive and psychotic character Alex lives in a grimy industrial 'loft' in Manhattan's meat-packing district, complete with exposed pipes and ceiling fans (in contrast to Michael Douglas's character's suburban marital home). Her kitchen is equipped with a restaurant-style six-burner hob, an RLM enamel metal factory light, an Abolite 'radio wave' lampshade and, of course, a set of chefs' knives – all essential 'industrial style' items featured in Kron and Slesin's High Tech book. In the film, the loft functions as a sign of Alex's unstable personality and the dangers of unsafe sex, and the kitchen is the setting for both erotic and violent encounters.

In 1987, the year Banham wrote his unpublished essay outlining his approach to High Tech, he called it the 'only real novelty to emerge from architecture in the 1980s'.[35] In the same year, Suzanne Slesin wrote an article for the *New York Times* describing its 'death':

> High Tech, the revolutionary design movement that brought the industrial style into thousands of American homes and apartments, seems to have vanished without a trace after a life span of less than 15 years. The look that celebrated innovation and resourcefulness, it was expressed in the beauty of exposed pipes, the plainness of restaurant ware and the practicality of hospital equipment. High Tech's birth was greeted with acclaim by the young and the avant-garde, yet today it is no more than a dim memory. Services will be minimal. Please omit flowers.[36]

According to designer Michael Schiable, the AIDS epidemic provides another context for the death of High Tech style: 'High Tech was for the new kids on the block', he said in Slesin's article. 'We used to have the best time. We had Studio 54 and great parties. We didn't care about coats and ties and wore red cowboy boots, Levis and Lacoste shirts.' He went on: 'The world has become very scary. We're scared about AIDS and the economy. We are too old to crawl around on the floor, and so are our clients.'

## Conclusion

It might be said that the engineer questions the universe, while the 'bricoleur' addresses himself to collection of oddments left over from human endeavours.[37]

In *The Savage Mind* (1966), Lévi-Strauss distinguishes between the 'scientific' mind of the engineer, who seeks to invent new solutions, and the 'anti-modern' approach of the *bricoleur*, who reconfigures the world from what is at hand. Reading Kron and Slesin's book through its images, the overall impression is that this is a source book for *bricoleurs*. Industrial elements are not combined to suggest seamlessness or unity; rather, they celebrate uncanny juxtaposition (sports locker as wardrobe, concrete birdbath as fruit bowl), obvious technical 'fixes' and flaws (visible cabling, exposed pipes) and the inversion of 'quality' signifiers (scaffolding as bed frame). Whereas High Tech architecture was a concept of building as advanced engineering, High Tech interior design was more about craft and improvisation. It was a practice of making that comes close to the definition of 'adhocism' first outlined by Charles Jencks and Nathan Silver in their 1972 book of that title:

> [Adhocism] involves using an available system or dealing with an existing situation in a new way to solve a problem quickly and efficiently. It is a method of creation relying particularly on resources which are already at hand ... beyond its utilitarian aspects, adhocism gives rise to new areas of inquiry and speculation.[38]

Libertarian and pluralistic, adhocism was a way of thinking beyond formal modernism, and suggesting that 'design might be entrusted to everyone'.[39] It was also a corrective to the Banham-esque argument for technology, and became a key technique of postmodernist design. In the UK in the 1980s, for example, bricolage was fundamental to the practices of designers such as Ron Arad, Tom Dixon and the 'Creative Salvage' collective, to the work of Nigel Coates and Narrative Architecture Today (NATO) and to the punk collages of Jamie Reid.[40] By the 1980s, the industrial aesthetic of the New York loft had also crossed over to the UK, as former warehouses were reconfigured for retail, residential and leisure uses.

It is clear in Banham's assessment of High Tech that Kron and Slesin's book played a troublesome role in the popularization of a stylistic label that stuck, unwanted, to a particular form of architecture, and that his planned book on the subject was a kind of corrective. Despite certain superficial similarities, the two High Techs were effectively two different entities.

Neither was derivative of the other. Although they shared a common interest in the use of prefabricated elements, they operated in different registers. Whereas architectural writing generally defined High Tech in opposition to postmodernism, incorporating it into a teleology of modernism, design writing was happier to let it take its place within a panoply of styles and fashionable behaviours. High Tech, in its NY loft sense, was improvisational, heterogeneous and fun. It was knowing in its fashioning of 'industrial chic'. It was transgressive, in that it helped to shape an alternative version of domesticity to the nuclear, suburban family ideal. It also helped to make the names of a number of designers associated with 1970s loft style, who moved on relatively quickly and did not appear wedded to any kind of design programme, nor interested in any kind of theorizing. In the end, High Tech style was happy to be expendable – yet as it died away, it left a definitional problem in architecture which is yet to be resolved.

## Notes

1.  See, for example, Reyner Banham, 'Grass Above, Glass Around', *New Society* 42, no. 783 (1977): 22–3; Martin Pawley, 'High-Tech Architecture: History vs. The Parasites', *AA Files*, no. 21, (Spring, 1991): 26–9.
2.  Joan Kron and Suzanne Slesin, *High-Tech: The Industrial Style and Source Book for the Home*, first published United States 1978 (UK edition, London: Allen Lane, Penguin Books Ltd, 1980).
3.  Speech given by HRH Prince of Wales at the 150th Anniversary of the Royal Institute for British Architects, Hampton Court Palace, 30 May 1984. See also Maxwell Hutchinson, *The Prince of Wales: Right or Wrong? An Architect Replies*, Foreword by Richard Rogers (London: Faber & Faber, 1989).
4.  Catherine Slessor, *Eco-Tech: Sustainable Architecture and High Technology* (London: Thames & Hudson, 1997).
5.  *Superstructures: The New Architecture 1960–1980* (Norwich: Sainsbury Centre for Visual Arts, 2018).
6.  Jane Pavitt and Abraham Thomas, *Superstructure: The Making of the Sainsbury Centre* (Norwich: Sainsbury Centre for Visual Arts, 2018), 20.
7.  Peter Reyner Banham, *Theory and Design in the First Machine Age* (London: The Architectural Press, 1960), 329–30.
8.  Todd Gannon, *Reyner Banham and the Paradoxes of High Tech* (Los Angeles: The Getty Research Centre, 2017).
9.  Gannon, *Reyner Banham*, 151.
10. See Lea-Catherine Szacka, *Exhibiting the Postmodern: The 1980 Venice Architecture Biennale* (Venice: Marsilio Editori, 2017).
11. Banham in Gannon, *Reyner Banham*, 244.
12. Colin Davies, *High Tech Architecture* (London: Rizzoli, 1988).
13. Kenneth Frampton, *Modern Architecture, A Critical History* (London: Thames & Hudson, 1980), 284.

14 Buchanan, 'High-Tech: Another British Thoroughbred', *The Architectural Review*, no. 174 (1983): 15–19.
15 John Thackera (ed.), *Design After Modernism* (Thames and Hudson, London, 1988), 22.
16 Sharon Zukin, *Loft Living: Culture and Capital in Urban Change* (Baltimore: The John Hopkins University Press, 1982), 64.
17 Kron and Slesin refer to High Tech as a term 'currently used in architectural circles'. Kron and Slesin, *High-Tech*, 1. Banham states their book was the 'first to use the phrase in its title' and as a fashionable style term. Banham in Gannon, *Reyner Banham*, 234.
18 Kron and Slesin, *High-Tech*, 1.
19 Kron and Slesin, *High-Tech*, inside cover text.
20 Kron and Slesin, *High-Tech*, 2.
21 Kron and Slesin, *High-Tech*, 1.
22 Kron and Slesin, *High-Tech*, 8–37.
23 Banham in Gannon, *Reyner Banham*, 234–5.
24 Kron and Slesin, *High-Tech*, 59, 55.
25 Kron and Slesin, *High-Tech*, 135.
26 *Machine Art*, Museum of Modern Art, New York, 6 March–30 April 1934.
27 Kron and Slesin, *High-Tech*, 2.
28 Victor Papanek. *Design for the Real World: Human Ecology and Social Change* (New York: Pantheon Books, 1971).
29 Zukin, *Loft Living*, 71.
30 Zukin, *Loft Living*, 73.
31 Suzanne Slesin. 'The 1970's Industrial Look: What Became of High Tech?' *New York Times*, Nov 19 1987, Section C: 1.
32 Frederic J. Schwartz (ed.), *Alan Buchsbaum, Architect & Designer, the Mechanics of Taste* (New York: The Monacelli Press, Inc., 1996), 14.
33 Schwartz, *Alan Buchsbaum*, 22.
34 Schwartz, *Alan Buchsbaum*, 132.
35 Banham in Gannon, *Reyner Banham*, 233.
36 Suzanne Slesin. 'The 1970's Industrial Look: What Became of High Tech?' *New York Times*, 19 November 1987, Section C: 1.
37 Claude Lévi-Strauss, *The Savage Mind* (Chicago: University of Chicago Press, 1966), 1.
38 Charles Jencks and Nathan Silver, *Adhocism: The Case for Improvisation* (Cambridge MA: MIT Press expanded and updated edition 1972/2013), 9.
39 Jencks and Silver, *Adhocism*, 9.
40 For further discussion of this, see Glenn Adamson and Jane Pavitt, *Postmodernism: Style and Subversion 1970–1990* (London: V&A Publishing, 2011), 32–9.

# CHAPTER THIRTEEN

# Shared and Not Contested:

# Modern Erasures in Design and Architecture – History, Practice and Education in Brazil

*Livia Rezende and Tatiana Pinto*

### Architecture and design in dialogue

In January 2016, the *Agência Brasil*, a Brazilian federal government communication outlet, posted a brief note on its news portal: a female toilet would soon be installed in Brasília's Federal Senate – the first in its fifty-five years of history.[1] The Federal Senate is best known to designers and architects as one of the white domes designed by Oscar Niemeyer for Brazil's National Congress. The *Agência Brasil* note explained that the toilet would support the plenary attendance of female senators who would no longer need to leave a session to use the facilities at a nearby restaurant. The note framed the amendment as an 'old necessity' given that thirty-three female senators have occupied seats since 1979 when Eunice Michiles, senator for Amazonas, became the first woman representative in the Brazilian Federal Senate.

The absence of a female toilet from Brasília's Federal Senate and the normalization of this abnormality for fifty-five years prompted a series of exchanges between us, the authors, shared here in a dialogue that captures our critical reflections on the implementation of modernism in Brazil since the 1960s. Our dialogue is a method of investigation, interrogation, exchange and reflection rather than simply a form of co-authored text. The difference is crucial. In retaining the texture and rhythm of our conversations, we aim to share how our argumentation unfolded; in retaining individual voices and forms of writing, we aim to capture the lived experiences of two professionals who have been interrogating their practice in the fields of design and architecture. Moreover, our dialogue is to be read as a statement of positionality from two Brazilian female practitioners – Livia in design history, Tatiana in architecture – frames what we have come to understand as 'modern erasures'.

Starting with the female toilet, erased as it were from the Federal Senate architectural plans, we analyse and expose further deleterious dimensions in modern practice in Brazil and propose that modern design and architecture have contributed to the widening of social, gender and racial inequalities. We dissect a decisive event in Brazilian architectural and design histories – Brasília's construction (1957–60) – to explore how we received this history, reflect further on our disciplinary fields, and question how we inherited, perpetuated and denied some of these modern practices in our professional trajectories. We propose, finally, that the uncovering of modern erasures through the research-led dialogical method prefigured here has the potency to bridge and transform the areas in between design and architecture, their conventional objects, practices and histories.

**Livia Rezende** For some time, we have been discussing how this recent toilet installation elicited deeply disturbing feelings in us. We read the absence of a female toilet in Brasília's Federal Senate as the presumed absence of women's representation in the modernist vision for political power in Brazil. In your research you have retrieved and analysed Niemeyer's technical drawings – was he responsible for this absence?

**Tatiana Pinto** The National Congress houses the legislative body of Brazil's federal government and comprises the Federal Senate and the Chamber of Deputies. It is located at the apex of the monumental axis (eixo monumental), the main avenue in Lucio Costa's master plan (plano piloto) for Brasília. Costa designed the avenue flanking seventeen identical ministerial buildings on each side to orientate one's focus to the two phallic towers and domes of the National Congress (Figure 13.1). Although it is but one of the three powers located at the monumental axis, architecturally the National Congress is the dominant focal point of Brasília.

The technical drawings for the National Congress show only one toilet facility in the Federal Senate.[2] It is not possible to ascertain the architect's intentions from the drawings alone. However, we should look at further evidence: it is unlikely that Niemeyer was proposing a gender-neutral toilet considering that in other parts of the building he had specified male and female toilets side by side. Also, gender-neutral toilets did not exist in 1960s public architecture in Brazil. Moreover, the drawing caption for this part of the building allocates the lone toilet for 'senadores', a term

FIGURE 13.1 *Brasília's National Congress Tower under construction (1959). Photograph by Marcel Gautherot/Instituto Moreira Salles Collection. Courtesy of IMS – Instituto Moreira Salles.*

that can denote 'male senators' only or 'female and male senators' in the plural. Again, given the unlikelihood that both genders were to use the same toilet, we can infer that the lone toilet was designed for male users only.

As a Brazilian woman who practises architecture, I see further evidence to support the thesis of a modern erasure of women's representation in Brasília in the rationale for building a federal district in the middle of Brazil. Juscelino Kubitschek, president from 1956 to 1961, transferred the capital from Rio de Janeiro on the southeastern coast to the western central plateau as part of his 'national integration through interiorisation' strategy.[3] Kubitschek wanted to inaugurate Brasília before ending his mandate, to conclude a project that would usher in a modern identity for the country, as well as crowning his developmentalist goals. In his inauguration speech, Kubitschek referred to Brasília as 'a presage of a fruitful revolution in prosperity'.[4] It is telling that this prosperity was continuously framed in male terms. Connecting the Chamber of Deputies and the Federal Senate is the Black Hall (Salão Negro). Reproduced on its wall – that is, inscribed in the architecture of this highly significant and busy passageway – are the words from Kubitschek's 1957 speech decreeing the transfer of the capital:

> This act represents the most virile, most energetic step that the nation takes, after its political independence, to fully assert itself as people who took on their shoulders one of the most extraordinary tasks that contemporary history has assigned to a collective: to populate and civilise the lands they conquered, vast as a continent; that of integrating, in the communion of peoples, for the common good of humanity, one of the richest territories in the world.[5]

Kubitschek clearly extols Brasília as a civilizing project on allegedly unoccupied land and as a triumph over nature through development and progress. In both speech and architecture, I can see the modern project – tightly connected with a particular political agenda – presented as 'virile': masculine, manly, made by men for men.

Niemeyer worked very closely with Kubitschek and held a significant amount of power over Brasília's design, construction and mediation. Niemeyer was the founder and chief editor of *Módulo*, an architectural magazine that made Brasília's construction visible and validated nationally and internationally. Another key mediator was the magazine *brasília* whose editorial mission was 'not only to document but to defend the plan'.[6] *brasília* was the mouthpiece of the Development Commission for the New Capital (Companhia Urbanizadora da Nova Capital), or NOVACAP, a group of contractors founded in 1956. Niemeyer was NOVACAP's chief architect. In addition, he took part in the jury who selected Lucio Costa's master plan via a public contest organized by Kubitschek. Niemeyer also designed the main administrative buildings in Costa's plan.

I interpret Niemeyer's collusion with Kubitschek as an omnipresence in the making of Brasília, not merely as an act of cronyism that jeopardizes the objectivity of the project. It is also a corroboration of his gender authority and evidence of the link between modernism and coloniality. 'Coloniality' is a term that refers to the structures of oppression and domination that linger from past colonial political forms. Walter Mignolo, understanding that colonialism as a historical phenomenon is over, says that 'we, and by *we* I mean ... the human species, are all today in the colonial matrix of power'.[7] The colonial matrix of power, referred to also as coloniality, perpetrates oppressions articulated through gender, sexuality, race, exploitation of labour and nature.[8] Niemeyer's control of both Brasília's project and its mediation, which overtly displayed male

FIGURE 13.2 *Worker on the 28-storey National Congress Tower without safety equipment (1959). Photograph by Marcel Gautherot/Instituto Moreira Salles Collection. Courtesy of IMS – Instituto Moreira Salles.*

figures as the heroes behind the city, evidences an accumulation of power in male authorities which is predicated on the silencing of others.

LR   You place the absence of the female toilet in the broader context of Brasília's construction framed as a manifestation of the colonial matrix of power. Hearing you talk about power, I think of the violence committed for Brasília to be erected in record time. A specific image comes to mind – one that exposes the experience of these others you just mentioned also erased from the modern project. It is a photograph taken by Marcel Gautherot, the Brazil-based French photographer hired by NOVACAP to document Brasília's construction.[9]

Gautherot was known for his working-class background, unfinished training in architecture and keen eye for photographing people at work.

This photograph is no different (Figure 13.2). A young construction worker is fixing a rope on a pulley. Below the man's arm we can discern at a distance the skeleton of an administrative building. The photo's viewpoint emphasizes that the worker is lifted high off the ground and brings to the fore the vast drylands of the Brazilian central plateau. Once we see beyond the sheer beauty of Gautherot's black-and-white contrasts, we note that the man's working conditions are extremely unsafe. He has no protective clothing or hard hat, he is not tied off or has any fall protection gear. But rather than an exception, this level of unsafety was the norm in Brasília's building sites. As a design historian, and after years of practising as a graphic designer trained under the aegis of modernism, I can no longer research the final formal products of design without interrogating the labour relations embedded in them. Often, in the Brazilian context, labour relations will have a dimension of violence, of stark inequality and exploitation, as seen in this photograph.

More than thirty thousand workers migrated from drought-stricken faraway regions to build Brasília in three years.[10] These were destitute men seeking the promise of a better life but finding work in labour-intensive and life-threatening building sites, a plight accentuated by the fact that Brasília's master plan simply did not include low-income housing to accommodate its workers after completion.[11] While key tenets of European modernism proposed rationalization of construction and materials and modular living as solutions to post-war public housing and urban densification, Brasília – and the Brazilian sociopolitical context – turned this modern logic on its head. Migrants built under outdated, unsafe and irrational working conditions a city that would be framed by historians and critics as rationally designed, a modernist masterpiece. Niemeyer's whimsical form-giving structures are, however, antithetical to any rationalization of construction. The white domes of the Chamber of Deputies and Federal Senate were hand-sanded; the techniques employed in making Brasília are frequently described as artisanal and unreproducible, predicated on a colossal amount of manual labour (Figure 13.3).[12]

Architect and historian Pedro Arantes refers to the smooth white-clad curves of Brasília as 'deletion of traces of labour'.[13] I find Arantes' assertion powerful and precise; he talks of artisanal practices that delete the traces of the artisan. This counter-reading of modernism's implementation in Brazil – that is, a reading that searches for deletions – has been transformative in my practice as a design historian. I've been questioning this official narrative of modernism through a feminist reading interested in exposing what has been erased or silenced from the records. For example, a common trope in design history hails the 1960s as a pivotal period in the establishment of design in Latin America, when modern design education and discourse became institutionalized and professionalized.[14] Existing records and narratives frame this institutionalization as a heroic achievement of a few pioneer designers,

FIGURE 13.3 Workers hand-finishing one of the domes of Brasília's National Congress complex (1959). Photograph by Marcel Gautherot/Instituto Moreira Salles Collection. Courtesy of IMS – Instituto Moreira Salles.

some émigrés, acting under favourable national economic policies and post-war industrial development. These narratives, however, underplay the complexity of local sociopolitical, cultural and postcolonial contexts. The national economic and cultural policies that favoured the emergence of modern design in Latin America happened alongside and because of the brutal military dictatorships that ravaged the region from the 1960s. The military ruled Brazil between 1964 and 1985, imposing social and political cohesion via cultural homogenization. One homogenization strategy employed was the adoption of a modern design language to communicate large infrastructural projects as the national pathway to progress. Through a cultural discourse centred on modernity, the military accelerated the intended erasure of indigenous people's and

Afro-Brazilians' lifeways from the official national culture, a project in course for centuries through overt racism, persecution and genocide. As with Gautherot's motivation for photographing all he encountered (and not only what he was expected to register), when historicizing design I am faced not simply with erased records, but frequently with records that have not been seen. Before going further, I wanted to ask you why we were not exposed to images from these working conditions in Brasília during our design and architecture training in the late 1990s. Did you say Gautherot's photographs had been censored?

**TP** I have not found evidence of an official censorship of these images but, as you say, the military dictatorship ruled Brazil under the motto 'love it or leave it'. Crucially, after the closing of the national congress and legislative assemblies in 1968, censorship became a violent but common method for image and narrative control. During Brasília's construction, though, I have found evidence that a 'moral censorship' was in place, as architectural and art historian Luisa Videsott notes.[15] Investigating unknown photographs and footage from this period coupled with oral history testimonies from workers, Videsott found insistent allusions to an unwritten but clear demarcation between what should and should not be registered and talked about. Likewise, historians Andréa Cristina Silva and Leila Beatriz Ribeiro refer to Gautherot's photographs of workers as 'silenced'.[16]

**LR** Reflecting on why these narratives and images were absent from our training, I note that most of the architectural research on Brasília's workers date from the 2000s.[17] This is a period in Brazilian historiography when architectural and design historians start to move away from investigating these disciplines through traditional primary sources: the outcomes of planning like objects and buildings, or planners' own testimonies and narratives. Since then, some historians – and I include myself in this effort – are no longer satisfied with writing histories that edify practice and practitioners, a task I frequently frame as a 'history of the profession'. Architectural and design historians have a more critical and productive task with which to engage, that is, grappling with the consequences of our creative professions. Niemeyer had great power over the making of Brasília, as you say. He was responsible for NOVACAP, for designing the administrative buildings and the mass-mediation of Brasília to the world. That power, I argue, spun off as violence rather than responsibility, the violence of ignoring the consequences of one's planning. A history of Brasília that exposes the erasures perpetrated by a modernization process and a modernism equated with coloniality is more meaningful to current designers and architects than a history that extols past designers' and architects' successes. A method for overcoming this 'history of the profession' bias lies in selecting primary evidence and sources not produced in our disciplines. In my critique of Brasília, for instance, the investigative works of filmmaker Vladimir Carvalho and sociologist Nair Bicalho Sousa, both creating knowledge situated outside of the design field, have been central to my contestation of modernist narratives in the field.[18]

Carvalho excavates the untold experiences of Brasília's migrant workers in an epic documentary that was nearly twenty years in production.[19] Through a series of on-camera interviews with workers, union leaders and architects, Carvalho exposes the chasm that existed between the Brasília conceived by Costa and Niemeyer and the Brasília built by the migrants. In one of many interviews, Niemeyer initially likens Brasília's construction to a 'crusade', a heroic act that would result in a 'city of equal men', evidenced by the fact that he – the NOVACAP chief architect – slept, ate and dressed alongside the workers.[20] Later on, however, Niemeyer concedes that when inaugurated, Brasília was already failing its promise to be 'a city of the future'.[21] He speaks of being disillusioned with a city that could not accommodate his 'working brothers'.[22] Throughout the film, Carvalho questions Costa's and Niemeyer's awareness of the appalling labour and living conditions, including a massacre of workers who protested against rotten food in the camps.[23] They deny knowledge of the massacre and Costa dismisses those dire conditions as 'a sociological problem given the flux of people brought to build the city'.[24]

FIGURE 13.4 *Migrants arriving to work on the construction of Brasília (1959). Courtesy of Arquivo Público do Distrito Federal.*

I read this trope frequently coming from planners and historians of Brazilian modern design and architecture. Modern efforts can be framed by the historiography as 'socially inclusive' projects within 'a socially exclusive society'.[25] This is, however, an unattainable and unrealistic dissociation between the practice of design and architecture and the society they serve. Returning to the artisanal, unsafe and time-consuming building methods required to erect the National Congress domes, I note that these building methods were made possible not despite the masses of disposable workers in a socially exclusive society but because of them. To some extent, it was Brazil's social inequality that produced the conditions for Brasília to exist and thrive as an example of modernism. To allow for Brasília's history to be focused on the building and objects of planning is to dehumanize the practice of architecture and design.

**TP** Absolutely! Brasília has been highly regarded for its aesthetic modernism. After years of architectural practice, my understanding of architecture has expanded beyond materiality and form. Currently, I understand architecture as a way of organizing bodies in space, therefore it is intrinsically social and political. The 'sociological problem' you mention is evident in another photograph of migrants arriving (see Figure 13.4). A group of men with only their body clothes and with few or no belongings, walking through hostile terrain towards a desolate end – this was a common image much exploited by the media to exalt migrants as pioneers and 'men of progress, brave, daring, persevering and dedicated to work'.[26] I can't stop thinking that the appalling working conditions you brought up are matched by another type of violence. The dissemination and trivialization of their struggle by the media – as in framing their working eighteen hours a day as a heroic act for the nation – is a further distortion and control of their narratives. Quijano discloses the domination and exploitation structures within coloniality, adding that the imagination of the dominated is a feat of colonization, 'that is, it acts in the interior of that imagination'.[27]

When I began researching historical and contemporary images of Brasília to interpret the absence of an architectural device, the female toilet, I was confronted with mostly male figures in nearly all images. In 1959, a year before the inauguration, the census reported that the city's population was 64,314 with 42,332 men and 21,982 women – that is, 192.6 men for every 100 women. This means a male population nearly twice the female one.[28] I realized that women's erasure from Brasília's history has been embedded early in its project.

Migrants who intended to work in Brasília were received by the National Institute for Migration and Colonization (Instituto Nacional de Imigração e Colonização, or INIC), a state agency created in 1954 to implement the alleged 'colonization' of Brazil. In hindsight, I read the existence of an official colonization institution as overt absurdity. My current intention is not to unravel the existence of such institutions but to unveil the fact that the violence intrinsic in colonization was normalized. It supported 'the control of knowledge, of authority, of the economy of the norms regulating gender and sexuality, and the assumptions regulating racial classification of people and of regions'.[29]

Alongside gender imbalance, the census also revealed that in 1959 Brasília's population doubled when compared to the previous year.[30] This had been a fact since pre-construction in 1956, when in one month the initial population of 250 workers doubled. Exponential population growth, however, was not anticipated by NOVACAP. In principle, NOVACAP would provide food, housing and healthcare for registered workers. But not every migrant was selected and registered by NOVACAP for Brasília's construction. A large surplus of migrants was not lodged in the existing accommodation schemes and infrastructure, which could not accommodate families either. Consequently, myriads of informal and spontaneous settlements grew around construction sites.

Viewed through a decolonial lens, Brasília's sumptuous inauguration in April 1960 now appears as a farce. There were two extremely opposite 'Brasílias' emerging simultaneously on the plateau: one for modern men and another for these others. The two cities were very different in their making processes, development and completion.

The settlement pictured in Figure 13.5 is known as Sacolândia (Sackland) as the houses were built with empty cement sacks discarded during Brasília's construction. The building/objects featured in the photo evidence how these two cities were intertwined and resulted from the same modern utopia. But like cement sacks, the poor, the families, the women were discarded.

One Brasília was born, as Bruno Zevi noted, of a 'governmental impulse, paternalistic, bureaucratic and authoritarian, therefore running the risk of not being a city, but a scenario to exhibit'.[31] The invisible and scarcely published other Brasília was built by the workers through 'vital necessity',[32] which contested the modernist utopian myth that design alone can define society and control social behaviour. Informal Brasília was built by and for the people, while modern Brasília was built by power, to perform and perpetuate power.

As a female architect, I recognize myself as having been 'pushed out of the tribe for being different'. And so, as Gloria Anzaldúa noted, we the others then 'become more sensitized' in identifying the injustices that modernism embodies and engenders.[33] I am aware of the structural exclusion of my body from the history and practice of architecture, and this provokes anger in me. Inspired by Audre Lorde, I creatively activate my anger and have been 'excavating honesty' in my architectural practice, reviewing and narrating the history of architecture from a woman's perspective.[34] As a decolonial feminist architect, I am empowered to disobey, subvert and expand the limits of an architecture

FIGURE 13.5 *Sacolândia, an informal settlement built by migrants and workers during Brasília's construction, since no housing projects featured in the city plan (1958). Photo by Marcel Gautherot/Instituto Moreira Salles Collection. Courtesy of IMS – Instituto Moreira Salles.*

framed within the colonial matrix of power. My architectural practice embraces 'pluriversalities';[35] this way, I recognize the houses in Sacolândia as another manifestation of architecture in Brasília, one that defends a 'democratic and humanising vision of architecture'[36] – something that the National Congress's virile towers do not.

## Brasília, shared and not contested

LR  Our dialogue uncovers structures, discourses, myths and social practices that resulted in the widening of social, gender and racial inequalities in Brazil, not despite the modern project but because of it.

I am wondering how Brasília was presented to you as an architecture student and when and how you developed a critical awareness of these modern erasures?

TP  Brasília and the modern project were handed to me without critique. Throughout my training, Brasília was an object to be admired, not contested. Later, this persistent centrality of an architectural canon where I did not belong as a creator or user produced in me a sense of not belonging to the profession. I studied architecture at the Federal University of Rio de Janeiro (UFRJ) at the end of the 1990s. The design of the UFRJ campus, originally called the University of Brazil, bore many similarities with Brasília's. The Faculty of Architecture building follows the same modernist precepts: the 'tabula rasa' approach to the site, functionality, rationality, pilotis, free floor plan and glass façade with brise soleil. Both stemmed from the ideals proposed by the generation of modernist architects influenced by CIAM and the Charter of Athens.

I spent five years inhabiting that modernist space while attending classes daily. My upbringing in this space, intentionally or not, denied me the tools to understand its deficiencies and absences, and denied me the right to contest modernism itself. Lorde brilliantly opened a path of emancipation for me with her famous statement that 'the master's tools will never dismantle the master's house'.[37] The Faculty of Architecture's building is the master's house. This structure was my source of knowledge, the model I was given to conceptualize what is architecture, how to practise architecture and, even more so, to appoint who has the right to practise architecture.

In the Faculty of Architecture, there was (and still is) a gender gap between teachers and students that caught my attention from the onset of my studies: students were mostly women, while teachers were all men. In my second year, I started an internship programme in architecture offices and noted that most offices in Rio de Janeiro were (and still are) run by men. The Brazilian Architecture Council's 2019 census revealed that among active architects under 40 years old, 61 per cent are women while 39 per cent are men. However, the census shows that most architects 60 years old or above are men, meaning that professional stability and longevity is still a male privilege.[38] Quijano speaks of the control of knowledge production as another engine that sustains the colonial matrix of power.[39] In fact, the imbalance in female professional references narrows the possibilities for women to succeed, while increasing the authority of the male gender in the architectural field.

Architectural historian Lauro Cavalcanti maintained that the modernist architect 'nourished a certain contempt for formal education, betting on the artistic vision of the career, valuing the innate gift and talent that would, by definition, be untransmissible'.[40] This view reinforces the myth of the individual genius architect who, not by chance, is a male icon. Consequently, this view undermines the potential for a transformative training in which access to knowledge, the power of knowledge and the agency of knowledge production are honestly shared.

In Brazil, this generation of (mostly male) modernist architects worked with or around Le Corbusier, who travelled to Brazil to present a proposal for the UFRJ campus.[41] The relationship between the Europeans and the others, such as Brazilians, continues to be one of colonial domination.[42] I experienced this mastery in myself when I was 'seduced' to continue my architectural studies in Europe, through what Quijano calls 'cultural Europeanisation'.[43] I reflect now on my displacement and my lack of acceptance of other epistemologies due to the 'imposition of the rulers' own patterns of expression, beliefs and images' in my training.[44] However, ironically, with my displacement I was able to detect the method of social and cultural control in my identity and architectural practice, which led me to confront this 'universal cultural model' with decolonial praxis.[45]

Currently, I understand architecture in a broader sense and advocate for the power of architecture to create a just society without dismissing its social and political dimensions. This entails the expansion of our understanding of any building, or object, beyond its formal aspects, thus claiming the architect's responsibility while making design decisions. How do you currently perceive your design training – was it detached from its contextual and political dimensions?

**LR** Although I see my design training detached from its sociocultural context at the time, I do not consider that it was depoliticized. To the contrary, twenty years after graduation, I came to realize that the decontextualization perpetrated by modern design and the education I received were themselves political positions within the design field, albeit ones that I do not embrace. Let me expand on this idea.

I studied graphic and product design in the mid-1990s at Rio's Superior School of Industrial Design (Escola Superior de Desenho Industrial, or ESDI), considered one of the first modern design schools in Latin America.[46] ESDI's opening in 1963 resulted from policies of industrial expansion and national development that peaked under Kubitschek's 'fifty years of progress in five' government. State-led investment in modern design intensified, not surprisingly, in the wake of Brasília's construction. ESDI's role in national development was 'to imprint in the Brazilian people, through the industrial products they consume, a form that is their own', as state governor Carlos Lacerda noted in his inauguration speech.[47] Lacerda's rationale for investing in modern design education reads primarily as an economic one: products designed in Brazil would foment import substitution and save the country from paying royalties to multinational corporations. But I read this role conferred to ESDI and to modern design through the perspective of anthropologist James Holston, to whom 'modernism [is] an aesthetic of erasure and reinscription' and modernization is 'an ideology of development in which governments ... seek to rewrite national histories'.[48]

To this effect, ESDI's curriculum was from the get-go adopted and adapted from the scientific-technical rationalist curriculum of the Hochschule für Gestaltung (HfG) in Ulm, Germany. Here I see the first decontextualization that I interpret as a political stance rather than an unintended consequence. The industrial and economic contexts in 1960's Brazil radically contrasted with those in Germany, yet ESDI's curriculum favoured a vision for design in Brazil predicated on industrialization and the consumption of industrial products. Currently, I see the adoption of this vision as another form of debasing and erasing methods of making and cultural expressions of social groups situated outside the privileged norm, notably indigenous peoples and Afro-Brazilians. In other words, and drawing from Lacerda's inaugural speech, this vision perpetrated in the 1960s proposed that through consumption of modern design the Brazilian people would develop a national form – or a national identity – necessarily different from those already practised in the country.

Historically, this disjuncture in adopting Ulm's curriculum to address Brazil's specific socio-economic challenges and cultural diversity was perceived by ESDI students who, amidst 1968's protests against the military dictatorship, suspended classes for several months and demanded a restructuring of the school's pedagogical model.[49] They installed a general assembly of students and staff to discuss and redesign the curriculum and reshape the school's future. Their discontent resulted from the premature installation of a modern design school in a country whose industrial parks and industrialists were unprepared to expand and innovate. Without the infrastructural framework to act upon production, ESDI graduates saw themselves constrained to work solely as makers of consumer goods.

Despite student protests and strikes, the official rationalist and industrialist design discourse became dominant in the school and to some extent nationally. Continuity with international modern design was maintained by key staff at ESDI who had studied in Ulm, including Karl Heinz Bergmiller (industrial design coordinator), Alexandre Wollner (visual communication coordinator) and Paul Edgard Decurtins. Cultural historian Ana Luiza Nobre speaks of their effort as the wish 'to rationalise the production of form, imposing its origin to an aesthetic and functional control that would not allow margins for daydreaming or intuitive creation'.[50]

This history is well trodden, but what happens a little later is politically foggy. A few years after its opening, ESDI was invited to participate in the organization of a series of International Biennials of Design held in Rio's Museum of Modern Art. The biennials were launched to promote modern design in Brazil and raise the international recognition of Brazilian design to the levels achieved by modern art in the previous decade. These events, however, were initiated by the Ministry of Foreign

Affairs of General Artur da Costa e Silva during the military intervention's most violent period. Soon after the International Design Biennial of 1968 opening, Costa e Silva promulgated the Institutional Act 5 (Ato Institucional 5, or AI-5) overruling the Brazilian constitution, closing the National Congress and State Legislative Assemblies, institutionalizing torture and CIA-backed state terror campaigns against dissidents.[51]

Despite a clear historical nexus between an oppressive state, economic development, modernization policies and the promotion of modern design in the country, this history has gone unwritten. Until recently, most of the historiography in the field – as with the teaching I received in the 1990s – was interested in framing the 1960s as a period of pioneers, progress, and the adoption of a modern language in design despite the odds, despite our living in 'a socially exclusive society'.[52] The installation and development of modern design in Brazil under a period of dictatorship is another example of decontextualization and historiographical silence which enables certain political gains. After returning to ESDI in 2012 as a design historian and teacher, however, I began to unpack these threads. This work became prescient and pressing after 2015, when an 'illegitimate, authoritarian and conservative' right-wing takeover resulted in the impeachment of Brazil's first female president, Dilma Roussef, and led to the country's current health and political crisis.[53] This may seem far-fetched to make a correlation between a threat to democracy in the 2010s and the installation of dictatorship in the 1960s. But it is not. Unlike other Latin American countries, Brazil did not prosecute the torturers, generals and captains from that period; one of them became Brazil's president in 2019.

## Reimagining otherwise

**LR** As we approach this point in our conversation, I want to ask you why and how was the absence of a female toilet in Brasília's Federal Senate finally repaired?

**TP** This act of reparation – that is, the installation of a female toilet in the Federal Senate after its fifty-five years of existence – was determined by Roussef working together with an all-party team of female legislatives. Clearly it is not a coincidence that this architectural and historical reparation happened during Brazil's first female presidency. The connection you just made between the installation of the military dictatorship in 1964, four years after Brasília's inauguration, and the 2010s right-wing takeover is crucial. The year 2015 marked the beginning of the end of Roussef's second mandate soon after her re-election, which had been contested by traditional power bearers, mostly male. Roussef was impeached in 2016 during what has been regarded as a coup d'état by Brazilian legislatives, those siting in the National Congress under smoothly finished white-clad domes. She did not survive the entrenched patriarchal structures of Brasília. Marielle Franco, a Brazilian politician, feminist and human rights activist, also did not survive. Due to her political actions and capacity to mobilize black women among other 'others', she was assassinated in 2018 by militia powers associated with the current extreme-right president Jair Bolsonaro. This was a brutal act of violence against democracy and women's rights. What I sense, though, is that we may have reached a historical period when these erasures, silences and absences are coming painfully to the fore and can no longer be ignored. In Franco's writings she called for a mobilization of 'the political creativity' of Brazil's marginalized groups, especially the *favelada*, the black women favela dwellers.[54] Our open dialogue to uncover modern erasures is a method to build ideas and dismantle current power structures in the fields of design and architecture collectively and creatively.

LR   I hear what you are saying ... that a collective tooling – in research, practice, thinking and writing – will help build other houses, to build otherwise. As a design historian, I have been accustomed to the form of intellectual practice and history writing that thrives in the entrenched patriarchal structures of academia and is predicated on individual achievement. The dialogical method we have used to reconsider modern erasures has elicited other forms of thinking and debate for me. It was through our dialogue that I could formulate an important switch in how I have been framing the installation of modern design in Brazil. Holston, in his ethnographic study of the city, interprets Brasília as a paradox: an 'imagined and desired future' that 'represented a negation of existing conditions in Brazil'.[55] However, through our reading of Brasília and the implementation of the modern project in Brazil as coloniality, I have arrived at a different interpretation. These modern paradoxes – the construction of a formally modern city but on archaic building methods; the promotion of modernism as socially transformative while perpetrating injustices and cultural exclusion – these paradoxes are not simply a 'negation of existing conditions in Brazil'.[56] These paradoxes are the very sustaining pillars, the intrinsic mechanism of ongoing inequality, that make modernity for a few happen. I am uncomfortable with calling the modern project in Brazil a paradox because it is not a self-contradictory project. These apparent contradictions are intrinsic to the logic of coloniality. Brasília's design and construction, as well as the powers emanating from their chambers, have been formed in this colonial logic; they reassert this logic incessantly.

# Notes

1   Mariana Jungmann, 'Senado constrói primeiro banheiro feminino no plenário' (2016) https://agenciabrasil.ebc.com.br/politica/noticia/2016-01/senado-constroi-primeiro-banheiro-feminino-no-plenario (accessed 30 September 2021).

2   Elcio Gomes Da Silva, *Os Palácios Originais de Brasília*, vols I and II (PhD diss., FAU Universidade de Brasília, 2012), 241–8.

3   James Holston, *The Modernist City: An Anthropological Critique of Brasília* (Chicago: Chicago University Press, 1989), 18.

4   Luíza Helena Nunes Pinto, *Presidente (1956–1961). Discursos selecionados do Presidente Juscelino Kubitschek* (Brasília: Fundação Alexandre de Gusmão, 2009).

5   https://www.camara.leg.br/visita-mobile/espaco/7;jsessionid=tHRF5rkYu+1JN EkGemUiHbEN.sepapn2.camara.gov.br (accessed 14 June 2021).

6   Maria Beatriz Camargo Cappello, 'A revista brasília na construção da Nova Capital: Brasília (1957–1962)', *Revista de pesquisa em arquitetura e urbanismo* 11, no. 1 (2010): 43–58.

7   Walter D. Mignolo and Catherine E. Walsh, *On Decoloniality: Concepts, Analytics, Praxis* (Durham; London: Duke University Press, 2018), 108.

8   Anibal Quijano, 'Coloniality of Power and Eurocentrism in Latin America', *International Sociology* 15, no. 2 (2000): 215–32.

9   Sergio Burgi and Samuel Titan Júnior, *Marcel Gautherot: Brasília* (São Paulo: Instituto Moreira Salles, 2010). Gautherot's collection of more than 25,000 items was acquired by the Instituto Moreira Salles in 1999: https://ims.com.br/titular-colecao/marcel-gautherot (accessed 14 June 2021).

10  Nair Heloisa Bicalho de Sousa, *Construtores de Brasília* (Petrópolis: Vozes, 1983).

11  Pedro F. Arantes, 'Reinventing the building site', in *Brazil's Modern Architecture*, eds. Elisabetta Andreoli and Adrian Forty (London: Phaidon, 2004), 175.

12  Arantes, 'Reinventing the building site', 172–5 and Sérgio Ferro, *Arquitetura e trabalho livre* (São Paulo: Cosac e Naify, 2006), 314.

13  Arantes, 'Reinventing the building site', 175.

14  Silvia Fernández, 'The Origins of Design Education in Latin America: From the hfg in Ulm to Globalization', *Design Issues* 22, no. 1 (2006): 3–19.

15  Luisa Videsott, 'Narrativas da construção de Brasília' (PhD diss., Universidade de São Paulo, 2009).

16  Andréa Cristina Silva and Leila Beatriz Ribeiro 'Imagens do Silencio, Imagens silenciadas–Marcel Gautherot e a construção de Brasília'. *XIII Encontro de História Anpuh Rio* conference proceedings (2008).

17  Ferro, *Arquitetura e trabalho livre*; Alexandre Pinto de Souza e Silva, 'As imagens que (re)significam a capital: os olhares de Gautherot e de Brasília sobre a construção cidade' *XIX Encontro de História Anpuh Rio* conference proceedings (2020).

18  See collections like IMS's Gautherot and Depoimentos, Programa de História Oral. Arquivo Público do Distrito Federal, 1991. Also: Nair Heloisa Bicalho de Sousa, *Construtores De Brasília: Estudo De Operários E Sua Participação Política* (Petrópolis: Vozes, 1983).

19  *Conterrâneos Velhos de Guerra* (1991) [Film] Dir. Vladimir Carvalho, Brasil. Also: *Brasília: Contradições de uma Cidade Nova* (1967) [Film] Dir. Joaquim Pedro de Andrade, Brasil.

20　Carvalho, *Conterrâneos Velhos*, 14:00'.
21　Ibid. 36:20'
22　Ibid.
23　Ibid. 1:45'00" to 1:55'00'
24　Ibid. 1:51'50"
25　Elisabetta Andreoli and Adrian Forty, 'Round Trip: Europe to Brazil & Back', in *Brazil's Modern Architecture*, eds. Elisabetta Andreoli and Adrian Forty (London: Phaidon, 2004), 19.
26　Videsott, 'Narrativas da construção', 193.
27　Aníbal Quijano, 'Coloniality and Modernity/Rationality', *Cultural Studies* 21, nos 2–3 (2007): 168–78.
28　Nelson Senra, *Veredas de Brasília: as expedições geográficas em busca de um sonho* (Rio de Janeiro: IBGE, 2010), 128.
29　Walter Mignolo, *The Darker Side of Western Modernity: Global Futures, Decolonial Options* (Durham; London: Duke University Press, 2011), xv.
30　Senra, *Veredas de Brasília*, 128.
31　Bruno Zevi, 'Inchiesta su Brasília: Sei ? sulla nuova capitale sudamericana', *L'Architettura: Cronache e Storia* 5, no. 51 (1960): 608–19.
32　Ibid.
33　Gloria Anzaldúa, *Borderlands/La Frontera: The New Mestiza* (San Francisco: Aunt Lute, 1987), 38.
34　Audre Lorde, 'The uses of anger', *Women's Studies Quarterly* 9, no. 3 (1981).
35　Mignolo, *The Darker Side*, 23.
36　Zevi, 'Inchiesta su Brasília'.
37　Audre Lorde, 'The Master's tool will never dismantle the Master's house' (1979), in *Gender Space Architecture: An Interdisciplinary Introduction*, eds. Jane Rendell, Barbara Penner and Iain Borden (London: Routledge, 2000), 53–5.
38　*Censo dos Arquitetos e Urbanista do Brasil*. https://www.caubr.gov.br/wp-content/uploads/2018/03/Censo_CAUBR_06_2015_WEB.pdf (accessed 14 June 2021).
39　Quijano, 'Coloniality and Modernity/Rationality', 168–78.
40　Lauro Cavalcanti in Henrique E. Mindlin, *Modern Architecture in Brazil* (London: Architectural Press: 1956), 15.
41　Ibid.
42　Quijano, 'Coloniality and Modernity/Rationality', 168–78.
43　Ibid.
44　Ibid.
45　Ibid.
46　Fernández, 'The Origins of Design', 3–19.
47　Ana Luiza de Souza Nobre, 'Fios cortantes: projeto e produto, arquitetura e design no Rio de Janeiro (1950–70)' (PhD Diss., Pontifical Catholic University of Rio de Janeiro, Rio de Janeiro, 2008).

48 Holston, *The Modernist City*, 5.
49 Pedro Luiz Pereira de Souza, *ESDI, biografia de uma idéia* (Rio de Janeiro: Editora UERJ, 1997), 148.
50 Nobre, 'Fios cortantes', 74.
51 Charles Green and Anthony Gardner, *Biennials, Triennials, and Documenta: The Exhibitions That Created Contemporary Art* (Chichester: Wiley-Blackwell, 2016). Also: Zuenir Ventura, *1968: O Ano que não terminou* (Rio de Janeiro: Nova Fronteira, 1988).
52 Andreoli and Forty, 'Round Trip', 19.
53 Marielle Franco, 'After the Take-Over: Mobilizing the Political Creativity of Brazil's Favelas', *New Left Review* 110 (2018): 135–40.
54 Franco, 'After the Take-Over'.
55 Holston, *The Modernist City*, 5.
56 Ibid.

# AFTERWORD – ON BORROWED TIME

## Ben Highmore

Few authors have traversed the fields of architectural and design history with such persistence and perspicacity as the German critic Walter Benjamin. The spirit of Benjamin hangs over this book, and while his name is only directly invoked in the introduction and in Swati Chattopadhyay's chapter on a set of bookshelves in colonial India, you can feel his presence in the constellation of objects and themes running through all the sections. Benjamin, and others, showed us the way to grasp the modern not 'directly' through its own self-image but from the side, by taking the epiphenomena of material actuality as our entry points. While freeways and televisions, convenience stores and air-conditioning units, high-tech architecture and portable emergency shelters, for instance, were either unknown or in development in Benjamin's lifetime, it is surely his spirit that has sensitized generations of historians of buildings and objects to look for illumination via the overlooked, the outmoded, and the seemingly incidental or banal. Benjamin liberates us from the auditor's exhausting demand for canonical histories *of* architecture and *of* design by steering us towards the generative pursuit of histories *through* architecture and design.[1] Benjamin shifts the ground; we are no longer burdened with having to account for the thing as a 'work' or a 'text' and positing it within hierarchies and taxonomies of established values. But with this liberation comes a much heavier obligation: we become answerable to the angel of history.

In his unfinished and unfinishable *Arcades Project*, which he worked on from 1928 until his suicide in 1940, Benjamin collated statements about nineteenth-century Paris, its buildings, its furnishings, its entertainments, its emergent consumer culture, and threaded this through with his own commentary, to create a vast montage for what he refers to as the 'capital of the nineteenth century'. And yet to recruit him and his work for a rapprochement or synthesis between the disciplines of architectural and design history would seem ill-advised: his subjects, after all, extended beyond buildings and objects to take in fashion, literature, advertising, philosophy, urbanism, memoir, technology, and the lingering presence of the ancient and outmoded in the new. In this Afterword my intention is not to corral Benjamin to the cause of multi-scalar accounts of our thingly environment, merely to pursue a central insight that governs his historical practice. This insight is in many respects a commonplace within the field of historiography – namely, that what we call history is not the reclamation of the past as it *really was* (there is no communion with the dead, no séance that would allow unmediated access to past experience), but a reconstruction of a past as it is *seen to be in the present*. Historians, whether their field is political history, literary history, architectural history, social history, or material history, are writers not time travellers, and they make 'history' by stitching together sources and interpretations. What Benjamin does, though, and what makes him a compelling voice for anyone interested in the practice of materialist history today, is to take this routine insight and return it to us as 'our' problem, 'our' potentiality.

In *The Arcades Project*, Benjamin writes that 'the events surrounding the historian, and in which he himself takes part, will underlie his presentation in the form of a text written in invisible ink'.[2] Aside from its masculinist presumption, Benjamin is declaring that the events of the present are unavoidably written into the writing of the past, but not in any straightforward manner. The events surrounding Benjamin (a German Jew) and the writing of *The Arcades Project* would include, most obviously, the rise of Nazism in Germany, Benjamin's exile in Paris, and the general precariousness of his material existence. You wouldn't need to be a cryptographer to sense the presence of these events in the tone and general approach of Benjamin in *The Arcades Project* – the sense of melancholy that pervades his commentary, for instance, and his refusal to reproduce ideas of historical progress in his account of nineteenth-century Paris. But Benjamin's point is that events would invisibly inscribe themselves in the historian's narrative whether or not the historian was a refugee fleeing from fascism or a supporter of Hitler, whether they were financially insecure or privately wealthy. The conditions of the present impinging on how the past is imagined and articulated is, for Benjamin, a universal, inescapable aspect of historical writing.

In his final essay Benjamin takes up this issue again, but now not as a universal condition, but as something that could drive the writing of a particular type of history: historical materialism. 'Articulating the past historically does not mean recognizing it "the way it really was"', writes Benjamin in 'On the Concept of History', 'It means appropriating a memory as it flashes up in a moment of danger. Historical materialism wishes to hold fast that image of the past which unexpectedly appears to the historical subject in a moment of danger.'[3] 'Events' are no longer just the invisible ink of history, instead they have become 'dangers' that animate the historian; instead of the universal condition of the present impinging on the articulation of the past, he poses the figure of a historian who struggles to grasp a past that 'unexpectedly appears' in a moment of danger. 'Danger', 'wishes' and the 'unexpected' are the terms for pursuing historical materialism. What seems clear (if this is the right word) is that this is no prescription for undertaking historical research, no roadmap for a 'correct' approach to history.

It is difficult to avoid the fact that today's 'events' and 'dangers' – which surround us and in which we are unavoidably involved – include a catalogue of competing emergencies: the rise of right-wing populism across the globe; misinformation peddled with alarming efficiency and effectivity across the internet; the continual hoarding of resources and opportunities to benefit structures of class, race and gender; the cavalier indifference by power blocks to swathes of suffering and poverty; pandemics and the long tail of their mutations, and so on. And overlaying all this an impending climate catastrophe that is already causing devastation and looks set to remake the world on a planetary, creaturely scale.[4] Given the scale and urgency of these 'events', it would be overreaching in the extreme to imagine that historians of buildings and objects are well placed to respond to these conditions in any practical or effective way. Yet the angel of history means that we can't look away either.

The humanities have a much slower rhythm than the world of social policy, politics and political activism. Cultural history takes time, its accomplishments are often slow accretions rather than sudden gains or losses (look how long Benjamin was working on *The Arcades Project*). The urgencies of the world imprint themselves on scholarly activity in the humanities in the name of 'new' sensitivities and attunements: queer theory, critical race theory, decolonization projects, digital humanities, environmental humanities, and so on.[5] These attunements and their amalgamations go some way to connecting the urgencies of the world to academic life. By way of these new concerns, researchers are sensitized to gaps and fissures in the historiographic record and are newly attuned to phenomena that might previously have gone unremarked. As part of this attunement, one necessary task for humanities researchers has been the scouring of the past for the voices of the unheard and unheralded: architects of colour, women designers, alternative modernities from the Global South, and so on, as well as the analysis of how processes of marginalization and erasure are maintained.[6] Alongside this, researchers have looked about for 'useable histories' – utopian and radical ecological projects from the past, accounts of forgotten forms of activism and collective effort – that might inspire new projects in the present, or can recalibrate an image of the past (for instance, by shifting the historical account of slavery by recognizing the resistance of chattel slaves to puncture the 'heroic' narratives of white abolitionists).

From the perspective of impending climate catastrophe, it is difficult not to look at most of the recent past of architecture and design as a catalogue of environmental disasters. For instance, 1950s car styling not only evokes dreams of a streamline future, but now comes heavy with the fumes of polluting emissions and the depletion of fossil fuels. The attempts of the 1960s and 1970s to give the furniture industry the same short-term modishness as the clothing industry now looks like the worst sort of wasteful profiteering. This is the other way that the present presses its own urgencies on a past that appeared (at the time) 'blissfully' unaware of them. Today Benjamin's assertion that 'there is no document of culture which is not at the same time a document of barbarism'[7] is an accusation that can put the entire history of modernity (powered by fossil fuels and its petrocultural imaginations) in the dock. But finger-wagging moralism was not Benjamin's scene. He was too much of a dialectician for that. Rather than imagining a clerisy of clean-handed historians driven by moral rectitude, Benjamin's melancholy method was always to try and glean the obscured and unfulfilled promissory notes hiding in plain sight amongst the material culture abandoned by the relentless drives of fashion, to resuscitate other possibilities within barbarous history and its ruins.

How will the events of the present inscribe themselves in the material and materialist histories that are being written now? Today's events are not only altering how we think about the past, they are also altering the very nature of time and how we experience it. In 1949 Fernand Braudel imagined three durations of historical time: the quickest of these was 'event time' – the froth of notable individual actions and interactions – a world of declarations, manifestoes, arguments, inventions, interventions, and so on. The much slower duration of social time was history measured across a lifetime, a generation. This might involve the slower roll-out of the irruptions of event-time (the mass take-up of a technology, for instance, rather than its spectacular invention) as well as the gradual build-up of cultural infrastructures such as comprehensive education and national health systems. The slowest duration was the *longue durée*: 'a history whose passage is almost imperceptible, that of man in his relationship to the environment, a history in which all change is slow, a history of constant repetition, ever-recurring cycles'.[8] Today the rhythmic identities of these three durations are being constantly unsettled: the climate and the geological, rather than heralding the slow, almost invisible changes that can only be registered across millennia, now behave more like the event-time of sudden explosive change; the slower infrastructural building that was so representative of social time can be undone in a blink of an eye. We are living a complex recalibration of time itself.

The Swedish ecologist Andreas Malm describes this recalibration as the discordant and inchoate activation of history:

> Now more than ever, we inhabit the diachronic, the discordant, the inchoate: the fossil fuels hundreds of millions of years old, the mass combustion developed over the past two centuries, the extreme weather this has already generated, the journey towards a future that will be infinitely more extreme – unless something is done *now* – the tail of present emissions stretching into the distance ... History has sprung alive, through a nature that has done likewise.[9]

If the study of objects, buildings and material infrastructures insists that we live across exponentially disparate scales of space (from the cellular to the global networks of communication and exchange), then the study of historical ecology insists we are living across disjunctive scales of time.[10] The fuels that took millions of years to form have powered our sense of the modern for a couple of centuries, and the effects of this combustion is shaping our present and *has already* shaped the future.[11] We are living on borrowed time – time borrowed from an expansive planetary history that we have used to pay for our carbon-fuelled modernity.

The recalibration of time undoes any neat parcelling out of historical periods: historical periods of invention, of human achievement, of aesthetic accomplishments. The invitation to historians is unclear. What can we make of this? What do historians of buildings and objects have to offer in this situation? Personally, I think that there are two temptations that are worth treating with caution. The first could be thought of as the 'funding-call' approach to the world's problems. This is the constant lurching towards different agendas: one year all the funding seems to be aimed at AI, the next year or two money is reserved for sustainability; one year the focus is on diaspora and refugees, the next on infrastructures. It seems to pander to an all-or-nothing logic: either you are concerned with environmentalism or you are not; either you are working towards racial emancipation or you are not. To see the present as caught up in conflicting and competing emergencies can produce a sense of chasing the research agenda that is currently most demanding (and most fundable). The second temptation that I would want to treat with caution is the lure of the overarching theory that could magically connect all the tensions and conflicts between, say, environmental depletion and anti-black racism, between a global class struggle and 'fake news'. Instead of a universal and universalizing theory, something more modest might be in order.

The spirit of Benjamin could be our guide. His work might continue to sensitize us towards a creative way of connecting across things and ideas, across different scales of time and space. Benjamin's spirit steers us away from the programme and the programmatic and points us towards the constellatory. It encourages us to adopt an intellectual nimbleness and fleet-footedness that could make way for the unexpected, the unanticipated, the unruly. It entreats us to look out for the surprising connection and to resist the path of least resistance. At their best, architectural and design history are empirical and connective ways of understanding the artificial environments that we inhabit. These artificial environments have been entangled in a vision of the earth dominated by an extractivist logic, but they have never been reducible to such a way of imagining the world and its resources.

Looking towards the year 2000 from the perspective of the mid-1980s, Raymond Williams offered a stark statement about what is at stake in extractivist logic:

> What is really at issue is a version of the earth and its life forms as extractable and consumable wealth. What is seen is not the sources and resources of many forms of life but everything, including people, as available raw material, to be appropriated and transformed. Against this,

the ecological argument has shown, in case after case, and then as a different way of seeing the whole, that a complex physical world and its intricate and interacting biological processes cannot for long be treated in such ways, without grave and unforeseen kinds of damage.[12]

Even if the future looks bleak, we need, in our small way, to be able to imagine a different way of seeing the complex lifeworld, of providing non-extractivist visions of the past and the future. Benjamin suggests that such seeing might be undertaken not from above, but glimpsed through constellations of seemingly disparate materials. What is at stake is not just a liveable planet for humans, but a creative capaciousness capable of imagining what a liveable planet might actually be like.

## Notes

1. I am borrowing Craig Clunas's formulation when he suggests that in the 'social history of art' tradition of scholarly research the most productive art history existed as 'a social history with or through or by means of art rather than a social history *of* art', in his 'Social History of Art', in *Critical Terms for Art History*, second edition, eds. Robert S. Nelson and Richard Shiff (Chicago: University of Press Chicago, 2003), 475.
2. Walter Benjamin, *The Arcades Project*, trans. Howard Eiland and Kevin McLaughlin (Cambridge, Mass. and London: Harvard University Press, 1999), 476. *The Arcades Project* was published posthumously and had Benjamin not died in 1940 would, no doubt, have been developed further.
3. Walter Benjamin, 'On the Concept of History', *Walter Benjamin Selected Writings, Volume 4, 1938–1940*, ed. Michael W. Jennings (Cambridge: Belknap/Harvard University Press, 2003), 391.
4. Achille Mbembe uses the deadly but evocative phrase 'necropolitics' to diagnose the overarching political climate orchestrating today's global society. See Achille Mbembe, *Necropolitics* (Durham: Duke University Press, 2019).
5. Of course, there is no reason to jettison older attunements and sensitivities: Marxism, semiotics, feminism, psychoanalysis, etc.
6. This isn't the place to catalogue this growing body of literature and the work of critical reclamation, but I have in mind books like Mabel O. Wilson, *Negro Building: Black Americans in the World of Fairs and Museums* (Berkeley: University of California Press, 2012).
7. Benjamin, 'On the Concept of History', 392.
8. Fernand Braudel, *The Mediterranean and the Mediterranean World in the Age of Philip II: Volume I*, trans. Siân Reynolds (London: Fontana Press, 1975), 20. First published in France in 1949.
9. Andreas Malm, *The Progress of This Storm: Nature and Society in a Warming World* (London: Verso, 2020), 11.

10 For an extended discussion of temporal disjunctures see my 'Disjunctive Constellations: On Climate Change, Conjunctures, and Cultural Studies', *New Formations* 102 (2021): 28–43.
11 Malm calls this the 'ongoing past' – Malm, *The Progress of This Storm*, 5. For a more extensive account of the ongoing past see Andreas Malm, *Fossil Capital: The Rise of Steam Power and the Roots of Global Warming* (London: Verso, 2016). An example of what this means is that if carbon emissions simply ended the oceans would continue to heat up, because the warming work of previous decades of carbon emissions would remain 'ongoing'.
12 Raymond Williams, *Towards 2000* (Harmondsworth: Penguin, 1985), 214–5.

# INDEX

*Page numbers in italics refer to Figures.*

Aalto, Alvar 161, 184
ad hoc/adhocism 13, 200, 202, 238, 244, 245, 249
advertisements
   brand signage 63, 68, 69
   print xv, 55, 65, 70, 71, 80, 82, 84, 153, 170–1, 172, *171, 173*, 273
   television xvi, 47, *49*, 55, 69, 72
aid 116, 162, 182, 183–4, 185, 186, 193, 194
AIDS epidemic 247–9
air 24, 77, 83, 87, 88, 90–1
air conditioning 20, 70, 77–91, 204, 209, 228, 273
Ant Farm 222, 226, 230
apartment block 20, 43, 44, 46, 49, 51, 52, 53, 167
appliances *see* home technology
Arantes, Pedro 258
Archigram 214, 222, 226, 240, 241
*Architectural Design* 223
architectural education 4, 9, 12–13, 141, 144, 145, 182, 193, 260, 265
*Architectural Forum* 169, 174
*Architectural Magazine* 141–57, *142, 149, 150, 151, 154*
architectural profession
   Societe Centrale d'Architecture de Belgique (SCAB) 166
   Royal Institute of British Architects (RIBA) 143–4
   *see also* education
*Architectural Review* 104, 156, 241
*Architecture* 167, 170, *171*

architecture and art 4, 5, 110, 122, 132–3, 155, 170, 171, 173, 175, 221–3, 226, 227, 246, 267
Archizoom 221
art history xiv, 4, 6, 8, 9, 98, 99, 132–3
artisan 116, 141, 143, 148, 149, 156, 202, 258
Arts and Crafts movement 13, 153, 156
as found 238
Ateliers Stephane Jasinski 172
Austen, Jane 1–2, 12
Austin & Seeley 153, *153*
avant-garde 185, 227, 233 n.3, 249

balcony 52, 57, 84
   *see also* veranda
Banham, Mary 100
Banham, Reyner xv, xvi, xvii, 6, 20, 85, 88, 97–104, *103*, 105–10, *108, 109*, 208, 209, 211, 227, 228, 237, 240, 242, 243, 248, 249
Barthes, Roland xvi
Bastin, Roger 170
Baudrillard, Jean 107, 110
Bauhaus 5, *5*, 242
*Bauwelt* 223
Behrens, Peter 13, *14*, 241
Bekaert, Geert 174, 175
Benjamin, Walter xv, 24–5, 273–4, 275, 277, 278
Berger, John xvi
Bertoia, Harry 162, 167, *168*
bibliomigrancy 23, 24–7, 32, 34
blueprint 187, *188*, 189

Bourdieu, Pierre 44
*Bouwen en Wonen* 168, 173
Bradbury, Ray 109
Braem, Renaat 173
brand 64–71, 162, 170, 171, 173–5, 209, 242
  *see also* advertisement
Brasília 253, 254, *255*, *257*, 255–8, *259*, 260–9, *261*
  *see also* NOVACAP
*brasília* 256
Braudel, Fernand 276
Bray and Schiable 247
Breuer, Marcel *168*, 168, 169
*bricoleur* 249
Brodzki, Constantin *168*, 168–9, 170
Brown, Denise Scott 97, 103, 110
Buchsbaum, Alan 247–8
building regulations
  *Independent Review of Building Regulations and Fire Safety* 201
  British Board of Agrément (BBA) 204
  British Standards Institute (BSI) 204, 207, 211, 212
  *see also* fire safety
building science
  Fibre Building Board Development Organisation (FIDOR) 211, 212
  Joint Fire Research Organisation (JFRO) 211, 212
building site 62, 194, 208, 265
buildings
  Administrative Centre of the Union Cotonniere textile company, Ghent 172, 173
  Banque Lambert, Brussels 172, *173*, 173
  Behrens House, Darmstadt 13, *14*
  British Museum Great Court, London 240
  Brussels Résidence, Brussels 166, 167, 174
  Centre Pompidou, Paris *238*, 238, 242
  Columbus Occupational Health Center, Columbus, Indiana 242
  Connecticut General Insurance Headquarters, Bloomfield, Connecticut 171–2
convenience store
  Retail Ice Station at Twelfth and Edgefield in Oak Cliff, Texas' (c. 1928) *64*
  'Tote'm Store of the late 1930s and early 1940' *65*
  A typical 7-Eleven Store of the early 1950s' *67*
  'A Fort Worth 7-Eleven Store' (1951) *69*
Crystal Palace, London 242
De Coene Model Home, *Expo 58, Brussels* 166, 167
Eames House, Los Angeles 239, 242
Eden Project, Cornwall 240
Eiffel Tower, Paris 242
Emergency House, Oxfam 116, 182–5, 186–7, 188–94, *188*, *189*, *190*, *192*
European Coal and Steel Community (ECSC) house, Charleroi 163, *164*, 165
European House, Ghent 165
Ishwar Chandra Vidyasagar's residence, Kolkata 21, 34–5, *36*, 36–8
Hongkong and Shanghai Bank, Hong Kong 239
Hopkins House, London *239*, 239, 242
Lloyds building, London 239
Maison de Verre, Paris 241, 242
National Congress Building, Brasília 253–5, *255*, *257*, *259*, *261*, 260, 262, 264, 268
Oriental Repository, East India House, London 27, *30*, 30–2, 38
Palais de Tuileries, Paris 125
Palace of Versailles, Paris 119, *120*, 127, 129
Reichstag Dome, Berlin 240
Reliance Controls electronics factory, Swindon 238
Sainsbury Centre for Visual Arts, Norwich 238, 240, 242

# INDEX

United Nations Headquarters, New York 168
UNESCO headquarters, Paris 168, 172
Bunshaft, Gordon 173
byelaws 206

California 106, 109, 243
canopy 66, 223, 224
Carrier, Willis 78, 91 n.4
cars and driving 62, 65, 70, 97–8, 100, 101, 102, 105, 107, 110
   'drive thru' 66
   Cadillac 99
   Chevrolet 99, 100
   Dymaxion 99
   Ford 99, 102, 106
   Jaguar 99
   *see also* freeway
Carvalho, Vladimir 261
*Casabella* 223
Castells, Manuel 105
censorship 47, 260
Chattopadhyay, Swati 13, 273
chimney 72, 54, 155, 208
cladding 210, 258, 260
Cold War 162, 185
colonialism/coloniality 13, 21–38, 79, 86, 87, 88, 145, 183, 184, 256–69, 275
   *see also* Global South; Third World'
comfort 45, 47, 53, 54, 73, 78–80, 87, 89, 90, 149, 167, 187
commodity/commodification xv, 2, 4, 6, 31, 32, 38, 64, 70, 72, 147, 155, 165, 166, 200, 202, 203, 205–6, 208, 209, 211, 212, 227
communication technology 104, 105, 220, 226, 230–1, 232, 276
   radio 47, 48, 50, 51, 102, 107, 167
   telecommunications 104, 230
   walkie-talkie 228, 229
components (building, factory-made) 44, 78, 88, 163, 165, 166, 174, 182, 184, 201, 203–4, 205–6, 207, 208–14, 239, 241, 244, 250
convenience store 64

Costa, Lucio 254, 256 261, 268
court festivities 119, 120, 121, 122, 123, 124, 127
Courtois, Robert 170
courtyard 28, 36, 41 n.42, 119, 123
craft xvii, 4, 7, 13, 122, 124, 201, 249
   *see also* Arts and Crafts movement
Cramer, Stuart W. 78
Crawford, Matthew 110
cultural history 8, 275
cultural studies xvi, 16
Cuny, Fred 193
cybernetics 100

*Daedalus* 104
Davis, Ian 184, 193
De Coene 164, 165–7, *166*, *168*, 172
deregulation 203, 206–8
Design Coalition 247
design education 125, 258, 266
   *see also* education
*Deutsche Kunst und Dekoration* 13, *14*
development/developmentalism 78, 79, 81, 181, 183, 184, 185, 186–7, 190, 193, 255–6, 266, 267
diagram/drawing 9, *121*, 125, 126, 132, 147, 148, 152, 169–70, 201, 222, 254
   *see also* blueprint
*disegno* 122, 132, 135
divertissements *see* court festivities
domes, dome culture 30, 130–1, *131*, 134, 190, 219, 220, 230, 240, 253, 254, 258, *259*, 262, 268–9
   *see also* geodesic dome
*Domus* 223
drug use 226
dwelling 11, 24, 186

East India Company Oriental Repository 30
ecology 11, 15, 98, 100, 101, 102, 103, 104–5, 107, 275, 276, 278
education
   École nationale supérieure des arts visuels (La Cambre), Brussels 168

Federal University of Rio de Janeiro (UFRJ) 265, 266
Hochschule für Gestaltung, Ulm (HfG) 267
Royal College of Art, London 185
Superior School of Industrial Design, Rio de Janeiro (ESDI) 266–8
Technical University of Vienna 223
*see also* architecture education; design education
Elmes, James 145
Elno, K.-N. 175
emergency housing 165, 182, 184
emergency shelter 184, 185, 188, 193
*see also* buildings, Emergency House
encyclopaedia 142, 147, 152, 153, 156
environment (built/human) 4, 10, 52, 56, 70, 91, 97, 98, 102, 107–8, 143, 169, 202–4, 225
environmental conditions 13, 20, 56, 77, 85–6, 182, 209, 219, 223, 229–31
*see also* air
environmental science 15
environmentalism 7, 53, 110, 240, 275, 276, 277
ephemeral structures *see* court festivities; emergency shelter; exhibitions; festival architecture; inflatable environments
equipment, and appliance 63, 79, 80, 81, 83, 84, 90, 141, 182, 187, 242, 244, 246, 248
*see also* object
*Esquire* 245, 245, 246
exhibitions 99, 165, 169, 170, 199, 240
'American Design for Home and Decorative Use', Helsinki (1953) 165
'Expo 58', Brussels (1958) 166, *166*
'From Aalto to Zumthor: Furniture by Architects', Köln (2012) 161
Industrialised Building Systems and Components Exhibition, London (1964) 212
International Biennials of Design, Rio's Museum of Modern Art 267
'Italy: The New Domestic Landscape', New York (1972) 226
'Machine Art', New York (1934) 244
'Salon de l'Enfance et de la Famille', Brussels (1953) 169
'The Presence of the Past', Venice (1980) 240

favela 269
Félibien, André 120, 122, 123, 124, 126
festival architecture 122, 124, 126, 133–4
fire safety 183, 191–2, 201–2, 204, 207, 208, 209, 211, 212
*flâneur* 107
Florence cathedral, lantern *131*
flow 104, 105
food packaging 62, 66, 70
Forty, Adrian 15
Foster Associates 240, 242
*see also* Team 4
Foster, Hal 6
Foster, Norman 238, 248
Franco, Marielle 269
freeway 98–9, 101, 102, 104, 107, 108, *109*
Fuller, Richard Buckminster 185, 241, 244, 248
furniture and domestic furnishing 1, 2, 20, 23, 33, 44, 50, 86, 87–8, 90, 148, 151–2, 155, 219, 221, 244, 275
and interior design 78, 148–9
and room layout 34, 46, 47, 48, *49*, 51, 56
furniture design 161–2, 163, 164–75, 222, 223, 226, 229
*see also* De Coene; home furnishings; Knoll; Tubax

gadget 228
  *see also* gizmo
gas stations 11, 20, 66, 68, 70
Gautherot, Marcel 255, 257, 257, 259, 264
gender xvi, 7, 15, 34, 70, 72, 143, 146, 152, 156, 245–6, 254, 256, 262–3, 264, 265, 269, 275
genre 11, 129, 134, 186
gentrification 72, 202, 241
geodesic dome 185, 188, 189, *188, 189, 190*, 241, 244
  *see also* domes
*Gesamtkunstwerk* 13
gizmo 228, 229, 231, 232
Global South 10, 116, 182, 193, 275
  *see also* colonialism/coloniality
Gothic 154, 155, 156
Grenfell Tower disaster 201, 202, 205, 211
Gropius, Walter 5, 184
Gruppo 9999 221
Guchez, Henri 165

Hackitt, Dame Judith 201, 202
Hall, Peter 97, 104, 105, 106
Hannoset, Corneille 169, 170, *171*, 171
Hardy Holzman Pfeiffer Associates 242
Harrison & Abramovitz 168, 169
Haus-Rucker-Co. 219–33, *220, 224, 225*
heating 46, 89, 152
  fireplace 44, 46, 47, 51, 56, 128, 248
  radiator 5, *5*, 16 n.8
  *see also* air
helmet 230, 231
High Tech 237–50, 273
Hollein, Hans 221, 229, 230
Holston, James 266, 269
home furnishings 163, 242, 243
  blinds 86, 90, 239
  bookshelf 22, 23, 24, 25, 33, 38
  carpet 1, 35, 88, *89*, 173, 246
  chair 13, 34, 37, 48, 52, 62, 87, 88, 116, 163, 166, 167, 171, 173, 242
  curtains 44, 87, 88, *89*, 166
  doilies 51
  lampshade 248
  loft-bed *243*
  piano 149, 150, *150*, 151, 154
  shower-bath 141
  sofa 48, 50, 88, *89*, 167
  table 34, 37, 51–2, 63, 119, 120, 123, 148, *149*, 151–2, *151*, 167, 242
  television cabinet 50, 51, 248
home technology
  electric fan 80
  gramophone 48
  radio 47, 48, 50, 51, 102, 107, 167
  refrigerator 72, 75 n.42, 80
  television 43–57
  washing machine 84
  *see also* air conditioning
Hopkins, Patty and Michael 239
housing 77, 78, 79, 80, 81, 83, 84, 88, 163, 164, 165, 167, 202, 206, 211, 232, 258, 263
  Flat Ownership Law of 1965, Turkey 53
  Housing Development Board (HDB), Singapore 79, 80, *85, 86, 89*
  Housing and Urban Development Company (HUDC), Singapore 89
  *see also* emergency housing
Howard, Jim 191
Hutton, Geoffrey 214

iconography 31, 99, 240
indigenous/indigeneity 259, 267
industrial aesthetic 237–49
industrial design 182, 184, 185, 193, 209, 214, 267
industrial processing (food) 63
industrial production 66, 141, 163, 167, 175, 187, 200, 267
  *see also* prefabrication
inflatable environments 181, 221, 223, 230
intermediate technology 192
international/internationalising 172, 174, 175, 238, 240, 256, 267
international aid 181, 182, 184, 186
Izenour, Steven 103

Jacobs, Jane 106, 112 n.27
Jasinski, Stéphane 170, 172
Jolles, André 12
Jones, Inigo 202
*Journal of Design History* 8
*Journal of Material Culture* 9

Kelp, Günter Zamp 223
Kelter, Theodore 172, 178 n.45
Knoll Associates, New York
Knoll, Florence 167, *168*
Knoll, Hans 164, 167, 168, 169
Knoll international Brussels 161–75, *166*, *168*, *171*, *173*
Knoll International France 167, 174
Kron, Joan 241–3, *243*, 244, 245, 246, 248, 249
Kubitschek, Juscelino 255–6, 266
*Kunstwissenschaft* 6

labour 4, 7, 12, 35, 56, 147, 187, 201, 203, 206, 208, 210, 211, 256, 258, 261
Lamb, Edward Buckton 147, 148, 149, 150–1, *150*, 154
landscape 2, 12, 13, 97, 98, 99, 103, 104, 225, 228, 229
*L'Architecture d'Aujourd'hui* 174
L'Art Décoratif Céline Dangotte 172
Le Brun, Charles 127, 128
Le Corbusier xiv, 99, 184, 209, 266
Le Pautre, Jean *120*, 121
Lerner, Max 228
Lévi-Strauss, Claude 249
library 21–2, 23, 24, 25, 27–38
lighting 66, 90, 127, 134, 169
    candle 119, 123, 124, 127, 129
    fluorescent 89
    halogen *89*
    neon 68, 238
Liu Thai Ker 79, 80
Llewelyn Davies, Richard xv, xvii
loft style 238, 241, *243*, 246–7, 248, 249, 250
Los Angeles 97, 98, 101, 102, 103, *103*, 104, 106, *108*, *109*, 109, 110, 239
Lorde, Audre 263, 265
Loudon, John Claudius 141–8, 152–7

Louis XIV 119, 120, 125, 126, 129
Lueg, Gabrielle 161, 163
Luhmann, Niklas 230, 231
Lukács, Georg 205, 208
Lyotard, Jean-François 221

Macaulay, Thomas Babington 25, 27
McLuhan, Marshall 100
Malm, Andreas 276
Marshall Plan 162, 165
Marx, Karl xv, 15, 205
Marxism 104, 105, 205, 206
mass culture iv, xv, xvi
mass production *see* industrial production
material culture studies 9
materials
    artificial stone 116, 153, 154
    bamboo 10, 84, 86, 87
    brick 10, 72, 86, 123, 173, 207, 208, 237, 246
    ceramic tile 2, 53, 70, 88, 207, 208
    concrete 10, 68, 84, 87, 88, 102, 107, 173, 204, 209, 249
    faux fur 223
    fibreboard *210*, 211
    glass 1, 15, 22, 33, 34, 44, 45, 62, 63, 66, 70, 79, 239, 240, 244, 265
    gold 30, 123, 124
    marble 46, 87, 119, 123, 151, *151*, 152, 248
    plasterboard 209, 246
    plastic xvi, 66, 193, 214, 219, 223
    plexiglas 219, 225
    polystyrene 182, 183, 187, *188*, *189*, *190*
    porcelain 31, 44, 145
    rattan 87, 88
    rubber 246
    silver 44, 123
    slate 151, 152, 207
    steel 70, 84, 163, 209, 237, 239, 240, 244
    Styrofoam 223
    stone 10, 123, 154, 207, 208
    wood 1, 2, 10, 22, 62, 63, 64, 84, *128*, 151, 165, 166, 208
Matter, Herbert 170, 174
Mechanics' Institutes 145

*Mechanics' Magazine* 145, 146, *146*, 147
*medianoche see* court festivities
metanarrative 221
Michiles, Eunice 253
Mies van der Rohe, Ludwig 162
Mignolo, Walter 256
migrant/migration 15, 72, 181, 182, 258, *261*, 261, 262–3, 264
modernism 133, 162, 184, 222, 237, 240, 249–50, 253, 256, 258, 260–3, 265–7, 269
modular architecture 184, 185, 188, 258
*Módulo* 256
Montois, Henri 170
Morris, William 4
Morsa design team *243*
Moses, Robert 106
museum 7, 66, 121, 153, 157, 181, 221, 223
    Casino in Ostend 165
    Design Museum, London 181
    Ghent Museum of Decorative Arts 165
    Museum für Angewandte Kunst, Köln 161
    Museum of Modern Art, New York 165, 226, 244
    Museum of Modern Art, Rio 267
music 54, 56, 124, 170, 225–6, 231
    *see also* sound

neoliberalism 6, 206
network
    knowledge 37, 231, 276
    of objects 62, 110, 204, 220, 221, 226, 227, 231–2, 244
    social/professional 143, 162, 167, 168, 169, 184, 220, 226, 229–30, 232
    transportation 20, 61, 63, 68
    *see also* system
*New Society* xv, xvi, 101, 104, 105
Niemeyer, Oscar 253, 254, 256, 258, 260, 261
*Nomadland* 12
Nonplace 104, 105
NOVACAP 256, 257, 260, 263

object-led sociability 220, 226, 229–32
object
    air conditioning unit 78, 81–5, *82*, 90, 204, 228
    aquarium 15
    *Battleship* 223, 224
    candelabra 123, 124, 127
    carton 62, 66, 70, 72
    cement sacks 263, *264*
    chimney pot 154, *155*, 208
    cordless shaver 228
    *Electronic Tomato* 226
    *Environment Transformers* 225, *225*, 226, 229
    Evinrude outboard 228, 229
    Franklin Stove 228, 229
    icemaker 228
    *Info-Gonks* 226
    ironing board 148, *149*
    Meccano 241
    *Media Van* 226
    *Mind Expander II* 219, 220, 221
    mosque lamps 2, *3*
    piano 149, *150*, 151, 154
    piping/pipework 83, 237, 240, 243, 246, 248, 249
    radio 47, 48, 50, 51, 102, 107, 167
    rotisserie 228
    seed drill 68, 244
    spray can 228
    Stetson hat 228, 229
    *Suitaloon* 226
    swing-out bar 228
    toilet 253–5, 257, 262, 268
    TV antennas 53, *54*
    walkie-talkie 228, 229
    *see also* cars; ephemeral structures; home furnishings; home technology; water feature
ornament/ornamentation 5, 124, 127, 130, 133, 143, 148, 153–5, *153*, 162, 210
Ortner, Laurids 223
Ortner, Manfred 223
Ove Arup & Partners *238*, 248
Oxfam 183, 186, 187, 190–2, 193
    Appropriate Technology Unit 192, 193

Oxfam Igloo/Emergency House 116, 182–5, 186–7, 188–94, *188*, *189*, *190*, *192*

Palm, Léon 163, *164*
Pamuk, Orhan 44, 45
Panofsky, Erwin 6, 99, 134
Papanek, Victor 193, 245
paper architecture 222
    *see also* diagram/drawing
parking lot 11, 66, 67, 68, 70, 72, 73
passive design 80
Pawley, Martin 237
Payne, Alina 125, 132, 133, 162
*Penny Magazine* 145, 147
Pevsner, Nikolaus 6, 134, 143
photograph/photography 13, 63, 87, 116, 163, 167, 171, 172, 173, 244, 257
Piano, Renzo 238, *238*, 242
Pichler, Walter 221
Pinter, Klaus 223
*Playboy* 228
post-disaster sites 181, 183, 186, 189, 191
postmodernism 221, 222, 223, 237, 239, 240, 241, 248, 249, 250
power
    colonial 23, 256–7, 258, 263–5
    electrical 11, 81, 83, 243
    relations 23, 25, 28, 116, 200, 260, 268, 275
prefabrication xvii, 141, 163, 165, 166, 182, 184, 209, 238, 241, 250
    *see also* buildings, Emergency House; Fuller, Richard Buckminster; industrial production; Prouvé, Jean
Price, Cedric 240, 241
print/printing/print culture 23, 24, 32, 69, 72, 141–57, 184
    *see also* blueprint
*Progressive Architecture* 169, 174, 223
projective drawings 201
product design 182, 227, 266
professionalisation 3, 4, 5–7, 8, 10, 15, 20, 34, 115–17, 122, 125, 132, 135, 144, 156, 169, 205, 206, 209, 238, 254, 258, 265

*see also* architectural education; design education
Prouvé, Jean 184, 241

Radical Architecture 221, 222–3, 226, 227, 229, 230, 232
readers/audiences xv, 23, 24, 25, 36, 56, 101, 104, 125, 126, 142, 143–5, 148, 152, 153, 155, 156, 169, 172, 174, 184, 193, 244, 246
ready-made 78, 141, 143, 152–6
    *see also* industrially produced; prefabricated
refrigeration 20, 78
    *see also* home technologies
reification 202, 203, 204–5, 206, 210, 211
relational objects 200, 232
    *see also* network
Riegl, Alois 6, 132, 134
Rogers, Ernesto Nathan 222
Rogers, Richard 238, *238*, 239, 242
Roma, Spiridione ('The East Offering its Riches to Britannia') *31*
Roussef, Dilma 268
Ruscha, Ed 11, 102, 110
Ruskin, John 154, *155*
*Rythme 166*

Saarinen, Eero 162, 166, 167, *171*, 171
salon 23, 34, 43–7, *45*, *46*, 48–9, 50, 52, 53, 56
Saverys, Jan 169, *170*
scale 2, 3, 12–15, 34, 61, 68, 72, 77–9, 80, 86, 87, 90–1, 122, 124, 126–7, 129, 131, 133, 134, 147, 219, 246, 275, 276, 277
Schiable, Michael 247, 248
Schumacher, E. F. 192
science 5, 7, 15, 34, 77, 132, 145, 186
    building science 211–12
Semper, Gottfried 6, 132, 134
sensation 78, 87, 88, 90, 110, 124, 222, 234
    *see also* air; heat; sound; taste
7-Eleven Store 67, *69*, *71*

## INDEX

shelter 4, 183–94, 222, 229, 232
  see also buildings, Emergency House
Shove, Elizabeth 78, 79
Simmel, Georg xv
simple forms 12
Skidmore, Owings & Merrill 172, 173
Slesin, Suzanne 242–3, *243*, 244, 245, 246, 248, 249
Smithson, Alison and Peter 97, 99, 100
Société Belge des Urbanistes et Architectes Modernistes (SBUAM) 169
sound 49, 52, 56, 124, 170, 219, 226, 231
  see also music
Sri Ramakrishna 24, 35–8
Stapels, René 166, 170
Stoller, Ezra 172
Stringer, Guy 191
Superstudio 221, 224, 226, 227, 230
systems
  circulation/transportation 64, 99
  classification 11, 122
  communication 105
  ecosystem/ecology 11, 100
  language 25
  regulatory 6, 202, 203, 205, 206, 211, 212, 214
  see also network
systems theory xv, xvi, 83, 100–1, 102, 103, 107, 110, 175, 224, 227, 230–2, 245, 249
  see also Barthes, Roland; Baudrillard, Jean; Luhmann, Niklas

Tafuri, Manfredo 221
taste
  cultural 1, 21, 25, 44, 126, 143, 144, 147, 155, 245, 246
  sensorial 73
Team 4 238
Tipu Sultan 23, 27–8, 29, 32, 38
Thackera, John 241
theatre 56, 125, 126
'Third World' 183, 186
topology 10
total design 4–5, 222
totem pole 64

Tote'm Store 65
Trajan's Column 129
Tubax company, Belgium 163, *164*
Turin, Duccio xvii

United States Information Agency (USIA) 165
UN Refugee Agency – UNHCR 181, 182
universal shelter 182–4, 194
  see also shelter
utility corner 84, *85*, 85, 90

Van Der Meeren, Willy 163, *164*, 165, 167, 175
Vandercam, Serge *168*, *171*, 171
Vasari, Giorgio 128, 132
Venturi, Robert 97, 103, 110
veranda 23, 52, 63, 87, 88
  see also balcony
Veranneman, Emiel 170
Vidler, Anthony 99, 103
Vidyasagar, Ishwar Chandra 21, 22, 24, 34–8, *36*
Vigarani, Carlo 119, 120–2, *121*, 124–7, 129, 131, 132–5
Vigarani, Gaspare 129, *130*
Vignelli, Massimo 175
Vitruvius 125, 128

Wabbes, Jules 170
Warburg, Aby 7
water feature
  bird bath 249
  fishpond 154
  fountain 119, 123–4, 152
wearable objects 226
  see also object, *Environment Transformers*
Webber, Melvin 97, 103–6
welfare state xv, 206, 207, 211, 212
*Whole Earth Catalog* 244, 245
Williams, Raymond 277
Wolff, Alfred 78
Wölfflin, Heinrich 132, 133, 134
Wright, Frank Lloyd 184

Zukin, Sharon 241, 246
Zweig, Stefan 1–2, 12